Anatomy of Film

Third Edition

Anatomy of Film

BERNARD F. DICK

Third Edition

St. Martin's Press

New York

Sponsoring editor: Suzanne Phelps Weir
Managing editor: Patricia Mansfield Phelan
Project editor: Deirdre Hare
Senior production supervisor: Dennis J. Para
Art director: Lucy Krikorian
Text and cover design: Delgado Design, Inc.
Cover photos: (clockwise from left) Sabrina (1954), courtesy of Paramount Pictures
and MOMA/FSA; *Malcolm X,* courtesy of Warner Bros. Inc. and David Lee; *All
About Eve,* courtesy of Twentieth Century-Fox; *Clueless,* courtesy of Paramount
Pictures and MOMA/FSA.

Library of Congress Catalog Card Number: 97-66542

Manufactured in the United States of America.
3 2 1 0 9 8
f e d c b a

For information, write:
St. Martin's Press, Inc.
175 Fifth Avenue
New York, NY 10010

ISBN: 0-312-15399-6

Acknowledgment

Review of *Evita* by Richard Corliss. Copyright © 1996 Time Inc. All rights reserved.
Reprinted by permission from *Time.*

Published and distributed outside North America by
MACMILLAN PRESS LTD
Houndmills, Basingstoke, Hampshire RG21 6XS and London
Companies and representatives throughout the world
ISBN: 0-333-72721-5
A catalogue record for this book is available from the British Library.

TO MY STUDENTS, PAST AND PRESENT

Preface

I was gratified by the response of instructors and students to the previous editions of *Anatomy of Film*, and I am pleased to have the opportunity to offer an updated and revised third edition. An introductory film course should be one of the most enjoyable courses a student can take. I hope this new edition of *Anatomy of Film* will contribute to that joy.

There are several basic differences between this edition and the previous ones. Where possible, examples have been drawn from films of the 1980s and 1990s (e.g., *Raging Bull, Forrest Gump, The Age of Innocence,* and *The Mirror Has Two Faces*). Instructors should also supply their own examples: Even if students are unfamiliar with a particular film element, its context will explain its meaning. All of us learned about simile and metaphor through examples; only later did we see how they functioned in specific poems.

Just as instructors should be free to add their own examples, so should students. Students should be encouraged to imagine themselves as filmmakers and asked how *they* would frame a shot, when they would use a close-up, or how they would compose a long take. If students have trouble understanding what is meant by a cut, they should count the number of times shots change in the course of, say, a half hour.

As schools are downsized, departments merged, and budgets curtailed, only instructors in institutions with extensive 16 or 35 mm holdings—or whose departments can pay the ever increasing rental fees from distributors—will be able to offer a film course in the true sense of the word. Naturally, a video is no substitute for a film projected in the proper aspect ratio. On the other hand, an introductory course is just that: an initiation into a particular subject. If using videos in the course inspires students to see films in theaters and seek out revivals at museums and film societies, then the medium has certainly served its purpose.

In a sense, illustrations in a film text are superfluous; if a film is a moving picture, reducing any segment of it to a still photograph is alien to the nature of the medium. Yet how appealing would a film text be without illustrations? Ideally, the illustrations should consist of frame enlargements rather than publicity stills. However, frame enlargements often reproduce poorly; there are also too many techniques that they cannot illustrate. For example, a wipe is a *moving* line that "wipes" one image away to make way for another. Even a frame enlargement showing what a wipe might look like on the frame is no substitute for viewing the wipe in operation. A frame enlargement, however accurate, reduces motion to a still devoid of other elements such as dialogue or sound that might be integral to the shot. Thus, frame enlargements are not the answer; the film is.

Furthermore, it is impossible to provide a frame enlargement or a still for every point being made. However, if examples are carefully explained, students will understand them even without corresponding illustrations in the text. Film is a wonderfully imaginative medium; it should therefore challenge a student's imagination in addition to appealing to his or her visual sense. Visual thinking is an intellectual act; it is not the passive watching of a "flick."

A text is a tool; it is a guide for the instructor, not a substitute. Accordingly, many instructors may prefer their own examples; some might use the chalkboard to illustrate film techniques. They might run a piece of chalk horizontally across the board to suggest a wipe or mark a spot at the top of the board and one at the bottom to indicate placement for high- and low-angle shots.

More important than illustrations is the act of seeing a film as a total work of art in which shots, transitions, sound effects, and music are parts of a whole. While *Anatomy of Film* analyzes the components of film, it also restores the parts to their proper place within the whole.

As in the first two editions, the third avoids the dreary jargon that has made so much film criticism unreadable. Plot and story are not synonyms; the "story" of a film in the form of a synopsis is not the same as its plot, which is an intricate mix of dialogue, sound, music, and various narrative techniques such as flashbacks and flashforwards. Understood in this sense, plot is a perfectly acceptable term and one that is universally accepted, as opposed to the Greek word, *diegesis*, which is sometimes used to describe the "world" of the film to distinguish plot from story. In Lillian Hellman's author's note to her published screenplay, *The North Star* (1943), the playwright-screenwriter noted that film terms "were invented by the early technicians in Hollywood and, like all terms which come from the desire to be clear . . . are simple. They say what they mean and they say it well."[1] *Anatomy of Film* has tried to preserve that simplicity.

There will always be disagreement about the way films should be cited. The first edition (1978) used a common designation at the time: the director's name in the possessive preceding the title with the release date in a parenthesis: John Ford's *Stagecoach* (1939). Since some directors deserve to be regarded as authors (while others clearly do not), in the second edition (1990) the director's name was placed in a parenthesis along with the release date: *Stagecoach* (John Ford, 1939). Students, however, rightly wonder whether every director's name in a parenthesis is a name to remember; also, a preponderance of such parentheses overloads the sentence, making it less readable.

The third edition has attempted a compromise; in most cases, the film is merely followed by the release date. However, some directors, who deserve the *'s* treatment, are acknowledged accordingly: John Ford's *Stagecoach* (1939). For students seeking the director's name, there is a list of all films discussed along with their directors in Appendix I.

For their criticism and advice, I would like to thank the reviewers of this third edition of *Anatomy of Film:* Roy M. Anker, Calvin College; Robert Brown, Northern Virginia Community College; David Gaines, Southwestern University; Ron Hoffman, Northern Kentucky University; David Jones, Drexel University; Gale Miller, Marquette University; Thomas Murray, Fitchburg State College; Jonah Raskin, Sonoma State University; Granetta Richardson, University of North Carolina–Wilmington; and Scott Stoddart, Nova Southeastern University.

As usual, I am grateful to my former student, Martin Nocente, for alerting me to the large number of recent films that evoke past films. I have drawn on his knowledge for some of the examples in chapter 4.

BERNARD F. DICK
Professor of Communications
Teaneck, New Jersey

[1] Lillian Hellman, *The North Star* (New York: Viking 1943), 12.

Contents

Preface vii

**1 FILM, CINEMA, OR MOVIE:
UNDERSTANDING THE MEDIUM   1**

Narrative Film 2
Time-Space Relationships 4
Movie Time 5

2 GRAPHICS AND SOUND   8

Graphics 9
    Logos 9
    Main Titles, Credits (and Precredits) Sequences, and End
       Credits 11
    Opening Titles and End Titles 16
    Intertitles 18
    Subtitles 20
    Other Uses of the Printed Word 20

Sound 22
    Actual and Commentative Sound 23
    Synchronization and Asynchronization 24
    Overlap 25
    Voice-over Narration 26
    Other Kinds of Voice-over 31

3 FILM, SPACE, AND IMAGE   **36**

Types of Shots 36
Close-ups and Long Shots 37
High-Angle and Low-Angle Shots 38
Subjective Camera 40
Shots as Parts of a Whole 44
Framing the Shot 45
The Moving Shot 54
Zooms and Freezes 57
Combining Shots: The Sequence 59
    The Linear Sequence 60
    The Associative Sequence 61
    The Montage Sequence 63

From Shot to Shot 64
    Cuts 64
    Transitions 65

Assembling the Shots 73
    Eisenstein's Theory of Montage 74
    Continuity Editing 75
    The Role of the Editor 78

Coloring the Image 80
    The Black-and-White Film 80
    The Color Film 82
    Colorization 83

Lighting the Image 84

4 FILM GENRES   **89**

The Musical 91
The Western 97
The Crime Film 103
Film Noir 105
Screwball Comedy 110
The Reflexive Film 113
The Woman's Film 115
The Horror Film 120
The Science-Fiction Film 124

5 FILM SUBTEXT 128

Mythic Associations 130
The Nature of Myth 130
The Transformation Myth in *Cat People* 132
The Savior Myth in *Shane* 134
The Genesis Myth in *The Big Carnival* 138

Visual/Iconic Associations 138
Humphrey Bogart as Screen Icon in *High Sierra* 139
Al Pacino as Christ Figure in *Serpico* 141
Jack Nicholson as Free Spirit and Louise Fletcher as Boss
Lady in *One Flew over the Cuckoo's Nest* 142
Barbara Stanwyck as Marlene Dietrich in *Double
Indemnity* 144

Intellectual Associations 144
Relating a Film to History 146
Relating a Film to Film History 148
Relating the Remake to the Original: *Sabrina Fair* (1953),
Sabrina (1954), *Sabrina* (1995) 151

Musical Associations 155

6 THE FILM DIRECTOR 162

Auteurism 163
The Beginnings of Auteurism 163
The Debate over Auteurism 165

Collaboration 167
Variety 169
Repetition 172
Quotations 173
Borrowings 175
An Interview with Billy Wilder 176
An Interview with Alan Alda 184

7 FILM AND LITERATURE 192

The Flashback 193
The Flashforward 195
Point of View 196
Omniscient Author 197
The Implied Author (Author's Second Self) 198

Film Adaptation 199
    Adaptation of Novels 200
    Adaptation of Plays 211

The Nature of Screenwriting 213

8 **FILM AS FILM**   **222**

Casablanca 224
The Godfather, Part II 225
Raging Bull 227
Natural Born Killers 231

9 **FILM CRITICISM: THEORY AND PRACTICE**   **235**

The History of Film Criticism 236
    The Russians 236
    The Grammarians 237
    The Apologists 238
    The Realists 238
    The Auteurists 243
    The Mythographers 244
    The Semioticians 246
    Feminist Criticism 251
    The Reviewers 253

Practical Criticism 259
    The Film Historian 260
    The Auteurist 261
    The Myth Critic 263
    The Social Historian 264

Guidelines for Film Criticism 266

APPENDIX I   **271**

Films Discussed and Directors 271

APPENDIX II   **282**

Art vs. Violence in *A Clockwork Orange*
    (Sample student paper) 282

A Basic Film Library 285
    Film History 285
    Film Criticism 286
    Auteur Studies 286
    Biographies 286
    Autobiographies 287
    Studio History 287
    Reference Works 288

Index 289

Anatomy of Film

Film, Cinema, or Movie

Understanding the Medium

*F*iction is a widely understood term; it means the invented, the imaginative, the fanciful—the opposite of fact. There is also *historical fiction*, as well as *historical drama:* terms for works of the imagination that draw on history for narrative or dramatic purposes (Gore Vidal's *Lincoln*, Shakespeare's *Henry V*). Thus, a novel or a play can still be considered fiction, even though it is derived from fact.

There are other forms of fiction as well—gothic, romantic, picaresque, detective, stream-of-consciousness, to name a few. *Fiction*, then, is an umbrella term—one with many different spokes.

Film is another word that means different things in different contexts: roll film, film stock, *a* film, *to* film. We were all exposed to some kind of film before we saw our first example of classic moviemaking. It may have been something we saw on television: a cartoon, a Three Stooges short, a *Lassie* rerun. Or perhaps it was an educational film we saw in school or a theatrical film (a film intended to be shown in movie theaters).

Yet, asked to define *film*, many of us would hesitate. But so would professional filmmakers. Animators, documentary filmmakers, and experimental filmmakers perceive themselves as working in the same medium—film. The films they produce, however, differ totally in look, subject matter, and style from those of mainstream Hollywood. To the general public, *film* means "movie"—a perfectly acceptable term (and one that the noted American critic Pauline Kael has always championed).

Unfortunately, *movie* suggests popular culture rather than art, while *cinema* suggests art rather than popular culture. Ironically, *cinema*, though it is a French word, is derived from the Greek *kinein* (to move); thus, whether we use *cinema* or *movie*, we are talking about an art form that was once known as "moving pictures"—appropriately named because the pictures really moved. There is nothing pejorative about the word *movie*; certainly some of the greatest examples of film art ever produced (many of which are discussed in this text) are, and always will be, movies. Although Kael finds *cinema* pretentious, it is commonly used to categorize films according to kind (contemporary cinema, world cinema) and origins (American cinema, French cinema, Third World cinema, and the like). *Movie*, then, is just a synonym for the narrative film and implies nothing about artistic worth.

Since we are dealing only with the narrative, or story, film, a definition is in order. However, a good definition is also a description. In attempting to define *film*, the American playwright, screenwriter, and critic John Howard Lawson offered this description: "A film is an audiovisual conflict; it embodies time-space relationships; it proceeds from a premise, through a progression, to a climax or ultimate term of the action."[1] Note that Lawson has not described film as such; he has described one of its particular forms: the narrative film, or what is commonly called a movie.

NARRATIVE FILM

What is a movie? To Lawson it is narrative, told through sound and image, that builds to a climax and culminates in a resolution. Note that Lawson does not make dialogue part of the definition: he merely says that a movie is audiovisual. A movie does not need spoken dialogue to tell a story. The silent films had no spoken dialogue, but they did have some kind of sound. Piano or organ accompaniment was common, and sound effects were necessary to complement the action on the screen. Even with the advent of sound, filmmakers who were truly creative knew that parts of the action could be told visually without any dialogue.

In a film, the images themselves can tell part of the story, independently of language. Some of the most unforgettable moments in film are wordless. We should not go so far as Norma Desmond (Gloria Swanson) in Billy Wilder's *Sunset Boulevard* (1950), who made only silent films and saw no need for spoken dialogue. "We had faces then!" she exclaims. On the other hand, the coming of sound ushered in the golden age of the American film (roughly 1930 to the end of the 1950s), during which a vast number of classic films appeared that were the result of outstanding screenplays. Orson Welles's *Citizen Kane* (1941) would never have been the masterpiece it is without the script that Herman J. Mankiewicz and Welles created. Even contemporary filmmakers such as Woody Allen and Joel and Ethan Coen realize the paramount importance of the script. Still, there are moments when words are unnecessary because the visuals are doing the narrating: the burning sled in *Citizen Kane* that reveals the meaning of "Rosebud"; a man, destined to be a loner, standing in the doorway of a house that everyone enters but himself (John Ford's *The Searchers*, 1956); an astronaut clearing the window of his spaceship at the same time that his wife is looking out of the window of their home so that it seems as if they see each other—if only in their imagination (*Apollo 13*, 1995). The great filmmakers always knew that the difference between theater and film was the difference between a play and a screenplay; the latter is precisely what the term implies: a play designed for the screen, where images can carry as much weight as words.

Joseph L. Mankiewicz's *All About Eve* (1950) and Alfred Hitchcock's *Psycho* (1960) illustrate the way images advance or enhance the action without the use of dialogue. *All About Eve* is the story of an aspiring actress, Eve Harrington (Anne Baxter), who deceives the Broadway star Margo Channing (Bette Davis) into befriending her. After she betrays Margo and becomes a star herself, Eve becomes the victim of a similar scheme: Phoebe, a star-struck student, will do to Eve what Eve did to Margo. As Phoebe stands in front of a three-way mirror, bowing to an imaginary audience as if she were accepting an award, her image is multiplied until the screen is filled with what seems to be an infinity of Phoebes. The final sequence is entirely without dialogue. None is needed; the visuals themselves make the point. As long as there are stars, there will be the star-struck, some of whom will stop at nothing to achieve fame.

Psycho will always be remembered for the shower murder of Marion Crane (Janet Leigh). The episode is completely wordless. There is sound, of course: music that really shrieks, as if anticipating the audience's reaction. As Marion prepares for a shower in her room at the Bates Motel, Norman Bates (Anthony Perkins) is in the adjacent parlor, where there's a peephole, covered by a picture of Susanna and the Elders. Removing the

Bette Davis (left) as Margo Channing; Marilyn Monroe as an aspiring actress; and George Sanders as a formidable critic in *All About Eve* (1950). *(Courtesy Twentieth Century-Fox)*

picture, Norman watches Marion undress. She goes into the shower, luxuriating in the spray of water. Suddenly a shadow, presumably of an elderly woman, appears against the shower curtain. The "woman" pulls the curtain aside and proceeds to stab Marion repeatedly as blood mingles with the water and swirls down the drain. Although the entire episode lasts less than a minute, a great deal of information has been imparted. Hitchcock's choice of painting was not arbitrary; just as the Elders in the Book of Daniel spied on Susanna as she entered her bath, so the voyeuristic Norman spies on Marion. A shower is a place of privacy, relaxation, and cleansing. Marion's privacy has been invaded. Instead of relaxation, she experiences the repose of death. Instead of her body being cleansed, it is defiled. Actually, it is the shower stall that must be cleansed, because it has been splattered with blood.

Writing down everything that happens in that episode would take longer than it does to see it. In his *Filmguide to Psycho*, James Naremore devotes five pages to a description of those forty-five seconds of film.[2]

TIME-SPACE RELATIONSHIPS

Like any narrative, a good movie involves conflict: personalities clash, goals differ, interests diverge, characters are at odds with each other or with society. In a movie, however, the conflict is audiovisual: it is heard and seen rather than written and read. A movie "embodies time-space relationships." While a written narrative can suggest that two events are occurring at the same time and in different places, a movie can do more than suggest: it can *show* them occurring.

In their accounts of the Passion, the four evangelists imply that Peter's denial of Christ coincided with Christ's interrogation by the

Sanhedrin: while Peter was outside in the courtyard denying Christ, Christ was within, being questioned by the chief priests and scribes. A film could make it clear that this was the case by switching back and forth from Peter's denials to the Sanhedrin's questions. In Shakespeare's *Romeo and Juliet* (V,1), Romeo buys poison from an apothecary and plans to commit suicide because he has not received a crucial letter. In the next scene, Friar John explains to Friar Laurence that he was unable to deliver the letter because he had been confined to a house that was under quarantine. Both actions—the purchase of the poison and the explanation about the letter—seem to be occurring simultaneously. A film could cut from Romeo's buying the poison to Friar John's detention; it could even do so without dialogue if the bottle were labeled poison and the house in which Friar John was confined were depicted as plague-ridden.

MOVIE TIME

Since a movie tells a story, it must do so within a certain period of time. Anyone who attends movies regularly checks the movie timetable in the newspaper. Television programmers are especially conscious of a movie's running time, since films are often cut to fit into a particular time slot. Running time, however, is real time—90 minutes, 105 minutes, and so on. Movie time is not; movie time manipulates real time, so that an event can be prolonged or shortened, and an action slowed down or sped up.

Movie time is arbitrary. In a movie, an entire day can be compressed into a few minutes or even seconds; likewise, a few minutes or seconds can be prolonged into what seems to be an entire day. In the famous Odessa steps sequence in *Potemkin* (1925), the Russian director Sergei Eisenstein distorts real time. He makes the massacre seem longer than it was because he wants to emphasize the atrocities the czarist troops committed against the people of Odessa. Toward the end of the sequence, a soldier swings his saber, striking the right eye of a women wearing a pince-nez. In reality, the soldier would have slashed her eye with one movement of his arm, but Eisenstein fragments the act. First, we see the soldier, his arm raised with the blade behind his head; then we see his savage face, but not the saber; now his face dominates the screen. Next, he shouts something as his raised arm begins to descend. Finally, we see the woman—her mouth gaping, the right lens of her pince-nez shattered, blood spurting from her eye and running down her face.

Removing a key from a key ring is a simple operation. In Alfred Hitchcock's films, however, nothing is simple. In *Notorious* (1946), Alicia (Ingrid Bergman) is an American intelligence agent whose job requires her to marry Sebastian (Claude Rains), an ex-Nazi. She has keys to every room in their house except the wine cellar. Since her coworker (Cary Grant) suspects that the cellar contains more than wine, Alicia must remove that key from her husband's key ring while he is in the bathroom getting ready for a party they are giving that evening. To create suspense, Hitchcock prolongs the action, making the audience wonder whether she will succeed; and if she does, what will happen when her husband discovers that the key is missing—which he does when the champagne runs out and he must make a trip to the wine cellar.

In real life, a wine bottle perched too close to the edge of the shelf will simply fall and smash. In *Notorious* a wine bottle does smash, but first it lingers on the edge, causing us to wonder if it will fall; and if it does, what its contents will reveal. In Hitchcock, things are not always what they seem; needless to say, this wine bottle does not contain wine.

The party in *Notorious*, which lasted several hours, occupies about ten minutes of screen time. Similarly, in Frank Capra's *Meet John Doe* (1941), a cross-country political campaign occurs in a few seconds. The climax of *Nickelodeon* (1976) is the premiere of D. W. Griffith's *The Birth of a Nation* (1915). To make the premiere as credible as possible, clips from the actual film were used. The premiere is so authentic, and the audience's reaction so spontaneous, that we forget that Griffith's three-hour epic has been reduced to a few minutes. Likewise, Robert Altman's *Nashville* (1975), which runs two and a half hours, is so absorbing that we forget we have spent five days with twenty-four people, whose destinies have been interconnected.

We must observe the laws of time, but movies do not; they can expand or contract time. If the film engages our attention, as James Whale's *Show Boat* (1936) does, we are oblivious to the fact that a story that spanned three generations took only 113 minutes to tell. A few films exhibit perfect unity of time: the running time coincides with the story time. Such films are, admittedly, rare, but Robert Wise's *The Set-Up* (1949) and Fred Zinnemann's *High Noon* (1952) run seventy-two and eighty-four minutes, respectively. Clocks are important markers of time in both films; as a result, we realize that there was no difference between the time it took to see the film and the time it took for the plot to unfold.

We have treated films like *All About Eve*, *Psycho*, and *Notorious* as texts—works to be analyzed and interpreted. A movie is a text, and it is similar to any other text, including a textbook used in a course. *Text* comes from the Latin *textus* (to weave). A text weaves the material together in an orderly and coherent fashion. A movie is a text that interweaves sound in any or all of its aspects (noise, music, speech) and image (everything from the printed word to physical action, movement, gaze, and gesture) for the purpose of telling a story.

NOTES

[1] John Howard Lawson, *Film: The Creative Process* (New York: Hill and Wang, 1967), 292.

[2] James Naremore, *Filmguide to Psycho* (Bloomington: Indiana University Press, 1977), 53-57.

Graphics and Sound

A movie's running time and the speed at which the action progresses are among the many decisions that are made before or after production. Who has made these decisions is not the point; often we do not know who was responsible for a particular image or line of dialogue. Some directors—Woody Allen and Robert Altman, for example—allow actors to improvise certain scenes. Several writers worked on the *Casablanca* (1942) screenplay, but the final line, "Louis, I think this is the beginning of a beautiful friendship," never appeared in any of the drafts. It was the inspiration of the producer, Hal Wallis, who also decided that the film (originally called *Everybody Comes to Rick's*) would be entitled *Casablanca*.

Although Victor Fleming is credited as the director of *Gone with the Wind* (1939), Sam Wood and George Cukor also worked on the film. But none of these three directors were responsible for the impressive burning-of-Atlanta sequence; that was the work of the film's art director, William Cameron Menzies. Thus, in writing about film, we use the general term *filmmaker* because it is often difficult to know who was responsible for what effect.

GRAPHICS

Logos

Although we may never know exactly how all the decisions involved in producing a film were made, we do know that a film is intended to begin and end with a certain image. In American films, the first image to appear on the screen is generally the studio's or the distributor's logo.

A logo is an example of graphics, the combination of print and design. It is also a studio's trademark. Although the studios are not what they were during Hollywood's golden age of the 1930s and 1940s, the logos of such studios as MGM, Warner Bros., Columbia, Paramount, Twentieth Century-Fox, and Universal have either remained the same or have been slightly modified. Universal's globe still spins in the sky, but it is no longer encircled by an airplane as it was in the early 1930s; nor is it made of Plexiglas as it was from 1936 to 1946. Columbia's lady-with-a-torch is intact, except that the torch shines more brightly and the lady is slimmer. In *Transparent Things*, Vladimir Nabokov claimed that contained within each word is its own history; if this is so, we might also say that encapsulated within each logo is the studio's history. In the 1930s and 1940s, moviegoers knew the differences between the studios. When they heard MGM's lion roar its greeting, they could expect a well-produced film with an outstanding cast; at that time, MGM was Hollywood's biggest studio, boasting of "more stars than are in the heavens." When an audience saw the Republic eagle, they knew they would be seeing a B movie; Republic was known for programmers (for example, Gene Autry and Roy Rogers westerns)—movies that filled out the second half of a double bill. Students of film should be able to distinguish between the studios whether they are studying films of the past or attending those of the present.

While it is true that filmmakers have no control over the logo, they often try to integrate it with the film so that it is not merely a trademark. Steven Spielberg's *Indiana Jones and the Temple of Doom* (1985) opens with Paramount's snowcapped mountain, which appears concurrently with the Indiana Jones theme on the soundtrack. The combination of logo (Paramount's mountain) and music (the familiar Indiana Jones theme) says that what follows is both a Paramount picture and an Indiana Jones movie.

Some filmmakers even start the action with the logo. In *That's Life!* (1985), the Columbia logo appears simultaneously with background conversation that continues throughout the credits. We do not know whose voices we are hearing; they seem to be surgeons performing an operation (they are indeed surgeons, as we discover when the credits are over). The surgeons have just performed a biopsy, the results of which will not be made known until the end of the movie. Since *That's Life!* was a Columbia picture, it had to open with the Columbia logo. However, director Blake Edwards made an imposition work to his advantage: he synchronized the opening action with the appearance of the logo. In effect, Edwards wanted the audience seated at the very moment the movie began.

In the Universal release *Waterworld* (1995), one of the most expensive pictures ever made ($175 million), the logo is directly related to the film's setting: the earth sometime in the future when it is completely covered with water. The first image to appear is the blue Universal globe in a sky of much darker blue. Gradually the globe begins to fall from the sky, filling the screen with an expanse of blue that resembles an ocean. Next comes the title, *Waterworld;* there are no further credits until the end of the movie.

Has the moviegoer missed anything by arriving just as *Waterworld* appears on the screen? Nothing in terms of plot, but certainly something in terms of a filmmaker's desire to establish a mood by using the studio's logo as more than a trademark.

Main Titles, Credits (and Precredits), Sequences, and End Credits

The main reason for being seated when the movie begins is that it is impossible to know exactly *how* it will begin. Take, for example, the *main title*—the film's title plus the opening credits (although in some cases it is simply the film's title). If you miss the main title when it consists only of the film's name, cast, key personnel, producer, and director, you will not have missed any of the plot. But you will have missed a certain part of the film—

Cry of the City (Robert Siodmak, 1948) opens with the Twentieth Century-Fox logo. *(Courtesy Margaret Herrick Library of the Academy of Motion Picture Arts and Sciences)*

After the logo, the main title begins with the movie's name, often against an appropriate background. *(Courtesy Museum of Modern Art/Film Stills Archive [hereafter abbreviated as MOMA/FSA])*

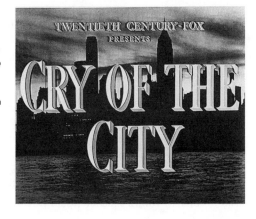

a part that is often imaginatively executed. Main titles can be quite creative and even witty. In Preston Sturges's *The Lady Eve* (1941), in which a female cardsharp pursues a timid herpetologist, the main title appears as a snake slithering across the screen; in Billy Wilder's *The Seven Year Itch* (1955), the main title—designed by Saul Bass, who is renowned for his main titles—consists of credits popping out of a jack-in-the-box. *Psycho*'s main title was also designed by Saul Bass; here, the credits intersect, coming onto the screen horizontally and vertically as the actors' first and last names split apart. The main title prepares the viewer for a movie about a split personality, as well as one in which slashing and cutting figure prominently.

A main title can also be educational; *The Front* (1975), which deals with one of the most shameful periods in American history (the McCarthy-inspired witch-hunt as it affected television in the early 1950s), begins with a 1950s montage of film clips of the Korean War, Marilyn Monroe's wedding to Joe DiMaggio, President Eisenhower and his wife, Mamie, entertaining at the White House, and Ethel and Julius Rosenberg (whose execution as Soviet spies is still a controversial subject) being led away by the police—all to the musical accompaniment of "Young at Heart" as sung by Frank Sinatra.

Although its basic function is that of a program or a playbill, the main title can establish the mood of the film, especially when it is artistically executed and appropriately orchestrated (as it is in *Psycho*, where the credits are accompanied by Bernard Herrmann's tense musical score). Missing a main title like *Psycho*'s or that of Bernardo Bertolucci's *The Last Emperor* (1987), whose credits unfold against exquisite artwork to evocative music, is like arriving at a performance of Wagner's opera *Die Meistersinger* after the prelude, which is a major piece of music in its own right. And to miss the main title of Martin Scorsese's *The Age of Innocence* (1993), designed by Saul and Elaine Bass and consisting of roses opening to the sun, is to miss one of the most elegant main titles ever designed. Here, the main title not only suggests a privileged existence but also prefigures the way flowers function in the film as both decorations and expressions of love.

Sometimes a film will dispense with graphic design and start immediately with a *credits sequence*, in which the credits are integrated with the main action. *The Four Seasons* (1981) opens with a credits sequence in which one couple picks up two other couples in their car. The credits come on during the sequence. By the time the sequence is over and the last credit has appeared, we have been introduced to three couples whose trips together constitute the plot.

Sometimes a credits sequence involves an image or object that takes on greater meaning in the course of the film. As the *Forrest Gump* (1994) credits start to roll, a feather floats through the air, eventually resting on

Forrest's (Tom Hanks) left shoe. Forrest retrieves the feather and places it in a children's book that he has been reading. Anyone who was not present during the sequence will not appreciate the ending, in which Forrest re-opens the book and the feather is released, returning to the sky from which it originally fell. The feather symbolizes the interconnection between chance and destiny, which is one of the film's themes. When the feather first fell, Forrest could never have known that he would become a national figure, much less meet American presidents. Then, he was simply drifting, much like the feather.

Sometimes a film opens cold with a *precredits sequence*—a sort of pro-logue preceding the credits. In this kind of sequence, the title does not ap-pear until *after* the sequence is over. If such a technique seems like a gimmick, remember that film is an art form, but it is also a business. And just as businesses experiment with various ways of attracting customers, so does Hollywood. One way to get an audience's attention is to vary the logo/main title/film proper format and offer the unexpected.

Exactly who was the first to alter the format is unknown, but film historians tend to credit Lewis Milestone, who directed the movie version of John Steinbeck's *Of Mice and Men* (1939). The film opens with neither logo nor title but with two men in flight, followed by a posse. The men manage to hop a freight train and scramble into an open boxcar, joining others riding the rails in search of work during the Great Depression. Someone pulls the door shut; then verses form Robert Burns's "To a Mouse," which inspired the title, appear, as if they had been inscribed on the door. The key phrase, "Of Mice and Men," is highlighted, thus be-coming the title. The remaining credits follow.

A filmmaker might choose a precredits sequence to keep the audi-ence guessing about the identity of the characters or the nature of some pivotal event that is later dramatized. After the Twentieth Century-Fox logo, *Phone Call from a Stranger* (1951) begins with a man rushing out of his home in the rain and entering a waiting cab. "Airport, hurry!" he in-structs the driver. Then the credits come on. The man becomes one of the main characters, and the plot hinges on a flight during a rainstorm. In *Hustle*'s (1975) precredits sequence, a body is washed up on a beach; we ex-pect to learn the corpse's identity—and eventually do.

Another reason for choosing a precredits sequence is to capture the viewer's attention with the hope of sustaining it for the film's duration. Thus some filmmakers deliberately attempt to draw the viewer into the ac-tion at the outset. After the Columbia logo, *Postcards from the Edge* (1994) begins without title or credits. The setting seems to be a Latin American country; a female tourist is stopped at customs, then brought to a police station, where she is brutalized. The viewer is shocked at this treatment but then discovers that the "tourist" is an actress and her beating is merely a scene in a movie being shot. Once the sequence ends, the title appears, and *Postcards from the Edge*—which dramatizes the difficult relationship between the actress in the precredits sequence and her famous mother—starts. To miss a credits or precredits sequence, then, is not merely to miss part of the film; it is to miss part of the text.

If important information is lost by arriving after the film has formally begun, significant elements may also be lost by leaving before it has formally ended. It is true that end credits have become longer than they were in the 1930–1950 period, when they consisted only of the cast of characters. Now the end credits acknowledge everyone from the star's fitness trainer to the caterers. While comics joke about end credits being longer than the movie and mock such job titles as "gaffer" and "best boy," the end credits show the complexity of contemporary filmmaking and prove conclusively that film is a collaborative art in which the gaffer (chief electrician) and best boy (the gaffer's first assistant) are among the collaborators.[1]

Since the end credits are prepared by the studio's legal department and must follow a specific format, they do not figure among the filmmaker's decisions. Filmmakers, however, have learned to use the end credits to the movie's advantage, so that they are not just the cue to exit the theater. End credits can also function in the following ways:

As epilogue. In *Sweet Liberty* (1986), which depicts the filming of a book about the American Revolution, the end credits are interspersed with scenes from the movie's premiere. Until the very end, the author, a university professor (Alan Alda), is appalled at what is being done to his book. During the end credits, he is interviewed by a reporter who congratulates him on writing history as it should be written. At that moment, a disclaimer appears on the screen to the effect that any similarity between the film and American history is purely coincidental. Anyone who leaves during the end credits misses the point: in the movies, historical truth may have to be sacrificed for the sake of entertainment.

As an informational or educational source. *The Front* is a highly accurate portrayal of blacklisting in the 1950s. The end credits not only list the actors, the director, and the writer but also identify those who themselves had been blacklisted—the actors Herschel Bernardi, Zero Mostel, and Lloyd Gough; the screenwriter Walter Bernstein; and the director Martin Ritt.

The end credits of *Married to the Mob* (1988) are interspersed with outtakes (shots deleted from the film) that make the audience aware of how much they did *not* see. Similarly, the outtakes of *Rumble in the Bronx* (1996) show martial-arts actor Jackie Chan sustaining bodily injuries while making the film, thus alerting audiences to the risks actors face when they perform their own stunts. Since *Chaplin* (1992) is based on fact, the end credits consist of shots of the main actors, along with a brief account of what happened to the historical figures they portrayed.

As a musical postlude. The end credits of Woody Allen's *Radio Days* (1987), which is set in 1941, are orchestrated with the music of the 1940s, thereby allowing a nostalgic mood to linger. During the end credits of Martin Scorsese's *GoodFellas* (1989), the popular song "My Way" is heard, suggesting that the narrator, who from childhood aspired to be a gangster, has no regrets about his profession. Anyone who exited during the end credits of *French Kiss* (1995) missed the chance to hear Kevin Kline sing in French; another lost opportunity (for those who automatically get up when the end credits start) comes during the *Postcards from the Edge* end credits, when Meryl Streep, known primarily as a dramatic actress, delivers a completely uninhibited rendition of "I'm Checkin' Out."

Priscilla, Queen of the Desert (1994), which recounts the adventures of three drag queens touring the Australian outback, not only has end credits worth staying for but an additional scene as well. The end credits roll as one of the performers lip-synchs "Save the Best for Last." When the credits are over, a short scene comes on that does not add to the narrative but is a delightful touch in its own way. Early in the film, the trio launch a kite made of pink crepe paper into the sky. In what can only be called a postcredits epilogue, the kite lands somewhere in Japan, piquing the curiosity of the locals who discover it.

The end credits are similar to a curtain call, except that in a theater the cast—not the crew—takes the bows; in a movie, everybody does. A serious theatergoer would never leave during a curtain call, and a serious moviegoer should not leave during the film equivalent of that. Students who develop this habit will not automatically rise from their seats when they think the film is about to end. Some people do this after Tom Joad (Henry Fonda) in John Ford's *The Grapes of Wrath* (1940) vows to fight for a better world, yet that is only the penultimate scene. By comparison, the final scene is anticlimactic, but it is the one that the producer, Darryl F. Zanuck, wanted. Likewise, *Citizen Kane* (1941) does not conclude with "The End." Since the director, Orson Welles, came from the stage, it is only fitting that his first film should end with a curtain call. The cast was relatively unknown, so Welles identified the important members by name as well as by repeating a shot in which each appeared. Peter Bogdanovich did the same at the end of *The Last Picture Show* (1971), and for the same reason: the unfamiliarity of the cast.

One might argue that the curtain calls in *Kane* and *The Last Picture*

Show are extraneous to the plot. That may be true, but they are not extraneous to the films in which they appear. The process of making a film entails many decisions. A filmmaker may choose to begin with a main title that consists of nothing but the most basic form of graphics: words on a plain background. A director may decide to open with an elaborate main title, a main title that foreshadows the action or includes part of it, or no title at all. A main title like *Psycho's* is implicitly part of the narrative, since it affects how we see what follows. No matter how a film begins, it should be seen as it was intended to be seen—in its entirety.

Opening Titles and End Titles

There are titles other than main titles. A title is simply printed material that appears in a film. Often, after the main title, there is an *opening title* that can serve several functions. It can be a time-place designation: "Shanghai, 1935," the opening title of *Indiana Jones and the Temple of Doom;* "Phoenix, Arizona. Friday, December the Eleventh. Two Forty-Three P.M.," *Psycho's* quite specific (and understandably so) opening title. An opening title can be used to attest to a film's authenticity ("This film is based on a true story," in *GoodFellas*); it can also be used as a preface to explain an event with which the audience might be unfamiliar. While World War II moviegoers knew the history of the conflict, later generations might not. Thus, in Steven Spielberg's *Empire of the Sun* (1987), the opening title explains the significance of December 7, 1941, and, more important, what Japanese aggression meant to British subjects living in Shanghai. An opening title can be stationary, as in *Empire of the Sun,* or it can roll up or down the screen, in which case it is known as a *roll-up title* or a *crawl.* Roll-up titles were common in the serials of the 1930s and 1940s. To evoke that era, the Star Wars trilogy—*Star Wars* (1977), *The Empire Strikes Back* (1980), and *The Return of the Jedi* (1983)—feature elaborate roll-up titles, in which the print moves up the screen.

An epigraph (literary excerpt) or a quotation is another common opening title. *The Picture of Dorian Gray* (1945) opens and closes with the same excerpt from the *Rubáiyát.* George Santayana's "Those who do not remember the past are condemned to relive it" is the epigraph to *Lacombe, Lucien* (1974), which shows how a French boy's apathy made him a pawn of the Nazis. Perhaps the most memorable opening title is the "Old Arabian Proverb" about Beauty and the Beast that appears in *King Kong* ("And lo the beast looked upon the face of beauty . . ."), which invites us to consider the film from the proverb's point of view.

Opening titles have also been used as disclaimers. *Hennessy* (1975), which is about an attempt to blow up the Houses of Parliament on Guy Fawkes Day, incorporates newsreel footage of the royal family. The open-

The end title of the World War II documentary *Prelude to War* (Frank Capra, 1942). *(Courtesy National Archives)*

No compromise is possible and the victory of the democracies can only be complete with the utter defeat of the war machines of Germany and Japan.

G. C. MARSHALL
Chief of Staff.

ing title states, "This motion picture incorporates extracts from a news film of the Queen at a State Opening of Parliament which, when photographed, was not intended for use in a fictional context." Similarly, the opening title of Martin Scorsese's *The Last Temptation of Christ* (1988) makes it clear that the film is based on a novel and is not a historical account of the life of Christ.

Just as an opening title can serve as a preface or a prologue, an *end title* can function as an epilogue. An end title is particularly useful as a means of informing the audience of the fate of the characters, especially if extending the action would prove anticlimactic, destroy the mood the ending was supposed to create, or (from a more pragmatic standpoint) send the film over budget.

At the end of Hitchcock's *The Wrong Man* (1957), which is based on a true incident, a musician's wife becomes mentally unbalanced after her husband is falsely accused of theft and imprisoned. The end title informs us that she was eventually cured and is living in Florida. The title is a bald statement of fact and nothing more; when it appears on the screen, it has the effect of a case stamped "Closed." Had Hitchcock shown the wife basking in the Florida sun, he would have shattered the film's somber mood, gratifying only those who want the storm clouds turned inside out so they can see the silver lining. The title he chose, however, provides neither a happy ending nor a triumph for the wrong man, even though he is now free.

Dog Day Afternoon (1975) is a film about a Vietnam vet (Al Pacino) with two children who holds up a Brooklyn bank to finance a transsexual operation for his second wife—a man he married in a wedding ceremony complete with celebrant and bridesmaids. The film ends on a Kennedy Airport runway, a few feet from the jumbo jet the vet has ordered to fly him to Algeria. Then three titles appear on the screen without any fanfare, as if they were being typed by someone concerned only with the accuracy of the transcription, not with its implications: the vet is serving a twenty-year prison sentence; his first wife is on welfare; and his second wife has become a woman and is living in New York. Similarly, in *GoodFellas* an end title tells the audience that the narrator, Henry Hill (Ray Liotta), and his wife have separated and the other mafiosi depicted in the film have either died or been paroled.

In Samuel Fuller's *Shock Corridor* (1963), the opening and end titles are identical: "Whom the gods wish to destroy, they first make mad." The double-duty quotation is appropriate for a movie about an ambitious reporter who feigns madness in order to solve a murder and ends up going mad himself.

Intertitles

The silent film made great use of *intertitles*, printed material that appeared periodically on the screen during the course of the movie. The intertitle was one of the ways in which the silent filmmaker supplemented the narrative or clarified the action; it is also a reminder of film's early dependence on the printed word. D. W. Griffith used intertitles for a variety of purposes, not just to reproduce dialogue and identify characters. He used them (1) to attest to the accuracy of a particular setting (e.g., the intertitle—"An historical facsimile of Ford's Theater as on that night, exact in size and detail with recorded incidents, after Nicolay and Hay in *Lincoln, a History*"—introduces the assassination-of-Lincoln sequence in *The Birth of a Nation*); (2) to comment on the action or play on the audience's emotions (e.g., the intertitle, "Dying, she gives her last little smile to a world that has been so unkind," accompanies the heroine's death in *Broken Blossoms*, 1919); (3) to define terms with which the audience might be unfamiliar (e.g., *Pharisee* and *Sanhedrin* in *Intolerance*, 1916); and (4) to reveal a char-

An intertitle from *The Birth of a Nation* (D. W. Griffith, 1915). Note the underscoring for emphasis and the DG trademark as a sign of authorship. *(Courtesy MOMA/FSA and Epoch Producing Corp.)*

acter's thoughts (e.g., the intertitle, "The Inspiration," appears after Ben Cameron sees some white children frighten black children with a sheet in *The Birth of a Nation*; the "inspiration" is the use of bedsheets to make the Klansmen's robes for the cross-burning vigilantes). Griffith treated intertitles as images, integrating them with the film so they would be part of the narrative.

A Woman of Affairs (1928) shows how silent filmmakers used punctuation, especially the dash, to suggest how the lines would have been spoken:

> My nerves have gone to pieces—I'm going out—somewhere
> I didn't mean to come here—I started driving—
> Why should a man—happy as David was—take his own life?
> David died—for decency.

Intertitles did not die with the advent of sound. Martin Scorsese used them in *Raging Bull* (1981) and *GoodFellas*, both of which are based on fact, to achieve a sense of authenticity. Each sequence in *Raging Bull*, which is told in flashback, is introduced by an intertitle (e.g., "New York, 1964"; "The Bronx, 1941"; "La Motta vs. Robinson, 1943"). Scorsese does the same in *GoodFellas* (e.g., "Brooklyn, 1953"; "June 11, 1970"; "Idlewild Airport, August 1963").

Woody Allen may well have chosen to use intertitles in *Hannah and Her Sisters* (1986) because, in addition to being an actor, a director, and a screenwriter, he is also a playwright and a short-story writer. Allen's stories are often vignettes, and *Hannah and Her Sisters* is a series of vignettes about three sisters. Thus, Allen segments the film, introducing each vignette with an intertitle that can be (1) a line of dialogue repeated in the segment (the opening intertitle, "God, she's beautiful!," is also the first line of dialogue, spoken offscreen); (2) a character introduction ("The Hypochondriac" introduces the Woody Allen character); a vignette title ("The Abyss" is the intertitle of the episode in which Allen thinks he has a brain tumor); and (4) a quotation ("The only absolute knowledge attained by man is that knowledge is impossible"—Tolstoy). By using intertitles in so many different ways, Woody Allen allies himself not only with the venerable tradition of the intertitle but also with the written word.

Since Philip Kaufman was both the screenwriter and the director of *The Unbearable Lightness of Being* (1988), he clearly intended the titles to serve a purpose. The film opens like a fairy tale. The first intertitle, "In Prague in 1968 there lived a young doctor named Tomas," is followed by a scene showing Tomas in a less than fairy-tale situation: making love to a nurse. The second intertitle, "But the woman who understood him best was Sabina," is followed by another lovemaking scene, this time between

Tomas and Sabina. After the third intertitle, "Tomas was sent to a spa town to perform an operation," the film turns serious, as one might expect of a film about the Soviet-backed invasion of the former Czechoslovakia in 1968. The intertitles, with their storybook connotations, run counter to the erotic scenes that succeed them. Once the intertitles end, the eroticism continues, but within a historical, not a storybook, context.

Subtitles

The *subtitle* shares one of the main functions of the intertitle: the transmission of dialogue. Although subtitles—in which the translation of dialogue appears at the bottom of the screen—are common in international films shown in the United States, they are also used in American films with scenes that require the characters to speak in a language other than English. For such scenes, filmmakers now prefer to have the actors use the characters' native tongue rather than to simulate an accent that suggests their nationality—which was the case until about 1970. *Tora! Tora! Tora!* (1970) is unusual among films about World War II because it was apparently the first Hollywood production in which the Japanese spoke their own language, with subtitles providing the translation. Since then, it has become standard to use a subtitle whenever a foreign language is spoken— e.g., Russian (*Red Dawn*, 1985), Sicilian (*The Godfather, Part II*, 1974), French (*The Last of the Mohicans*, 1992), Sioux (*Dances with Wolves*, 1990). When a hearing-impaired character used sign language in *Four Weddings and a Funeral* (1994), the translation was given in a subtitle. In context, the translation is quite funny, since the character is expressing sentiments about someone who, if he understood sign language, would not be amused.

Other Uses of the Printed Word

Printed matter in a film is a visual; as such, it can make a valuable contribution to the narrative. The entire plot of *Citizen Kane* revolves around an attempt to discover the meaning of Charles Foster Kane's dying word, "Rosebud!" Until the end, no one—neither the characters nor the audience—knows what "Rosebud" means. The characters never do, but the audience eventually does. After Kane's funeral, workmen begin clearing out his cluttered basement, throwing what they consider to be junk into a blazing furnace. One of them tosses in a sled, which, as it burns, allows us to see that it bears a name: "Rosebud." The film's resolution is a word, but one that must be seen—a word that symbolizes Kane's lost childhood.

Another example of the symbolic use of print occurs in *Casablanca* when Rick (Humphrey Bogart), standing in the rain, reads a letter from

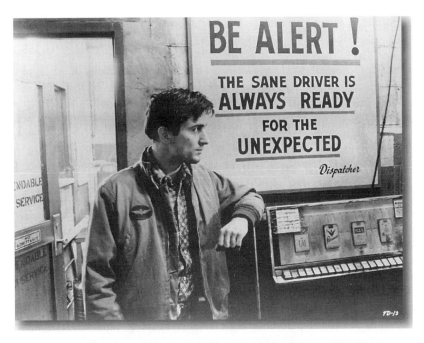

The ironic juxtaposition of print and image in *Taxi Driver* (1976), in which Travis Bickle (Robert De Niro) may be ready for the unexpected but is not exactly sane. *(Courtesy Sony Pictures Entertainment and MOMA/FSA)*

Ilsa (Ingrid Bergman) informing him that she cannot leave with him for Marseilles. As Rick reads the letter, the rain falls on it, causing the ink to run, tearlike, down the page. The running ink provides the tears that the stoic Rick cannot show; it also signals the end of an affair that has faded like the words of the letter. In both films, print has been dramatically embellished—by flames in *Citizen Kane* and by rain in *Casablanca*.

Naturally, print does not always operate so symbolically. Generally, print is a visual shorthand that enables the filmmaker to identify locales and impart important information without having to resort to awkward exposition. Thus signposts, street signs, newspapers, and plaques are used to pinpoint setting. Since much of *The Grapes of Wrath* consists of a drive from Oklahoma to California along Highway 66, signs along the way tell the audience which state the Joads are in. A San Francisco newspaper seen at the opening of Hitchcock's *The Birds* (1963) immediately identifies the setting.

It is possible to formulate a general rule about the best use of print in film: print should be used as a means of supplying information that either cannot be imparted in any other way or that will reduce the amount of exposition. Sometimes the script calls for print. In *Dark Victory* (1939), Judith Traherne (Bette Davis) learns that she is terminally ill when she comes across her medical file and sees the words "PROGNOSIS NEGATIVE." In a similar film, *An Act of Murder* (1948), a woman learns from a letter her physician has written to her husband that she is dying. When Bob Woodward (Robert Redford) realizes that Carl Bernstein's (Dustin Hoffman) apartment is bugged in *All the President's Men* (1976), he turns up the stereo and types: "Deep Throat says our lives may be in danger. SURVEILLANCE. BUGGING."

Since computers are now part of our everyday life, the computer screen has also become an important narrative tool, capable of advancing the plot in the same way the typewriter once did. The computer that the villain in *Ghost* (1990) uses to transfer funds becomes the means of revealing his identity; *The Net* (1995) revolves around an attempt to use computer technology to alter a character's identity.

Film, then, uses print in a variety of ways (signs, plaques, posters, headlines, ticker tape, letters, notices, invitations, telegrams, notes, typewritten or computer-generated texts, and so on). Thus, print can perform an important narrative function; as visual shorthand, it minimizes the need for expository dialogue.

SOUND

Seeing a narrative film without sound would be an abomination. Even the silent films (which were silent only in the sense that there was no spoken dialogue) had some kind of sound effects as well as musical accompaniment. *Nickelodeon* illustrates the importance of sound in the silent film by showing the world premiere of *The Birth of a Nation*, in which men fire cap pistols backstage to simulate the gunfire in the battle scenes.

Gunfire, a staple in westerns, war films, and crime movies, is one of many sound effects used in films. Under the heading of sound effects come all the sounds heard in a film except dialogue, music, and offscreen narration. Noise is an important sound effect in a film, and it can be a legitimate, even powerful, device. Jacques Tourneur's *Cat People* (1942) would not be the horror classic it is if noise were absent in two crucial scenes. As Alice (Jane Randolph) walks home at night, she hears the ominous sound of footsteps. Just when we think that whatever is following her will catch up with her, we hear the sound of brakes; a bus has pulled up alongside Alice, and she quickly boards it. Later, as she is swimming in an indoor pool, she hears growling sounds, as if a ferocious beast were nearby.

The noise in *Cat People* is atmospheric; it is intended to heighten the suspense. In many films, however, noise is essential to the plot. A scene from Hitchcock's *Marnie* (1964), for example, demands noise—a noise that the audience and Marnie must hear but that another character in the scene cannot hear. After taking money from her employer's safe, Marnie (Tippi Hedren) stealthily leaves the office. In the adjacent area, a cleaning woman is washing the floors. In order not to be heard, Marnie removes her shoes, placing them in the pockets of her jacket. One of her shoes falls to the floor. Anyone in the vicinity would have heard the sound, yet the cleaning woman does not look up from her work. As we wonder whether Marnie will be discovered, the janitor calls to the cleaning woman in an unnaturally loud voice, making it clear that she is hard of hearing.

And Now Tomorrow (1944) contains an interesting example of noise that, under ordinary circumstances would be audible but which, in the context of the film, must be inaudible. When Emily Blair (Loretta Young) wakes one morning, she sees the windowpanes streaked with rain but does not hear the rainfall. The audience discovers that Emily has lost her hearing at the same moment she does: when the rain silently beats upon the window.

Actual and Commentative Sound

As a form of sound, noise can emanate from a source that is either on or off screen. We do not have to see the source of the noise; we only have to know there is a source. We never see the foghorns in *Long Day's Journey into Night* (1962), but we hear them, and know they are coming from nearby ships. In Joseph L. Mankiewicz's *A Letter to Three Wives* (1949), everything in the Finney kitchen shakes when the train passes by. We never see the train, but we hear it and witness the results of the vibrations it causes.

Sound, then, can be actual (or natural) in the sense of coming from a real source that we may or may not see. It can also be commentative in that it may come from a source outside the physical setting of the action. Perhaps the most familiar type of commentative sound is background music, the recurring motifs or signature themes that can identify a character (Lara's theme in *Dr. Zhivago*, 1965), a place (the Tara theme in *Gone with the Wind*, 1939), a physical state (the blindness theme in *Dark Victory*), or an obsession (the power theme in *Citizen Kane*). In *Dark Victory*, when Judith Traherne discovers that she will experience a short period of blindness prior to death, the blindness theme is heard on the soundtrack. Judith cannot hear the music because it is not coming from a source within the action, but the audience hears it and, having heard it before in various forms, recognizes it as a sign of Judith's fate.

Synchronization and Asynchronization

Another way of looking at sound is from the perspective of synchronization and asynchronization. In synchronization, sound and image are properly matched; the sound comes from within the image or from an identifiable source. Synchronization is not just limited to a literal correlation of sound and image. In many films, characters may be in transit (e.g., in a car or a plane) and the audience will see the car on the freeway or the plane in the air but not see the characters. Yet we hear their conversation. In postproduction, the dialogue has been added and synchronized with the image.

There are, however, more sophisticated forms of synchronization. For example, a nonhuman sound may be combined with the image of a person. In *Cat People*, Irena (Simone Simon) tactfully tells her husband on their wedding night that she is not ready to consummate their marriage. As they retire to separate rooms, Irena, who is a descendant of a Serbian cat cult and periodically reverts to panther form, falls to her knees, assuming an animal posture. At that moment, the snarl of a panther is heard. The audience knows the source of the sound: the Central Park Zoo, which Irena frequents. However, within the new context of an unconsummated wedding night, the combination of a sound coming from an identifiable source and the image of the crouching Irena adds another dimension to the narrative: her repressed sexuality is given "voice." While sound and image have been synchronized in this instance, we know the sound source and see the image before us; it now seems as if the image is making the sound. The combination (growling panther + crouching woman) suggests that within Irena there is something waiting to be unleashed.

Synchronization, then, can be quite imaginative. It can be particularly effective when a character remembers the past. The voice of the person remembering can be combined with the image of what is remembered, or the face of the person remembering can be combined with the sound that is remembered. In *A Streetcar Named Desire* (1951), Blanche du Bois (Vivien Leigh) periodically recalls the music that was played the night her husband committed suicide. At the end of *Forever Amber* (1947), Amber (Linda Darnell) watches her son go off with his father, never to see either of them again. Earlier, the child's father—Amber's former lover—had said, "May God have mercy on both of us for our sins." In the final scene, Amber, standing at the window, recalls his words—her image synchronized with the sound of his voice.

In synchronization, sound and image are related contextually, spatially, and temporally. In asynchronization, sound and image are related symbolically, metaphorically, or ironically. With the latter, the image the viewer expects to see after hearing a particular sound turns out to be some-

Asynchronization in *M* (1931). When Mrs. Beckmann calls, "Elsie!," the response is not verbal but visual: a place setting never to be used again. *(Courtesy MOMA/FSA and Janus Films)*

thing quite different. Asynchronization allows filmmakers to contrast sound and image, substitute a sound for an image, or juxtapose sounds and images that would not normally occur at the same time.

In Fritz Lang's *M* (1931), Mrs. Beckmann is waiting anxiously for her daughter Elsie to return from school. She leans out of the window, calling, "Elsie! Elsie!" On the screen we do not see Elsie but rather a series of images: an empty stairwell, an empty attic, Elsie's place at the dinner table, her ball on the grass, and, finally, a balloon that is momentarily caught in some telephone wires and then floats away.

The asynchronization is remarkably subtle. Ironically, Mrs. Beckmann's call is heard, but she is answered only by images that denote absence and emptiness. Elsie will never return. Like the balloon that was caught in the wires and then blown skyward by the wind, she was enticed by a child molester and led away to her death.

Overlap

What might seem to be asynchronization could be overlap—sound or dialogue that either carries over from one scene to the next or anticipates the new scene by starting at the end of the previous one. Thus, *overlapping sound* is really synchronous, since it emanates from a known source. Bridging scenes through sound was rare in the 1930–1950 period, mainly because such a device would have struck audiences as illogical. If *The Age of Innocence* had been released in 1943 instead of in 1993, there would never have been the scene in which Newland Archer (Daniel Day Lewis) stands in front of a flower shop and, before he even enters, a voice says, "Oh, Mr. Archer. Good evening." The florist would have extended the greeting *after* Archer had entered. Today, however, overlapping sound has become so commonplace that it is just a cue for a scene change.

Still, there are instances in which the scenes being bridged are connected in ways that develop the narrative rather than merely link segments of it together. In Spike Lee's *Malcolm X* (1992), as Malcolm walks along a street thronged with prostitutes, we hear the words "What has happened to our women?" Is this what Malcolm is thinking? The next scene clarifies the situation: the question is part of a sermon that is about to end. The incident in the first scene inspired the subject matter of the sermon in the second, with the question becoming the link between them.

In *Three Days of the Condor* (1975), a CIA official in Washington is asking questions about an agent, who at that moment is hiding out in a Brooklyn Heights apartment. The official's voice carries into the next scene, which takes place in the apartment. The overlapping voice gives us the unsettling impression that the CIA is present everywhere, including Brooklyn Heights.

At the end of *Medium Cool* (1969), set in Chicago during the 1968 Democratic convention, the director, Haskell Wexler, allows the audience to hear about an event before it happens. As a TV cameraperson and an Appalachian schoolteacher are driving away from a bloody confrontation between the police and Vietnam War protesters, a newscaster's voice describes their death in a car crash before it is actually shown. Like the film, the untimely newscast is disturbing; it is not just a matter of overlap but of omniscience. It is as if the "cool medium," as media critic Marshall McLuhan called television, knows our destiny and can therefore compose our obituary before we die.

Filmmakers seeking alternatives to the sound bridge might consider what Robert Zemeckis did in *Forrest Gump*. On a summer night, as Forrest and Jenny (Robin Wright) are sitting together in Alabama, fireworks light up the sky. This is not a fireworks display in an Alabama town, however, but in Liberty Park in Jersey City, New Jersey; and the occasion is the American bicentennial, as we learn from the next scene, a live telecast of the event. Even though these are the Liberty Park fireworks, the transition is not jarring; such a display on July 4 was as common in Alabama as it was anywhere in the country, including Liberty Park.

Voice-over Narration

Voice-over, off-camera narration or commentary, has been a standard feature of film since the beginning of the sound era and is now so common in film and television that we scarcely notice it. We have become accustomed to the television voices of unseen individuals promoting products, reading labels, or attesting to the miraculous results of a headache remedy. In airports and train stations, we continually hear voices announcing arrivals and departures. We seldom inquire about the source or identity of the voice because we are usually interested only in the information the voice is conveying. Because disembodied voices are everywhere, we tend to give little thought to voice-over narration in film. It is another case of accepting the familiar uncritically.

Voice-over is also one of the most abused techniques in film. A gifted filmmaker like Woody Allen uses voice-over intelligently; in *Radio Days*, Allen makes voice-over integral to the film, which is a reminiscence by a narrator whose younger self appears as a character. Unfortunately, voice-over can also be a convenience for writers who cannot think of any other way of imparting information. Voice-over is understandable in a memory film like *Radio Days*, but there are other movies that are not reminiscences in which the technique is used without any consistency or logic. In John Ford's *When Willie Comes Marching Home* (1950), the main character's voice keeps intruding even though there is no reason for him to tell his own story.

Historically, when the movies learned to talk, filmmakers seized upon voice-over as a narrative device and attempted to use it as they had used titles. As often happens, the quest for novelty led to eccentricity, and soon voice-over narration was being entrusted to everyone—and everything. *The First Time* (1952), narrated by an unborn baby, dramatizes the disruptions that come with a first child. A variation on the same device occurs in *Look Who's Talking* (1989), which is told from the point of view of a newborn baby (with Bruce Willis providing the voice-over). The film had a certain charm, unlike the 1990 and 1993 sequels, which had little audience appeal, suggesting that once may have been enough.

Since voice-over has become so widespread, its appropriateness deserves assessment. Is it a convention like a soliloquy in a play? Does it function as an expository prologue? Or is it an emergency cord a filmmaker pulls when he or she is unable to think of another way to convey information? There is no manual a filmmaker can consult to determine whether to use voice-over or titles, or to use neither and work the exposition into the dialogue. Sometimes voice-over needs some kind of aural reinforcement: a few sounds, some chords, a musical theme. Sometimes the necessary information can be incorporated into the dialogue so that both voice-over and titles are unnecessary.

The best filmmakers know intuitively when to use voice-over and when to use some kind of title. They also know that in some instances a combination is required. The 1935 adaptation of Charles Dickens's *A Tale of Two Cities*, directed by Jack Conway, is a good example of the sensible use of print and voice-over. The novel includes two of the most famous lines in English literature: the opening line ("It was the best of times, it was the worst of times") and the closing line ("It is a far, far better thing that I do, than I have ever done: it is a far, far better rest that I go to than I have ever known"). The opening appears as a title without voice-over. This is fitting because these are the words of Dickens, not one of his characters; thus, the text alone is sufficient. At the end, however, voice-over is necessary. The last words of the film, like those of the novel, are the thoughts of Sydney Carton, the main character; they are not Dickens's reflections. Since these are Carton's thoughts, the audience must hear them. Since Carton does not verbalize his thoughts, the audience hears them through voice-over.

The dominant forms of voice-over are the narrating "I" and the voice of God.

The Narrating "I"

The narrating "I" tells the story, or a portion of the story, that we see on the screen. There can be one "I" or several. Some films are narrated by one character (*Murder, My Sweet*, 1944); others by multiple narrators (*Citizen Kane; Sorry, Wrong Number,* 1948). Since anyone can tell a story in the movies, even a corpse has the opportunity in Billy Wilder's *Sunset Boulevard* (1950). Narration by a dead person would pose severe problems of credibility in a work of fiction unless it were a tale of the preternatural; yet the narration works in *Sunset Boulevard*, which, for all its realism, is similar to many other films about old Hollywood that resemble tales of the unearthly. In the film, Norma Desmond (Gloria Swanson), a former silent-screen star half crazed by memories of a past that will never return, believes she can make a comeback in a movie about Salome. She hires an out-of-work screenwriter, Joe Gillis (William Holden), to write the script in which she plans to star. When Gillis decides to leave her, Norma kills him. *Sunset Boulevard* begins with Gillis's body floating in a pool; Gillis's voice then proceeds to tell the story of his fatal association with Norma Desmond. The narration is ironically fitting: a corpse talking about the living dead.

Another Billy Wilder film, *Double Indemnity* (1944), is considered a classic of "I" narration. It opens with Walter Neff (Fred MacMurray) entering a Los Angeles office building shortly before dawn. Neff describes himself as having "no visible scars"—none, that is, that can be seen *now*. Actually, he has just been shot by his mistress, whom he then killed. While Neff still has the strength, he recites his whole story into a dictaphone. The film then becomes a flashback in the form of a testimony that is being recorded and dramatized at the same time.

In "I" narration, if there is only one narrator, the narrator's voice will recur periodically throughout the course of the film. Narration by one character is a more difficult method, since the narration must unify the film, bridging the scenes as the action shifts from present to past. Neff's

Walter Neff (Fred MacMurray) as the narrating "I" in *Double Indemnity* (1944), one of the finest examples of first-person narration in film. *(Copyright Paramount Pictures, Courtesy MCA Publishing Rights, a Division of MCA Inc.)*

narration in *Double Indemnity* succeeds because the flashbacks frequently end with a cue line, a line that triggers the next bit of dialogue so that the action can return to the present without an awkward transition. When Neff and Phyllis Dietrichson (Barbara Stanwyck) are in a supermarket plotting her husband's murder, Phyllis says, "Remember, we're in it together." "Yes, I remember," Neff answers into the dictaphone.

Sometimes the "I" tells his or her story in the hope of learning from it. Robert Bresson's *Une Femme Douce* (1969) opens with a suicide. Someone rushes to the veranda, a chair is overturned, a white shawl flutters through the air, and a woman's body falls to the pavement. A man, later revealed to be the woman's husband, begins to speak of her. Bresson keeps returning to her body, which now lies on a bed, to remind us that her husband is narrating the film. The approach is psychologically valid, for the husband is not so much recalling his wife as trying to understand why she committed suicide. At the end, he knows no more than he did at the beginning.

If the voice of the "I" is flat and dispassionate, the narration will have a distancing effect, which may be desirable in a film in which the characters are not empathetic. "I" narration works well in *Badlands* (1973), whose characters are far from endearing. The heroine is a fifteen-year-old with cornflower eyes that look as if they have lost their physical and moral center; the hero, her boyfriend, can shoot a man in the back and then talk to him as if nothing had happened. Holly (Sissy Spacek), the heroine, narrates *Badlands* in a voice as flat as the western plains she and Kit (Martin Sheen) traverse. She is presumably telling the story to us, but it sounds as if she might be writing it for a pulp magazine. Some of the narration is grimly amusing, particularly when Holly tries to turn a phrase and instead produces a cliché ("Little did I realize that what began in the backways and alleys of this little town would end in the badlands of Montana"), or when she tries to be poetic and succeeds only in being trite ("When the leaves rustled overhead, it was as if the spirits were whispering about all the little things that were bothering them"). Her boyfriend's inclinations cause Holly to remark, "Suddenly I was thrown into a state of shock: Kit was the most trigger-happy person I ever met." The line is delivered so apathetically that audiences laugh, perhaps without realizing the implications of their laughter. At any rate, Holly's monotone prevents us from sympathizing with her and Kit.

The Voice of God

Between 1945 and the early 1950s, the semidocumentary was a popular type of film. While a documentary is nonfiction, a semidocumentary is fiction based on fact (e.g., *The House on 92nd Street*, 1945; *Boomerang*, 1947). In the semidocumentary the credits often appear in a "typewriter" typeface to give the movie a "case history" look. An authoritative voice delivers the prologue, reminding the audience that the film sprang from today's headlines or the FBI's files and that it was shot on location. Since the voice belongs to no character, it is completely disembodied. As a result, it can weave in and out of the action, commenting, reflecting, even questioning. In the semidocumentary the disembodied voice (or voice-of-God technique, as it is sometimes called) has two advantages: it can impart a feeling of objectivity, which is required by a film of this kind, and it can insinuate itself into the characters, noting their moods and emotional states. The voice in *The Naked City* (1948) speaks directly to the characters as if it were an alter ego, confidant, and conscience combined. "How are your feet holding out, Alan?" it asks, or, "Lieutenant Muldoon, what's your hurry?" It even speaks to the audience: "Ever try to catch a murderer?" Since the voice had the first word, it is fitting that it should have the last: "There are eight million stories in the naked city. This has been one of them."

The disembodied voice is not restricted to the semidocumentary.

This scene from *Barry Lyndon* (1975) between Barry (Ryan O'Neal) and his son (David Morley) was introduced by the off-camera narrator who said: "Barry had his faults, but no man could say of him that he was not a good and tender father. He loved his son passionately, perhaps with a blind partiality. He denied him nothing." *(Courtesy Warner Bros., Inc.)*

Stanley Kubrick used it ingeniously in his 1975 adaptation of Thackeray's novel *Barry Lyndon*. Both the novel and the film have a narrator; however, in the film, the narrator is not Lyndon—as it was in the novel—but a voice behind the scenes, very much like the one in *The Naked City*, but much wittier and more urbane. It is actually the voice of the British actor Michael Hordern, which, like the traditional voice of God, is omniscient. The voice tells us about something before it happens or informs us of the outcome of an event without dramatizing it for us. When Lyndon is about to die, the voice even reads his obituary. The voice can speak with authority at this moment because it has been speaking with authority since the film began.

Other Kinds of Voice-over

Voice-over is often used in movies that are not narrated by one of the characters but, for purpose of plot, require a character's voice to be heard. Such voices are variously labeled the *epistolary voice*, the *subjective voice*, the *repetitive voice*, and the *voice from the machine*.

The Epistolary Voice

Advancing the plot through letters is a device common to both fiction and film. The epistolary novel has a long tradition that reaches back to Samuel Richardson's *Pamela* and *Clarissa*, written in the mid-eighteenth century. In film, the letter is a familiar means of setting the plot in motion (William Wyler's *The Letter*, 1940; *A Letter to Three Wives*) or of bridging the years (*Sea of Grass*, 1947). When an exchange of letters is used to mark the passage of time, voice-over is sufficient. In François Truffaut's *The Story of Adele H.* (1975), the epistolary voice is put to a variety of uses. We hear Adele's voice as she writes to Lieutenant Pinson, whom she has pursued to

Halifax in an attempt to regain his affection. When she writes to her father (later discovered to be Victor Hugo), we hear his reply. In addition to Adele's correspondence, we also hear her diary entries. When Pinson reads the love notes Adele has concealed in his pockets, her voice discloses their contents to us. After following Pinson to Barbados, she collapses in the street. A native woman brings Adele to her home. After learning that she is Victor Hugo's daughter, the woman writes a letter to the novelist, informing him of his daughter's pitiful condition.

In an era of film censorship, the epistolary voice was one way of having a character repent by voice-over confession. Robert Anderson's play *Tea and Sympathy* was considered unfilmable in the 1950s because of its subject matter: Tom Lee, a prep-school student thought to be homosexual because of his fondness for music and poetry, is initiated sexually by Laura Reynolds, the headmaster's wife. The play is best remembered for the final scene, in which Laura comes to Tom's room and slowly begins to unbutton her blouse. Pressing his hand against her breast, she makes one request: "Years from now, when you talk about this, and you will, be kind." When MGM decided to film the play in 1956, the Johnston Office* felt that any woman who would offer her body to an adolescent should die. After much wrangling, the director, Vincente Minnelli, decided to make the plot a flashback occasioned by a class reunion at which Tom discovers a letter Laura had written to him. As Tom reads the letter, Laura's repentant voice is heard, urging him to forget what they have done (which is "wrong") and go out into the world and write edifying novels.

What we have been discussing are films in which the letter is a plot device whose contents must be heard. There are few films that are totally epistolary; that is, in which the entire film is a dramatization of a letter or a series of letters. In *A Walk in the Sun* (1945) and *Platoon* (1986), the narrator is writing letters to his sister and grandmother, respectively; however, it does not follow that each film is a dramatization of the letter the character is writing.

If a film is totally epistolary (and such films are rare), it really is an example of the narrating "I," since the epistolary voice is used only to tell the contents of a letter. Max Ophuls's *Letter from an Unknown Woman* (1948), which revolves entirely around a letter Lisa (Joan Fontaine) has written to her former lover as she lay dying, is totally epistolary. Because the letter is such a personal document, we see only its powerful beginning ("By the time you read this letter I may be dead") and its unfinished ending. Otherwise we hear Lisa's voice, and experience the visualization of her

---

*The Motion Picture Producers and Distributors of America, Hollywood's self-censorship organization, was called the Johnston Office when it was headed by Eric Johnston from 1945 to 1963; previously it had been called the Hays Office and the Breen Office.

words. Yet the letter that is being dramatized is also being read by Lisa's lover, who never even bothered to learn her name. Thus, the audience and the lover learn about Lisa at the same time.

The Subjective Voice

Movies abound with examples of the inner voice that literally speaks its mind (called *subjective voice*) because the audience requires access to the character's thoughts. Pip in *Great Expectations* (1947) wonders how Joe Gargery, the blacksmith, will greet him when he returns home dressed as a gentleman. In *The Accused* (1948), we hear what a psychology professor, who has killed a student in self-defense, is thinking when she realizes the consequences of her act. During her flight from Phoenix in *Psycho*, Marion Crane imagines what her employer will say on Monday morning when she fails to report for work.

A more complex form of the subjective voice appears in the stream-of-consciousness film. Although *stream of consciousness* has been applied to everything from inarticulate rambling to incoherent prose, it is really the unbroken flow of thoughts, memories, and associations in the waking mind. *Hiroshima Mon Amour* (1959), a stream-of-consciousness film, opens with a man and a woman making love. At first their skin looks charred, like that of the Hiroshima victims; then it becomes dewy, as though cleansed by the act of love. She is a French actor, and he is a Japanese architect she meets in Hiroshima while making a film. As their bodies move toward fulfillment, we hear their voices—his denying that she knows the significance of Hiroshima, hers insisting that she does. But these are not their actual voices; they sound distant, anesthetized. We are hearing the rhythms of poetry, not prose. It is each character's interior that we hear, an interior expressing itself in the language of memory, which is made up of both words and images. When the architect's voice says, "You know nothing of Hiroshima," her consciousness replies with pictures of the artifacts she has seen at the museum and with newsreel footage of the bombing of Hiroshima. When the woman says, "Who are you?," instead of a verbal reply we see a street in Hiroshima. The man is Hiroshima, the only name she will ever associate with him.

The Repetitive Voice

A character, often the hero or the heroine, tosses restlessly in bed while someone's voice reverberates in his or her unconscious, repeating key dialogue from an earlier scene (in case the audience missed its significance). This kind of repetition, called the *repetitive voice*, occurs in Hitchcock's *Rebecca* (1940) when some comments made about Rebecca give Joan

Fontaine's character a sleepless night. The same technique appears in *Cat People* when Irena keeps hearing the voice of her psychiatrist as Halloween cats prowl across the screen.

The repetitive voice has become so familiar that it runs the risk of becoming a cliché. Yet at times some kind of recapitulation is necessary, and the filmmaker must decide whether the repetition should be aural or visual. If the character's words are important, then it is only necessary to hear what he or she has said. At the end of *Gone with the Wind*, Scarlett recalls the words her father had spoken earlier about the value of land and the importance of Tara. Hearing his words is sufficient. On the other hand, in *Murder on the Orient Express* (1974), the repetition is visual. Since the film is a whodunit, crucial shots are repeated: guilt is often a question not of what one says but of how one reacts, so the passengers' reactions, not just their words, are recalled for us visually.

The Voice from the Machine

Some filmmakers regard voice-over as the modern equivalent of the *deus ex machina* (god from the machine) of Greek theater. In certain Greek tragedies, a god would descend from a crane to resolve the action and bring the play to a conclusion. Some movies feature a "voice from the machine"; it belongs to none of the characters and materializes near the end to tie up any loose plot threads or offer some commentary on the action. The voice from the machine is not the voice of God, which is consistent throughout the film; the voice from the machine is heard only at the end. At the end of *The Lady and the Monster* (1944), a voice intrudes to remind us that Patrick Cory (Richard Arlen) has been sent to prison for his role in an experiment to keep a dead man's brain alive. The voice also reminds us that this is to be a film with a happy ending, and that Cory will emerge from jail to find his beloved waiting for him. Since no voice has been heard up to this point, we wonder whose it is. It must belong to a supernatural power that knows more about the script than the screenwriter does.

Despite its title, Jacques Tourneur's *I Walked with a Zombie* (1943) is a superior horror film. Initially, the movie is narrated by the "I" of the title—a Canadian nurse who has come to the West Indies to tend to a woman who turns out to be a zombie. At the end, the zombie is killed by her brother-in-law, who then commits suicide. Suddenly, a male voice asks God to pardon the unholy couple. The switch from the nurse's voice to the voice from beyond imparts a moralistic tone to a film that otherwise has remained aloof from moral issues. Perhaps the coda was a sop to the Legion of Decency, which frowned on suicide. (The Legion of Decency was a Catholic organization that rated films along moral lines from 1934 through the mid-1960s.) Still, it vitiates the artistry of an unusually intelligent B movie.

Voice-over, then, is not just faceless sound; it is a narrative device that can serve different purposes. It can be personal (the narrating "I") or impersonal (voice of God); it can reveal the contents of a letter or the contents of the unconscious; it can refresh a character's memory or our own. Because of its versatility, voice-over is often abused; for this reason, one should always be sure to approach its use critically.

NOTES

[1]For a readable guide to all the individuals involved in the making of a movie, see Eric Taub, *Gaffers, Grips and Best Boys* (New York: St. Martin's Press, 1987).

Film, Space, and Image

3

A s discussed in chapter 1, film can manipulate time. But it can also manipulate space. The subject can be near or far, partial or full, stationary or moving. How we see the image, and how much of it we see, are the result of the filmmaker's choice of shot.

TYPES OF SHOTS

A shot is simply what is recorded by a single operation of the camera. Shots can be defined in terms of distance. Does the camera appear to be close to the subject? If so, the shot is a close-up (CU)—in terms of human anatomy, a shot of the head, for example. Perhaps it is a head-and-shoulders shot, in which case it is a close shot (CS). If it is a specific part of the body—an eye, a mouth—the shot is an extreme close-up (ECU). A shot of the complete human figure, with some of the background visible, is a full shot (FS) or a long shot (LS). If the camera is so far away that the result is a broad, panoramic view, it is an extreme long shot (ELS). A shot that is neither a close shot nor a long shot but something in between is a medium shot (MS), showing, for example, the subject head to waist or waist to knees.

Perhaps the shot defines an area—a room, say, with all its appointments; such a shot is an establishing shot (ES), a type of long shot that is often broken down into its components. *Establishing shot* can also mean a shot that establishes location (e.g., the Golden Gate Bridge in San Francisco; the Eiffel Tower in Paris), so that the viewer knows the setting and where the action takes place.

Shots can also be defined by what they contain. A two-shot includes two characters; a three-shot includes three characters. "Shot/reverse shot" is the principle of alternating shots of characters in a conversation so that first one character, then the other is seen.

CLOSE-UPS AND LONG SHOTS

Jean-Luc Godard was fond of saying that the close-up was invented for tragedy, the long shot for comedy. This is something of an oversimplification, since long shots and extreme long shots are staples of the western. But at least Godard was suggesting that filmmakers have reasons for choosing one shot over another depending on the kind of movie they are making or the type of scene they are shooting. A close-up can reveal a particular emotion for which, under the circumstances, a long shot would have been inappropriate. When Lucy (Lillian Gish) is denounced by her father in *Broken Blossoms*, Griffith uses a close-up to express her fear.

The close-up is also a means of emphasis. Hitchcock found it ideal for objects like a suspicious glass of milk (*Suspicion*, 1941), an envelope dropped by a Nazi agent (*Saboteur*, 1942), and a wine bottle filled with uranium ore (*Notorious*, 1946). These objects are so crucial to the plot that Hitchcock was unwilling to assume they would be noticed unless their presence was emphasized.

Hitchcock also used the extreme close-up for reasons having to do with genre. *Psycho* is a horror film; audiences expect the proverbial chill up the spine, and Hitchcock does not fail them: the extreme close-ups of Marion Crane's screaming mouth and staring eye in the shower sequence stay in the memory. Extreme close-ups of the eye are, in fact, standard in horror films, especially if it is the eye of the killer spying on a prospective victim through a peephole, as is the case in *Psycho* and *The Spiral Staircase* (1946).

The extreme close-up is not just an embellishment; like any shot, it can have a direct bearing on the plot. The words "Prognosis Negative," which confirm Judith Traherne's terminal condition in *Dark Victory*, must be visible, and that can only be done in extreme close-up. If a scar identifies a murderer, as it does in *A Stranger Knocks* (1963), the scar needs to be photographed in ECU.

The ECU should be used sparingly, however; too many such shots create an imbalance in the film. They are such an extreme form of emphasis that a preponderance of them is like the speech pattern of someone who gives equal emphasis to every word, including *a* and *the*.

While the close-up is useful to point up the intense emotion of tragedy, the long shot—despite Godard's assertion—can be ideal for tragedy as well, since it makes death less painful to watch. The death of Santiago (Arthur Kennedy) in Edgar G. Ulmer's *The Naked Dawn* (1955) is photographed in long shot. Santiago is on horseback when the bullet strikes him; we see neither stunned eyes nor spurting blood. The shot has a formalized beauty about it that is reminiscent of a painting like Breughel's *Fall of Icarus*, in which the death of Icarus is made part of the setting.

Western filmmakers favor long shots and extreme long shots because these shots make the subject part of the environment in addition to conveying the vastness and awesomeness of nature. In George Stevens's *Shane* (1953), a deer laps water from a stream with snow-fringed mountains in the background. A man bids farewell to a woman who merges with the landscape as he rides off in John Ford's *My Darling Clementine* (1946). Many of Ford's long shots have an intensely pictorial quality. In *Clementine*, we see a stretch of sky brooding over the dusty main street of Tombstone, a bar thronged by men—sometimes in silhouette, sometimes illuminated by the kerosene lamps that hang overhead—and Monument Valley with its cliffs and mesas rising skyward from a flat plain and dwarfing all who pass beneath them.

HIGH-ANGLE AND LOW-ANGLE SHOTS

Shots are also defined by the position of the camera in relation to the subject. When Lillian (Jane Fonda) looks out of her hotel window in *Julia* (1977), what she sees on the street below is rendered as a high-angle shot. In a high-angle shot, the camera is positioned above (sometimes "high above") the subject. This is occasionally referred to as a *God's eye view*, a type of shot used by Hitchcock to suggest an unseen presence looking

Orson Welles prepares for a low-angle shot, below floor level, in *Citizen Kane* (1941). *(Courtesy MOMA/FSA and RKO)*

down on the subject. If the camera shoots up at the subject from below, it is a low-angle shot.

A low-angle shot makes the subject loom larger than it actually is. Such a shot can suggest dominance or power, as it does in *Citizen Kane* when Kane's guardian hovers over him as he presents the young Kane with a sled. Conversely, a high-angle shot makes the subject seem smaller than it is. When a member of the French underground interrogates the title character in *When Willie Comes Marching Home*, the high angle from which Willie is photographed suggests the feeling of helplessness that the intense cross-examination produces.

The high angle-shot of the president pacing the floor in D. W. Griffith's *Abraham Lincoln* (1930) reminds us that the burdens of the office dwarf even the great. In *All the President's Men*, as reporters Bob Woodward and Carl Bernstein are sorting out library slips, the camera watches them from above; indeed, they seem to grow smaller as they realize the enormity of their task. The scene ends with the camera's peering down at the reading room of the Library of Congress, which looks like a magnified snowflake.

Sometimes the script requires a high- or low-angle shot for reasons that have nothing to do with symbolism or imagery. In *Julia*, the shot following Lillian at the window had to be a high-angle shot; an eye-level shot would have made no sense. If a man is waiting at the foot of a staircase for a woman to descend, as Gabriel (Donal McCann) waits for Gretta (Anjelica Huston) near the end of John Huston's *The Dead* (1987), the woman must be photographed in a low-angle shot to match the man's angle of vision.

In *The Blue Dahlia* (1946), Mrs. Harwood (Veronica Lake) is on the mezzanine of a hotel when she phones down to Johnny Morrison (Alan Ladd) at the registration desk in the lobby; the camera had to shoot *down* at Morrison in order to match the angle from which Mrs. Harwood saw him. The context of the action determines the nature of the shot.

The same holds true of other types of shots; the screenplay and its interpretation by the filmmaker dictate the nature of the shots.

SUBJECTIVE CAMERA

An objective shot represents what the camera sees; a subjective shot (sometimes referred to as subjective camera) represents what the character sees. As the Joads drive into a Hooverville in *The Grapes of Wrath*, the residents are looking straight ahead as they step aside for the truck. At whom are they staring? one might ask. They are looking at the Joads, whom we cannot see. Thus, they are looking at *us*: we have been put behind the wheel in order to see poverty and squalor through the Joads' eyes. When, through voice-over, Henry Hill in *GoodFellas* recalls the time he entered a Mafia restaurant, director Martin Scorsese used subjective camera. Instead of showing Hill personally making a round of the tables, the diners looked directly into the lens as if they were acknowledging Hill's presence. Subjective camera implied that Hill, though unseen, is still a force to be reckoned with.

Sometimes in a film we experience sheer motion without a corresponding image. In *Marnie*, for example, Mark (Sean Connery) is seated at his desk when Marnie enters the room. Mark looks straight into the camera, acknowledging Marnie's presence. We do not see her, however; we only experience some sense of movement toward the desk. For a moment we have become Marnie, but we cease to be Marnie when she comes into view.

Robert Redford and Dustin Hoffman prepare for the Library of Congress scene in *All the President's Men* (1976). The camera is set for a high shot. *(Courtesy Warner Bros., Inc.)*

Because subjective camera offers a one-sided take on reality, it should never dominate a film as it did in *Lady in the Lake* (1946)—the textbook case of how not to make the audience a participant in the action. The main character in the film, Philip Marlowe (Robert Montgomery), is never seen except in a mirror. As a result, there are scenes in which the other characters, supposedly looking at him, stare straight into the camera, which represents Marlowe and, by extension, the audience. When a woman kisses Marlowe, she has to purse her lips into the lens, which makes it seem as though she is kissing the audience. When she lights Marlowe's cigarette, she thrusts the lighter into the lens as if she were about to ignite the viewer.

Subjective camera should be restricted to specific scenes or sequences, as is the case in *Dark Passage* (1947), in which the plot requires subjective shots. Unjustly convicted of his wife's murder, Vincent Parry (Humphrey Bogart) escapes from San Quentin to track down the real killer. He cannot solve the murder looking as he does because his picture

A low-angle shot of Gretta (Anjelica Huston) descending the stairs in *The Dead* (1987). *(Frame enlargement courtesy Vestron Pictures)*

is in every newspaper, so he chooses to undergo plastic surgery. Director Delmer Daves, who also wrote the screenplay, had two options. He could use another actor in the early scene and, after the operation, introduce Bogart, or he could use a combination of subjective camera and Bogart's voice for the first thirty minutes and then drop subjective camera after Bogart finally appears. Daves was pretty much forced to do the latter: in 1947, Humphrey Bogart was too big a star to make his initial appearance thirty minutes into the picture.

Parry escapes by concealing himself in a barrel that has been loaded onto a prison truck. The camera is totally subjective, jostling us as Parry maneuvers the barrel from the truck and making us reel with dizziness as it rolls down a hill. When the barrel comes to rest, we peer out of it cautiously but get no more than a tunnel-like view of the outside. Parry is now a presence. When he hitches a ride, the driver speaks to the presence, who answers but is still unseen. When the driver recognizes him, the presence knocks him unconscious. Later, the presence scans the highway and climbs into Irene Jansen's (Lauren Bacall) waiting car.

When the presence showers, a hand adjusts the shower head and a

A low-angle shot from *Suddenly, Last Summer* (1959), showing Violet Venable (Katharine Hepburn) ascending in her private elevator. *(Courtesy Margaret Herrick Library of the Academy of Motion Picture Arts and Sciences)*

jet of water sprays the camera lens. Camera movements express the presence's emotional state. When the presence is wary, the camera darts in the same direction as his apprehensive eyes. A telephone rings, and the camera swings around the way a tense person does at an unexpected sound. Gradually, Daves begins to switch from subjective to objective camera, from Parry as a presence to Parry as a character. The transition begins in a cab at night, so Bogart's face is kept in shadow. The sympathetic cabdriver recommends plastic surgery and refers Parry to a reliable doctor. After the operation, Bogart's voice returns to his body, and the camera ceases to be subjective.

Related to subjective camera is the point-of-view (POV) shot. A POV shot represents the point of view of the character, or what the character sees. A famous shot of this kind occurs at the end of Hitchcock's *Spellbound* (1945) when Dr. Murchison (Leo G. Carroll) is unmasked as the murderer of the former director of a mental institution. Murchison aims a gun at his accuser and then turns it around to fire at himself. The close-up of the gun with which Murchison commits suicide is a POV shot, representing the way he saw the gun when he turned it on himself.

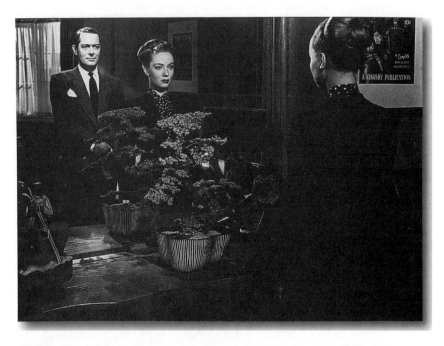

Philip Marlowe's (Robert Montgomery) reflection in *Lady in the Lake* (1946), the subjective camera film in which Marlowe is visible only when a mirror catches his image. *(Courtesy WCFTR)*

SHOTS AS PARTS OF A WHOLE

It is easy to become enamored of particular shots, especially those that are strikingly photographed. The close-up of the burning crucifix in *Amadeus* (1986) is a powerful moment in the film. It would still have an impact, though perhaps not the same kind, if one saw a still or a frame enlargement of it without having seen the film. It is the context that makes the shot not only powerful but chilling: Salieri, realizing Mozart's superiority, is so angry with God for giving him a rival that he destroys a symbol of his faith. The clock without hands that the main character sees in his dream in Ingmar Bergman's *Wild Strawberries* (1957) is a shot that would still have an effect if it were taken out of context. If one were shown a still or a frame enlargement of it and asked what it meant, the reply would be something like "time has stopped" or even "death"—a good answer, and not all that different from what it means in the film. But in *Wild Strawberries*, the clock without hands is one of the film's many death symbols; it therefore takes

Tight framing in *Detour* (1946). The camera tracks in for a close-up of Roberts (Tom Neal), who looks imprisoned within the frame. *(Frame enlargement courtesy John Belton)*

on its deepest meaning within the context of the film, which is a death odyssey.

At the end of *Radio Days*, a father holds his son lovingly on his lap. Anyone who saw a still of that scene without knowing anything about the film would assume that the character was a caring father. Yet throughout the movie, it is obvious that the father is not especially affectionate toward his son. The reason the boy is on his father's lap is that he is getting a spanking. As he is being spanked, a report comes over the radio that a child who had fallen into a well has died. Suddenly the father's attitude changes, and instead of punishing his son he caresses him. The death of someone else's child has made the father feel warmer toward his own.

Shots are like excerpts; just as some excerpts communicate more information than others, so, too, do shots. The excerpt is part of the work, just as the shot is part of the total film in which its meaning resides.

FRAMING THE SHOT

The concept of framing is easily understood by anyone who has either studied painting or has actually painted. Framing is the act, and sometimes the art, of composing a shot, reflecting decisions similar to those painters make about how their canvas will ultimately look. The filmmaker's canvas is the frame, the strip of celluloid on which the image is captured. Like a painter, the filmmaker must arrange the details of the frame in terms of the visual or dramatic points being made, or the ideas being expressed.

Although there are no ironclad rules of framing, certain principles are widely followed.

Tight framing gives a feeling of oppression. In tight framing, the subject appears confined within the horizontal and vertical borders of the frame so that there is not even a hint of offscreen space. To create an atmosphere of

The juxtaposition of strong verticals (the soldiers' legs) and stable horizontals (steps) with broken lines (sprawled bodies and hands raised in supplication) suggest the dominance of the Cossacks and the helplessness of the people in *Potemkin*. *(Courtesy MOMA/FSA and Janus Films)*

fatalism, Edgar G. Ulmer chose tight framing for several shots of Roberts (Tom Neal) in *Detour* (1946). When Roberts's face is trapped within the frame, destiny seems to be closing in on him.

The frame should be slightly asymmetrical. Whatever is to be emphasized should occupy a position of prominence, but not in the center of the frame. If the image were dead center, a sense of depth would be lost because the subject would seem to be stamped on the frame. If a disorienting or unusual effect is sought, the extremity of the frame might be used. For example, in *Detour*, when Roberts discovers that Vera (Ann Savage) has accidentally strangled herself with a telephone cord, her body is seen right of frame, the head hanging over the bed.

Vertical and horizontal compositions denote solidarity; diagonals and oblique compositions denote tension. In *Potemkin*, the masts of the ships, the raised arms of the sailors, and the waving arms of the people suggest a solidarity that is destroyed when the Cossacks appear at the top of the Odessa steps. Their shadows falling on the steps create a diagonal that breaks the unity. A canted shot (also known as a Dutch angle shot) results in an

A canted shot of Orson Welles as Harry Lime in *The Third Man* (1949). *(Courtesy MOMA/FSA)*

oblique composition in which the frame looks lopsided. Edgar G. Ulmer uses canted shots in *Bluebeard* (1944) to emphasize the madness of the central character; the canted shots in *The Third Man* (1949) imply a world in which things are askew. In the violent argument between the title character and her mother in *Carrie* (1976), the frame looks as if it will tip over.

When an IRA hostage speaks wistfully of his "special friendship" with a hairdresser in *The Crying Game* (1992), director Neil Jordan chooses a canted shot, which should cause us to wonder why the frame is tipped. Is Jordan suggesting that their relationship is not entirely conventional? Eventually we discover that this is the case: the hairdresser is a transvestite.

Sometimes vertical framing is intentionally ironic. In *Address*

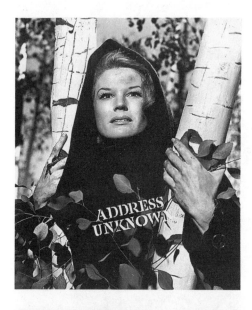

DECEPTIVE AND DEBARRING VERTICALS

Griselle (K. T. Stevens) in *Address Unknown* (1944) is framed between two trees, expecting to be saved from the mob that is pursuing her. Here the verticals are a support, but only a temporary one. *(Courtesy Sony Pictures Entertainment)*

Griselle before the gate leading to the home of a family friend who will not receive her *(Address Unknown)*. *(Courtesy Sony Pictures Entertainment)*

Unknown (1944), Griselle (K. T. Stevens) flees from a mob that has discovered she is Jewish. She hopes to find refuge in the home of a family friend. Framed by trees, she looks hopefully into the distance where the friend lives. Ordinarily, such a composition, with its strong verticals, would imply hope. However, Griselle is a Jew in Nazi Germany, and the man she assumes is a friend has become a Nazi.

Vertical bars across the face, on the other hand, have another connotation: mystery, imprisonment, exclusion. When Carmen (Rita Hayworth) appears behind a beaded curtain in *The Loves of Carmen* (1948), the verticals give her face an exotic yet dangerous look. When Griselle, in *Address Unknown*, finally arrives at the friend's house and stands before the gate, the composition recalls the earlier one in which she was framed by trees. Here, however, the gate is a barrier, and even though she reaches it she still does not gain access to the house. The use of verticals in this different composition, as bars across the face, suggests exclusion: prevented from entering, Griselle is killed by the Gestapo.

Geometrical compositions can be symbolic as well as visually interesting. In Jungian psychology, the circle is a symbol of wholeness, suggesting unity and commonality. Such is the case in *Sahara* (1943) when Sergeant Joe Gunn (Humphrey Bogart) passes a cup of water around to his thirsty men, who stand in a circle. If a composition involves three characters, triangular arrangements can make a statement about their relationship, as is the case in François Truffaut's *Jules and Jim* (1961), in which two men share the affections of the same woman.

Iconography should be unobtrusive. If the filmmaker is imitating a painting or a sculpture, the composition should look natural even though it is a replica of, or an homage to, a favorite work of art. The beggars' banquet in Luis Buñuel's *Viridiana* (1961) is an obvious parody of *The Last Supper*, made even more so by the use of the "Hallelujah Chorus" as background music. A less blatant parody of *The Last Supper* occurs in Robert Altman's *M*A*S*H* (1970) when the medics stage a literal last supper for the dentist who plans to commit suicide because he thinks he is impotent. Christ imagery with crucifixion and "way of the cross" motifs tends to call attention to itself: when the bloodied Terry Malloy (Marlon Brando) staggers along the dock at the end of *On the Waterfront* (1954), one might recall Christ on his way to Calvary. A more subtle "way of the cross" appears in Capra's *Meet John Doe* (1941) when the title character makes his lonely way through a crowd that reviles him.

The angle at which the subject is viewed is determined by two factors: narrative logic and symbolic implications. As we have seen, if a character is looking out of a hotel window onto the street below, the shot that follows must be a high-angle one. Similarly, if a character is on the ground looking up at someone, the person at whom the character is looking must be pho-

TRIANGULAR COMPOSITIONS IN *JULES AND JIM* (1961) SHOWING CATHERINE (JEANNE MOREAU), JULES (OSCAR WERNER), AND JIM (HENRI SERRE), WHO BECOME *A MÉNAGE À TROIS.* The *ménage* running. *(Courtesy MOMA/FSA and Janus Films)*

The *ménage* shot from below. *(Courtesy MOMA/FSA and Janus Films)*

tographed at a low angle, with the camera shooting upward. Since subjects photographed from a high angle look small and those photographed from a low angle look large, high-angle shots can imply inferiority, defeat, or oppression; low-angle shots, power, dominance, superiority. Susan Alexander Kane is often photographed at a high angle in *Citizen Kane* because she is dominated by her husband, who is often photographed from a low angle.

The focus within the frame depends on how much or how little is to be seen. If the filmmaker decides that in a particular shot, foreground, middle ground, and background should be equally visible, the shot will have a deep focus. In *Citizen Kane*, Orson Welles used deep focus for several reasons: to convey a greater sense of depth, to minimize the need to cut from one shot to another, and to bring out meanings that might not otherwise be apparent. The classic deep-focus shot in *Kane* shows Mary Kane making arrangements with a banker who is to raise her son as a gentleman because she and her husband cannot. The position of the mother

A different triangular composition from *Citizen Kane* (1941), showing Kane (center) flanked by Thatcher (left) and Bernstein (right) as he is about to relinquish control of his enterprises after the crash of 1929. The position of Kane at the apex of the triangle makes him both the focus of attention and an object of defeat, since he is dwarfed by the more prominent figures of Thatcher and Bernstein. *(Courtesy MOMA/FSA)*

(foreground), banker and father (middle ground), and son (background, seen through the window blissfully playing in the snow) says infinitely more about the way young Kane's life is being signed away without his knowledge than would be the case if the action were broken down into four separate shots: mother, father, banker, son.

Sometimes shallow focus is preferred—for example, when the background should not be as distinct as the foreground because it would detract from the foreground. At other times, the background must remain indistinct until the time for it to be clear. In such a case, the filmmaker will pull focus: first, the background will be a blur and the foreground sharp; then the background will be sharp and the foreground blurry. This technique, known as *rack focus*, is used in *Time After Time* (1976). Someone is behind the heroine, but the person's face is a blur. Then the face comes into focus, and we realize that it is Jack the Ripper's.

Focus may be deliberately erratic, with the image going in and out of focus, as might happen if a character is hallucinating, disoriented, or drunk. In *Detour*, when Roberts realizes that Vera has accidentally strangled herself, objects go in and out of focus as he looks around the room in a state of shock.

Iconographic Framing: *The Last Supper* parody in *Viridiana* (1961). (*Courtesy MOMA/FSA and Janus Films*)

Another *Last Supper* parody in *M*A*S*H* (1970). (*Courtesy Margaret Herrick Library of the Academy of Motion Picture Arts and Sciences*)

If the frame is to be masked—that is, if its shape is to be altered—the same considerations that govern other framing techniques apply: narrative logic and symbolic value. If a character is peering through a pair of binoculars, a telescope, a microscope, or a keyhole, the next shot should assume the appropriate configuration.

If a character is positioned in a doorway, the result is a frame-within-a-frame, or double framing; within the film frame is another frame—the frame created by the doorway. Double framing may reveal something about the character so framed. John Ford often uses the frame-within-the-frame, especially in *The Searchers* (1956). When Ethan (John Wayne), who will always be a loner and a searcher, returns with Debbie, the object of his search, he remains in a doorway while the others go inside the house.

Because doorways and archways resemble the proscenium arch of a theater, they have a dramatic effect. In John Ford's *The Quiet Man* (1952), Mary Kate (Maureen O'Hara) is framed in the doorway as Sean (John Wayne) pulls her toward him. In William Wyler's *The Little Foxes* (1941), the Hubbards do their plotting in the archway of the drawing room, thus seeming like the stage villains they were in Lillian Hellman's play.

The long take—a shot that lasts more than a minute—can also be framed. Recall the definition of a shot: a single run of the camera. The camera can accommodate ten minutes' worth of film, although few filmmakers would allow it to run for that length (Hitchcock did so in *Rope* [1948], an eighty-minute film consisting of eight ten-minute takes. *Rope*, however, was an experiment—and not an especially successful one.) The average shot lasts between ten and twenty seconds, but many shots are often longer, and even a three-minute shot can be framed.

The most famous long take in American film is the three-minute credits sequence in Orson Welles's *Touch of Evil* (1958). Someone puts a time bomb in the trunk of a car. Two people get into the car and proceed down the street of a Mexican border town, past Mr. and Mrs. Vargas (Charlton Heston and Janet Leigh). The Vargases reach the customs booth before the couple do. In their conversation with the customs officer, we learn that Mrs. Vargas is American and Mr. Vargas, soon revealed to be Mexican, is a narcotics agent. Then the car with the couple pulls up to the booth. The driver, Mr. Linnekar, is known to the customs officer. The woman with him, who admits that she is not an American citizen, complains about a "ticking noise," but the customs officer does not take her seriously. The Vargases, who behave like newlyweds, are more interested in each other than in the occupants of the car. The car crosses the border, continues a short distance, and then explodes into flames. Within three minutes of uninterrupted camera movement, we have had the credits, been introduced to two of the main characters, discovered that the drug trade will be an important element of the plot, learned that Mrs. Vargas is American while her husband is Mexican, witnessed a car bombing that will have to be explained, and entered a world where the unpredictable and the incalculable are the norm. Welles chose to make the credits sequence of *Touch of Evil* a long take and framed it accordingly, creating an atmosphere of restlessness with a camera that is continually moving.

In *GoodFellas*, there is a long take that lasts well over a minute. It begins with Henry Hill and Karen entering the Copacabana through the kitchen; as they do, the camera follows them, proceeding through a labyrinth of corridors and past stoves, ovens, and sinks—up a flight of stairs into the foyer, where, despite a reservations line, the couple are immediately escorted to a table to which a waiter brings their specially prepared meal. But the shot does not end there; Scorsese pans right to left—to the next table, where a party is seated that obviously knows Henry; and then diagonally to the bandstand, where the comedian Henny Youngman is set to perform. The beauty of Scorsese's long take is its ability to capture the unbroken rhythm of an action through camera work of incredible fluidity.

Shots can be framed graphically in terms of lines (horizontals, verticals, diagonals); they can be framed geometrically or iconographically; in deep or shallow focus; from a high or a low angle; in a frame that has been masked or doubled. A shot can last a second or run ten minutes. Guided by a script that requires a scene to be filmed in a particular way and by aesthetic considerations that will enhance the script and enrich the narrative, the filmmaker makes his or her decisions. These decisions, however, should not be accepted on faith; rather, the viewer should ask if the decisions were the right ones.

THE MOVING SHOT

Movement in film can be deceptive. In the three-minute long take in *Touch of Evil*, the camera was literally moving. However, when the camera rotates horizontally on a fixed axis (pan shot) or vertically (tilt shot), it is not, strictly speaking, moving. The camera head—but not the camera itself, which is probably on a tripod—is moving. For mobile camera shots, the camera is on a moving vehicle such as a dolly, a truck, or a crane, or on specially built tracks. The mobile camera has the advantage of being able to add to the narrative by opening up more space, thereby augmenting what is seen. The pan and the tilt can add to our knowledge, too.

Pan shots generally move left to right in imitation of the reading eye, but they can also go from right to left. In *The Thin Man* (1934), it does both in the same shot. As Nora Charles (Myrna Loy) opens a door on the right, the camera pans right to left, from the doorway to the interior, where her husband is comforting a weeping girl. When the husband catches sight of his wife, the camera pans left to right, back to Nora in the doorway, as if it, too, were embarrassed at what it has discovered. Through panning, a filmmaker can have the camera comment on a situation, thus making the camera almost a character. As David Locke (Jack Nicholson) in Michelangelo Antonioni's *The Passenger* (1975) cries aloud in desperation because his Land Rover is stalled in the sand, the camera answers by panning the indifferent desert. Martin Scorsese uses slow, almost languid pans of the characters' living rooms in *The Age of Innocence*—the slow panning suggesting lives of leisure. A swish pan (unusually rapid panning that produces a momentary blur) can suggest a sudden change or a transformation. In Rouben Mamoulian's *Dr. Jekyll and Mr. Hyde* (1932), there is a swish pan immediately after Dr. Jekyll drinks the potion and becomes Mr. Hyde.

When the camera pivots vertically, the result is a tilt shot (sometimes called a vertical pan; hence the expression *pan up/down*). Tilting also mimics eye movement: in this case the eye's tendency to move up the face of a building to take in its height, or down a column of names. In *Jane Eyre* (1944), the camera tilts down from a plaque that reads "Lowood Institution" to the figure of the sleeping Jane Eyre, who is being carried into it. In *Citizen Kane*, the camera tilts up to the entrance gate of Kane's estate, Xanadu, past the No Trespassing sign, reminding us that the warning applies to everyone but itself. At the end of the film, the camera tilts *down* the gate to the No Trespassing sign as it returns to its starting point.

Like the pan, the tilt shot can be a silent spectator, commenting visually on a situation. As the vampire is about to sink her teeth into a victim's neck in *Dracula's Daughter* (1936), the camera begins tilting up the wall, leaving the rest to the viewer's imagination. A tilt shot can even suggest the actual or potential fate of a character. When Phillip Vandamm (James Mason) in Hitchcock's *North by Northwest* (1959) discovers that his mistress is an American agent, he decides to kill her aboard a plane: "This matter is something that is best disposed of at a great height—over water," he remarks. At the mention of *height*, the camera tilts up—to nothing but empty space.

As it pans or tilts, the camera guides the eye horizontally or vertically, determining both the direction and the object of the audience's vision. Tilt-pan and pan-tilt combinations are also possible, to direct the viewer's or the character's gaze across one surface and up or down another. In *The Passenger*, the camera is in the process of tracing the curve of a surface wire up the wall of a hotel room when a sudden knock at the door interrupts its ascent, causing it to backtrack over to the door to see who is there.

A combination of panning and tilting occurs in the notorious flashback in Hitchcock's *Stage Fright* (1950), which is later revealed to have been a total lie. Jonathan Cooper (Richard Todd) is explaining to his bewildered girlfriend how Charlotte Inwood (Marlene Dietrich) begged him to go to her flat and bring her a new dress; it seems the one she was wearing is stained with her husband's blood. As Cooper enters the flat, the camera pans across the room to Mr. Inwood's body and then tilts up a closet door. At first the camera's tilting up a clothes closet seems odd, but it is part of Hitchcock's plan to make Cooper's story believable. Thus, Hitchcock has the camera guide Cooper to the closet, from which he removes the dress, as if Cooper did not know where the closet was. If Cooper had headed straight for the closet, the audience would sense that he was more familiar with Charlotte's flat than he should be and would therefore not accept his story.

As we have seen, in panning and tilting the camera itself does not move. Strictly speaking, then, a pan or a tilt is not a moving shot, since the camera merely rotates on a tripod. In a moving shot, the camera moves with, toward, alongside, or away from its subjects. There are several kinds of moving shots, depending on the way in which the camera moves. If it moves on tracks, it is a tracking shot; if it is mounted on a dolly, a dolly shot; if it moves up and down, in and out of a scene on a crane, it is a crane shot, which is easily identified by its ascending or descending motion, although a crane can move laterally as well.

Preparing for a crane shot in *Cover Girl* (1944), with the camera in a mechanical arm. *(Courtesy MOMA/FSA)*

Some writers use the terms *dolly shot* and *tracking shot* interchangeably; the camera dollies in (tracks in) when it moves toward the subject and dollies out (tracks out) when it moves away from the subject. Other writers simply call any shot in which the camera is moving on a vehicle (a truck, a dolly, a bicycle) a tracking shot, which is identified by the direction of the camera: forward tracking shot, vertical tracking shot, diagonal tracking shot.

Tracking shots have distinct advantages over other types because they can encompass a greater area and supply more detail; thus, they can sustain a mood for a longer period of time. While the pan and tilt can act as a silent commentator, the track can be a character's alter ego or unseen companion. Max Ophuls was a master of the moving shot. In his films, the camera seems to waltz and glide; it can rush up the stairs with the breathless lovers or accompany them on a stroll, occasionally slipping behind a fountain so as not to be conspicuous. In *Letter from an Unknown Woman*, Ophuls makes the camera almost human. As a provincial band ruins Wagner's "Song to the Evening Star," the camera, unable to stand the tinny sound, rises up fastidiously and leaves the square. In the same film, the camera accompanies the operagoers up the grand staircase as if it were escorting them.

The moving camera can draw viewers physically into the action, and it can even lure them into a character's consciousness, as it does in the film version of Eugene O'Neill's *Long Day's Journey into Night.* The crane shot that ends the film is one of the great feats of moviemaking; in it Lumet manages to incorporate almost all of Mary Tyrone's great monologue. Mary (Katharine Hepburn) is in her parlor with her husband and two sons. She recalls how a nun had dissuaded her from entering the convent because she claimed to have visions of Our Lady of Lourdes. If regression could be visualized, it would consist of gradual diminution. Almost as soon as Mary begins her monologue, the camera starts pulling back from her; then it rises up as her thoughts leave this world. As Mary grows smaller, so do her husband and sons. As the monologue draws to a close, Mary appears in close-up as she speaks the final lines: "That was in the winter of senior year. Then in the spring something happened to me. Yes, I remember. I fell in love with James Tyrone and was so happy for a time." Mary's close-up is followed by close-ups of the other Tyrones; then there is one last close-up of Mary's face, now strangely peaceful.

Many filmmakers today favor the Steadicam for moving shots because it reduces the need for complex camera setups. The principle is simple: the camera is attached to a body harness worn by the cameraperson, enabling him or her to achieve the fluidity of a mobile camera without the jerkiness that usually results from a handheld camera.

ZOOMS AND FREEZES

Likewise, many filmmakers prefer the zoom to the moving shot because it is both economical and timesaving. Technically, the zoom is not a moving shot because the camera does not move; rather, an adjustable lens gives the impression of its moving close to, or far away from, the subject (hence, the terms *zoom in/zoom out*). There are occasions when a zoom is useful: to single out someone in a crowd, to pinpoint the criminal's hiding place in the woods, to capture a facial expression without the person's being aware of the camera's presence. Zooming also flattens the image, creating an unreal sense of depth. However, some filmmakers may prefer such a two-dimensional effect. Stanley Kubrick clearly did in *Barry Lyndon,* in which he deliberately zoomed out of close-ups to reveal scenes that resembled paintings—a technique in keeping with his purpose of portraying the eighteenth century as if it were on exhibit at an art gallery.

The opposite of the zoom, which represents deceptive motion, is the

The most famous freeze frame in film: the final shot in *The 400 Blows* (1959). *(Courtesy MOMA/FSA and Janus Films)*

freeze, which is a form of stopped motion. In a freeze, all movement suddenly halts, and the image "freezes" as it turns into a still photograph. The most famous freeze occurs at the end of François Truffaut's *The 400 Blows* (1959). Antoine Doinel (Jean-Pierre Léaud) escapes from a reformatory and heads toward the ocean. When he reaches the water's edge, he walks into the shallows; then he turns and faces the shore. At that instant Truffaut freezes the frame, trapping Antoine between the reformatory and the ocean, between the past and the present. The freeze implies immobility, helplessness, or indecison.

The zoom and the freeze are similar in that they can call attention to details more dramatically than other devices do. Because of their strong underscoring power, they are as easily misused as italics are by inexperienced writers. Since many contemporary films end with a freeze frame, which then becomes the background for the end credits, examples of an intelligent use of the freeze frame are hard to come by. A great filmmaker will freeze for a reason; a mediocre one will freeze for effect. The freeze at the end of *Women in Love* (1970), the film version of D. H. Lawrence's novel, is perfectly motivated. The novel comes to no real resolution. The film duplicates the unresolved ending by repeating Lawrence's dialogue, which leads to a natural freeze. When Birkin (Alan Bates) tells Ursula (Jennie Linden) that he wants an "eternal" relationship with another man, Ursula, who cannot conceive of such a relationship, says, "You can't have it, because it's false, impossible." Birkin replies, "I don't believe that," and with these words the novel ends. The same dialogue appears in the film, but when Birkin says, "I don't believe that," Ursula's face freezes into utter bafflement. His words have left her speechless, and what conveys speechlessness better than a freeze?

COMBINING SHOTS: THE SEQUENCE

In film, shots combine to form sequences, or what we generally think of as scenes. Note that some writers prefer to distinguish between a scene and a sequence. A scene, they would say, is a unit of the action that takes place in the same location and is made up of one shot (e.g., a long take) or many shots. A sequence is a group of shots forming a self-contained segment of the film that is by and large intelligible in itself.

From the above definitions, *scene* and *sequence* appear to be virtually synonymous, and for all practical purposes they are. The chief difference is that there can be scenes within a sequence, but not sequences within scenes. In the key sequence in *Notorious*, there are several scenes. The sequence begins in the bedroom with Alicia's removing the key to the wine cellar from Alex's key chain (scene 1); next, she gives the key to Devlin downstairs (scene 2); finally, Devlin and Alicia go down to the wine cellar (scene 3).

There are several kinds of sequences, two of which have already been discussed: credits and precredits sequences (chapter 2). Someone who has not seen Sam Peckinpah's *The Wild Bunch* (1969) and is shown only the credits sequence would still be able to make some sense of it. What appears to be a detachment of cavalry troops rides into a small town. Some children are feeding a pair of scorpions to a horde of ants. The soldiers ride past the children and proceed up the main street toward the payroll office. On the rooftops of the buildings flanking the street is a band of armed men crouching behind the parapets. The soldiers dismount at the payroll office, enter it, flash their .45s, and pistol-whip the employees. By the time all the credits have appeared, a drama in miniature has unfolded in the form of a sequence. The peaceful tenor of the town has been established and threatened. We now know that the troops are bandits; the rooftop crowd, bounty hunters in the employ of the railroad; the townspeople and children, unsuspecting victims of the crossfire that will certainly erupt.

Sequences can also be identified as linear, associative, and montage. Note that these types of sequences are not mutually exclusive. Credits and precredits sequences can be linear (with a beginning, a middle, and an end); they can also be a montage of various shots (like the New York montage that accompanies the credits of Woody Allen's *Manhattan*, 1979). Similarly, an associative sequence can be linear (although a linear sequence is not associative). When a sequence is designated as associative, it means that the links between beginning, middle, and end are not so much narrative as visual.

The Linear Sequence

In a linear sequence, one action links up with another, creating a miniature drama with a beginning, a middle, and an end. Let us return to the key sequence in *Notorious*. The beginning of the sequence initiates the action: Alicia removes the key. The middle adds to the action: Alicia slips the key to her coworker, Harry Devlin, during the party; they proceed to the wine cellar, where they discover that one of the bottles contains uranium ore; meanwhile, the champagne supply dwindles, and Alicia's husband and the wine steward go down to the cellar. The end follows and completes the action: the husband discovers his wife with Devlin. In a linear sequence, then, the connections between the incidents are like links in a chain.

After *The Age of Innocence* main title with its rose motif, the action begins with a shot of a basket of daisies—another instance of the role flowers play in the film. A hand plucks one of the daisies; it is the hand of the soprano-singing Marguerite in a performance of Gounod's *Faust*. The setting, then, is an opera house. Everyone is elegantly attired, as shots of bejeweled hands and necks indicate. And the audience is less interested in the opera than in who is sitting next to whom, as the camera imitates the way gossipmongers might use their opera glasses. Newland Archer (Daniel Day Lewis) is seated in a box, wearing a white rose in his lapel. In another box are three women, two of whom will play important roles in his life: his fiancée, May (Winona Ryder), and the Countess Olenska (Michelle Pfeiffer), whose colorful past has made her an object of speculation and, among the self-righteous, scorn. Although Newland insists that his engagement be announced at the ball following the performance, he chooses to sit behind the countess. Indifferent to the opera, they recall their childhood together. *Faust*, which will be heard again, was not an arbitrary choice on Scorsese's part. In the opera, Faust gives up his soul to possess Marguerite. In the film, Archer sells his soul, one might say, to respectability by choosing to marry the conventional May rather than the unconventional countess, whom he really loves. Although the opening sequence lasts only a few minutes, it establishes the setting (mid-nineteenth-century New York) and introduces the characters (New York society), three of whom (Archer, May, and the countess) become the principal ones. The beginning introduces us to a privileged world; the middle, to a world where appearances alone count; and the end, to a world where a man who cannot wait to announce his engagement to an innocent young woman chooses to sit next to one whose innocence is questionable.

In some linear sequences, however, a few links may be missing; thus, the sequence is *elliptical*. A linear sequence is designated as elliptical when certain details have been omitted because the viewers are expected to make the connections for themselves. The "Wedding of Angharad" sequence in John Ford's *How Green Was My Valley* (1941) comprises three episodes that appear, on the surface, to be loosely related: "The Courting of Angharad," "The Visit to Gruffydd," and "The Wedding." In the first episode, Evans, a mine owner's son, comes to court Angharad (Maureen O'Hara) after his pompous father has made the initial arrangements. Since Angharad appears to have a mind of her own, there is little likelihood that Evans will win her despite his wealth. Thus, we do not take the courting seriously. In the second episode, Angharad calls on Mr. Gruffydd (Walter Pidgeon), the minister, whom she really loves. There is something disturbing about this episode—it hints at love never to be consummated. Angharad speaks of her affection for the minister to discover if he feels the same toward her. But his only concern is his low salary, which makes marriage impossible. In the third episode, Angharad steps wraithlike into a carriage, her bridal veil billowing in the breeze.

The three episodes become linked by the impressions they create in the audience's mind. Initially, there seems to be no connection between the courting and Angharad's visit to Gruffydd, but the link becomes clear with the final episode: *money*, which means nothing to Angharad but means a great deal to the minister. In choosing Evans, she chose what Gruffydd considered the prerequisite for marriage. The folly of her choice is a mirthless wedding where the wind makes sport of her veil as if it were a kite. The tragedy of her choice is mirrored in the minister's face as he watches the wedding party drive away.

The Associative Sequence

In an associative sequence, the scenes are linked together by an object or a series of objects. In another sequence in *Notorious*, Alicia, who has fallen in love with Devlin, plans an intimate dinner for the two of them. As Devlin leaves for headquarters, Alicia asks him to pick up some wine. In the next scene, Devlin enters his supervisor's office with a bottle of champagne, which he leaves on the desk. When he discovers that Alicia's assignment requires her to seduce Sebastian, he is so disturbed that he forgets the cham-

Harry Devlin (Cary Grant) on the verge of forgetting the champagne in *Notorious* (1946). Hitchcock ends the scene with a close-up of the bottle, the object that unifies the entire sequence. *(Courtesy ABC Picture Holdings, Inc.)*

pagne. Scene 2 ends with a close-up of the bottle. In the third scene, Devlin is back in Alicia's apartment, where the dinner is burned and there is not even any wine to salvage the evening. He looks around for the champagne: "I guess I left it somewhere," he mutters. These three episodes coalesce into a sequence that might be entitled "The Ruined Dinner," whose three scenes might be called "The Bottle Suggested," "The Bottle Purchased," and "The Bottle Forgotten." It is an object that unifies the sequence: the close-up of the bottle in scene 2 links scenes 1 and 3, bringing them into dramatic focus.

A similar sequence occurs in Hitchcock's *Rebecca*. Maxim de Winter's new bride lives in the shadow of her husband's first wife, Rebecca, whose presence is everywhere. In a sequence that might be called "The Ubiquitous Rebecca," we first see a shot of Rebecca's room, closed since her death and guarded by her dog; then a napkin with Rebecca's initials; finally, Maxim de Winter (Laurence Olivier) and his young bride (Joan Fontaine) at opposite ends of a long table. What separates them is not just distance but the spirit of Rebecca, who is present even in the napkins on the table. Hitchcock has fashioned a sequence out of three different shots, each dominated by an object associated with the late Rebecca de Winter: a bedroom door, an embroidered napkin, and a dining-room table.

In the sequence that ends another Hitchcock film, *North by Northwest*, Eve Kendall (Eva Marie Saint) is holding on to the hand of Roger Thornhill (Cary Grant) to keep from sliding off Mt. Rushmore. Thornhill encourages her to "hang in there" and, as an added incentive, proposes marriage. In one of the smoothest transitions in film, the hand to which Eve was just clinging is now helping her climb to the upper berth of a compartment on the Twentieth Century Limited. Without the audience's suspecting it, the scene changed from Mt. Rushmore to the train compartment. Thornhill's hand was the unifying image; it rescued Eve from death and saved her for marriage.

The Montage Sequence

Montage is a word that has many meanings. When it is used to describe a sequence, *montage* can be defined as a series of shots arranged in a particular order for a particular purpose. In a montage sequence, the shots are arranged so that they follow each other in rapid succession, telescoping an event or several events of some duration into a couple of seconds of screen time. *A New Life* (1988) contains a dating montage that shows a newly divorced woman trying to resume a form of socializing she has not done in twenty-five years. Another kind of montage, called *American montage* because it was so prominent in American films of the 1930s and 1940s, works from the same principle: time is collapsed as shots blend together, wipe each other away, or are superimposed on each other. A typical American montage might consist of calendar pages blowing away as one month yields to another, then one year to another, while over the blowing pages are superimposed headlines giving the main events that happened during that time period. Finally, the montage ends, and the action resumes.

Just as an associative sequence can also be linear, a montage sequence can have features of the linear and the associative sequence. A montage sequence compressing a decade into ten seconds could be linear in its chronological arrangement. The World War II montage was common in films of the 1940s. First, one would see a headline announcing the Japanese attack on Pearl Harbor, then subsequent headlines would enumerate key battles, and the last headline would proclaim the Japanese surrender.

A montage can also be unified by images. For example, the tour-of-Washington montage in Capra's *Mr. Smith Goes to Washington* (1939) combines shots of the Capitol, the White House, the Washington Monument, the Lincoln Memorial, and excerpts from Lincoln's Second Inaugural Address and the Gettysburg Address, all of which are associated with the spirit of American democracy.

FROM SHOT TO SHOT

Cuts

Cut is one of the most commonly used terms in film. It can be a verb a director shouts to terminate a shot ("Cut!") or a noun meaning a strip of film or a joint between two separate shots. It can also be a version of a movie in its various stages (rough cut, director's cut, final cut). In the context of this chapter, a cut is the joining of two separate shots so that the first is instantaneously replaced by the second, showing something the preceding shot did not. There are five basic kinds of cuts: straight, contrast, parallel (cross), jump, and form.

In a straight cut, one image instantaneously replaces another. Straight cuts are the most common kind of cuts: shot B replaces shot A. In *The Lady Eve* (1941), Preston Sturges cuts from Charlie Pike (Henry Fonda) sitting at a table in a ship's dining room (shot A) to a group of women staring in his direction (shot B). In a contrast cut, the images replacing each other are dissimilar in nature; for example, the cut from the manacled feet of slaves to the galloping hooves of horses in *Slaves* (1969) contrasts the enslaved and the free.

The parallel cut, or crosscut, presents two actions occurring simultaneously. In *Saboteur,* an attempt to sabotage a battleship at a christening in the Brooklyn Navy Yard is crosscut with the ceremony itself. In *Moonstruck* (1987), a mother is having dinner with a university professor, while her daughter is at the Metropolitan Opera with her lover. *King and Country* (1964) includes two actions that are crosscut: the mock trial of a rat the soldiers are staging in the rain, and the actual trial of a deserter that is being conducted in the barracks. Thus, the plight of the soldier is equated with the plight of the rat. Both the soldier and the rat are victims—the former of a dubious military code and the latter of the soldiers' cruelty, which stems from boredom.

A break in continuity that leaves a gap in the action constitutes a jump cut. In *Darling* (1965), a shot of a couple about twenty yards from the entrance to a building is followed by a shot of them going through the door to the interior of the building. Obviously not everything has to be shown in a particular scene or sequence, but excessive jump-cutting can give a film the continuity of a comic strip. On the other hand, when a knowledgeable director jump-cuts, there is probably a reason. In Jean-Luc Godard's

Breathless (1959), the main character shoots a police officer in Marseilles, runs across a field, and emerges in Paris. Godard is too talented a filmmaker to break continuity without a reason. *Breathless* is the kind of movie that calls attention to itself as a movie: It is dedicated to Monogram Pictures, which produced low-budget films during the 1930s and 1940s, and re-creates the style of the low-budget American film in which a character can move from one location to the other without being seen in transit.

A form cut is a cut from one object to another that is similarly shaped. In *Detour*, there is a cut from a record in a jukebox to a drumhead—one circular object replaces another. Similar in principle to the form cut is the match cut, in which one shot "matches" the other, following it so smoothly that there is no break in continuity. Often a match cut is similar in shape to the shot it matches, although it need not be. In *Indiana Jones and the Last Crusade* (1989), Steven Spielberg uses a match cut to bring Indiana from youth to adulthood. In the first shot, Indiana, the boy (River Phoenix), bows his head to receive the famous hat; as the head lifts in the second shot, the hat is now worn by Indiana, the man (Harrison Ford). Probably the most famous match in film is the one in Stanley Kubrick's *2001: A Space Odyssey* (1968) when an ape hurls a bone into the air in one shot, and a space station in orbit appears in the next. The match condenses the history of evolution into two images.

Transitions

In a cut there is no bridge between shots; one shot simply replaces another. Just as writers use transitional phrases (*however, moreover, in fact*) to bridge ideas, filmmakers use transitional devices to bridge scenes. And just as one can spot transitional phrases, one can also spot transitional devices in film because they are more noticeable than cuts. The following are the chief transitional devices in film.

The Fade

The fade-out is the simplest kind of transition: the light decreases, and the screen goes dark. The opposite is the fade-in, where the light increases as the picture gradually appears on the screen. (The term *fade* generally refers to a fade-out.) Most fade-outs are no more profound than a blank screen, but some can bring an action to an artful close much the way a gifted orator rounds out a sentence. A good illustration is the first fade-out in William Wyler's *Mrs. Miniver* (1942). The first sequence covers a day in the lives of the Minivers. Husband and wife feel guilty for having purchased something the other might find frivolous: Kay (Greer Garson) has bought a new hat, and Clem (Walter Pidgeon) a new car. At the close of

Harry Devlin as the uninvited guest at Alicia's (Ingrid Bergman) party in *Notorious*. Hitchcock will fade out on the back of Grant's head and fade in on his face. *(Courtesy ABC Picture Holdings, Inc.)*

the day, the camera pans the bedroom, pausing at the hat smartly perched on the bedpost. The scene fades out with the hat in silhouette. Fading out on the hat brings the sequence full circle: it began with Kay's buying the hat and ends with its being displayed. We smile at the fade because it provides the same pleasure of recognition we receive when a speech begins and ends with the same image. But we also smile at its wisdom, for it represents one of those little domestic triumphs that seems more meaningful at the end of the day than at the beginning.

In the theater, the curtain sometimes descends between the scenes of an act to mark the passage of time. In film, a fade can function in the same way. The first fade in *Notorious* occurs at a particularly dramatic moment. There is an unidentified guest at Alicia's party, sitting with his back to the camera. Curiously, he remains after everyone leaves. Hitchcock fades out on the back of the man and fades in on his face, which is none other than Cary Grant's. Hitchcock interrupts the party with a fade to indicate a lapse of time; but the fade is also a clever way of introducing the male lead by linking two scenes in which he appears—one ending with his back to the camera, the other beginning with his face coming into view. The fade produces a more natural rhythm than would be the case if Hitchcock had cut from the back of Grant's head to a close-up of his face.

A fade can also be commentative. In *Mr. Skeffington* (1944), the aging Fanny Skeffington (Bette Davis) reassembles her former suitors, who are now either married or balding. The scene fades out as the men enter the dining room and fades in on a gentleman's hat and gloves. A cut would spoil the mood, which is one of genteel hypocrisy. The hat and gloves belong to Edward (Jerome Cowan), an impoverished suitor who has returned to court Fanny. The fade-out allows us to see a connection between the two scenes. In the first, Fanny has invited her suitors to dinner to reassure herself that she is still beautiful. However, Edward is not interested in her beauty, which is nonexistent, but only in her money, also nonexistent although he does not know it. One charade fades out and another fades in. A cut would have been too abrupt, and it would also not have conveyed the idea of one farce rising out of another.

The Dissolve

A fade denotes demarcation—it indicates the end of a narrative sequence. A dissolve denotes continuity by the gradual replacement of one shot by another. This kind of transition, in which the outgoing and incoming shots merge, serves a variety of functions. Sometimes a dissolve simply has the force of "in the meantime" or "later." In *North by Northwest*, Hitchcock dissolves a shot of Roger Thornhill bribing his mother to get a key from the desk clerk at a hotel to a shot of the two of them walking down the corridor toward the room Thornhill was so anxious to enter.

A dissolve can also mean "no sooner said than done." The Mother Superior in *The Song of Bernadette* (1943) no sooner asks to see Bernadette than the shot dissolves into Bernadette's room. In Max Ophuls's *Caught* (1948), a shot of a woman gazing at a picture of a model in a mink coat dissolves into a shot of the woman, who has become a model herself, wearing a mink.

When is a dissolve a transition and when is it more than a transition? This is like asking when a word is simply a conventional sign and when it is a symbol. Water can simply be a liquid, or it can be a sign of birth, rebirth, or fertility. It depends on the context: in T. S. Eliot's poems, water is never just water. It is the same with a dissolve. What a dissolve means— if, in fact, it means anything—is determined by the context. The dissolve in *North by Northwest* was just a way of getting two characters from the hotel lobby to one of the floors.

When two images blend in such a way that their union constitutes a symbolic equation, however, the result is a metaphorical dissolve. This is a visual form of synecdoche (or metonymy, with which synecdoche is very similar), a species of metaphor in which the part is substituted for the whole (roofs for houses, sail for ships) or a sign for the thing signified (green = Go, crown = royalty). We often use this figure of speech without knowing it: "Give us this day our daily *bread*" (bread = food); "All *hands* on deck" (hands = crew); "He addressed his comments to the *chair*" (chair = chairperson).

In *The Two Mrs. Carrolls* (1947), Geoffrey Carroll (Humphrey Bogart) is a wife poisoner. Early in the film, Sally (Barbara Stanwyck) discovers a letter he dropped, addressed to his wife. Because Sally is in love with Geoffrey, she questions him about his marriage. He replies that he is getting a divorce. The letter dissolves into a neatly wrapped package of poison Geoffrey has just purchased from a pharmacist. The merging of the two images, the letter and the package, results in the equation: Mrs. Carroll + package = death. Dissolving an envelope bearing a woman's name into the means that will make her only a name is an ingenious touch.

The dissolves in George Stevens's films have an effect similar to the homogenization of cream and milk. In *Shane*, when Starrett (Van Heflin) and Shane (Alan Ladd) succeed in uprooting a stubborn tree trunk, Stevens slowly merges their triumphant faces into the landscape, making the men one with nature. Later, when Starrett watches a homesteader's property go up in flames, Stevens dissolves his vengeful face into the burning house. The resulting equation—man + nature = natural man; face + burning house = consuming rage—do not advance the plot; their purpose, rather, is to illustrate one of the film's main themes: the pioneer's oneness with nature, which enables him to become part of everything he sees or does.

A dissolve can sometimes have the effect of dramatic foreshadowing if the filmmaker prepares the audience for subsequent events by hinting at their outcome earlier. In *King and Country*, a skull mired in mud dissolves into the face of a soldier playing a harmonica. The dissolve prefigures the fate of the soldier, who later dies in the mud, his voice silenced by a pistol shot in the mouth.

Just as dissolves foreshadow, so can they recapitulate. At the end of *The Last Picture Show*, Sonny (Timothy Bottoms) returns to the house of Ruth Popper (Cloris Leachman), the coach's wife, with whom he has been having an affair. The movie house has closed its doors forever; Sam the Lion and Billy are dead; Duane is on his way to Korea. All that remain are Ruth and the dreary Texas town where the tumbleweed rolls down the main street. As Sonny and Ruth look at each other, their eyes forge the only bond that can unite them—loneliness. At that moment, Sonny and Ruth dissolve into the town and the vast Texas flatlands. There is no difference between a young man without prospects, a middle-aged woman without hope, and a town without a future. Their destinies have become one.

At the end of *Colorado Territory* (1949), Raoul Walsh's western remake of his earlier success, *High Sierra* (1941), the hands of Wes (Joel McCrea) and Colorado (Virginia Mayo), touching in death, dissolve into a shot of a ringing bell. The dissolve does not so much connect two images as two events that the lovers' hands and the bell represent. Earlier in the film, Wes had hidden some stolen money in an abandoned church. After the deaths of Wes and Colorado, a priest discovers the money and uses it to restore the church bell, telling the villagers it was the gift of two lovers who passed by.

The Form Dissolve

A filmmaker can merge two images with the same shape or contours through a form dissolve. Often a form dissolve is merely easy on the eyes. For example, in *Jane Eyre* the figure of a ballerina on top of a music box dissolves into a little girl dressed in the same costume. A form dissolve can also be directly related to the plot. In Hitchcock's *The Wrong Man*, a jazz musician is falsely accused of committing a holdup. As the musician (Henry Fonda) prays in front of a picture of Jesus Christ, the scene gradually changes to that of a man walking down a dark street. Then the man's head merges with the musician's, which in turn becomes hollow enough to accommodate the other's face. The man whose head fits into the musician's is the real criminal. The dissolve shows how easy it is to mistake the innocent for the guilty; it is just a matter of superimposing one face upon another.

The Wipe

Some television news programs change news items by means of a line traveling vertically across the screen. That traveling line is a wipe, and in the 1930s and the 1940s this device was the most stylish of the transitions. Since the screen is rectangular, the wipe can move vertically, horizontally, or diagonally; it can create a theatrical effect by rising or falling like a drop curtain, as it does in a scene in *The Thin Man*, where it moves from the bottom of the screen to the top, revealing a stage full of dancers.

Sometimes wipes complement each other: One shot ends with a wipe that travels from left to right; the next with a wipe that moves across the screen from right to left. The best example of complementary wipes can be found in the opening of *The Petty Girl* (1950).

More fluid than a cut and faster than a dissolve, the wipe is ideal for presenting a series of events in quick succession. Frank Capra, a frequent user of the wipe, employed it in the opening sequences of *It Happened One Night* (1934), *Mr. Deeds Goes to Town* (1936), and *Mr. Smith Goes to Washington*. In the handwriting sequence in *Mr. Smith Goes to Washington*, for example, one expert after another testifies to the authenticity of Jeff Smith's signature. After each expert speaks, Capra simply "wipes" him off the screen, thereby showing the inanity of the investigation.

Rouben Mamoulian's excellent use of the wipe is apparent in *Dr.*

Jekyll and Mr. Hyde. After Jekyll (Fredric March) becomes Hyde, he goes off into the night, deserting Muriel Carew (Rose Hobart), his fiancée, who expects him at her dinner party. A wipe opens like a fan, dividing the screen diagonally: on the left is the departing Jekyll; on the right, the party in progress. When Jekyll leaves the Carew estate, Mamoulian wipes him out of the frame, which expands to disclose the dinner guests and the worried Muriel. At that point, the frame divides diagonally again: on the right is Ivy (Miriam Hopkins), the woman Hyde will kill, sipping champagne; on the left is Muriel, the woman Jekyll yearns to marry. The wipe acts as a parallel cut, informing us that while Muriel was at her party, Ivy was at home. But the split screen also represents the protagonist's ideal woman, who is similarly halved. It is only fitting that for a double man (Jekyll/Hyde) there should be a double woman (Ivy/Muriel).

When Muriel's father, furious at Jekyll's absence, cries, "Muriel, you will have nothing more to do with that man," a wipe begins to move him from the left of the screen to the center, revealing the "man" himself. However, it is not Jekyll but Hyde whom we see. The wipe is an ironic commentary on the father's outburst; clearly, he did not mean that Muriel should have nothing to do with Hyde (whom he cannot know) but with Jekyll. At this point, however, Jekyll is Hyde.

Some writers compare the wipe to a windshield wiper. Hitchcock uses it as such in *Rebecca*, when the second Mrs. de Winter sees Manderley for the first time through the windshield as the wipers clear away the rain. He repeats the technique in *Psycho:* as Marion drives in the rain, the sign for the Bates Motel materializes on her windshield. In each film, the wipe introduces a new phase of the character's life by bringing the future before the character's eyes. In Mrs. de Winter's case, it was the house where she learned the truth about Rebecca, her husband's first wife; in Marion's, it was the motel where she met her death.

The Iris

Mt. Rushmore as seen through a telescope in *North by Northwest* appears inside a circle in the middle of the darkened screen. This is a masking shot, or, to be more accurate, an iris shot, in which everything is blacked out except for what is to be seen telescopically. The frame can also be altered to simulate other shapes (e.g., the view from a keyhole, a crack in a door, binoculars, a submarine periscope) depending upon the form in which the director wants the audience to see the image.

In addition to the iris shot, there is what is known as irising in and irising out. Irising in consists of opening up the darkened frame with a circle of light that keeps expanding until the picture fills the frame. Irising out is the opposite; it is as if darkness were seeping into the frame from all

A frame enlargement of an iris shot from *The Birth of a Nation.* In an iris shot, the image appears within a circle on an otherwise dark screen. *(Courtesy MOMA/FSA and Epoch Producing Corp.)*

sides, forcing the diminishing picture into some part of the frame until it becomes a speck and disappears.

A director can dolly in or out of a scene or, today, zoom in or out of one; but there is nothing quite like an iris to open the frame. In *The Birth of a Nation*, Griffith used the iris breathtakingly in Sherman's March to the Sea. The frame opens from the upper-left-hand corner to reveal a mother and her children on a hill; at first we do not know why they are huddled in fear, but as the frame opens we see Sherman's soldiers in the valley below. In *Intolerance*, Griffith gradually disclosed the splendor of Babylon by expanding the frame, starting at the lower-right-hand corner.

The iris is especially effective in death scenes. Lucy of *Broken Blossoms* and the Mountain Girl of *Intolerance* both die in iris. Irising out can suggest death because of the way in which darkness creeps into the frame, reducing the size of the image to a pinpoint and then annihilating it. Orson Welles chose the iris to symbolize both the death of Wilbur Minafer and the end of the horse and buggy era in *The Magnificent Ambersons* (1942). A horseless carriage moves in long shot across the snow. The passengers sing merrily, but their song is in sharp contrast to the landscape, which is dominated by a dead tree with wiry branches. As the motor buggy moves out of frame, Welles starts irising out until it disappears in the darkness that floods the screen. Welles irises out into a fade. One would have expected him to iris out of one scene and into another, but the shot that follows the fade is of a black wreath on the door of the Amberson house. The iris and the fade imply finality in different ways—the iris gradually and poetically, the fade irrevocably.

The principle of the iris unifies the flashbacks in George Stevens's *Penny Serenade* (1941). Julie (Irene Dunne) recalls incidents from her marriage by playing recordings of popular songs that had meaning for her and her husband. Each flashback begins with a close-up of the center of the disc, which then opens up, irislike, to reveal the scene.

Because of their fondness for the movies of the past, both François Truffaut and Jean-Luc Godard used the iris more readily than did many of their peers. Truffaut irises out repeatedly in *The Wild Child* to make the scenes resemble the stages of a scientific experiment conducted as dispassionately as possible. Godard uses the iris for sheer nostalgia in *Breathless*. In one scene, he irises out on Michel gazing idolatrously at a poster of Humphrey Bogart in his last film. One is tempted to say that Godard is irising out on the old Hollywood—except that irising is still being practiced, although not as regularly as it was in Griffith's day or during the 1930s and the 1940s. However, we do find irising on certain television programs and in movies where techniques of the past function as period touches. When George Roy Hill irises out on the two con men at the close of *The Sting* (1973), it gives the ending a deliberately old-fashioned look. Similarly, Peter Bogdanovich's use of irising in *Nickelodeon* lends an air of authenticity to the film, which is set in the early days of the movie industry.

Contemporary filmmakers such as Steven Spielberg, Francis Ford Coppola, and Martin Scorsese, who are also immersed in films of the past, understandably use the techniques of the past. They use wipes, irises, and fades both because they respect these techniques as vestiges of a past they admire and because those techniques can still be effective narrative devices. Brian De Palma uses the fade as a sign of demarcation at the beginning of *Dressed to Kill* (1980) when he fades to white after Kate's sexual fantasy. Steven Spielberg fades to black in *Empire of the Sun* to indicate that the first part of the action is over. Francis Ford Coppola uses a wipe in *Peggy Sue Got Married* (1986) to take Peggy Sue (Kathleen Turner) from high school, where she is talking with a male student, to her bedroom, where she is talking with her girlfriends. Scorsese uses two iris shots in *The Age of Innocence*—one of May's unusual engagement ring, an emerald in a diamond setting; the other of Newland and the countess at the opera, either to suggest intimacy by placing them within a circle of privacy or to imply that they may have come within the range of some gossip's opera glasses. Wipes and irises abound in the Star Wars trilogy, which evoke the old movie serials where wipes and irises were common. Here they have the double function of evoking nostalgia and promoting the narrative. Alan Alda ends *Sweet Liberty* with a variation on the iris out; the image does not narrow into a circle but into a rectangle that grows progressively smaller until it disappears. As more film disciples go on to become filmmakers, their work will reflect what they have learned and what they have seen.

ASSEMBLING THE SHOTS

When Alfred Hitchcock said that a film must be edited, he meant that the shots making up the movie had to be assembled and arranged in such a way that the action proceeds in a logical and coherent manner. Editing involves selecting and arranging the shots based on the following considerations: their place within the narrative, their contribution to the mood of a particular scene or to the film as a whole, their enhancement of the film's rhythm, their elucidation of the film's deeper meaning, and their fulfillment of the filmmaker's purpose.

The most common form of editing in the narrative film is continuity editing, which entails assembling shots so that they follow each other smoothly and without interruption, as opposed to the piecemeal way in which a movie is filmed. Although movies are shot out of sequence (with location filming usually done before soundstage filming, and scenes involving actors with other commitments shot when the actors are available), filmgoers do not care which scenes were shot first or that the climax in the Grand Canyon was shot on the second day of shooting because the weather happened to be ideal. Continuity editing preserves the illusion of an ongoing narrative.

Eisenstein's Theory of Montage

While *montage* is sometimes used as a synonym for *editing* (e.g., montage and American montage sequences), it had deeper implications for the great Russian filmmaker Sergei Eisenstein, who believed that shots should not so much connect as collide, and that the viewer should be affected by their collision. Thus, montage calls attention to itself, unlike continuity editing, which is supposed to be unobtrusive. If a man postures like a peacock, cut from the man to the peacock; if he is figuratively a horse's ass, pair him with a real one. If the purpose of a scene is to show people being killed like animals, cut from workers being massacred to an ox being slaughtered. If one wishes to state visually that all wars waged in the name of God are immoral, arrange a series of shots starting with a baroque Christ and ending with an idol, thereby making militarism a form of regression. This is the kind of montage that Eisenstein practiced.

Eisensteinian montage is based on contrast and conflict, which can exist both within the film as a whole and within a particular shot or scene. In the Odessa steps massacre in Eisenstein's *Potemkin*, a body lies diagonally across the steps; the Cossacks cast shadows that fall menacingly at oblique angles to the steps; the steps form three contrasting planes, with the Cossacks at the top firing at a woman on a landing behind which lies a trail of bodies.

Eisenstein discovered how ideas could arise from the contrast and conflict of images. Without creating an actual series of cause and effect, he opened *Potemkin* with a shot of breaking waves and followed this image of turbulence with shots of men sleeping in hammocks that formed a shroud-like tangle, mess tables swinging back and forth, meat crawling with maggots—each image jarring us, disquieting us, but ultimately preparing us for the sailors' revolt.

Eisenstein's influence was enormous but not always beneficial. Instead of producing an artistic effect, sometimes the collision of images produced only pretentiousness. There is an embarrassing scene in Mamoulian's otherwise excellent *Dr. Jekyll and Mr. Hyde* when Jekyll, exulting over his impending marriage to Muriel, cries, "If music be the food of love, play on!" as he sits down at the organ and pounds away. Five shots appear in rapid succession, commenting on his rapture: a lighted candelabra, an illuminated art object, a smiling statue, the butler's beaming countenance, and a blazing hearth. Jekyll's rapture is evident from the way he plays the organ; the accompanying montage is superfluous.

To Eisenstein, *montage* meant the visual conflict of images. On the Continent, it means editing: selecting and editing the shots that will form the scenes and sequences of the film. In England, the same process is called *editing*, or *cutting*, but with a slight difference: *editing* means the step-by-step assembling of the shots in the cutting room, while *montage* refers to the process considered as a whole. A further complication is that, during the 1930s and 1940s, American films employed what has become known as *American montage*, which, as we have already seen, is a convenient way of collapsing time. In a typical American montage scene, newspapers would spin across the screen announcing a murder trial as one headline obliterates the other. The face of the judge would dissolve into the defendant's; during the trial, one shot would wipe away another. Superimposed over the defendant's face would be that of his anguished wife, and over hers, the face of the real murderer, who is hiding out in a sleazy room above a bar. Although this form of montage, in which time is telescoped through a blend of dissolves, wipes, and superimposures, is not in vogue today, in its time it was highly effective and was regarded as sufficiently important to warrant screen credit for the montage editor. Slavko Vorkapich was especially adept at montage (*Mr. Deeds Goes to Town, Mr. Smith Goes to Washington*), and Don Siegel began in montage at Warner Brothers before going on to become a well-known director (*Invasion of the Body Snatchers*, 1956; *Dirty Harry*, 1971; *Escape from Alcatraz*, 1979 and so on).

Continuity Editing

While montage may seem to be more exciting intellectually than continuity editing, it would be a mistake to dismiss continuity editing as merely the sequential arrangement of shots. Continuity editing is based on other editing principles that affect a film's rhythm, time, space, tone, and theme.

Rhythm

No great film is rhythmically uniform. Some shots remain on the screen longer than others; some sequences move more rapidly than others. One sequence may be uncommonly slow, while another may be unusually fast. The best filmmakers vary speed, movement, and pace, knowing that long strips of film produce a slower rhythm, short strips a more rapid rhythm. The process itself is not the issue here; the effects are, as one can see in the first two sequences of *Citizen Kane*, "The Death of Kane" and "News on the March."

The film begins with the camera ascending the gate of Xanadu, defying the No Trespassing sign. A series of dreamlike dissolves culminates in a shot of a lighted window that suddenly goes dark. A mouth utters "Rosebud!" through a veil of falling snow, and a glass paperweight with a snow-covered house inside it smashes without making a sound. A nurse enters a room and folds a dead man's arms across his chest. The mood of the first part of "The Death of Kane" is slow and languid. As the camera

FROM THE DEATH OF KANE IN *CITIZEN KANE*
Frame enlargement of the glass paperweight that falls
from Kane's hand. The lighted window of Kane's bedroom goes dark. Suddenly snow begins to fall; it is the
artificial snow in the glass paperweight that falls from
Kane's hand as he utters his last word, "Rosebud!"
(Courtesy MOMA/FSA)

draws closer to the window, the rhythm accelerates. Snow falls to the
sound of crystal-pure music, evoking Kane's Colorado boyhood. The paperweight breaks, and the nurse enters. Then the rhythm decelerates, and
the mood becomes solemn as she places Kane's arms on his chest.

Without warning, a voice bellows "News on the march!" as a newsreel of Kane's life unfolds. In the second scene the pace is frenetic; fifty
years of a man's life are compressed into a few minutes. The pace builds
inexorably until the "News on the March" is over and the camera sputters
out, as if in exhaustion.

Time

Parallel cutting makes it possible for two concurrent actions to be depicted
on the screen without one's being completed before the other begins—the
filmmaker simply cuts back and forth between them. Most novelists would
never narrate two simultaneous episodes by completing the first before
going on to the second; the novelist would bring the first to a certain point
and, leaving the reader in suspense, proceed to the second. The novelist
would then gradually add to each episode until the episodes are resolved
either separately or jointly. D. W. Griffith understood this principle when

As the nurse enters Kane's room, her image is refracted through a piece of the shattered paperweight. (*Courtesy MOMA/FSA*)

he made *The Lonely Villa* (1909), in which he cut back and forth between a mother and her daughters being terrorized by thieves who have broken into their home, and the father en route to rescue them. The action is resolved by the last-minute rescue.

Space

Film's ability to alter our perception of space is well known. A filmmaker can combine a shot of a tractor trailer that has jackknifed on the New England Thruway with a shot of a girl who has just gotten off the Cyclone at Coney Island, looking appropriately dazed. The combination could lead one to conclude that the girl witnessed the jackknifing even though one event occurred outside of Boston and the other took place in Brooklyn.

D. W. Griffith's *Intolerance* is a four-plot film about the theme of injustice as seen in four different periods: the early twentieth century, the time of Cyrus the Great (sixth century B.C.), the time of Christ, and the St. Bartholomew's Day massacre of the Huguenots in 1572. Although the film depicts events in four different parts of the world, at the climax everything seems to be occurring within the same location. By alternating between shots of Christ proceeding toward Calvary, the mountain girl in her chariot on her way to warn Cyrus, the car's attempt to catch up with a train to prevent an innocent man from being executed, and Prosper the Huguenot rushing through the streets of sixteenth-century Paris to rescue his beloved, Griffith makes it seem that all of these events are occurring not only at the same time but also in the same general area. The parallel cutting has affected our sense of space as well as time. It also suits the film's theme: the existence of intolerance at all times and in all places.

Morphing—a computer-graphics effect that allows the filmmaker to create a situation in which, say, a movie character interacts with a historical figure—might seem to challenge our perception of film space. The result, virtual reality, is, like any innovation, a novelty when first seen. It worked well in *Forrest Gump*, in which Forrest is seen interacting with Presidents Kennedy, Johnson, and Nixon, and John Lennon of the Beatles. The reason is that Forrest, who gave every indication of being one of life's losers, eventually triumphs, achieving a familiar version of the American dream: going from obscurity to fame. However, the danger is that once audiences catch onto the device, they will dismiss it as a gimmick. The extent to which morphing can engage audiences depends upon how intelligently it is handled. Far more realistic is the digital placement of an actor in a disaster scene. First, the actor is photographed at the site; then the disaster is photographed; finally, the actor is situated digitally in the scene. Despite the perennial interest in special effects, they can only be a means to an end; if the end is to falsify reality, mock history, or compensate for a mediocre script that is devoid of human emotions, special effects are the equivalent of trick photography: gimmickry, not art.

Tone

Just as tempo should vary in a film, so too should tone, which is primarily light, shade, and color. Again, *Kane* is an excellent example. The first sequence, "The Death of Kane," is dark and eerie. The second sequence, "News on the March," is the exact opposite; it is a newsreel, and looks as grainy as any newsreel ever made.

Theme

A filmmaker might deepen a film's theme by juxtaposing contrasting shots. As we have seen, there is a cut in *Slaves* from the manacled feet of slaves to the galloping hooves of horses. Whether the horses are in the same vicinity as the slaves is irrelevant; the point of the cut is the contrast between the enslaved and the free. In *A Doll's House* (1973), there is a cut from Nora's upper-middle-class home to Krogstad's hovel; seeing how Krogstad lives makes it easier to understand his blackmailing Nora.

The Role of the Editor

Since it is a common fallacy that films are made in the editing room, students often have difficulty distinguishing between the editor's role and the filmmaker's. We have seen that editing involves selecting and arranging the shots in a particular order. But who does the arranging, the editor or the filmmaker?

Let us use an analogy from student life. After you have written an essay or a term paper, you submit it to your instructor. Even before submitting it, you have edited it: removed superfluous words, substituted the right words for the wrong ones, corrected spelling and grammar. Still, your essay may not be perfect; you have been too close to it to catch all the mistakes. Since your instructor has not written it, he or she can be more objective. You may have sentences, or even paragraphs, that should be transposed. What you thought was an introduction might work better if you made it your conclusion. Perhaps you did not prune the paper of all its excesses; your instructor will note that. A good instructor can take what you have submitted and, by making the proper corrections and suggestions, show you how it can be improved. Your instructor did not write the paper, yet he or she has done something for it that you could not do: your instructor has made it better.

An editor performs a similar task: an editor takes what has been shot and improves upon it. The ideal film editor is the director's alter ego, carrying out what the director would do if he or she had the time to be all things to the film. Thus, an editor may select the shots or decide which portion of a shot should be used. An editor can give an action scene its distinctive rhythm by alternating tempo and varying directional movement. If a sequence needs greater momentum, an editor can cut it in such a way that it acquires it. If a scene is especially violent, an editor can cut it so rapidly that the movie will receive a PG-13 instead of an R rating. If shot A shows the cavalry pursuing the Indians left to right, shot B must show the Indians fleeing left to right; otherwise, it would look as if the cavalry and the Indians collided. If a character exits shot A from the left, the character must enter shot B from the right.

Because all films require some form of editing, the importance of editors has often been exaggerated and their role sometimes equated with that of directors. Lee Bobker compares editors with painters, working in isolation to create the movie's pace, mood, and rhythm. Yet, despite Bobker's respect for the editor's function, he is forced to admit it is a subservient one: "The editor should always enjoy a wide creative latitude, but he should never fall prey to the illusion that he is creating a new film from scratch. His primary purpose is to bring to completion an artistic work already in progress."[1]

In the first edition of *The Technique of Film Editing*, Karel Reisz dubbed the editor "the interpreter of the small details rather than the prime creator of the continuity."[2] For the second edition, Professor Thorold Dickinson provided an introduction to the second part of the book in which he stated that "the modern editor is the executant for the film-maker and no longer his equal on any self-respecting film."[3]

Most good editors would agree. The best answer to the question "What is film editing?" was given by the British editor Anthony Gibbs: "Film editing is putting into dramatic form the basic filmed material given to the editor by the director."[4] However, just as there are average, good, and great directors, there are average, good, and great editors. Gibbs would call a good editor someone who can achieve "the total interpretation of the director's and the writer's intentions," and a great editor as someone who is capable of "taking their intentions even farther, showing them a dimension to their project which even they may not have imagined to be there."[5]

True greatness is rare in any profession; thus, great editors are probably at a premium. It is not unlikely that an editor capable of bringing to the surface what the filmmaker did not even know was there would go on to become a director. The motto of Edward Dmytryk, who began his career as an editor and then went on to direct some fifty films between 1935 and 1975, is relevant: "Substance first—then form."[6] The filmmaker must provide the substance if the editor is to provide the form.

COLORING THE IMAGE

The Black-and-White Film

Film theorist Rudolph Arnheim has argued that color is accidental to film, and that audiences can accept the absence of color in black-and-white movies. The history of film proves that a movie photographed in black and white can render all of the important plot details without loss of verisimilitude. Just as sound films cannot be considered superior to silent films simply because the dialogue can be heard, color films cannot be considered superior to black and white because all the colors can be seen. Nor are black-and-white films that include references to color less effective because the color cannot be seen; the color can be imagined. In William Wyler's *Jezebel* (1938), a black-and-white film, Julie (Bette Davis) arrives at a ball in a red dress that she has been forbidden to wear. The dress photographs as nonwhite, and white was the color Julie was expected to wear. Julie's act of rebellion is as effective today, when color films are the norm, as it was in 1938, when color films were the exception.

One should always remember that it is only since the late 1960s that color has been the norm. Yet, even when black and white was the norm, filmmakers could work within the parameters of monochrome and achieve something akin to color. In *Twelve O'Clock High* (1949), Gregory Peck plays an Air Force general whose inflexibility results in a nervous breakdown. He tolerates no deviation from the rules—he might even be described as someone who thinks in "black and white." When the general breaks down, the blackness of his hair and leather jacket and the stark whiteness of his face set against a translucent gray background imply that

The creative use of black and white in *The Merry Widow* (1934). *(Courtesy MOMA/FSA)*

the gray area in human affairs that lies between the extremes of black and white was something the general had relegated to the background. It was his inability to perceive shades of difference that led to his breakdown.

In Ernst Lubitsch's *The Merry Widow* (1934), the black-and-white photography produces a color scheme that even the most advanced form of color technology would find hard to rival. Since the film is based on a Viennese operetta, everything looks as if it has come from a confectionary. It is impossible not to think of chocolate, icing, and whipped cream when watching the film: the widow's mansion looks like a tiered wedding cake; her boudoir is like a pastry shell; the walls of her boudoir are creamy and incandescent. When the widow wears a black negligee, the dramatic contrast of her attire and the appointments of her boudoir satisfy whatever craving for color a viewer might have.

Although *Citizen Kane* was photographed in black and white, it is rich in color symbolism. Throughout the film, white is an ambivalent symbol. It suggests innocence as well as the loss of innocence; it is the color of the real snow that Kane knew as a boy in Colorado, and the color of the artificial snow in the glass paperweight he keeps as a memento of that happy time. White is also a symbol of freedom; when Susan leaves Kane, a white cockatoo screeches and flies away. But white also evokes sterility and death. Xanadu, Kane's palatial home, is adorned with useless statues and white marble; the nurse who enters Kane's room at the moment of his death wears a white uniform. The symbolic values of white can be rendered so artfully by black and white that color is not missed.

The Color Film

If black-and-white photography can achieve such art, it would seem that color can go even further. Color can be simply part of the way a film is made, or it can be used creatively by those who think creatively. There are, also, some outstanding uses of color as a means of deepening the narrative. Although the heroine of Hitchcock's *Marnie* has suppressed all memory of a murder she committed as a child, the guilt persists in the form of an intense aversion to red. Instinctively, she removes red gladioli from a vase and replaces them with white mums. A drop of red ink on her white blouse sends her rushing to the washroom; the red polka dots on a jockey's uniform petrify her. Not until the end of the film do we learn that Marnie's aversion to red is the result of her having killed a sailor with a poker to protect her prostitute mother from possible harm.

The title character in Federico Fellini's *Juliet of the Spirits* (1965) is a housewife whose fantasies are dominated by erotic reds. When we first see Juliet, she is trying on a red wig; then she sets the table with red candles. When she visits a clairvoyant, she wears a red scarf. Yet red is not her color; it is the color of the women of her fantasies. At the end of the film, Juliet reverts to white, the color that typifies the ordinary person that she is.

The title character in *Carrie* is a high-school senior with telekinetic powers. Her mother is a religious fanatic, and both have reddish hair. When Carrie menstruates for the first time, she thinks she is bleeding to death. Her naïveté makes her an object of derision to her classmates, who humiliate her publicly at the senior prom by dropping a bucket of pig's blood on her. The blood reddens Carrie's pink dress, and Carrie literally sees red. Her revenge, as one might suspect, is appropriately bloody.

Red predominates in Nicholas Ray's *Rebel Without a Cause* (1956), the film that gave James Dean his first starring role. Despite the title, the three main characters—Jim (Dean), Judy (Natalie Wood), and Plato (Sal Mineo)—who bond together have a reason to rebel: parental indifference. In Jim's case, it was a weak father and a domineering mother; in Judy's, an affectionless father; in Plato's, the absence of a father, which caused him to seek a surrogate in Jim. Red has always been the rebel's color; *Jezebel*'s Julie

Marsden was certainly rebelling against convention when she insisted on wearing red to the ball. In *Rebel Without a Cause*, the credits are in red; when Judy is first seen, she is wearing a red coat and bright red lipstick. Despite his meekness and emotional instability, Plato even tries to play the rebel by wearing red socks. Jim dons a red windbreaker during the "chickie run," a dangerous coming-of-age ritual in which teenage males prove their manhood by driving their cars to the edge of a bluff. When Plato is killed, Jim uses the windbreaker as a shroud, placing it on his friend to suggest that at least Plato died a rebel.

The Godfather, Part II integrates the lives of Vito Corleone and his son Michael by contrasting the immigrant world of Little Italy, where Vito grew to manhood, with the world of modern Lake Tahoe, where Michael lives. Michael's world has a dark mahogany look; everything about it is forbidding and austere. Vito's world is one of pastels; the colors are soft, delicate, warm. Not only are father and son contrasted, but their respective eras as well: a sunlit past as opposed to a somber present. A similar contrast occurs in *The Wizard of Oz* (1939). To convey the disparity between the colorless real world and the colorful world of the imagination, the Kansas scenes were photographed in sepia and the Oz scenes in color. Likewise, the garden in *The Secret Garden* (1949) is in color, while the film itself is black and white.

One of the most poignant uses of color in a predominately black-and-white film is Steven Spielberg's *Schindler's List* (1993), which opens with a color shot of two Sabbath candles. Imperceptibly, the background darkens to monochrome, with the candles providing the only color. The darkening of the frame suggests the coming of the Holocaust. But since the film is not merely a catalogue of Nazi atrocities but the story of survival in a hell that even Dante could not have imagined, the initial use of color implies that the powers of darkness will not prevail. Color returns to the film in the epilogue, in which some of the actual Holocaust survivors, who owed their lives to Oskar Schindler, appear.

Color can embellish, suggest, characterize, and forge symbolic connections; so can black and white. An astute filmgoer will know when color is decorative or functional and when monochrome is perfunctory or motivated.

Colorization

Colorization is the use of a computer-aided process to apply color to black-and-white movies. Colorization requires the film to be analyzed shot by shot and scene by scene so that the colorization is consistent. The colors of the opening frames must be determined first by consulting sketches, memos, and set designs if they are available. Once the colors for the opening frames are selected, a computer applies the same colors throughout, varying the hues in terms of the lighting pattern in the original. Still, there is no guarantee that a color sketch provided for a black-and-white film would be valid if the studio had decided to shoot the film in color. Thus, the claim that a colorized version of a black-and-white film would have proved satisfactory if the filmmaker had the opportunity to shoot it in color is false.

The foes of colorization—and there have been many, including James Stewart, Burt Lancaster, Woody Allen, Frank Capra, and Martin Ritt—contend that colorization vitiates the principle of creative choice that is essential to art. When a studio chose to film a movie in black and white rather than color, that choice entailed several factors, the chief one being, no doubt, the cost. During Hollywood's golden age, there was no aesthetic policy that dictated what kinds of movies should be made in black and white as opposed to color. One cannot say, for example, that color is more suited to westerns than black and white since some of John Ford's classic westerns were photographed in black and white: *Stagecoach* (1939), *My Darling Clementine, Fort Apache* (1948), *Wagonmaster* (1950), *The Man Who Shot Liberty Valance* (1962). Nor was color considered mandatory for musicals; the great musicals of the 1930s, notably those starring Fred Astaire and Ginger Rogers, were black and white. Color was expensive and was not lavished on every film, only on films that the studio deemed important enough to warrant it or on those that needed color to realize their dramatic potential to the fullest. *Gone with the Wind* was intended to be in color; another film set in the South and released the previous year, *Jezebel*, was not.

When the decision is made to shoot a film in color, everything—costumes, lighting, makeup, settings—is planned and executed in terms of that choice. That choice, however, was to shoot the film in a color *process* such as Technicolor, Trucolor, Warnercolor, and so on. Colorization is not a *color* process; it is a *computer-aided* process that, in the absence of any guiding intelligence, allows a computer to make the choices that should be the prerogative of the filmmaker.

LIGHTING THE IMAGE

The classic Hollywood film is an example of three-point lighting—key, fill, and back lights used in combination to light the subject. These are not the only lights; still, three-point lighting is a standard lighting scheme that, if understood properly, explains how lighting can affect one's perception of a character or a setting.

The key light, the principal source of illumination, leaves shadows if

High-key lighting in *Meet Me in St. Louis* (1944). *(Courtesy MOMA/FSA)*

it is used alone. Thus, another light is necessary to fill in the areas the key light has left unlit and to soften the shadows it has cast: the fill light, an auxiliary light of slightly less intensity placed at eye level. But even a combination of key and fill light is not sufficient if a sense of depth is desired. Hence, a back light, placed above and behind the subject, is required. The back light alone would produce merely a silhouette. But in combination with the key and fill lights, the back light separates the subject from its environment, thereby creating a feeling of depth.

Low-key lighting in *Crossfire* (1947). *(Courtesy WCFTR)*

In terms of effect, lighting can be categorized as high key and low key. A low-contrast ratio of key and fill light will result in an image of almost uniform brightness, or what is called *high-key lighting*, the kind used in musicals, comedies, and for scenes of tranquillity and peace. Conversely, a high-contrast ratio of key and fill light will result in *low-key lighting* and create a shadowy effect and a nighttime aura, often with intensely white faces against an onyx-black background. Directors of horror films, melodramas, and film noir (a type of melodrama where passions run high in urban settings that are grimy and often fogbound and where streets are dark, mean, and continually rain-slick) prefer low-key lighting for its shadows and its strong contrast of light and darkness.

In addition to these two general categories of lighting, there are five other types, distinguished by the angle from which the light source illuminates the subject: front, back, top, side, and bottom. Front lighting has a softening effect that makes whatever we are viewing seem more attractive than it actually is. Front lighting of the face creates an ageless look, but it also robs the face of character. Back lighting, as we have seen, adds

Back lighting in *Sunset Boulevard* (1950). The back light is coming from a projector during the screening of a silent film starring Norma Desmond (Gloria Swanson), who, in the middle of it, stands up and with arm raised vows to return to the screen. *(Courtesy WCFTR. Copyright © 1949, Paramount Pictures Corporations. All rights reserved.)*

depth and brings out subtleties of design and pattern. When a character is backlit, as Esther (Barbra Streisand) is when she sings "Evergreen" at the end of *A Star Is Born* (1976), a halolike aura is produced that gives an ethereal quality. Similarly, top lighting creates an atmosphere of youthfulness or spirituality, as it does in *The Song of Bernadette*, where it emphasizes Bernadette's saintliness. Side lighting leaves the subject half in light, half in shadow; thus, it can denote a split personality, a morally ambiguous character, or a femme fatale. Greta Garbo and Marlene Dietrich were often photographed in this fashion. Bottom lighting gives the subject a sinister air; it was the kind of lighting D. W. Griffith employed in *Dream Street* (1921) to bring out the villainy of Sway Wan.

In a black-and-white film, the interplay of light and darkness can produce visual symbolism. Throughout *Citizen Kane*, Thompson, the reporter trying to decipher the meaning of Kane's dying word ("Rosebud!")

is always seen in shadow. He is literally in the dark, and remains in that state throughout the film. Just as darkness can denote ignorance, so light can intimate knowledge. When Thompson enters the Thatcher Memorial Library to read the memoirs of Kane's guardian, shafts of light illuminate the mausoleum-like room. Perhaps the memoirs will explain the meaning of "Rosebud." But the light is deceptive, and Thompson leaves the library as much in the dark as ever.

Thompson is not the only character who suffers from ignorance. Although Thompson is ignorant of the meaning of "Rosebud," Kane is ignorant of himself. When Kane delivers his Declaration of Principles, promising to be a "fighting and tireless champion" of the people, his face is in darkness. Kane does not know that he will never live up to his declaration, and the lighting states as much.

Lighting is also used effectively in Preston Sturges's *Sullivan's Travels* (1941). In that film, some black parishioners invite the white prisoners of a local chain gang to their church to watch a movie. When we see the prisoners making their way to the church, they are in darkness; for a moment they look like black men. The lighting establishes a bond between the black congregation and the prisoners; it also reinforces the film's theme that moviegoing is a form of brotherhood that erases all distinctions, including racial ones. Movies are the great leveler; in the dark everyone is equal.

NOTES

[1]Lee R. Bobker, with Louise Marinis, *Making Movies: From Script to Screen* (New York: Harcourt Brace Jovanovich, 1973), 209.

[2]Karl Reisz and Gavin Miller, *The Technique of Film Editing*, 2nd ed. (New York: Focal Press, 1968), 84.

[3]Ibid., 277.

[4]"Film Editors Forum," *Film Comment* 13 (March–April 1977): 24.

[5]Ibid.

[6]Edward Dmytryk, *On Film Editing: An Introduction to the Art of Film Construction* (Boston: Focal Press, 1984), 145.

Film
Genres

CHAPTER

4

S o far we have been talking about techniques, using examples from such films as *My Darling Clementine*, *Detour*, and *Carrie*. While these films illustrate certain principles of moviemaking, they also illustrate certain types of films. Each of these films represents a particular genre: *Clementine*, the western; *Detour*, film noir; and *Carrie*, the horror film.

When English professors speak of a genre, they mean a literary form with certain conventions and patterns that, through repetition, have become so familiar that readers expect similar elements in works of the same type. In the Greece of the fifth century B.C. and Elizabethan England, the two great ages of tragedy, audiences attending a performance of *Oedipus the King* or *Hamlet* were not witnessing a wholly new dramatic form. The protagonist embarking on a quest that will result in his or her undoing was already a familiar one. Equally well established was the tragic progression from ignorance to self-knowledge, and from prosperity to catastrophe.

The conventions of tragedy (protagonist with a tragic flaw, fatal mistake, reversal of fortune, and the like) appear in all tragedies; they do not, however, always appear in the same way. The Elizabethan tragic heroes, for example, exercise free will to a greater degree than did their Greek counterparts. Modern tragedy, on the other hand, seems to be deterministic, with characters such as Blanche du Bois of Tennessee Williams's *A Streetcar Named Desire* and Willy Loman of Arthur Miller's *Death of a Salesman* destroyed by forces over which they have no control. Yet *Death of a Salesman* is as much a tragedy as *Oedipus* or *Hamlet*, even though it may not be written in verse and the protagonist may not be of royal descent. The same basic elements that make *Hamlet* a tragedy also make *Salesman* one.

Thus, a genre is not monolithic. Just as a genus admits of species, so a genre has subcategories. There are various kinds of tragedy: Greek, Elizabethan, French neoclassical, historical, modern. There are also tragedies that blur into melodrama, where chance occurrences seem more important than causality. Genres are never simple. Even comedy admits of various kinds: slapstick, bedroom farce, romantic comedy, drawing-room comedy, and Chekhovian comedy (which blends pathos and humor in a unique way). Similarly, mystery fiction can be subdivided into crime fiction, detective fiction (soft-boiled and hard-boiled), gothic fiction, espionage fiction, and the police procedural.

It is not easy, therefore, to pigeonhole a work of literature. While a long work of prose fiction can be classified as a novel, the crucial question is what kind of novel. Film genres are equally complex. While some literary genres reappear in film, not all do. Comedy is itself a genre in literature, but not in film, where genres tend to be more specific. Not all kinds of comedy have succeeded on the screen. While a book can be written about theatrical drawing-room comedy or comedy of manners, neither has produced enough examples in film to warrant a study of film drawing-room comedy or film comedy of manners. On the other hand, screwball comedy, which is not a literary genre, is a well-established film genre. But perhaps the greatest difference between literary and film genres is that literary genres represent a hierarchy created by critics, while film genres represent the studios' response to the marketplace. By the sixteenth century, a hierarchy of literary forms had been established, beginning with the lowly pastoral and culminating in the lofty epic. While this particular hierarchy no longer exists, the mentality behind it does. There are still many literary scholars who rank poetry above fiction and drama below it; there are also some who would relegate the essay to the category of expositional or informal prose and deny it literary status. In film, on the other hand, there is no hierarchy of genres: there are only types of movies that succeed and types that do not. (Traditionally, for example, sports films do not succeed, while horror films do.) Furthermore, genres that succeed in one era may not succeed in another unless they can adapt to the changing times.

The woman's film was popular in the 1930s, and especially in the 1940s, when women constituted the majority of the moviegoing public. The woman's film still exists, as we shall see, but it is not what it was when stars like Bette Davis and Joan Crawford reigned supreme.

Finally, while the best examples of a genre may be pure (e.g., *Stagecoach* and *My Darling Clementine* are pure westerns), there are also films that cross genres. Raoul Walsh's *Pursued* (1947) is a western that crosses over into the whodunit genre; Mitchell Leisen's *Easy Living* (1937) is a screwball comedy that is implicitly critical of "easy living" during the Great Depression and thus takes on overtones of the social-consciousness film; the musicals *A Star Is Born* (the 1954 and 1975 versions) and Martin Scorsese's *New York, New York* (1977) end unhappily.

The point is not to come up with a definitive classification of a particular movie; categorizing a movie is not like categorizing a biological species. Nominally, *Pursued* is a western, *Easy Living* screwball comedy, and *New York, New York* a musical. What gives each an added distinction is that it embodies elements of another genre besides its own. Rather, the point is to see how various kinds of movies have survived over the years by repeating, varying, or altering their conventions.

THE MUSICAL

The musical is a good genre with which to begin because its plot conventions are relatively simple. It is axiomatic that in a musical emotions are expressed, and the plot advanced, through song and dance. Although this may seem self-evident, there are still moviegoers who look down on the musical for its unreality. Historically, there is some justification for this view: the frequent lack of integration of song and action in many musicals results in an interruption of the plot for a production number. For example, in *Lady Be Good* (1941), there is no motivation for Eleanor Powell's tap dance except that Powell was a superb tap dancer whose role in the movie was minor but whose fans expected her to dance—which she did in a show-stopping number.

Ideally, Eleanor Powell's tap dance should have been a natural outgrowth of the action, not a diversion. However, the seamless blending of song and narrative is rare in film musicals. Indeed, in early movie musicals, integration did not exist. The plots were thin; rather, what is memorable about the musicals of the thirties are the chic dancing of Fred Astaire and Ginger Rogers and the production numbers in which the chorus formed intricate geometric patterns. We may have vivid memories of Astaire and Rogers dancing the carioca in *Flying Down to Rio* (1933), but few of us can reconstruct the plot.

Whether the first integrated musical was *On the Town* (1949) or *Singin' in the Rain* (1952) is a matter of debate. *On the Town* was based on a Broadway musical that was itself superbly integrated with music by Leonard Bernstein and book by Betty Comden and Adolph Green. *Singin' in the Rain*, which was neither a Broadway show nor a play set to music, is something of a rarity: an original screenplay with songs that flow out of the action. While the film is remembered for the title song, danced in the rain by Gene Kelly, the sequence is related to the plot: the boy is so in love with the girl that he dances for joy despite the elements.

If we recall that genres are not simple, we can better appreciate the diversity of the movie musical. Here are some familiar types.

The revue. While the stage revue was a popular musical form from the 1920s through the mid-1950s, its amorphous nature (sketches interspersed with song and dance) did not lend itself to the movies, whose audiences require some kind of plot. When the Broadway revue *New Faces of 1952* was filmed, a wisp of a plot was added, but not enough to conceal the fact that the film was a photographed stage show. Some movie musicals (e.g., *Star Spangled Rhythm*, 1942; Vincente Minnelli's *Ziegfeld Follies*, 1946) were disguised revues that offered a number of stars an opportunity to do their specialty within a loosely plotted format.

The operetta. Most movie operettas have been adaptations of stage operettas (e.g., *Naughty Marietta*, 1935; *Bittersweet*, 1940; *The Student Prince*, 1954; *The Vagabond King*, 1956). Occasionally, one comes upon an operetta-like film such as Billy Wilder's *The Emperor Waltz* (1948) with a fairy-tale plot shored up by music, or *The Umbrellas of Cherbourg* (1964), in which everything, including the dialogue, is sung but operettas are rarely written for the screen.

The comedy with music. One of Paramount's most successful series was the Road movies of the 1940s and early 1950s, featuring Bing Crosby, Bob Hope, and Dorothy Lamour in zany adventures that took them across the world. Since all three performers could sing, musical numbers were inserted into the plot, most of which had no relation to the narrative—which itself had no relation to reality. Many of the so-called Elvis Presley musicals were really comedies and, in a few cases, dramas with music.

The drama with music. Neither a dramatic musical nor a musical drama, the drama with music is rarer than the comedy with music because it provides a true fusion of music with a serious plot. In George Cukor's *A Star Is Born* (1954), a musical version of the 1937 nonmusical film about the price of Hollywood fame, the basic plot remained intact: a fading male star marries an unknown talent, whose career skyrockets while his plummets. This remake, with Judy Garland and James Mason, includes some excellent musical numbers, all of which fit neatly into the action. The third version of *A Star Is Born* (1975) also had no choice but to feature music, but of a different sort: rock, because the main characters had been changed to rock stars. The same plot device of the heroine's career eclipsing the hero's was used in another drama with music, *New York, New York*, in which the songs (the title song as well as standards of the 1940s) were expertly interwoven with the plot.

The show-business musical. Sometimes called *backstage musicals*, musicals of this kind chronicle the joys and heartaches of show business. The backstage musical has five common plot pegs: the "overnight sensation," breaking up the act, writing the song, the crucial song, and career versus marriage.

The overnight sensation is the "unknown" who substitutes for the star and, on the basis of his or her initial exposure to the public, achieves instant stardom. The best-known overnight sensation is the understudy (Ruby Keeler) in *42nd Street* (1933), who is told by the director (Warner Baxter): "Sawyer, you're going out a youngster, but you've got to come back a *star*." She did, and a Hollywood cliché was born. The "Born in a Trunk" sequence in the 1954 *A Star Is Born* parodies the overnight-sensation theme.

The breakup theme often gets under way when a producer hires one of the members of an act for a Broadway show but not the other(s). In *The Jolson Story* (1946), Steve Martin (William Demarest) stays in vaudeville while his protégé, Al Jolson (Larry Parks), goes on to become a star. A family act breaks up when the children go their separate ways in *There's No Business Like Show Business* (1954); a husband-and-wife team breaks up when the wife wants to do serious drama instead of musical comedy in *The Barkleys of Broadway* (1949); a marriage breaks up when a husband prefers an adoring audience to his wife in *The Jolson Story*.

Several backstage musicals revolve around pairing the right lyrics with the right melody. This kind of situation assumes that the audience knows the right lyrics and will therefore be amused by all the difficulties the lyricists are having: the songwriters working out the lyrics to "Lady Be Good" for *Lady Be Good*, the lyricist trying to find the "three little words" for the title song in *Three Little Words* (1950).

Some musicals feature a crucial song that is heard so often during the film and acquires such associative properties that it becomes inseparable from the plot (e.g., "You'll Never Know" in *Hello Frisco, Hello*; 1943). Sometimes the crucial song is either sung incorrectly or at the wrong tempo until the singer is forced to sing it correctly. In

Coney Island (1943), Betty Grable ruins "Cuddle Up a Little Closer" with her flamboyant gestures until George Montgomery handcuffs her, thereby forcing her to tone down her delivery and sing the song as a ballad.

The backstage musical generally climaxes in a big production number, which illustrates a convention of the genre: the stage on which the number is performed would never be found in a Broadway theater because it is a large Hollywood soundstage doubling as a Broadway stage. No Broadway theater could ever accommodate the winding ramp down which Rita Hayworth rushes in *Cover Girl* (1944) or the gigantic platform on which Frank Sinatra sings "Ol' Man River" at the end of *Till the Clouds Roll By* (1946). A movie musical that is an adaptation of a stage musical clearly shows the difference between a soundstage and a theater stage. Vincente Minnelli's movie version of Lerner and Loewe's *Brigadoon* (1954) was shot entirely on an MGM soundstage. In both the stage and screen versions, the lovers walk through the heather on the hill as they sing the duet "The Heather on the Hill." No stage designer could have created such spectacular heather, nor could there ever have been so much of it on the stage as there is in the movie.

The dance musical. In the theater, *dance musical* refers to a type of musical in which the cast functions as a kind of chorus that both sings and dances. *A Chorus Line* and *Cats* are both dance musicals in that they have no real stars and give the appearance of having been choreographed rather than staged. In film, a dance musical is one in which dance is a means of furthering the action as well as expressing the characters' emotions and psychological states. Since dance is as central to the action as song, such a film is really a *song and dance musical*, for unlike a stage dance musical like *Cats*, which has no real plot, the movie dance musical does.

Of the various kinds of dancing in the dance musical, the courting dance is the most famous. Its effectiveness depends on star chemistry. In the Astaire-Rogers musicals, the chemistry is complementary. Astaire courted an aloof Rogers, who gradually responded as he encircled her, wooing her with every step. Their dancing was the epitome of Art Deco, stylized and sleek. When Astaire appeared later in his career with the long-legged Cyd Charisse, the dancing became more erotic, since Astaire had a more sensuous partner. When Gene Kelly and Rita Hayworth danced to the music of "Long Ago and Far Away" in *Cover Girl*, their dancing took on elements of yearning, as if each were looking for the dream lover suggested by the lyrics ("I dreamed a dream one day").

Fred Astaire (in his signature clothes) and Ginger Rogers, the musical film's most popular dancing team, in *Swing Time* (1936), with a score by Jerome Kern. *(Courtesy MOMA/FSA)*

Gene Kelly, who combined athleticism with a ballet dancer's gracefulness, and Rita Hayworth in *Cover Girl* (1944). *(Courtesy Sony Pictures Entertainment and MOMA/FSA)*

The two great exponents of the dance musical, Fred Astaire and Gene Kelly, had diametrically opposed styles. Astaire was cool and aristocratic; he was born for top hat, white tie, and tails. On the other hand, Kelly, who once played ice hockey and taught gymnastics, was more athletic. Yet Kelly could work aspects of ballet into his dancing, which was something Astaire couldn't do. While each performer represented a different style, together they epitomized the golden age of the Hollywood musical.

Whether or not the traditional musical will return to its glory days is debatable. On the other hand, genres never die; they simply reinvent themselves, emerging in other forms. Take the animated musical, for example. The first full-length animated feature, *Snow White and the Seven Dwarfs* (1937), was also a musical that introduced such perennial favorites as "Whistle While You Work" and "Some Day My Prince Will Come." Since then, there have been frequent attempts to create not so much an animated musical as an animated film with songs (e.g., *Pinocchio* [1940], with its famous "When You Wish upon a Star"). There have also been attempts to combine animation with live action and music (e.g., *Anchors Aweigh*, 1945; *Song of the South*, 1946; *Mary Poppins*, 1964). If the animation is realistic enough, audiences will accept it in the same way they accept comic-strip characters as stand-ins for real people; and if the score is at least on a par with the classic Hollywood musical, no one can claim that the musical has died—only that it has undergone a sea change.

The team of Alan Menken (music) and Howard Ashman (lyrics) must be credited with the revival of interest in the animated musical. Their collaboration has resulted in a form that was traditionally considered to be little more than a full-length animated feature with songs. Although Menken and Ashman changed that perception with *The Little Mermaid* (1988), it was really *Beauty and the Beast* (1992), the first animated feature to receive an Academy Award nomination for best picture (it won for best score and best song), that captivated the public in a way that no other film had since *Snow White*. One reason for its popularity was its structure. Except for the animation, *Beauty and the Beast* resembles a typical fiction film. It begins, as any contemporary film might, with a precredits sequence: immediately after the Walt Disney Pictures logo, there is a prologue, at the end of which comes the title.

If you miss the prologue, you learn nothing about the background—specifically, why a handsome young prince has been transformed into a beast. The prologue, dramatized with voice-over narration, portrays the prince as a self-absorbed young man who mocks a beggar woman who comes to his castle seeking shelter. When she suddenly metamorphoses into a beauty, the prince relents. But it is too late: a spell has been cast on both the prince and his household. The prince's only hope is a rose that will bloom until he is twenty-one. If he has learned to love before the last petal falls, he and his household will be released from the spell.

How Beauty—or Belle, as she is called—encounters the Beast and aids in his reverse transformation constitutes the main action of the film. There are several reasons that *Beauty and the Beast* is generally considered to be the quintessential animated musical, the most important of which is the credibility of the characters. It is easy to imagine a heroine like Belle, who is not the typical ingenue of operetta but a fearless young woman devoted to her widower father and an avid reader as well. She shares a love of reading with the Beast, which makes her his double. After a series of complications (e.g., the rescue of Belle's father, whom her jealous suitor, Gaston, tries to institutionalize), the spell is broken, and Belle and the (former) Beast pledge their love for each other.

Not only is *Beauty and the Beast* a tightly constructed narrative; it is also an integrated musical. The musical numbers bear directly on the action. For example, the title song is sung by the enchanted teapot, Mrs. Potts (the voice of Angela Lansbury) to her favorite cup, Chip. First, one hears Mrs. Potts's voice on the soundtrack, explaining how two dissimilar people could be attracted to each other—particularly a beautiful woman to a grotesque. The song, motivated by the desire of the maternal Mrs. Potts to explain an important fact of life to Chip, also expressed the film's eternal theme: "Tale as old as time/Song as old as rhyme."

THE WESTERN

The American western is more complex than the overworked and often misleading distinction between the black-hatted villain and the white-clothed hero suggests. In fact, some westerns totally disregard that color code. In *My*

Darling Clementine, Doc Holliday (Victor Mature), who is far from evil, dresses in black, but so does the true villain, Old Man Clanton (Walter Brennan). In Fred Zinnemann's *High Noon* (1952), the marshal (Gary Cooper) wears a black hat; so does Ethan (John Wayne) in *The Searchers*.

As James Kitses has demonstrated in his study of the western, *Horizons West*,[1] the western is not so much a matter of good vs. evil as wilderness vs. civilization. Within these extremes are three others: the individual vs. the community, nature vs. culture, and West vs. East. The tension between the wilderness and civilization is evident in *Clementine* when the civilizing institutions of the church and the school begin to encroach on the frontier, bringing order and stability into lives that have neither. As the film shows, the frontier is changing: the one-street town of Tombstone sports a barbershop where a haircut is capped by a spray of cologne; a church is being dedicated; an actor gives a Shakespeare reading; Clementine (Cathy Downs) becomes Tombstone's first teacher.

In the western, opposites continually confront each other: freedom/responsibility, self-concern/commitment, ignorance/education, the desert/the garden. The western hero is a loner, often fiercely independent. If he is to develop as a person, he must assume a sense of responsibility—for example, by marrying or by serving the community as peace officer, educator, or wagon-train leader. Nor can retirement stand in his way if he is needed, as Captain Brittles (John Wayne) is needed in John Ford's *She Wore a Yellow Ribbon* (1949).

Initially, the western hero avoids marriage because it is an institution that curtails freedom. Thus, the hero can be comfortable only with a woman who is his alter ego or his complement. If the hero has a criminal past, he may be drawn to a social outcast, as Ringo (John Wayne) is to the prostitute Dallas (Claire Trevor) in *Stagecoach* or as Link (Gary Cooper) is to Billie (Julie London) in Anthony Mann's *Man of the West* (1958). If he is an upright man, like Wyatt Earp (Henry Fonda) in *Clementine*, he will be attracted to a virtuous woman.

The frontier encourages a survival instinct that is so strong it can cause a community to abandon its lawman, as the townspeople do in *High Noon* when they refuse to come to the aid of their marshal. The frontier is also parochial: easterners are regarded with suspicion because they bring with them education and a knowledge of the law. In *The Man Who Shot Liberty Valance*, an eastern lawyer is an object of ridicule; in Anthony Mann's *The Man from Laramie* (1955), a frontier woman dismisses her rival as "a piece of fluff from the East." The East, however, is necessary to the West; it can bring the garden to the desert in the form of irrigation. In *Liberty Valance*, the cactus rose is all that can bloom in the desert until the arrival of irrigation—the result of legislation initiated by the eastern lawyer, who was dismissed as a "dude."

John Wayne as the black-hatted but hardly villainous Ethan in *The Searchers* (1956). *(Courtesy MOMA/FSA and Warner Bros., Inc.)*

Still, there are those who cannot adapt to the wilderness turned garden: outlaws, uncompromising individualists, romantic idealists. For the unassimilated, there are two choices: flight or a return to the wilderness. In *Stagecoach*, Ringo and Dallas are "saved from the blessings of civilization," as one of the characters observes—they head for Mexico, bringing the individualism of the frontier with them. In *The Searchers*, Ethan spends five years trying to find Debbie, who had been abducted by Indians as a child. When he brings her back at the end, he stands in the doorway momentarily as the others enter the house. He does not enter, because home and community are not meant for him; instead, he returns to the wilderness like the gods of myth, who descend to earth to help humankind and leave when their job is done.

In *Beyond Formula*, Stanley Solomon offers a single explanation for the plots, characters, and locales of the western: the landscape, which not only determines setting but also the kind of people who would be attracted to it and the kinds of situations they would encounter there.[2] Because the West is rugged, only the hardy can survive there. But even they need protection from unscrupulous bankers, cattle barons, crooked lawyers, and land speculators. Hence, they need the cavalry, lawmen, crusading newspaper editors, honest lawyers, fearless clergymen—the traditional heroes of the western.

The landscape also explains a certain sameness of setting: plains, valleys, mesas, deserts, ranches, trading posts, forts, and towns with a single street that features a combination saloon, gambling house, and brothel and, if civilization has made any incursions, a barbershop and a newspaper office. The landscape also accounts for modes of travel—stagecoach, horseback, wagon train, railroad—and helps to explain recurring plot devices and rituals. The western plot often revolves around a quest or a journey: a search for a loved one in *The Searchers*, or for a loved one's killers in *The Bravados* (1957) and *Last Train from Gun Hill* (1956). It can also include a trek across inhospitable terrain: the trip through Apache territory in *Stagecoach*, the cattle drive in Howard Hawks's *Red River* (1948), the Mormons' journey across the mountains in *Wagonmaster*.

Those embarking on the quest or making the journey are a varied lot, usually a mix of individualists and traditionalists, the educated and uneducated, moral people and amoral ones, romantics and realists. The passengers in *Stagecoach* are representative: the loner hero with a criminal past, the prostitute, the good woman, the drunken doctor, a southern gambler, a whiskey salesman, an embezzling banker, a kindly lawman, and a driver with a Mexican wife. Other films broadened the list to include homesteaders, cavalry officers, miners, trappers, prospectors, geezers, bullies, and matriarchal and patriarchal figures. As the genre matured, unusual variations on traditional character types were introduced: the sheriff turned bounty hunter in Anthony Mann's *The Tin Star* (1956); bilingual and trilingual Indians (*Fort Apache* and *She Wore a Yellow Ribbon*); the white men who marry Indian women in *Broken Arrow* (1950) and *Broken Lance* (1954); and the loner heroine in Nicholas Ray's *Johnny Guitar* (1954).

Despite its realistic nature, the western is also ritualistic. Certain acts are invested with a ceremonial quality, as if they were being performed according to a rite or a liturgy. Such rituals include gunplay, confrontations, dress, returns, departures, and burials. In a western, one does not just reach for a gun and shoot; one draws from the hip, with style. The gun is more than a weapon; it is an extension of one's personality. Sometimes a character removes it slowly from the holster with a cool gracefulness; at other times, the character whips it out and fires it by thumbing or fanning. A character might even fire two guns, standing defiantly with legs apart and holding the guns at different angles. The gun is also an icon—an image that inspires awe—to be held as one might hold a talisman or a sacred object.

In a western, clothes make the character. The virtuous woman is dressed primly and simply, covered up to her neck. The prostitute is usually dressed provocatively in an off-the-shoulder blouse and ruffled skirt, plumes and feathers, or a low-cut gown with a rhinestone bodice. In symbolic westerns like *Shane* and *The Searchers*, the hero's dress is so striking that it gives him the aura of a medieval knight or an epic warrior. Shane, who materializes like a god descended to earth to aid a homesteader and his family, wears white buckskins that set him apart from the others. Ethan in *The Searchers* makes his first appearance wearing a black neckerchief and a Confederate cloak, and carrying a saber. His rifle is in a fringed buckskin cover that resembles an aegis. His dress, a vestige of his Civil War days, marks him as an anachronism in postbellum Texas, but it also gives him heroic stature.

Ever since the first western, E. S. Porter's *The Great Train Robbery* (1903), the shoot-out has been a dramatic, sometimes an operatic, event. In *The Great Train Robbery*, when one of the outlaws is shot he does a balletlike twirl, firing his gun as he falls. Sam Peckinpah's westerns continue the tradition of choreographed death, often in slow motion, that adds a macabre quality to the bloody climax. Perhaps the most operatic death occurs in King Vidor's *Duel in the Sun* (1947) in which Pearl and Lewt (Jennifer Jones and Gregory Peck) are firing away at each other when suddenly they realize they are in love; thereupon Pearl crawls up rocks and boulders to die, blood-splattered, in Lewt's arms.

Most shoot-outs, though less bizarre, are still theatrical. Even those that seem to be conventional usually have a theatrical touch: Doc

Alan Ladd in his white buckskins in *Shane* (1953). *(Courtesy MOMA/FSA and Paramount Pictures)*

Holliday's handkerchief fluttering in the wind after he has been killed at the O.K. Corral in *Clementine*, McCabe's solitary death in the snow in Robert Altman's *McCabe and Mrs. Miller* (1971). Sometimes the shoot-out takes the form of a long walk: the hero walks down a street that the townspeople have cleared or deserted to confront the villain or the villain's gang, as in *High Noon*. A variation on the shoot-out is the climax of *Red River*, when Tom Dunson (John Wayne) strides down a street intending to challenge his surrogate son, Matt (Montgomery Clift), only to discover that Matt has too much respect for him to retaliate.

Homecomings, departures, and burials in the western are also acts of ritual. The homecoming is often a *nostos*, a return in the epic sense. When Ethan returns from the Civil War at the beginning of *The Searchers*, it is as a hero; he walks toward his brother's house as if in a one-person processional, with each member of the family looking at him with awe. When Wyatt Earp takes leave of Clementine, and Shane of Marion, each behaves like a knight bidding farewell to his lady. In John Ford's cavalry films, the cavalry does not merely leave the fort; it troops out in the grand manner to the music of "The Girl I Left Behind Me" or "She Wore a Yellow Ribbon." Burials are strikingly framed, with the mourners set against the horizon as if they were figures in a painting. Occasionally a touch of pathos is added. In *Shane*, the dead man's dog stretches out a paw to touch his master's casket as it is lowered into the ground; in *She Wore a Yellow Ribbon*, a woman uses part of her red petticoat to make a flag for an officer's burial.

The western, then, is far from a gathering of the good, the bad, and the ugly; it is a complex genre that, in its own way, records the history of America.

Throughout the 1960s, the Vietnam War polarized the nation as no other conflict had. However, except for *The Green Berets* (1968), which glorified America's involvement in Vietnam, filmmakers tended to avoid the war until well after it ended in 1973. Yet the war was not entirely absent from the screen; since the public was not interested in Vietnam War movies (they could see the war on the television news), the western performed a double function: it became a metaphor for an ugly war as well as a mirror of an America that civil rights had made more sensitive to the portrayal of minorities. The two functions were related: Vietnam was perceived as a war that discriminated against minority males who were unable to attend college, thereby qualifying for a deferment, and ended up being drafted.

If the West became less mythic in the 1970s, and the movie western more violent, part of the reason was the documentation of the atrocities American troops had committed in Vietnam. The 1968 My Lai massacre inspired *Soldier Blue* (1970) and *Ulzana's Raid* (1972), which contained some of the most graphic violence seen in a western—but nothing compared with what had happened in Southeast Asia.

The Indian, in the past the perpetrator of violence, was now the victim. *Little Big Man* (1971) challenged the legend of the heroic George Custer and his last stand at Little Big Horn; far from being the romantic figure Errol Flynn played in Raoul Walsh's *They Died with Their Boots On* (1941), the Custer of *Little Big Man* was almost deranged, and the Indians were the victims of his madness. The revisionist western was already established when *Dances with Wolves* (1990) appeared; *Dances with Wolves* marked the culmination of two decades of revisionism, which succeeded in reversing the familiar character types of the savage Indian and the civilized white man. The film's popularity also suggests that audiences are now less inclined to think of good and evil in terms of race and ethnicity.

THE CRIME FILM

Filmmakers have always been intrigued by the gangster and the criminal. The gangster era coincided with the beginning of Hollywood's golden age in the late 1920s, thereby providing screenwriters with fresh plot material. The plots often came straight from the headlines—and with Al Capone, Bonnie Parker and Clyde Barrow, John Dillinger, and "Lucky" Luciano making headlines, there was no dearth of subject matter. Filmmakers were not the only ones who were attracted to criminals—the public was also. Gangsters were colorful figures amid the bleak Great Depression, doing what moviegoers could not do, even if they wished. Gangsters did not so much break the law as flaunt it. But they flaunted it in accordance with the American success scenario. They practiced their own form of upward mobility, beginning with holdups and graduating to bank heists. They started as lackeys and ended up as heads of syndicates. As they advanced, they acquired the trappings of success—overcoats, fedoras, and dark or pinstriped suits. But most of all, gangsters exercised their freedom, the quality Americans prize most dearly. Unrestrained by conventional mores, they gloried in their independence, achieving an emancipation that moviegoers might envy but could never experience because the price was too high.

Thus, the crime film portrays gangsters and criminals with a combination of fascination and compassion, stopping just short of exoneration. As the Production Code insisted, crime could not pay; but this stricture did not stop Hollywood from giving gangsters a sinister charisma and making their lives high drama until the last few minutes when it came time for retribution. And even then, the gangster died in a grand manner, whether in the street or on a sidewalk, the surface of which was always elegantly black, as if specially prepared for those who revealed their dark side.

In addition to being gunned down in the streets (Howard Hawks's *Scarface*, 1932) and on sidewalks (*He Ran All the Way*, 1951), gangsters often met their ends on steps and cliffs, symbolizing their fall from power. In Raoul Walsh's *The Roaring Twenties* (1939), Eddie Bartlett (James Cagney) dies on the steps of a church, cradled in the arms of his mistress. When a police officer asks Eddie's identity, his mistress replies, "He used to be a big shot." Roy Earle (Humphrey Bogart) in *High Sierra* plunges from the top of a cliff. His death is a literal fall from the heights, as opposed to the figurative fall in classical tragedy. Sometimes when a criminal and his beloved die, one body folds over the other (Robert Siodmak's *Criss Cross*, 1948). If physical union is impossible, their hands attempt to touch (Arthur Penn's *Bonnie and Clyde*, 1967).

Like the western, the crime film has inspired theatrical death scenes. Two of the best occur in James Cagney films. In Michael Curtiz's *Angels with Dirty Faces* (1938), Rocky Sullivan (Cagney) agrees to feign cowardice to discourage the teenagers who idolize him from turning to a life of

Stylized death in the classic crime film as seen in *The Public Enemy* (1931). *(Courtesy WCFTR)*

crime. Walking cockily to the electric chair, Rocky suddenly turns craven and begs hysterically for his life. In Raoul Walsh's *White Heat* (1949), Cody Jarett (Cagney) dies amid an apocalyptic explosion of chemical tanks, yelling, "Top of the world, Ma!" Cody Jarett made it to the top, only to go up in flames.

The crime film has other features in common with the western. In both, the gun is an icon. Just as the gun in the western can be a reflection of the user's personality, the gun in the crime film can be projection of the user's neurosis or sexuality. Cody Jarett brandishes a gun as a child would who fancies himself an adult. Jarett's behavior is understandable: he has a relationship with his mother that is so oedipal that he sits on her lap. In *Bonnie and Clyde*, the gun is sexual. For the impotent Clyde, it is a substitute for potency; for Bonnie, who fondles Clyde's gun provocatively, it is the equivalent of a sexual thrill.

The crime film unfolds within a world of back rooms, bars, diners, sleek cars, mean streets, sleazy hotel rooms, speakeasies, nightclubs, tenements, gaudy apartments, and mausoleum-like homes. Unlike the western, which allows loners—even if they have been on the wrong side of the law—to find a mate and live happily ever after, the crime film cannot. Usually gangsters find their true love (another criminal or a person like Marie in *High Sierra*), only to die in their loved one's arms.

The classic American crime film depended for its effectiveness upon performers who were themselves icons: James Cagney, Humphrey Bogart, Edward G. Robinson, John Garfield. With actors who were able to ignite a human spark in characters that could be otherwise flat or unlikable, the gangster and the criminal become both lower and higher versions of ourselves. They are our dark side, doing what we would never dare, and yet achieving the American dream of success, wealth, and fame. While we are glad we are not they, at the same time we cannot help but envy their daring because, as one film scholar has noted, the gangster is "the archetypal American dreamer whose actions and behavior involve a living out of the dream common to most everyone who exists in the particular configurations and contradictions of American society, a dream in conflict with the society."[3]

FILM NOIR

While film noir has its roots in hard-boiled detective fiction, it can take the form of either a private-eye story or a crime film without a private eye. Note, however, that neither a private-eye film nor a crime film is necessarily film noir. *Murder, My Sweet* is a private-eye film that is also a classic

THE NOIR NIGHT AND THE NOIR CORPSE IN *MILDRED PIERCE* (1945). (SEE PAGE 107.)
Wally (Jack Carson) and Mildred Pierce (Joan Crawford) on the pier. *(Courtesy WCFTR)*

film noir; *Meet Nero Wolfe* (1936) is just a private-eye movie. *Criss Cross* and Joseph H. Lewis's *Gun Crazy* (1950) are crime films and film noir; *Angels with Dirty Faces* and *The Roaring Twenties* are just crime films.

Film noir is virtually impossible to define, yet its characteristics are among the most recognizable of any genre. Literally, the term means "dark film"; film that is both dark in its look, with the look of nighttime rather than daylight, and dark in the sense of revealing the dark side of humankind and society. In film noir, the interplay of light and dark is accomplished by high-contrast photography and low-key lighting, which create a monolinear world of white and black. Street lamps shed circles of light on glistening black pavements; neon signs illuminate dark skies; blondes wear black gowns decorated with silver stripes; the hoods of dark cars look glazed by the moonlight. Murders are committed in darkness or in shadow, but during the struggle a table lamp is often knocked over so that when the body is discovered the victim's face is illuminated by the overturned lamp.

Wally discovering Monty Berrigan's (Zachary Scott) body. Note the overturned lamp, a typical noir prop in a typical noir framing. *(Courtesy WCFTR)*

The world of film noir is one of paranoia and entrapment, of forces bearing down on the individual that are too overwhelming to resist. Tight framing encloses characters within a universe from which there is no escape. Slow tracking shots create a mood of uncertainty; long backward tracks suggest continuous movement, pursuit, life on the run. Canted shots imply a world gone haywire. That world is often enshrouded in fog. Riverside Drive in New York is seldom fogbound, but when Roberts and Sue walk down it in *Detour*, they seem to be walking through a fog bank. The fog is not so much real as symbolic of a universe whose workings are impenetrable and whose design, if there is any, can never be known. The stock characters of film noir—private detectives, insurance salesmen, prostitutes, murderous housewives, two-time losers, ex-convicts, or gamblers—are essentially reducible to two: a man and a woman caught up in a chain of circumstances from which only the death of one—or both—can extricate them. When the woman is a femme fatale, the man can either follow her to his—or their—fate, or free himself from her snares. In either case the end is violent, sometimes dramatically so. While O'Hara (Orson Welles) does free himself from Elsa Bannister (Rita Hayworth) in Orson Welles's *The Lady from Shanghai* (1948), Elsa dies in a hall of mirrors where she shoots it out with her husband as their images, reflected in the mirrors, shatter with the glass. (Mirrors are a favorite prop of film noir because the characters are often mirror images of each other.) Before he fires at his wife, Bannister, appropriately, tells Elsa that in killing her, he is killing himself.

Sometimes the climax of a film noir is a *Liebestod* (love-death). Common to film noir is the theme of *amour fou*, or "mad love"—love generated by a combination of passion and infatuation that takes a perverse turn, causing one lover to kill or attempt to kill the other. At the end of *Double Indemnity*, the adulterous lovers plan to kill each other. Phyllis fires at Neff, wounding him; then, suddenly regretting what she has done, she

The hall of mirrors in *The Lady from Shanghai* (1948). *(Courtesy MOMA/FSA and Columbia Pictures)*

moves toward him. Neff takes her in his arms and embraces her while at the same time firing a bullet into her heart.

Film noir plots are convoluted, reflecting the intricacies of fate. Voice-over narration and flashbacks are common; in *The Locket* (1946) there are flashbacks within flashbacks. Chance—in the sense of a character's being in the wrong place at the wrong time—is more significant in film noir than in most other genres. In *Gun Crazy*, a young man whose fascination with guns landed him in reform school, wanders into a carnival featuring a female sharpshooter; the chance encounter changes both their lives, as they become bank robbers in the tradition of Bonnie and Clyde and end up dying in a foggy swamp. In *Detour*, Roberts, hitchhiking from New York to Los Angeles, is picked up by a man with a heart condition who dies en route. Thinking the man's death will be misconstrued as murder, Roberts adopts the dead man's identity. He later makes the mistake of picking up a woman who knew the dead man and who therefore knows that Roberts is not the owner of the car. The woman, Vera, makes Roberts her prisoner and dies in a manner that is bizarre even by film noir standards. Drunk, Vera grabs the phone, rushes into the bedroom, and locks the door behind her. Falling on the bed, she becomes entangled in the telephone cord, which is coiled around her neck. Outside, Roberts pulls at the part of the cord that is under the door, not knowing the rest of it is around Vera's neck. When he finally breaks the door open, he bursts into the bedroom as we see the reflection of the prostrate Vera in the mirror. This is Roberts's second brush with fate; he is now a two-time loser.

Unlike the western, whose popularity is intermittent, film noir has never gone out of fashion because its stylistic elements are applicable to a wide range of plots: the whodunit, the man/woman in hiding, the old dark house, the cover-up, the murderous couple, the murderous lover, and so on. The familiar husband/wife/wife's or husband's lover plot admits of several possibilities: wife and lover can plot to kill husband in the tradition of *Double Indemnity* (or *Body Heat*, 1981); the husband's lover can terrorize the husband's household until his wife takes action and kills her (*Fatal Attraction*, 1989); the husband's lover can be killed when she accidentally discovers that the government is using American service personnel as guinea pigs for atomic tests (*Mulholland Falls*, 1996). An interesting variation on the adulterous trio occurs in *The Grifters* (1990), in which the three are a mother, her son, and the son's lover, who is as amoral as his mother.

While purists may argue that true film noir is black and white, the same high contrast can be obtained by creating a color scheme where black and white predominate. It was not intentional that in *Body Heat* and *The Grifters* the *femmes noires* (Kathleen Turner and Anjelica Huston, respectively) wore white, which was striking against a dark background.

SCREWBALL COMEDY

Like tragedy, comedy has its own conventions: mistaken identity, lovers' quarrels and reconciliations, marital mixups, the deflation of the pompous, trickery, deception, and masquerade. It also has its own gallery of stock characters—irate fathers, errant husbands, clever servants, fops, foundlings, and amorous wives—all of whom speak in maxims, non sequiturs, puns, double entendres, and malapropisms—the traditional sources of verbal humor.

Although film comedy draws on the same sources of humor as stage comedy, it has a genre that is peculiar to itself: screwball comedy. While screwball comedy may have overtones of drawing-room comedy or romantic comedy because of its witty and sophisticated dialogue, screwball comedy also contains elements of farce and slapstick that are alien to the comedy of the drawing room: a food riot in an automat (*Easy Living*), a leopard on the loose (Howard Hawks's *Bringing Up Baby*, 1938), destruction of property for comic effect (the shooting spree that leaves a club car in shambles in Preston Sturges's *The Palm Beach Story*, 1942).

Like film noir, screwball is better described than defined. One or both of the leading characters is a screwball—an oddball whose unconventional nature is responsible for the equally unconventional situations in which the characters find themselves. In *It Happened One Night*, an heiress rebels against her father, ends up hitchhiking with a reporter, masquerading as his wife, and finally discarding the masquerade for marriage. In *Easy Living*, a young working woman is riding on the top deck of a double-decker bus at the very moment an irate husband hurls his wife's sable coat from their penthouse terrace. The coat lands on the young woman, who is then mistaken for the husband's mistress and ensconced in a luxury hotel.

Clark Gable as a reporter and Claudette Colbert as a runaway heiress in *It Happened One Night* (1934). *(Courtesy Sony Pictures Entertainment and MOMA/FSA)*

She later falls in love with a worker at an automat who turns out to be the son of the man who threw the coat from the terrace. A socialite and a paleontologist become involved with a leopard that responds to the song "I Can't Give You Anything but Love, Baby" in *Bringing Up Baby*. A couple in the process of divorcing vie for custody of their dog and vie to sabotage each other's prospects for remarriage in *The Awful Truth* (1937).

The hero in screwball is usually a professional: a reporter in *It Happened One Night* and *Nothing Sacred* (1937); an editor in Howard Hawks's *His Girl Friday* (1940); a herpetologist in *The Lady Eve*; a film director in *Sullivan's Travels*; a professor in Howard Hawks's *Ball of Fire* (1941). The heroine can be a socialite, as in *It Happened One Night*, *Bringing Up Baby*, and *My Man Godfrey* (1936); a Cinderella figure, as in *Easy Living*; a reporter, as in *His Girl Friday*; or a gold digger, as in Mitchell Leisen's *Midnight* (1939) and *The Palm Beach Story*. Rarely are hero and heroine from the same social class. Sometimes the heroine is from the

Cinderella (Jean Arthur) in the automat in the classic screwball comedy *Easy Living* (1937). *(Copyright by Paramount Pictures, Courtesy MCA Publishing Rights, a Division of MCA Inc.)*

higher class (*It Happened One Night*, *My Man Godfrey*); at other times the hero is (*The Lady Eve*, *Easy Living*). In any event, class barriers never stand in the way of a happy ending.

One distinguishing feature of screwball comedy is dialogue that is sharp, fast, and witty. One character picks up on what another says to put the other down and score a point. In *Sullivan's Travels*, Sullivan (Joel McCrea) is trying to convince a studio executive of the importance of making social-consciousness films. When he is told that one such film failed in Pittsburgh, he scoffs, "What do they know in Pittsburgh?" "They know what they like," the executive replies. "If they knew what they liked, they wouldn't live in Pittsburgh" is Sullivan's capping retort. Later, he makes the same appeal to an unemployed actor, extolling a somber movie called *Hold Back Tomorrow*. "You take a picture like *Hold Back Tomorrow*," he begins. "You hold it," she replies dryly.

Screwball comedy delights in non sequiturs. In an attempt to fend off Susan's (Katharine Hepburn) advances in *Bringing Up Baby*, Henry (Cary Grant) informs her that he is engaged to be married. Susan replies with screwball logic: "Then she [his fiancée] won't mind waiting. If I was engaged to be married to you, I wouldn't mind waiting. I'd wait forever."

Double entendre, too, is common in screwball. Since the Production Code frowned on suggestiveness in dialogue and situations, writers encoded the dialogue with double meanings with the expectation that audiences would choose the right meaning; most did. In *The Palm Beach Story*, a millionaire tells the fortune-hunting heroine that he admires women who can cook. "You should taste my popovers," she says playfully. "I'd love to," he replies. Somewhat more subtle but also more suggestive is a character's slip of the tongue in referring to a boys' magazine in *Easy Living*; instead of calling it by its correct name, *The Boy's Constant Companion*, the character calls it *The Boy's Constant Reminder*.

Like film noir, screwball comedy will never become extinct. Audiences are always ready for "meet cutes." In *Only You* (1994), a high-school teacher (Marisa Tomei), who is convinced that her soul mate's name is Damon Bradley, expects to find him in Italy, where, instead, she finds her true love, a shoe salesman (Robert Downey, Jr.). *French Kiss* (1995) reverses the classic screwball situation, in which the bride-to-be bolts from the altar because she cannot say "I do." (The paradigm is *It Happened One Night*.) In *French Kiss*, the prospective bridegroom (Timothy Hutton) phones his fiancée (Meg Ryan) from Paris to inform her that he has found someone else. En route to Paris to reclaim him, she finds herself seated next to a Frenchman (Kevin Kline), who happens to be a thief (which will not stand in the way of romance).

One of the best contemporary screwball comedies is *While You Were Sleeping* (1994), in which a subway employee (Sandra Bullock) comes to the aid of a handsome passenger (Peter Gallagher) when he is mugged on the platform. When the passenger becomes comatose, his family assumes that the employee is his fiancée. The subway employee is not meant to marry the passenger, although she does become part of the family. In screwball there is only one constant—true love, which rarely occurs at first sight; everything else is a variable.

THE REFLEXIVE FILM

Reflexive literature calls attention to itself as literature: a reader, for example, may sense that the novel he or she is reading is really a novel about the art of the novel or about the act of writing a novel, and not just a work of prose purporting to tell a story. Iris Murdoch's *Under the Net* is such a novel; it is both about the nature of fiction and an implicit criticism of existential fiction, which the author feels has sacrificed the personal for the philosophical. Robert Frost's "The Wood Pile" seems to be about a wood pile but is really about the way poetry transforms the ordinary. An extreme example of reflexivity is Jean Anouilh's *Number One*, in which the play a dramatist is trying to write turns out to be the play we have been watching.

A reflexive film calls attention to itself as a film. Reflexivity appears in varying degrees in the following kinds of films:

Films about the nature of film. Woody Allen's *The Purple Rose of Cairo* (1985) explores the consequences of mistaking the illusion of the screen for the reality of life. During a movie, which also has the same title, a character steps off the screen and into the audience, leaving the other characters stranded in mid-plot. The other characters then become autonomous, refusing to continue with the plot until he returns. The character's adventures in the real world point up the difference between life and art: one cannot live art, only life.

Films that refer to specific films. Sometimes called "movie movies," such films depend for their effectiveness upon an audience's knowledge of film. It is true that one can enjoy *The Last Picture Show* for its plot alone; however, anyone who is knowledgeable about film will have a deeper appreciation of Bogdanovich's movie. "The last picture show" of the title is *Red River*, which serves two purposes: it allows the movie theater to close with a bang rather than a whimper—with an epic western and not, as was the case in the original novel, with a minor one. *Red River* is also a metaphor for the film itself. In *Red River*, the John Wayne character befriends a fatherless boy with whom he develops a close relationship. In *The Last Picture Show*, Sam the Lion (Ben Johnson) befriends two boys who might as well be fatherless. With its references to *Red River, The Last Picture Show* establishes itself as a film that, at least on one level, is about America's film heritage, reflecting not only the way generations of Americans behaved but also the way generations of filmmakers portrayed America.

Likewise, to appreciate—rather than merely enjoy—Steven Spielberg's *Raiders of the Lost Ark* (1981), some knowledge of the old movie serials is essential, especially *Nyoka and the Lost Tablets of Hippocrates* (1942), which, along with the anti-Nazi films of the 1940s, inspired *Raiders.*

Films that visually evoke other films. This category differs from the previous one the way an echo differs from a sound. There are some films that have been clearly influenced by other films and reveal their debt through visual quotations—not necessarily by incorporating actual shots from the film, as was the case with the *Red River* footage in *The Last Picture Show.* The much-admired assembly-line sequence in Chaplin's *Modern Times* (1936), in which mechanization comes in for some sharp satire, was not original; it was derived from an earlier French film, René Clair's *À Nous la Liberté* (1931). The climax of *The House on Carroll Street* (1988) was modeled on that of Hitchcock's *Saboteur;* but since staging it atop the Statue of Liberty, as Hitchcock had done, would be too obvious, the screenwriter Walter Bernstein chose another New York landmark—Grand Central Station. The result, however, was the same: the villain plunges to his death from a high place.

When Martin Scorsese decided to remake *Cape Fear* (1991), he knew he would be inviting comparison with the 1962 original, in which Robert Mitchum played Max, an ex-convict who terrorizes the family of the judge who convicted him. Since one of Scorsese's favorite actors, Robert De Niro, would be playing Max, Scorsese incorporated elements of another Mitchum characterization, Harry Powell, the murderous preacher Mitchum played in *The Night of the Hunter* (1955), and had De Niro play Max as a sadist who is also a Bible-spouting religious fanatic. Thus, Scorsese fashioned a character that brings to mind two of Mitchum's best-known roles; still, Scorsese's Max is neither Mitchum's Max nor Mitchum's Powell but merely evokes them.

Films about the filmmaking process, including a behind-the-scenes look at the movie world and those who work in it. *Nickelodeon* is historically accurate in its portrayal of silent filmmaking; *Sweet Liberty* and Vincente Minnelli's *Two Weeks in Another Town* (1962) are valid depictions of contemporary on-location filming.

"What price Hollywood" films that demythologize the industry by stripping away the glamour and exposing the grim reality beneath the painted surface. All three versions of *A Star Is Born*, even though the third is about the rock scene, show how stars are constantly replaced in the pantheon. *Sunset Boulevard* dramatizes a silent star's descent into madness because she cannot adjust to a Hollywood that is not the one she remembers. Vincente Minnelli's *The Bad and the Beautiful* (1952) and Robert Altman's *The Player* (1992) reveal the awesome power movie executives have over writers; *The Player*, a darkly satiric look at corporate Hollywood, goes so far as to have an executive kill a writer.

There is always the danger that a reflexive film will become so obscure in its illusions and quotations that it will appeal only to film buffs. No one enjoys being trapped in a conversation that's so specialized that only experts can participate in it. The films mentioned in this section can be appreciated by anyone, regardless of his or her knowledge of movies or lack of it. On the other hand, a film like Godard's *Detective* (1985), which expects the viewer to be familiar with all of the incongruities of the private-eye movie that Godard renders even more incongruous, is a parody of reflexivity; by its elitism, it alienates moviegoers who can accept the incongruous but not the incomprehensible.

THE WOMAN'S FILM

While *woman's film* is an accepted term in film criticism as well as legitimate film genre, *man's film* is neither. The woman's film became a genre for two main reasons: Hollywood's early attempts to woo female audiences, and the emergence of female stars whose personalities elevated them to the level of icons. Female audiences were always special to the industry either because it was assumed that women had more time for moviegoing than men or that women were more inclined to be movie fans than men. Whatever the reasoning, in the early days of film some nickelodeon owners attempted to attract middle-class women to their theaters by offering them free admission for prenoon shows. Others, less generous, allowed women in for half price.

Theater owners used a different tactic in the 1930s and 1940s: they sponsored "dish nights." Once or twice a week, a free piece of dishware was included in the ticket price and, in the course of time, a complete set of dishes could be acquired. With women comprising such an important— and during World War II, a major—segment of the audience, Hollywood responded by giving them their own genre, with such stars as Bette Davis,

Joan Crawford, and Barbara Stanwyck—actresses who became so inseparable from their personas that one often speaks of a "Bette Davis movie"
or a "Joan Crawford movie."

Bette Davis and Joan Crawford could not play subservient women.
They played women who were the equal and, at times, the superior of
men. In Michael Curtiz's *Mildred Pierce* (1945), Mildred (Joan Crawford)
goes from being a housewife to owning a restaurant chain; in *The Corn Is
Green* (1944), Miss Moffat (Bette Davis) establishes a school for Welsh coal
miners and sends her prize student to Oxford.

In a woman's film, the plot revolves around the woman, and her only
limitations are those imposed by her mortality. Yet, even when faced with
death, the woman dies nobly. In *Dark Victory*, Judith Traherne (Bette
Davis), dying of a brain tumor, not only manages to conceal her imminent
death from her husband; she also chooses to die alone. In *No Sad Songs for
Me* (1950), a wife faces terminal illness with a spirit of resignation that puts
her husband to shame.

The woman's film of the 1930s and 1940s promoted self-sacrifice.
When a daughter decides to marry above her class, her mother disappears
from her life but reappears to watch the wedding ceremony through the
window (King Vidor's *Stella Dallas*, 1937). Women struggled to provide a
better life for their children (*Mildred Pierce*) or raise a friend's illegitimate
child (*The Great Lie*, 1941). They even give up their own illegitimate chil-

Bette Davis as Judith Traherne
and George Brent as Dr. Steele
in *Dark Victory* (1939), a major
"woman's film" *(Courtesy Movie
Star News)*

dren (*The Old Maid*, 1938) and stand by watching the child address someone else as mother.

While women suffered nobly in many films throughout the 1930s and 1940s, they also succeeded in male-dominated professions. The woman's film of the period portrayed women in a variety of occupations: lawyers, copywriters, reporters, actors, surgeons, nurses. By the 1960s, however, there was nothing unusual about a successful woman lawyer or entrepreneur. Terminal illnesses had become standard television fare and were no longer special. The cancer victim had become the cancer patient, and resignation to the inevitable was no longer the noble gesture it was in *Dark Victory* but, rather, the final stage of a process that begins with denial and ends with acceptance.

The portrayal of women on the screen has changed through the years. In the classic woman's film, women did not so much have friends as confidantes who were either supportive sisters or wisecracking sidekicks. Genuine friendship between women was rare on the screen; women who seemed to be friends were actually rivals (*Old Acquaintance*, 1943). It was not until *Julia*, in 1977, that American audiences saw a true friendship between women depicted on the screen. The title character and her friend Lily are not at odds with each other; they complement each other. Thus, the politically committed Julia inspires the apolitical Lily to take a stand against the spread of fascism that is soon to bring about a global war.

When Barbara Stanwyck played a young widow in *My Reputation* (1946) who refused to wear black as a sign of mourning, she scandalized her friends. In Martin Scorsese's *Alice Doesn't Live Here Anymore* (1975), Ellen Burstyn plays a widow who would no more wear black than she would mourn in silence. Instead, she takes her son on the road in an attempt to resume her singing career but eventually has to work in a diner. The point is that each of these women, although they belong to different eras, exercised the same kind of independence; one defied her mother and refused to have her dresses dyed black (*Reputation*); the other defied convention and took off with her son in search of work (*Alice*). Thus, it is not entirely correct to say that contemporary films portray women more realistically than did those of the past—unless realism is measured by explicit language, nudity, and overt sexuality. On the other hand, had the Production Code not inhibited filmmakers, the dialogue of the films of the 1940s and 1950s would have been far less subtle, and the portrayal of sexuality more direct.

It is important to remember that the women depicted on the screen during Hollywood's golden age were often strong-willed, but various factors (the Production Code, audience expectations, a general suspicion—if not bias—against a woman who succeeds in a male-dominated profession) necessitated either a last-minute conversion to marriage, always regarded

Rosalind Russell, the quintessential career woman of the 1940s, in *A Woman of Distinction* (1950). *(Courtesy Sony Pictures Entertainment)*

as more satisfying than a career, or some sign of imperfection on the woman's part.

Rosalind Russell was known for her career women, who were always elegantly dressed, witty, and the equal of any male. Yet, in movie after movie, she ended up preferring marriage to a career. In *Tell It to the Judge* (1949), Russell played the title character, who is in every way the intellectual superior of her ex-husband. However, the script called for Russell not only to take him back but also to utter the incredible line "A woman's place is in the home." To her credit, Russell tossed the line off as if she didn't believe it—and hoped the audience agreed with her.

MGM's *Woman of the Year* (1942), the first pairing of Spencer Tracy and Katharine Hepburn, was to end with Tess Harding (Hepburn) telling her husband, Sam Craig (Tracy), that she prefers to be known not as Mrs. Sam Craig but as Tess Harding Craig. While this should have posed no problem, MGM thought audiences would leave thinking that Tess had scored a victory over Sam. Instead, a scene was added in which Tess tried to make breakfast for Sam and proved to be totally incompetent in the kitchen. Her inability to brew coffee was apparently a cardinal sin, despite her awesome intelligence and fluency in various languages.

MGM insisted on some sign of Tess's vulnerability; unfortunately, the kitchen scene marred what might have been a truly feminist film. Still, there were films in the 1930s and 1940s in which women defied convention but paid the price for it, which was often death. *Back Street* (both the 1932 and the 1941 versions) portrayed a woman who accepted her role as mistress, even sailing to Europe with her married lover (but always boarding the ship after he and his family had done so). However, the prevailing mentality—that the wages of sin is death—meant that both husband and mistress died at the end.

In 1968, an event occurred that affected all of the genres, but especially the woman's film: the movie ratings. The changeover really began in the 1950s, when filmmakers, motivated by the need to offer audiences something different from what was available on television, started challenging the Production Code. Thus, language and subject matter that were once forbidden ("You go to hell!" spoken to a priest in *On the Waterfront*; heroin addiction in *The Man with the Golden Arm*, 1955) found their way to the screen. By the early 1960s, another taboo subject, homosexuality, was implied—though not depicted—in *Suddenly, Last Summer* (1959) and *The Children's Hour* (1962). As a result, the Production Code proved to be obsolete and was replaced by a rating system, which originally consisted of G (general audiences), M (mature audiences), R (restricted to viewers over 16, unless accompanied by parent or guardian), and X (under 16 not admitted). As film content became more explicit, the designations changed, eventually becoming G, PG (parental guidance), PG-13 (parental guidance for children under 13), R (restricted to anyone under 17 unless accompanied by an adult), and NC-17 (no children, only 17 and older).

These changes, combined with the attack on female stereotypes mounted by women's groups, allowed filmmakers to explore a theme in the woman's film that had been treated superficially in the past: female bonding. The traditional woman's film never denied the possibility of close relationships between women; however, the notion of women bonding like the title characters in *Butch Cassidy and the Sundance Kid* (1969) was unthinkable in the 1935–1960 period. Women could be friends or rivals. If two women were friends, at least one of them would marry (*These Three*, 1936); if they were rivals, they would resolve their differences, realizing that they might have to spend the rest of their lives together (*Old Acquaintance*, 1943). But in *Julia* (1977), Lily (Jane Fonda) and Julia (Vanessa Redgrave) are the closest of friends but not rivals; they differ only in their degree of social commitment. Prior to the ratings, if there was the slightest chance of a woman's having a relationship with another man after her husband left her, she would never forgo it to open an art gallery; but that is exactly what happens in *An Unmarried Woman* (1978). In 1946, the year after World War II ended and Hollywood turned its attention to the problems of returning veterans, no studio would have considered a film about a married woman who falls in love with a paraplegic veteran. But

Vietnam was not World War II, and a situation that was unthinkable in 1946 worked some thirty years later in *Coming Home* (1978).

Although the woman's film has undergone many changes since a woman was expected to give up her career for marriage or her lover to preserve the family name (always the man's family), it is not entirely accurate to say that women are no longer depicted as victims; rather, women are at least allowed to retaliate against their victimizers. In *Thelma and Louise* (1991), a female bonding film in which the women become fugitives from justice, Louise (Susan Sarandon) comes upon her friend Thelma (Geena Davis) as she is about to be raped. Louise might have spared the rapist's life if he were repentant, but when he becomes verbally abusive, she shoots him in the face. Thelma and Louise thus become women on the run. Pursued by the police, they take a suicidal drive over the Grand Canyon; the car heads into space, the frame freezes, and Thelma and Louise move out of time into eternity (or at least myth). The ending recalls *Butch Cassidy and the Sundance Kid*, in which the pair, outnumbered and about to be killed, also freeze into a composition that is slowly drained of color until it becomes monochrome. If men can bond, turn outlaw, and freeze into myth, why not women?

The chief obstacle to the woman's film is presently the dearth of decent scripts for middle-aged women. The woman's film will never die out, but it will never regain the popularity it once had until producers realize there can be as much drama in a movie about a middle-aged woman as there is in a movie about a younger one.

THE HORROR FILM

The classic horror film involves a metamorphosis: an individual is transformed into an animal (panther, ape), insect (fly), semihuman (werewolf), antihuman (somnambule, ghoul, zombie, vampire), antiself (Dr. Jekyll), shrunken self (homunculus), or, as in the Frankenstein themes, a synthetic creation is turned into a living creature. The inanimate can also be an object of transformation: a house can change from a habitation for humans to a habitation for ghosts (*The Uninvited*, 1944); it can even acquire an evil personality that affects those who live there (*Burnt Offerings*, 1976; *The Amityville Horror*, 1979).

The ghost story is transformation in reverse, with the ghosts taking on human qualities. The ghosts may be benign or vengeful; both types are featured in *The Uninvited*. If they are not at rest, they may work through the living until they are vindicated (e.g., the mother's ghost in *Lady in White* [1988] that cannot be reunited with her daughter in the hereafter until her daughter's murderer is apprehended).

The prototypical horror film is *The Cabinet of Dr. Caligari* (1919), whose visual style, pruned of its exaggerations, became standard for the genre. Visually, *Caligari* is expressionistic; its asymmetrical and bizarre settings suggest a world out of joint, a world not so much of our dreams as our nightmares. Chimneys look as if they will topple over, windows are shaped like diamonds, walls seem on the verge of caving in. The American horror film uses a less extreme form of expressionism; the high-contrast photography of the German-made *Caligari*, in which there are no grays but only black and white, was not entirely discarded by American filmmakers but made less pronounced through low-key lighting that allowed for the interplay of light and shadow.

Caligari also features two plot devices that have become conventions of the horror film: the team of the mad doctor and his subhuman accom-

THE MONSTER AND THE GIRL

Caesare the somnambule and Jane in *The Cabinet of Dr. Caligari* (1919). *(Courtesy MOMA/FSA)* plice (whose most familiar successors were Dr. Frankenstein and his hunch-back assistant in James Whale's *Frankenstein*, 1931); and the creature's desire for a mate. In *Caligari*, the doctor's accomplice may be a somnambule, but he is not impervious to the heroine's charms; nor are the Wolf Man and Dracula of later films unaffected by the presence of a beautiful woman. Moreover, embalming does not stop the mummy from searching for his beloved Princess Ananka, even if she happens to be in the United States (*The Mummy*, 1932). A synthetic creature like Frankenstein's monster needs a bride: when his bride rejects him (James Whale's *Bride of Frankenstein*, 1935), he retaliates by destroying the laboratory where he was created. The monster's attraction to women is easily explained; the creature is the personification of the id, or the libido, which is virtually all that is left after the transformation. The creature's libido may even be more active because it is no longer under the control of reason.

The basic types of horror films—ghost, creature, dual personality, and mad scientist—had been established in the 1930s and 1940s along with the conventions of low-key lighting, shadowy surfaces, dissolve transformations, cellar laboratories with overflowing test tubes, fogbound woods, and Gothic mansions. While the musical and the western were photographed in either monochrome or color, the horror film was shot almost exclusively in black and white. In the 1950s, the use of color began with *House of Wax* (1953) and *Phantom of the Rue Morgue* (1954), but it was the British-made *Curse of Frankenstein* (1957), the first of Hammer Films' horror series, that set the trend toward the color horror film.

While color and horror are not incompatible, as Roman Polanski's *Rosemary's Baby* (1968) and *Carrie* prove, color cannot capture the shadowy

Larry Talbot (Lon Chaney, Jr.), whose transformation does not diminish his interest in the heroine in *The Wolf Man* (1941). *(Copyright by Universal Pictures, a Division of Universal City Studios, Inc. Courtesy MCA Publishing Rights, a Division of MCA Inc.)*

world of the unconscious as well as black and white, which is also more conducive to horror by suggestion. Color is suited to gore, the hallmark of the latest kind of horror film: the slasher film. Like every addition to a genre, the slasher film is not without precedent: its parent is *Psycho*, which was a genuine horror film with a subtle transformation. The oedipal Norman Bates becomes so closely identified with his mother that he assumes her personality, even to the extent of dressing in her clothes and murdering in her name. Significantly, Norman does not die at the end of *Psycho*; and as the years passed and *Psycho* became a classic, the need for a sequel arose—*Psycho II* (1983), then *Psycho III* (1986). As long as there is an audience for horror, there will be a *Psycho* of some sort.

The *Psycho* sequels illustrate a time-honored tradition in horror: the monster is destroyed only when the series or the cycle dies. Even though the monster clearly dies at the end of *Frankenstein* in the fire that destroys the mill, he is discovered in the mill's cellar at the beginning of *Bride of Frankenstein*. And even though the monster clearly perishes again in the inferno at the end of *Bride of Frankenstein*, he is resurrected for *Son of Frankenstein* (1939) four years later and paired with the Wolf Man in *Frankenstein Meets the Wolf Man* (1943) four years after he was revived by Frankenstein's son.

The same principle applies to the slasher film, the most popular being *Friday the 13th* (1980), although it is hardly the most inventive. That distinction belongs to *Halloween* (1978), which introduced a plot device that *Friday the 13th* and similar films (e.g., *Prom Night*, 1980; *Terror Train*, 1979) imitated: a prologue depicting a murder that has occurred prior to the main action and has definite bearing on the plot. *Halloween* led to three sequels (1981, 1983, 1988), but it was clear that the public was more taken with *Friday the 13th*, which, within eight years after its release, had spawned seven films.

The *Friday the 13th* cycle works from the same premise as other horror cycles and series: the premise of the undying monster. In *Friday the 13th*, two teenage camp counselors are killed because they were making love when they should have been rescuing the drowning Jason. The killer is Jason's mother, who is herself killed at the end. The sequels feature Jason himself, who emerges from the mud to continue his mother's work.

In addition to the obligatory prologue, the slasher film practices its own form of voyeurism: subjective camera. The camera is often stationed outside a window representing the point of view of someone looking in; it tilts up to a bedroom, as if someone were spying. The slasher film also uses off-center compositions and framing that excludes the killer, leaving only the victim in the frame. While the slasher film is a lesser form of horror, its use of subjective camera is a feature worth noting.

THE SCIENCE-FICTION FILM

"There is no clearly recognized border between SF [science fiction] and such genres as fantasy and horror," notes a science-fiction expert.[4] Such a statement is not surprising, since, as we have seen, genres often overlap or share conventions. While the western and the crime film portray both sides of the law, the designations are different: bandits in one, criminals in the other; sheriffs in one, police officers in the other. Moreover, what one critic would call horror, another might term science fiction. In *Science Fiction in the Cinema*, John Baxter considers *The Birds* to be science fiction even though it is neither futuristic nor a fantasy. *The Birds* does, however, deal with an invasion—not of Martians but of killer birds. The invasion motif justifies its inclusion under science fiction; the transformation motif (benign creatures turning malevolent) merits it a place in horror. On the other hand, utopian, fantasy, and doomsday films, as well as those about space travel and warring planets, are never mistaken for anything other than science fiction.

Nonhumans, often extraterrestrials, play a major role in science fiction; they are also a diverse lot and even differ in their attitude toward humans. While some extraterrestrials seek the destruction of the planet (*War of the Worlds*, 1953), not all are treacherous. Some have come to warn mankind of the dangers of nuclear testing (*The Day the Earth Stood Still*, 1951); others, to enlighten humans about the nature of aliens in the hope of bridging the gap between Us and Them (*Close Encounters of the Third Kind*); still others to use Earth's resources for their own purposes (*This Island Earth*, 1955). The aliens in *It Came from Outer Space* (1953) mean no harm; they merely wish to repair their spaceship.

The creatures themselves represent various life forms: plant life (*The Thing*, 1951); aquatic life (the gill-man in *The Creature from the Black Lagoon*, 1954, and *Revenge of the Creature*, 1955; a protoplasmic mass (*The Blob*, 1958); birds (*The Giant Claw*, 1957); spiders (*Tarantula*, 1955); grasshoppers (*Beginning of the End*, 1957); and ants (*Them!*, 1954).

In *Seeing Is Believing*, Peter Biskind argues that just as the western is bipolar (wilderness vs. civilization, West vs. East, and the like) so is science fiction, with its political extremes of right and left.[5] Conservative science fiction portrays science, the federal government, and the military as forces for the good. In conservative science fiction (*It Came from Beneath the Sea*, 1955; *The Thing*), science succeeds in destroying the alien. Liberal science fiction either depicts science, the federal government, and the military as ineffectual or criticizes their methods. In *I Married a Monster from Outer Space* (1958), salvation comes not from the government but from a dog. In conservative science fiction, aliens have no redeeming features. In liberal science fiction, they are portrayed sympathetically. In *The Seven Year Itch*, The Girl (Marilyn Monroe) remarks on how moved she was by *The Creature from the Black Lagoon*.

Since creatures are often found in horror films as well as in science fiction, there should be some method of determining whether a film is more properly classified as science fiction than as horror. One must determine the role that science and technology play in the film, the sense of time reflected in it, and the effects of the experiments—individual, local, or global—conducted in it.

While neither horror nor science fiction mirrors the real world, science fiction tries to convince us that it does by dealing in specifics. Horror tends to be more general. In *Bride of Frankenstein*, we never know how Dr. Pretorious shrinks humans to the size of miniatures. In *Dr. Cyclops* (1940), on the other hand, we know that the physicist creates his homunculi by subjecting humans to atomic radiation. Because science is the film's point of departure, *Dr. Cyclops* is viewed as science fiction.

The horror film, like the gothic novel, tends to be set in remote times. Even when a horror film is set in the present, it recalls cults (the cat cult in *Cat People*) and practices (devil worship in *Rosemary's Baby*) that go back centuries. Science fiction, on the other hand, can either reflect the present or evoke the future. The futuristic film is easily recognized. Less evident is the way science fiction can mirror the present.

In the 1950s, science-fiction movies preyed on Americans' two deep fears: flying saucers and the atomic bomb. The possibility of extraterrestrial life resulted in one of the era's best science-fiction movies, Don Siegel's *Invasion of the Body Snatchers* (1956), in which aliens descend upon a California town and take possession of the inhabitants by an ingenious

Science fiction as mythology in *Return of the Jedi* (1983): The confrontation of Good and Evil, Luke Skywalker (Mark Hamill) and Darth Vader (David Prowse). *(Courtesy Lucasfilms Ltd.)*

method of transformation: pods are placed under their beds, absorbing the inhabitants' personalities and leaving them as parodies of human beings. The implications of the film were far-reachng: aliens threatened the race with a unique form of extinction—the extinction of the human personality. The threat to civilization posed by the atomic bomb triggered a host of science-fiction movies that imagined the results of atomic detonations: mutants in the form of giant ants, creatures dislodged from the ocean depths, humans turned into steel.

In the 1950s, a villain that was a computer would have made sense only to a few. By 1968, the name of Hal, the dispassionate computer of Stanley Kubrick's *2001: A Space Odyssey*, had entered the movie vocabulary, joining such unforgettable names as Rick Blaine and Rhett Butler.

In the 1970s, the science-fiction movie took an interesting turn. The threat of the atomic bomb had mushroomed into the fear of nuclear destruction. Since, as T. S. Eliot observed, "humankind cannot bear very much reality," George Lucas in *Star Wars* (1977) amalgamated science fiction, which was never a pure genre to begin with, not with horror but with adventure. The result was not mindless escapism but a return to myth in its earliest stage: fairy tale or dream narrative with stock characters rather than individuals—heroes, princesses, villains, half-humans, nonhumans, animal-like humans, and humanlike animals—that we have met many times before in our dreams. In the Star Wars trilogy, the characters include the pure-hearted Luke Skywalker, the virginal Princess Leia, the evil Darth Vader, the 900-year-old Yoda, the patriarchal Ben (Obi-Wan) Kenobi, Chewbacca the Wookie, the treacherous Jabba the Hut, the porcine Gammorean guards, the reptilian Admiral Ackbar, and a lovable pair of robots, C3PO and R2-D2.

Equally important are the contributions of Steven Spielberg to the genre. While Lucas added adventure and an uncritical form of myth to science fiction, Spielberg humanized the genre. *Close Encounters of the Third Kind* portrays real people—a man, a woman, and a child—whose response to aliens reflects the film's philosophy. The child and the childlike characters in the film do not fear the aliens. What Spielberg is arguing for is the tearing down of the wall that divides one group from another, one race from another, and humans from extraterrestrials. The aliens bring love; thus, one can learn from them. Those who return at the end of *Close Encounters* have clearly been changed—for the better. Likewise, in Spielberg's *E.T.: The Extra-Terrestrial* (1982), a human—again a child—learns from an alien.

It is important to remember that genres never really die; a genre may go out of fashion for a while or reconstitute itself. When it reappears, it might seem like a totally new creation, when it is really "old wine in a new bottle." All that has happened is that, in addition to reflecting its own conventions, the genre also mirrors the conventions of the age. In 1936, the notion of strong language in a musical like *Swing Time* would have been laughable; in 1996, Woody Allen's *Everyone Says I Love You* was R-rated for its language. Each film observes the conventions of the musical; each also reflects the era in which it was made.

NOTES

[1]James Kitses, *Horizons West* (Bloomington: Indiana University Press, 1969), 8–27.

[2]Stanley J. Solomon, *Beyond Formula: American Film Genres* (New York: Harcourt Brace Jovanovich, 1976), 12–15.

[3]Jack Shadoian, *Dreams and Dead Ends: The American Gangster/Crime Film* (Cambridge, Mass.: MIT Press, 1977), 2.

[4]William Johnson, "Journey into Science Fiction," in *Focus on the Science Fiction Film*, ed. William Johnson (Englewood Cliffs, N.J.: Prentice-Hall, 1972), 1.

[5]Peter Biskind, *Seeing Is Believing: How Hollywood Taught Us to Stop Worrying and Love the Fifties* (New York: Pantheon Books, 1983), 102–59.

CHAPTER

Film
Subtext

5

H ow often have you read a story or seen a film that you felt was not entirely what it seemed to be about? Many college freshmen read "The Widow of Ephesus," a tale from Petronius' *Satyricon*, written in the first century A.D. In this frequently anthologized story, a woman is so shattered by her husband's death that she cannot practice the ancient rites of mourning (breast-beating and hair-tearing). Instead, accompanied by her maid, she retires to the underground tomb where the body lies. A soldier, patrolling a crucifixion site nearby to prevent the bodies from being taken down from the crosses, notices her presence, enters the tomb, quotes Virgil, and finally wins her attention. When a corpse disappears from one of the crosses, the soldier fears his negligence will cost him his job. But after three consecutive nights of lovemaking, the widow of Ephesus offers him her husband's body as fair exchange.

What was just summarized was the story's plot, which consisted of a situation (a widow in mourning), its complication (the soldier's appearance), and its resolution (the substitution of the husband's body for the criminal's). However, a classic tale like "The Widow of Ephesus" cannot be reduced to its story line. In every narrative worth studying, whether it's a work of fiction or a work of film, there is a subtext, a complex structure beneath the narrative consisting of the various associations the narrative evokes in us. In other words, there is a surface meaning and a deeper meaning. "The Widow of Ephesus" has a surface wit that cannot mask the underlying cynicism. The surface meaning is that love conquers all; the deeper, or subtextual, meaning is that love conquers lovers, generating such passion in them that they think nothing of sleeping three nights in a row next to a corpse.

Film also has a subtext, or what might be called an infranarrative. Whether we realize it or not, film has a dual nature. There is the film projected *on* the screen and the film projected *from* the screen. The first is the narrative in the traditional sense: a text that is the result of the collaboration between a director, a writer, a cast, and a crew; in other words, what audiences would think of as the "movie" they are about to see.

The situation is analogous to a novel that has just been published; prior to publication it was revised and edited. Now it awaits readers. The text is there, but readers, reviewers, and scholars must find their own way into it. When they do, they will be entering the infranarrative and experiencing the text more deeply, finding levels of meaning (symbols, image patterns, references to other works, including the author's) that are there but must be discovered through sensitive reading.

Film infranarrative, or subtext, is the result of what occurs from the various associations we make during the film. It is comparable to the symbolic or metaphorical level in literature. In a literature class, a professor might say that while Dante's *Inferno* is, *literally*, about a man's descent through the nine circles of hell, *symbolically* it is about a man trying to put his life in order by envisioning what awaits him in the hereafter; or though Robert Frost's "Stopping by Woods on a Snowy Evening" might seem to be a poem about a man stopping to observe the snow-covered woods, it is actually about a man contemplating death on the longest night of the year.

Naturally, the narrative and infranarrative (or text and subtext) are not two separate entities (there is, after all, only one film); think of them, rather, as two concentric circles, the infranarrative being *within* the narrative. But just as, for the sake of definition, English teachers distinguish between form and content, and philosophers between matter and form, we can also make a similar distinction between the two narratives. Beneath the primary narrative (the plot conceived as the ordered arrangement of the incidents) is a secondary one. The first can be summarized as one would a novel or a play. But the infranarrative has no place in a synopsis. Asked for a plot synopsis of *Psycho*, for example, one would never say it is about an Oedipus complex gone haywire, sexual repression, voyeurism, transvestism, schizophrenia, and necrophilia, although these are all part of the film's subtext. But saying that *Psycho* is about such matters implies that we must have made certain associations between what we saw on the movie screen (a film about a woman who absconds with a $40,000 bank deposit and ends up in a motel, where she is murdered by a young man who can kill only by dressing as his mother) and what we saw on our own personal screen: a man so obsessed with the spirit of his dead mother (whom he killed, along with her lover) that he dresses like her and kills women of whom his mother would have disapproved; an indentation in his mother's bed, suggesting that her corpse had occasionally been placed there; and an identification so deep that, finally, the young man believes he has become his mother. The film may remind us of a famous story about necrophilia, Faulkner's "A Rose for Emily." It might even remind us of certain Greek myths in which sons murder mothers—e.g., Alcmaeon killing his mother Eriphyle, Orestes killing his mother Clytemnestra and her former lover (now her husband) Aegisthus; or of a novella like Stevenson's *Dr. Jekyll and Mr. Hyde,* in which the respectable Henry Jekyll is incapable of doing what his evil alter ego, Mr. Hyde, does. By making certain associations between *Psycho*, mythic figures, and literary characters, we have gone beneath the film's surface into its infranarrative.

These associations can be *mythic, visual/iconic, intellectual,* and *musical;* they can even exist in some combination. For example, an iconic association (one in which the actor's screen persona is associated with the character, so that the actor *is* the character) can also be mythic in the sense of reminding us of some mythic type or mythological figure; but it is primarily iconic. For example, the character that Barbra Streisand plays in *The Mirror Has Two Faces* (1996)—a plain-looking college professor who transforms herself into a chic and highly attractive woman—might recall the story of the ugly duckling or the crone, who is really a beautiful woman in disguise. But Streisand herself has become such a screen legend, and has capitalized on her metamorphosis from gawky performer on early 1960s television to world-class singer-actor-writer-director-philanthropist, that we are more apt to identify her with the character than with the underlying myth of transformation.

MYTHIC ASSOCIATIONS

The Nature of Myth

To understand how myth is part of a film's subtext, we must reconsider our concept of myth. In the popular mind, myth is synonymous with falsehood. In literary and film criticism, however, it has another meaning altogether. William York Tindall defined *myth* as "a dreamlike narrative in which the individual's central concerns are united with society, time, and the universe."[1] Erich Fromm called myth "a message from ourselves to ourselves."[2] The film critic Parker Tyler regarded myth as "a free, unharnessed fiction, a basic prototypic pattern capable of many variations and distortions, even though it remains imaginative truth."[3] Lillian Feder's definition is the most detailed: "Myth is a narrative structure of two basic areas of unconscious experience which, of course, are related. First, it expresses instinctual drives and the repressed wishes, fears, and conflicts that they motivate. These appear in the themes of myth. Second, myth also conveys the remnants within the individual consciousness of the early stage of phylogenetic development in which the plots were created. This characteristic is evident mainly in its plots."[4] In other words, myth is a form of racial history—a narrative distillation of the wishes and fears of both ourselves and the human race.

Common to all four definitions are the following:

1. Myth is a narrative and as such obeys the rules of narrative (e.g., the beginning-middle-end structure).
2. Myth also operates on an unconscious level, presenting us with characters (questers, the enchanted and the enchanter, ogres, scapegoats, monsters), themes (the homeward journey, the quest, ancestral curses, revenge, patricide, matricide), and settings (caves, wastelands, subterranean rivers, enchanted islands, flat-topped mountains, ominous castles, desolate moors) that we recognize without having experienced them because they tap into our racial memory and recall early stages in the development of humankind as well as events that occurred during those stages and are now regarded as stories.
3. The themes of myth are universal: the return of the hero, the desire for forbidden knowledge, the quest for identity, the rebellion against tyranny. No single age has a monopoly on such themes. Thus, myth transcends time and place and can never be said to be dated.
4. Myths are ultimate truths about life and death, fate and nature, God and humans. For this reason, they can never be false, even though the characters they portray may not have existed. Myths also endure long after the civilizations that produce them have vanished because they crystallize, in narrative form, unchanging patterns of human behavior. There will always be rebels like Antigone and Prometheus, homeward-bound voyagers like Odysseus, vengeance seekers like Medea, those who pursue reason

and favor Apollo over Dionysus, and those who favor emotional release at the expense of reason and prefer Dionysus to Apollo.

Film is receptive to myth for two reasons. First, film and myth can speak the same language—picture language. Long before myths were written down, they were transmitted orally through epics and visually through artwork on walls, vases, bowls, and wine vessels. Thus, from the very outset myth was oral and visual; and so was film, for even during the silent period there was always some form of sound, as we have seen. Another reason film and myth are so compatible is that both are intimately associated with dreams. Parker Tyler coined a phrase for film: "the daylight dream." It is also not coincidental that Hollywood has been dubbed the "dream factory." We dream individually, of course; but we also dream collectively. The stuff of our dreams is the stuff of fairy tales, legends, and romances: quests, evil enchanters, enchanted princes and princesses, talking animals, transformations of humans into beasts and the ugly into the beautiful (and vice versa), apparitions, conversations with the dead, and so forth. Such dream material belongs to the human race, and thus our dreams make us one with humankind. The psychologist Carl Jung compared the dream to a screen on which the history of the race is projected; the same can be said of the movie screen. When mythic figures appear on the screen, they strike a responsive chord because they are familiar: we have encountered them before—if not in actual myths or fairy tales, then in our dreams.

Film has a dream level to which we respond the way we respond to myths: we respond instinctively, never questioning their origins or even their existence. Making a mythic association involves remembering a pattern of experience that is universal. Sometimes we can determine the specific myth; *King Kong* evokes Beauty and the Beast; *The Blue Angel* (1930), in which a respected teacher is destroyed by a seductive singer, recalls myths about such temptresses as Circe, Calypso, and the Lorelei. More often, you will not be able to isolate the specific myth but only a mythic type (the searcher, the exile, the knight errant, the blessed damsel, the earth mother, the eternal child, the messiah/liberator/savior/deus ex machina) or a mythic theme (the descent to the underworld, the quest for the grail, the journey into the unknown, the homeward journey, the birth of the hero, the life force vs. the force of reason, wilderness vs. civilization, and the like).

The Transformation Myth in *Cat People* (Jacques Tourneur, 1942)

The transformation myth is one of the most common myths, as anyone who has ever read Ovid's *Metamorphoses* knows: Daphne is transformed into a laurel tree, Philomela into a nightingale, Chiron the centaur into the constellation Sagittarius, Niobe into stone, and so on. There are also instances of mythological figures who are capable of changing form (Proteus, the sea nymph Thetis). In *Cat People*, Irena (Simone Simon), the ill-starred descendant of a Serbian cat cult, is doomed to revert to a panther whenever her passions are aroused; the reason could be anything from jealousy to sexual desire—not so much on her part as on the male's.

The script, as might be expected of any early-1940s script, skirts the issue of Irena's frigidity; instead, the assumption is that Irena, who bears the curse of the cat women (her ancestors who rejected Christianity and embraced pagan rituals and black masses), is unable to consummate her marriage because she is afraid of turning into a panther and killing her husband. Rather, she insists on a relationship of friendship; her husband tries to understand but eventually turns to a female coworker, Alice, who recommends a psychiatrist, Dr. Judd. The psychiatrist is so intrigued by Irena that he tries to seduce her, not realizing that a man's touch can release the panther in her. The panther emerges and attacks Judd, who mortally wounds Irena with his sword cane.

The narrative seems a Freudian reworking of a transformation myth. But the infranarrative points to something far deeper: a woman who wants a man only as a friend, not as a lover; who cannot bear a man's touch; who, after taking on animal form, pursues Alice through Central Park (always unseen, thanks to the ingenious direction of Jacques Tourneur) and later to a health club, where—also unseen—she terrorizes Alice while she is swimming. Discerning audiences now regard *Cat People* as more than just another horror movie: some see elements of lesbianism in the way Irena stalks Alice; others see Irena as a mother goddess to whom men are meant to be subservient; still others view her as a woman who yearns in vain for a healthy relationship with a man; a woman who, when she commits an act

Irena (Simone Simon) and her husband in name only (Kent Smith) in *Cat People* (1942). *(Courtesy MOMA/FSA)*

of violence (which she does when, as a panther, she attacks a herd of sheep), must cleanse herself by taking a hot bath. For a movie that was not taken seriously in its time, *Cat People* now enjoys critical respect.

The Savior Myth in *Shane* (George Stevens, 1953)

Every critic who has written about *Shane* has sensed a mythic subtext in the film. In *Shane*, there appear to be at least three mythic levels.

Shane as a Christ Figure

Shane begins with the credits, with Alan Ladd as Shane entering on horseback from the left to the "Shane theme," a melody that suggests cantering horses and deer drinking peacefully from a stream against a background of snow-decked mountains. Shane is descending into a valley; he is not moving horizontally across the frame like a gunfighter, although he will later change both speed and direction during his ride of vengeance. For the moment he is moving *downward*—in symbolic terms, he might be said to be lowering himself—as he descends into the lives of the Starretts, a family of homesteaders.

Shane can be seen as a Christ figure. Just as Christ descended from heaven and humbled himself by assuming human nature, Shane descends into the valley, temporarily putting aside his divinity to serve humanity. Shane's resemblance to Christ has been noted by the critic Donald Richie:

> Shane . . . came from nowhere and he is going nowhere—like the vagrant Jett Rink in *Giant*, like the hitchhiking George Eastman [in Stevens's *A Place in the Sun*], like Jesus Christ. . . . His difference from the romantic hero is that he—like Christ himself—rather than merely feeling that he ought to do something to express his inner values and to affect the world, actually does something about it.[5]

Shane's past is as enigmatic as Christ's. Christ's life before he began his public ministry at thirty is a mystery. And so is Shane's; he simply appears one day, looking like a god in white buckskins. As part of his ritual incarnation, he sheds his divine trappings and dresses in the clothes of mortals—blue denim and dark trousers. But he will not retain that outfit forever. Before he avenges the death of Torrey (Elisha Cook, Jr.), he changes back into his buckskins, becoming a god once more.

Jesus Christ preaches meekness: "If someone strike thee on the right cheek, turn to him the other also" (Matt. 5:40). Shane displays his meekness when Chris (Ben Johnson) challenges his manhood after Shane orders a bottle of soda pop for young Joey Starrett. Chris offers Shane a "man's drink" by spilling a jigger of whiskey on his shirt. At that moment, Shane does not retaliate; but later, when he returns to the saloon, he reciprocates by buying Chris a drink and disposing of its contents in the same way. In the ensuing brawl, the abandon with which Shane swings his fists suggests a wrathful god not unlike the Christ who overturned the tables of the moneychangers as he drove them out of the Temple of Jerusalem. Meekness and righteous anger are not incompatible.

Shane's message is for the chosen. It is for the homesteaders, not for the cattle ranchers. Sometimes, as history has proved, the chosen must take up arms. Thus, Shane teaches young Joey how to shoot. When Marion Starrett (Jean Arthur) finds Shane teaching her son how to handle a gun, Shane's explanation is simple: "A gun is as good or bad as the man using it." Joey, who has a male child's notion of manhood (men do not

Shane's farewell to Joey in *Shane*. Shane leaves Joey (Brandon de Wilde) with the command to grow up "strong and straight," as he departs, presumably to aid another family of homesteaders. *(Courtesy Paramount Pictures)*

flinch when turpentine is applied to an open wound, and they settle disagreements with their fists), is given a rare opportunity to see his theory put to the test when he watches Shane kill Wilson (Jack Palance), the gunfighter. Shane leaves Joey with the command to grow up "strong and straight." Now Shane is no longer a man but a god delivering one of his commandments before he disappears from view.

Shane as Apollo-Hercules

One writer has called Shane "the frontier Christ, coming down from a Western Olympus."[6] This description characterizes Shane as part Christ, part Greek deity.

In Greek mythology, Zeus punished Apollo for killing one of his sons by forcing him to spend a year of servitude in the household of Admetus, the king of Thessaly. Admetus respected Apollo's godhead, and in gratitude Apollo allowed him the privilege of living beyond his allotted time, provided he could find someone to die for him. Unable to find a volunteer, Admetus turned to his wife, Alcestis, who agreed. During the funeral, Hercules stopped off at the palace on one of his labors, learned what had happened, wrestled with Death, and restored (or so the legend goes, although Euripides' *Alcestis* is intentionally vague on this point) Alcestis to her husband.

Although Shane's golden hair is a good metaphor for Apollo's radiance, Shane is as much a Hercules as he is an Apollo. Shane's power of endurance is Herculean; in one scene a stubborn tree trunk is uprooted, a task that required Shane's perseverance as well as Starrett's brawn. Two themes are common to both *Shane* and the Greek myth: a god's bondage in a mortal's household in expiation for a crime, and a god's saving a mortal's life. As we have seen, Shane's life is a mystery, yet from the way he draws when little Joey Starrett clicks the trigger of his unloaded rifle, he seems to be an ex-gunslinger. That he humbles himself through voluntary servitude suggests that he is atoning for his past.

Just as Apollo served the family of Admetus, Shane serves the Starretts; just as Hercules restored Alcestis to her husband, Shane restores Starrett to his wife. Instead of allowing Starrett to kill Wilson (and lose his life in the bargain), Shane knocks him unconscious and goes in his place, thus increasing Starrett's life span and saving him for Marion and Joey.

Shane as Knight-Errant

According to André Bazin, the subtext also encourages us to think of Shane as a "knight errant in search of his grail," pursuing the ideals of courtly love in the American West.[7] While it is Starrett whom Shane aids, it is Marion whom he serves. But in the tradition of courtly love the knight not only served the lady but tried to emulate her gentleness and thus acquire some for himself to offset his rough ways. Physically, there is a great resemblance between Shane and Marion. Both have golden hair, blue eyes, and a diminutiveness that suggests a gentle heart, not a natural failing. It is significant that Shane chooses to wear blue, one of the lady's favorite colors. However, the medieval knight was a living paradox; the lady he honored as the embodiment of natural perfection was frequently the unsatisfied married woman he took to his bed.

Here the analogies cease; the closest Shane comes to Marion is to dance the Varsouviana and to shake her hand in a farewell gesture. Yet *Shane* is a magnificently subtle film. When Marion is tucking Joey into bed, we hear his voice from behind the closed door: "Mother, I just love Shane." Good-nights are exchanged; Marion enters her bedroom, and Shane retires to the barn. "Goodnight, Shane," Joey calls, but there is no answer. A declaration of love has taken place, shared by mother and son, but in different ways. Marion's graceful entrance into the bedroom is neither slinking nor erotic but willowy and feminine. She may be retiring to her husband's bed, but she is clearly thinking of Shane. The mythic hero has many faces. Three of Shane's have been described here.

Chuck Tatum (Kirk Douglas) of *The Big Carnival* (*Ace in the Hole,* Billy Wilder, 1951), unearthing his story. Tatum allows cave-in victim Leo Minosa (Richard Benedict) to remain entombed longer than necessary so he can win fame as a reporter. *(Courtesy Paramount Pictures)*

The Genesis Myth in
The Big Carnival (Billy Wilder, 1951)

In *The Big Carnival* (or *Ace in the Hole,*) an unscrupulous reporter deliberately allows the victim of a cave-in to remain entombed for a longer period of time so that he can cover the rescue operations. Chuck Tatum (Kirk Douglas) is en route to cover a rattlesnake hunt when the victim's wife (Jan Sterling) informs him of the cave-in. Sensing a story, he accompanies her to the site of the cave-in, where he strikes up a friendship with Leo, the entombed man, promising to immortalize him in print. Tatum never gets to the rattlesnake hunt, but in a perverse way the rattlesnakes come to him in the form of the pet rattler of the local sheriff, who carries the animal around in a cardboard box. Tatum convinces the sheriff that a dramatic rescue would ensure his reelection. As the pact is ratified across a table where a snake moves restlessly in his box, it suddenly becomes clear what Wilder is doing: he is using as the film's subtext one of the oldest myths known to man—the lost paradise, the Eden infiltrated by the evil serpent. We are back in an archetypal garden, here a New Mexico desert community, where an innocent Adam lies transfixed in a cave, his Eve bites into an apple as if she were glorying in the taste of forbidden fruit (an unforgettable shot), and a serpent's coils vibrate against cardboard.

The film then becomes an inversion of the book of *Genesis*, complete with a parody of the six days of creation. Had the rescue operations taken place as planned, Leo would have been freed in sixteen hours. But he cannot last the week. A priest administers the last rites; a host is placed on the end of a long-handled device, which resembles a serpent creeping toward the dying communicant. Leo succumbs on the sixth day, his death bringing the grotesque parody of the creation myth to a close as the shadow of a snake passes across his resigned face. The desert is still; presumably the seventh day will be one of rest.

VISUAL/ICONIC ASSOCIATIONS

Sometimes we make associations on a visual level; for example, some performers have such a strong screen persona (e.g., Katharine Hepburn, John Wayne, Bette Davis, James Dean, Marilyn Monroe, Sean Connery) that we make no distinction between them and the characters they play. Bette Davis was not playing Margo Channing in *All About Eve*; she *was* Margo Channing; and John Wayne was always John Wayne. The similarities between Madonna and Eva Perón (both of whom rose from obscurity to fame as they transformed themselves into celebrities) made it impossible to think of *Evita* (1996) as the story of Eva Perón but, rather, as that of Madonna.

Davis and Madonna are icons. In medieval art, an icon is a pictorial representation of a religious subject invested with such a spiritual aura that it becomes worthy of veneration. An icon of the Virgin Mary, for example, is not just a picture of a woman but of a special woman, the mother of Jesus Christ. An icon therefore has a dual nature: it depicts not just a person but a person who stands out from the ordinary, as indicated by a halo, a nimbus, or a gilded background.

Humphrey Bogart as Screen Icon in *High Sierra* (Raoul Walsh, 1941)

Bogart is a true screen icon, inseparable from the cool, unemotional types he played—characters who seemed totally indifferent to the plight of humanity ("I stick my neck out for no man," Rick, perhaps his most famous character, says in *Casablanca*). Yet when Rick's help is needed, as it is by two Bulgarian refugees in the film, he comes to their aid but is embarrassed when they show gratitude. Bogart's screen persona was forged with his first starring role, Roy Earle, in *High Sierra* (1941). Bogart might never have appeared in the film, which made him a star, if George Raft, who was originally slated for the lead, had not refused to be in a movie in which he had to die. Raft, however, could never have suggested the inward drive for freedom that propels Earle to the summit from which he falls. *High Sierra* is a film about existential freedom—that freedom to which a human being is condemned, as Jean-Paul Sartre would say. It is not surprising that Bogart became an existential cult hero. Throughout his career, he projected the image of a man living in the present, striving for freedom, and performing meaningful actions to achieve it—financing an operation for a girl with a club foot (*High Sierra*); relinquishing the woman he loves to her freedom-fighter husband, who can do more for the world than he can (*Casablanca*); leading a detachment through the desert like Moses (*Sahara*, 1943); refusing to allow his love for the woman responsible for his best friend's death to stand in the way of justice (*Dead Reckoning*, 1947); and defending an underprivileged youth (*Knock on Any Door*, 1949) when no other lawyer would.

At the end of *High Sierra*, Earle lies dead at the foot of a mountain; when Marie (Ida Lupino), the woman who stood by him, asks Healy what it means when a man "cracks out," he replies that it means he is "free." "Free," Marie says as she walks triumphantly into the frame, knowing that Earle has won his freedom—and his essence—in death. The existential implications of "crack out" would have eluded a mediocre actor like George Raft. Bogart understood them and embodied them in his perfor-

THE ACTUAL AND INTENDED STARS OF *HIGH SIERRA* (1941).

Humphrey Bogart, who played Roy Earle in the film. *(Courtesy Collector's Book Store)*

George Raft, who was slated for the part of Roy Earle but refused to be in a movie where he had to die. *(Courtesy Collector's Book Store)*

mance, thus giving the film its existential character. Even Bogart's face was extraordinary and fittingly existential. It was not a neighborhood face, nor was it especially handsome. It was a face that knew the mixed blessings of life; a face that did not slacken with age but grew tauter, the eyes retreating into their sockets until by the end of his career they had settled into omniscience.

Not every actor becomes an icon like Humphrey Bogart; screen icons, in fact, are rare. But that does not rule out other kinds of visual associations. We make visual associations when (1) an actor's portrayal coincides with the traditional perception of a historical figure (e.g., an actor playing a Christ figure in a film in which his appearance evokes the traditional representation of Christ; an actor playing a rebel in a manner consistent with the popular image of the rebel); and (2) an actor's performance style recalls that of another actor, who is not in the film but whose presence is clearly felt. For example, a generation of actors that came of age in the late 1980s and early 1990s (the late River Phoenix, Brad Pitt, Val Kilmer, Jason Patric) recall the brooding intensity of James Dean; although Dean made only three films that were of any importance, young actors still aspire to achieve the same blend of aggressiveness and sensitivity, detachment and warmth, and indifference and compassion that he exhibited in his films. Dean could not be pigeonholed; if he seemed androgynous, it was because he embodied the best qualities of both male and female and revealed them in his portrayals of Cal Trask in *East of Eden* (1955), Jim Stark in *Rebel Without a Cause* (1955), and Jett Rink in *Giant* (1956). When the latest version of Shakespeare's *Romeo and Juliet* (1996) opened, several critics compared Leonardo diCaprio's (Romeo) acting style with James Dean's—simple, direct, intense without seeming overwrought.

Al Pacino as Christ Figure in *Serpico* (Sidney Lumet, 1973)

When *Serpico* opened, several critics noted a resemblance between Al Pacino, who interpreted the title role magnificently, and pop art pictures of Jesus Christ. The critic Vincent Canby also compared Pacino with St. Francis of Assisi. All sensed that there was more to Pacino's Serpico than just great acting; behind his Serpico they saw either a god-man doomed to suffer for his love of humanity or a saint who resisted the attempts of the religious establishment to interfere with his mission.

It was not merely Al Pacino's beard, his mesmeric eyes, or his uncontrollable rage at corruption that caused critics to think of Jesus Christ. Certain details of Serpico's life also recalled similar details in Christ's; thus, the text (Serpico) is coordinated with the subtext (Christ), and both come together in the person of the star (Pacino). Such coinciding of actor and historical figure does not occur in every movie with a police officer hero. The identification of Christ with Serpico (a cop who found his apostolate on the streets and underwent the traditional scapegoat cycle of harassment, betrayal, and desertion) was present in Pacino's performance in a way that it was not in the performances of Stacy Keach in *The New Centurions* (1972), Robert Duvall in *Colors* (1988), and Morgan Freeman in *Seven* (1995), all of which were hero-cop movies.

Al Pacino as Frank Serpico (*Serpico*, 1973*)*, one of the few visually acceptable Christ figures in film. *(Courtesy Paramount Pictures)*

Jack Nicholson as Free Spirit and Louise Fletcher as Boss Lady in *One Flew over the Cuckoo's Nest* (Miloš Forman, 1975)

The impression made by an actor's performance is based on many factors, including such seemingly irrelevant details as hairstyle and wardrobe. Yet it is through such details that filmmakers realize their intentions; it is also through such details that we see in characters what directors want us to see.

When Miloš Forman was about to direct *One Flew over the Cuckoo's Nest*, he was faced with the task of making a movie out of a cult book of the 1960s. During the last few years of that decade, Ken Kesey's novel seemed a tragically accurate mirror of America. The animosity between Randle P. McMurphy and Big Nurse paralleled similar confrontations between the pacifist and the draft board, the militant Students for a Democratic Society and the police, the student activists and the campus administration.

In 1975, however, Vietnam was a memory, the draft had been suspended, and campuses were quiet. To make the film meaningful, Forman had to deemphasize all the political overtones the novel had acquired in

HAIRSTYLE AS A VISUAL ASSOCIATION

Nurse Ratched (Louise Fletcher) and Randle McMurphy (Jack Nicholson) in *One Flew over the Cuckoo's Nest* (1976). Louise Fletcher's hairstyle is a throwback to the 1940s. *(Courtesy Fantasy Films)*

Sheila Ryan in an authentic 1940s hairdo. *(Courtesy Twentieth Century-Fox)*

the 1960s. The film's text emphasized the humanism and comedy of Kesey's novel; the subtext transformed the conflict between McMurphy (Jack Nicholson) and Nurse Ratched (Louise Fletcher) into a battle between man and woman. Forman capitalized on Nicholson's exposed and often vulnerable masculinity, but he also saw more in it than locker-room bravado. There is an impishness about Nicholson; at times he seems to be putting us on, challenging us to make the hackneyed connection between a man's height (Nicholson is not tall) and his ego. Little details about Nicholson's portrayal of McMurphy suggest the imp: the cap pulled down over the ears, the hornlike tuft of hair that gives the impression of a satyr, the eyes that dart from one direction to another as if they, too, were free spirits.

Although the time of the film is the 1960s, Louise Fletcher's hairstyle came out of another era. Forman had her wear her hair the way women did in "lady executive" movies of the 1940s, which were typified by such movies as Mitchell Leisen's *Take a Letter, Darling* (1942) and *They All Kissed the Bride* (1942). These films, however, were a harmless type of screwball comedy featuring women as executives and men as their subordinates. *Cuckoo's Nest* is hardly screwball comedy, and Nurse Ratched, by her hairstyle and manner, is a savage parody of the female executive of the 1940s.

Barbara Stanwyck as Marlene Dietrich in *Double Indemnity* (Billy Wilder, 1944)

The name of the femme fatale in James Cain's novel *Double Indemnity* is Phyllis Nirdlinger. When Billy Wilder was working on the screenplay for the film version, which he also directed, he changed the character's last name to Dietrichson. He wanted audiences to think not of Marlene Dietrich herself but of Dietrich's persona, the embodiment of the extremes of desire and danger, passion and aloofness, femininity and masculinity. Wilder even had Barbara Stanwyck, whom he cast in the role, wear a blond wig. Thus, throughout the film one senses something about Stanwyck that suggests Dietrich—behind Stanwyck's performance lurks Dietrich's persona.

INTELLECTUAL ASSOCIATIONS

When we make a mythic association, we are reminded of universal patterns that are true of all human beings at all times. When we make an iconic or visual association, we perceive a likeness between an actor's persona and the character, or between the actor's performance and another's

BARBARA STANWYCK AS MARLENE DIETRICH

Fred MacMurray and Marlene Dietrich in *The Lady Is Willing* (1942). *(Courtesy Columbia Pictures)*

Fred MacMurray and Barbara Stanwyck in *Double Indemnity* (1944). Wilder changed the name of Stanwyck's character to Dietrichson and had the actress wear a blond wig to evoke the Dietrich persona. *(Copyright ® by Paramount Pictures, Courtesy MCA Publishing Rights, a Division of MCA Inc.)*

persona. When we make an intellectual association, we relate the film as a whole—not just one aspect of it—to history, to another medium (literature, opera, and so on), to another film, or even to an earlier version of itself.

Relating a Film to History

John Schlesinger's film of Nathanael West's novel *The Day of the Locust* has a historical subtext. West intended his novel as an anti-Hollywood tract, but it was also a subtle indictment of the political apathy that breeds moguls in the movie colony and dictators in the world at large. The 1975 film version followed a similar course. Nothing in the script's language implied that there was a political dimension to the plot. Therefore, Schlesinger had to supply that dimension visually; he had to show a Hollywood where life is a soundstage and where reality becomes illusion and remains so even as the armies of Europe are preparing for World War II. Sometimes Schlesinger's cutting is so abrupt that it blurs the distinction between the real and the illusory. For example, he cuts from a father calling his daughter to passengers waving from a ship. At first this is puzzling, until the ship is shown to be a soundstage prop whose passengers are movie extras.

The climax of the film is the brutal death of Homer Simpson (Donald Sutherland) on the night of a Hollywood premiere. Homer's death is a grim reminder of the price a nation pays when it turns inward upon its myths (where the dream is more glorious than the reality) and worships those who promise to make the dream come true. Schlesinger prepares us for the apocalypse earlier in the film with images of decay and perversity: a boy with platinum curls unsexed by his fame-hungry mother so he can look like Shirley Temple; a dead horse in a swimming pool; a death face peering into Homer's backyard; a bloody cockfight intercut with flashes of the gaudy dress Faye Greener (Karen Black) waves in front of Homer with a rhythm that matches, beat for beat, the quick jabs the roosters are giving each other.

The Hollywood depicted is an insular community that resents the intrusion of history and reality. Faye and her beaux leave the movie theater before the newsreel begins; having seen a film in which she had a bit part, Faye is uninterested in a newsreel about the rise of Hitler. On the night of the premiere, a newspaper blows down Hollywood Boulevard, its headlines announcing the advent of World War II. The master of ceremonies for the event is a Hitler look-alike, and the fans are the kind that would turn out for a premiere or a Nazi rally. Again Schlesinger crosscuts, this time between the premiere and the death of Homer. He is not crosscutting between illusion and reality but between two forms of madness, as in the cockfight/swirling dress scene.

In the climax, all the associations merge: political detachment, fascism, and the mob's need for a scapegoat. Adore, the boy who's too old for his feminine curls, strikes Homer in the head with a stone. In a rage, Homer pursues him into a parking lot and stomps him to death. His reaction is our reaction: we want this unnatural product of a twisted dream destroyed before it grows up to be something worse. But the mob is so crazed by the sight of the gods and goddesses at the premiere that it turns on Homer and tears him apart. As Tod the art designer watches in horror, he envisions the fans as zombies with death-mask faces, American grotesques mobilized to kill the destroyer of the dream.

By crosscutting between the premiere and Homer's ritual dismemberment, Schlesinger creates associations that are implicit only in the script. In the text, the crowd destroys Homer because he kills Adore; in the subtext, it destroys him because he kills what Adore represents—the necessity of perverting one's nature to become a star. And if one must become dehumanized to be a star, one must do the same to worship the star; thus movie fans can be as grotesque as the objects of their worship, knocking down barricades to get a touch of mink or a piece of shirt. There is another motive for their behavior, a motive as old as the one that impelled the worshipers of Dionysus to kill the intruder who witnessed their sacred rites. Homer has wandered into a sacred ritual, the ritual of the Hollywood premiere; but Homer is also unclean from the blood of Adore. Thus, the fans turn on him because he has polluted their rites and shed the blood of one of their own.

A film, therefore, can be set in a particular era and yet evoke that era only indirectly. Such a film does not declare itself "historical" in the sense of dramatizing a historical event the way, for example, *Tora! Tora! Tora!* recreates the Japanese attack on Pearl Harbor. Yet, to appreciate this kind of film, one has to know history; unlike the historical film, the script does not provide the information.

A knowledge of the Great Depression enables one to look at *It Happened One Night* as something more than just a screwball comedy. And yet it is not coincidental that screwball comedy was born in the Great Depression; its breeziness and happy endings offered escape and enjoyment to the beleaguered audiences of that era. This kind of comedy, in which social barriers crumbled like the walls of Jericho, was ideal for Depression audiences, who delighted in seeing a society woman put in her place by a man who didn't even wear an undershirt. *It Happened One Night* is pure fairy tale, a variation on "The Princess and the Commoner" set in the early 1930s. The associations we bring to the film—breadlines, soup kitchens, strikes—enable us to see it as a fable of the Great Depression.

Easy Living, another screwball comedy, is best remembered for the automat sequence in which Mary Smith, swathed in the sable that has literally dropped to her from the sky, is sitting by herself, eating a beef pie, completely oblivious to the fighting that goes on when the food suddenly becomes free. In the context of the film, the scene is uproarious; in the context of Depression America, the sight of people sliding on a food-covered

Cinderella in sable (Jean Arthur) is exposed to the grim realities of the Great Depression in the automat sequence of *Easy Living* (1937). *(Copyright ® by Paramount Pictures, Courtesy MCA Publishing Rights, a Division of MCA Inc.)*

floor is disquieting. When the camera roams around the automat, observing a fur-clad Mary eating in the foreground with the masses fighting in the background, it does more than record a comic free-for-all. By highlighting the extremes of affluence and poverty, it defines the Great Depression as a time of sable for the lucky and rags for the luckless.

Relating a Film to Film History

Bernardo Bertolucci's *Last Tango in Paris* (1972) is ostensibly about a woman caught between two men, one of whom debases her while the other idealizes her. Bertolucci used this narrative structure to work out a theory of film that he illustrates with references to movies of the past. Thus, when Pauline Kael reviewed *Last Tango*, and alluded to the film's constant "feedback," she meant that much in the film—the performances as well as the imagery—recalled other films.

"Movies are a past we share, and, whether we recognize them or not, the copious associations are at work in the film and we feel them," Kael observed.[8] As we have already seen, the way a movie is cast can create certain associations between the actor and his or her role. In *Last Tango*, Marlon Brando plays Paul, an American in Paris, who meets Jeanne (Maria Schneider) when both of them show up to look at the same apartment; Jean-Pierre Léaud is Tom, the TV director and movie nut who is using Jeanne for a television film he is making. Brando and Léaud are not ordinary actors. Each epitomizes a style of acting and a type of film that revolutionized the cinema. Brando will always be synonymous with the Method, a system of acting that requires the performer to draw on past experiences, emotions, and memories for a particular role. Brando was the definitive Method actor of the 1950s—brooding, introspective, often inarticulate. Léaud was the discovery of François Truffaut, who cast him as Antoine Doinel, the problem child of *The 400 Blows*. Léaud and Truffaut then went on to make other films: the "Antoine and Colette" episode in *Love at Twenty* (1962), *Stolen Kisses*, *Bed and Board* (1970), and *Day for Night* (1973). Physically, Léaud had even begun to resemble the director. Truffaut typifies the New Wave—that extraordinary burst of creativity that started in France at the end of the 1950s, when directors like Truffaut and Jean-Luc Godard rejected literary scripts for shooting scripts and improvisation, filmed in the streets rather than in studios, demanded naturalistic acting instead of old-fashioned emoting, and quoted liberally from the movies of the past.

Just as Brando and Léaud represent two different eras of filmmaking, the characters they portray represent two different ways of life. Paul isolates himself in the apartment, where he works out his sexual aggression on Jeanne; Tom roams the streets of Paris, scouting for locations for his movie. Jeanne is trapped not just between two men but between their worlds: Paul's closed world of the apartment and Tom's open world of the

ASSOCIATIONS BETWEEN ACTOR
AND ROLE

Jean-Pierre Léaud as Antoine
Doinel in *The 400 Blows* (1959),
perhaps the most famous of the
New Wave films. *(Courtesy Janus
Films)*

Léaud as Tom, the TV director in
Last Tango in Paris (1973), with
Maria Schneider. Even as Tom,
Léaud typified the casual,
naturalistic form of acting that the
New Wave directors encouraged.
(Courtesy United Artists)

city. Yet filmmakers are in the same predicament: Do they remain within the closed world of the studio set, as their predecessors did, or do they venture outside, where an entire city can be their soundstage?

What Kael calls "feedback" is not limited to the eras Brando and Léaud evoke. Bertolucci used *Last Tango* as a vehicle for his ideas on film in the same way Paul and Tom were using Jeanne for their respective purposes. Thus, in the film Bertolucci invokes movies of the past that have some bearing on his own film. When Jeanne and Tom are on a barge, there is a life preserver with *L'Atalante* inscribed on it. *L'Atalante* is the title of Jean Vigo's classic film (1934), and the barge scene in *Last Tango* pays homage to Vigo's exquisite production, in which a young bride leaves her barge captain–husband to experience the excitement of Paris, only to return to the secure world of the barge at the end. However, Bertolucci is also replying to Vigo's optimism: Vigo's bride can be reunited with her husband, but once Paul and Jeanne leave the apartment, no reunion is possible.

Last Tango is like a course in film history. The scene in which Paul looks out on the roofs of Paris before he dies recalls René Clair's *Sous les toits de Paris* (*Under the Roofs of Paris*, 1931), which the director made when he was thirty, the same age Bertolucci was when he made *Last Tango*. When Jeanne shoots Paul, the scene is not only a part of *Last Tango* but of all those Hollywood movies in which a woman pulls a revolver and pumps her lover full of bullets. *Last Tango* purports to be about male-female relationships, but subtextually it is about the relationship between filmmakers and their art.

With its mix of animation and live action, Robert Zemeckis's *Who Framed Roger Rabbit* (1988), set in 1947, seems to have a double subtext: the animated cartoons of the 1930s and 1940s and the private-eye films of the 1940s. While *Roger Rabbit* has been enjoyed by children who have never seen a private-eye movie and who know cartoons only from television, it speaks most directly to those who have a knowledge of film history. The dancing hippos bring back memories of Walt Disney's *Fantasia* (1940); Roger's sexy wife, Jessica, with her red tresses and low-cut gown, recalls Rita Hayworth in *Gilda* (1946); Eddie Valiant (Bob Hoskins), the private eye hired to trail Jessica, whose infidelity is causing Roger to forget his lines, is a seedier version of the 1940s private detectives Sam Spade and Philip Marlowe.

However, the plot of *Roger Rabbit*—a detective's discovery of a scheme that would, if executed, change the face of Los Angeles—is not to be found in any cartoon or 1940s detective movie, but in one particular film, Roman Polanski's *Chinatown* (1974), the true subtext of *Roger Rabbit*. In *Chinatown*, the private investigator J. J. Gittes (Jack Nicholson) uncovers a shady land deal involving Noah Cross (John Huston), who is buying up property in the San Fernando Valley, where a projected reservoir will turn the area into choice real estate. In *Roger Rabbit*, Eddie Valiant discovers that Judge Doom (Christopher Lloyd) plans to transform Los Angeles from a city that relies on trolley cars for transportation into a city of freeways. To do so, he must destroy Toontown, the enclave in which the cartoon characters live. If he succeeds, he will be destroying a venerable film tradition: the animated cartoon and the characters, like Bugs Bunny, Donald Duck, and Porky Pig, who are part of it.

Judge Doom's plan is thwarted through the combined efforts of Eddie and the Toons. The actual history of Los Angeles and Hollywood, however, has proved otherwise. Thus, moviegoers who remember a time when theaters featured a cartoon, two movies, a newsreel, and a chapter of a serial find *Roger Rabbit* bittersweet: the film conjures up a Hollywood of another time and place—to many, perhaps a better time and place.

Relating the Remake to the Original: *Sabrina Fair* (1953), *Sabrina* (1954), *Sabrina* (1995)

First there was Samuel Taylor's *Sabrina Fair,* a Broadway hit of the 1953–54 season. Paramount Pictures produced the film version, *Sabrina,* almost immediately; *Sabrina's* popularity had as much to do with the script—coau-

Margaret Sullavan, who created the role of Sabrina Fairchild on Broadway in Samuel Taylor's *Sabrina Fair* (1953). *(Courtesy Margaret Herrick Library of the Academy of Motion Picture Arts and Sciences)*

thored by Taylor, Ernest Lehman, and the film's director, Billy Wilder—as with Audrey Hepburn's performance in the title role. *Sabrina* was a variation of the Cinderella story in which a chauffeur's daughter, Sabrina Fairchild, finds her Prince Charming in the son of her father's employer, a shipping tycoon who lives on a Long Island estate. The 1995 remake followed the same narrative path; both versions are interesting examples of the way the same plot can be adapted to the era in which the film was made.

Sabrina Fair opened with a prologue spoken in semidarkness, beginning "Once upon a time." Both film versions use a voice-over prologue with the same words, suggesting that what follows is a contemporary fairy tale.

In the play, Sabrina goes to Paris to work for the American government; since *Sabrina Fair* is a single-set play, her pre-Paris life is narrated, never dramatized.

The two film versions begin in much the same way: Sabrina is in a tree, observing a party that is in progress at the Larabees, for whom her father is the family chauffeur. In both versions, she is secretly in love with David Larabee, but Fairchild wants his daughter to learn a trade. Since, in the play, Sabrina had spent time in Paris, it makes sense to show her there rather than just have her talk about it. Thus, in the 1954 version Fairchild sends Sabrina (Audrey Hepburn) to Paris to study cooking; in the 1995 remake, Sabrina (Julia Ormond) leaves to work as a photographer's assistant at *Paris Vogue*. The change was in keeping with a 1995 audience's association of Paris with high fashion and also explains Sabrina's metamorphosis into a glamorous young woman.

Another change occurred in the 1995 version regarding David's fiancée and her family's business. In the play, David was divorced; in Wilder's film, David (William Holden) is a playboy engaged to a sugar heiress. In the nutrition-conscious 1990s, no one would be impressed by anyone's marrying into a sugar dynasty. Moreover, a 1990s audience, aware of such media empires as Time Warner, Viacom, and ABC-Disney, would be more interested in a family that made its money in telecommunications. Thus, in the 1995 version David's fiancée belongs to a family whose telecommunications company David's brother, Linus (Harrison Ford), would like to merge with Larabee Communications.

There was a significant plot change in the 1954 version that was also reflected in the 1995 remake. Instead of following the play, in which Sabrina suddenly realizes that she loves David's brother, Linus, Wilder initially prejudices us against Linus. When Linus senses David's interest in Sabrina, he starts courting her himself—not out of love but to divert his brother's attention from her to the sugar heiress, who represents a more profitable match. But Linus soon succumbs to Sabrina's charm, and what began as a ruse ends in love. The new characterization worked because

Audrey Heburn as Sabrina and Humphrey Bogart as Linus in *Sabrina* (1954). *(Courtesy Paramount Pictures and MOMA/FSA)*

Julia Ormond as Sabrina and Harrison Ford as Linus in the 1995 remake. *(Courtesy Paramount Pictures and the Margaret Herrick Library of the Academy of Motion Picture Arts and Sciences)*

Humphrey Bogart, who rarely played comedy, was cast as Linus. The audience, given its image of Bogart as the unsentimental "tough guy," was delighted when he fell under Sabrina's spell.

In the play and the 1954 film, the Larabee household is patriarchal, but not in the 1995 remake, in which there is no Linus Larabee, Sr.—only his widow (Nancy Marchand), the matriarch of the clan. This change also worked because Marchand, best known as Mrs. Pynchon of the television series *Lou Grant*, excelled at playing matriarchs.

In the play and the two movie versions, it is Linus, Jr., whom Sabrina grows to love. The play, which is a comedy of manners, ends with a double revelation: Fairchild discloses that his prudent investments have made him a millionaire and his daughter an heiress; and Sabrina confesses that it is Linus, Jr., she really loves and even goes so far as to propose to him. Linus realizes his need for Sabrina, who is the embodiment of liberation, and admits his love for her.

Altering the plot so that the cynical Linus could mellow into a romantic meant eliminating Fairchild's disclosure, which, under the circumstances, would be anticlimactic. Also, Sabrina's proposing to Linus would detract from a confession of love that Linus alone can make. Wilder therefore has Sabrina, disillusioned because she thinks Linus lavished attention on her only to effect a better match for his brother, sail back to Paris. Once Linus locates the ship, in a recklessly romantic gesture, he hails a tugboat and catches up with it. In 1995, plane travel was more common, so Sabrina flies back to Paris. Since the Concorde is faster, however, Linus (who can afford the luxury) arrives there before she does. How he finds her is never really plausibly explained, but in a fairy tale all that matters is that Cinderella is reunited with Prince Charming.

Whether Sabrina sails or flies to Paris, or whether the Larabees are in shipping or media, the basic plot remained unchanged. All that was required was updating. As with any remake, the original becomes the subtext. However, with the 1954 *Sabrina*, Samuel Taylor's *Sabrina Fair* was the subtext for those who knew the play. And if anyone had seen the play with Margaret Sullavan, who created the role, it would be hard not to make comparisons between Sullavan and Hepburn, each of whom brought undeniable charm—but in different ways—to the part: Sullavan was mischievous and witty, while Hepburn was dreamy and vulnerable. For those who know Wilder's film but are unfamiliar with the play, the 1954 *Sabrina* is the subtext of the 1995 version. Moreover, in her personification of elegance, grace, and romantic longing—the very qualities we associate with a fairy-tale princess—Julia Ormond was as close to Hepburn as anyone could be.

"I've seen this before," we often say of a particular movie; quite possibly we have. Twentieth Century-Fox constantly remade its musicals: To see *Wabash Avenue* (1950) is to see *Coney Island*. *Three Blind Mice* (1938) was set to music and became *Moon over Miami* (1941), which was remade as *Three Little Girls in Blue* (1946) and later as *How to Marry a Millionaire* (1953). Often time and place were changed, but the basic plot remained the same: Raoul Walsh's *Colorado Territory* was *High Sierra* in a western setting; *I Died a Thousand Times* (1953) was *High Sierra* again, with Jack Palance in the Humphrey Bogart role. *High Society* (1965) was George Cukor's *The Philadelphia Story* (1940) with a Cole Porter score; *Against All Odds* (1984) was not only a remake of Jacques Tourneur's *Out of the Past* (1947) but also featured one of the stars from the original, Jane Greer. *The Preacher's Wife* (1996) was *The Bishop's Wife* (1947) from an African-American perspective. The classic *Detour*, which starred Tom Neal, was remade as a less-than-classic movie of the same name in 1992; it starred Neal's son, Tom Neal, Jr., and proved that unless filmmakers can enhance, surpass, or at least equal the original—by clarifying ambiguities or bringing out details that were only hinted at initially—they would be advised to stay with less familiar material.

MUSICAL ASSOCIATIONS

Music has two main functions in a film: it either advances or enhances the narrative. When it advances the narrative, it is a plot device and is not subtextual. In Mitchell Leisen's *Lady in the Dark* (1944), a childhood song the heroine tries to remember is the key to her neurosis. Many a Twentieth Century-Fox musical included a tender ballad the heroine was belting out until the hero taught her how to sing it properly (*Coney Island*, *Wabash Avenue*). We have already seen how in many musicals working out the melody or the lyrics to a song was the significant moment in the film. There are also songs that drift in and out of the characters' lives, becoming *their* song and playing at appropriately dramatic moments; the classic example is "As Time Goes By" in *Casablanca*. Some movies have a classical score, usually a ballet or an opera, that catapults an unknown to stardom (*The Red Shoes*, 1948) or notoriety (the synthetic opera *Salammbô* in *Citizen Kane*). Sometimes a piece of music forms the film's climax, achieving an effect that words cannot: "Remember My Forgotten Man" in *Gold Diggers of 1933* (1933), George Gershwin's Concerto in F in *Rhapsody in Blue* (1945), the title ballet in Vincente Minnelli's *An American in Paris* (1951).

Music is even more functional as an element of the subtext when it does not so much advance the narrative as deepen it. Take, for example, a musical phrase that is repeatedly associated with a character, a mood, or a situation. Such a recurring musical phrase is a *leitmotif*. When a leitmotif identifies a character, it becomes the character's musical signature. Heard in conjunction with the appearance of a character, or representation of an idea, the leitmotif is inseparable from the individual with whom it is associated or the idea it underscores. It also enjoys a kind of autonomy. A leitmotif can confirm a declaration of love, but it can also recur when the lovers are quarreling or parting, mocking what it had previously celebrated. As part of the character, a leitmotif can remind the audience of what the character is feeling at a particular moment. In Hitchcock's *I Confess* (1952), when Ruth (Anne Baxter) tells her husband she does not love him, we hear the leitmotif that is associated with the man she really loves.

The leitmotif expresses aspects of the character that lie beyond the capacity of language. The nursery tune that opens the 1942 version of *Cat People* is the first indication that the movie is not an ordinary horror film. It is fitting that such a singsong motif should be Irena's signature, for she is emotionally a child.

The leitmotif also concretizes abstract themes. Power is an abstraction, yet Bernard Herrmann, who composed the music for *Citizen Kane*, called one of the leitmotifs of the film "power." As a musical phrase, "power" is no longer abstract because we hear it. The power motif is heard for the first time as the camera ascends the gate of Xanadu, taking us into the pleasure dome and then to Kane's deathbed. But it is a *synesthetic* experience: we see, feel, and hear power. We watch its calculatingly slow rise, feel the isolation it brings, and hear the grim consequences it holds for those who seek it.

There are all kinds of motifs—love motifs, death motifs, and even love-death, or *Liebestod*, motifs. At the end of *Duel in the Sun* (1947), which must have one of the lushest scores ever composed, Pearl Chavez (Jennifer Jones) crawls over sunbaked rocks to die in her lover's arms. As their blood mingles, the love motif heard when they first met seems to surge out of some chasm in the great Southwest to become their Liebestod.

For *The Private Life of Sherlock Holmes* (1970), Billy Wilder fashioned a love motif out of a few measures of Miklos Rozsa's Concerto for Violin and Orchestra. It is a bittersweet but dignified theme expressing a yearning never to be satisfied—in this case, Holmes's love for Ilse von Hofmannstahl. When Holmes receives the news of Ilse's death, the same theme is heard, no longer an expression of unfulfilled love but of love irretrievably lost.

Music is also capable of forging ethnic and national connections. In the pre–civil rights era, blacks were stereotyped both dramatically and musically. When they appeared on the screen, the original soundtrack often ceased, and a spiritual was heard, presumably because it was more fitting. Even in such a brilliant film as *The Little Foxes*, blacks were given this kind of musical treatment, which not only equated them with their music but also perpetuated the misguided image of southern blacks as passive. Music, whether it wishes to or not, equates, and a moviegoer's earliest associations are equations: "Deep River" = blacks; "The International" = Soviet Union; a few gongs = the mysterious East; "Deutschland über Alles" = Nazi Germany; a tarantella (or "O Sole Mio") = Italy, and so on. Although only the slightest references were made to the title character's being Jewish in *Mr. Skeffington* (1944), a leitmotif that was vaguely based on traditional Jewish melodies left no doubt of it.

During World War II, movie music programmed its audiences to patriotism. People not only saw flag-wavers; they also heard Old Glory hymned on the soundtrack. Planes streamed across the sky to the accompaniment of "Wild Blue Yonder," which also doubled as death music for the marines who went off to be executed by the Japanese at the end of *The Purple Heart* (1944). To evoke American values, Frank Capra frequently incorporated typical American songs like "Red River Valley" and "Buffalo Gals" into his films.

Using classical music that was written centuries ago is a special case, since it is music not composed for a specific film. Yet the media have made extensive use of classical music. In the 1930s and 1940s, when radio was a mass medium, listeners were exposed to classical music without being aware of it. Rossini's *William Tell* Overture ushered in *The Lone Ranger;* Sibelius's "Valse Triste" introduced *I Love a Mystery;* Prokofiev's March from *Love for Three Oranges* was the theme of *The FBI in Peace and War;* the second movement of César Franck's Symphony in D Minor heralded the opening of *Quiet, Please.* Thus, associations were created between the radio programs and their introductions, which were the equivalents of musical signatures.

Movies used classical music in the same way. Before many moviegoers even knew what Rachmaninoff's Second Piano Concerto was, they had heard it as background music in *Brief Encounter* (1946). In fact, for people who know the film, the concerto has such indelible associations that it never fails to evoke a dingy railroad station where two married people, on the verge of committing adultery, choose to say good-bye and never meet again.

Thus, the Rachmaninoff Second Piano Concerto took on associations of extramarital love, and was used for that purpose in *September Affair* (1950), where it forms the background for a story of adultery. Like any venerable device, the Rachmaninoff Second ended up being parodied; still, parody attests to its associations. In *The Seven Year Itch*, in which a husband whose wife is away for the summer imagines himself seducing the woman upstairs, Billy Wilder parodies the tradition. In a fantasy sequence, the husband fancies himself a great pianist, sitting down at the piano and breaking into the concerto to impress his potential conquest.

Since classical music is added to a film rather than being composed for it, it may already have produced certain associations within us; the film may either reinforce those associations or change them, so that thereafter we associate the music only with the movie. Certainly it is difficult to disassociate the Rachmaninoff Second from *Brief Encounter* and, in a totally different way, from *The Seven Year Itch*. Similarly, anyone who has seen *Shine* (1996), based on the life of the gifted but troubled pianist David Helfgott, will always associate the Rachmaninoff Third, Helfgott's signature concerto, with the film. This type of association should not be surprising, since few *Lone Ranger* fans can separate the *William Tell* Overture from the program.

Wagner's music occupies a peculiar place in the American film. There has always been a connection between Wagner and the Third Reich. Wagner was Hitler's favorite composer; in fact, Hitler identified with Wagner's Siegfried and maintained that to understand National Socialism (Nazism) one must first understand Wagner. To the Hollywood of the 1940s, then, Wagner was the composer of the Third Reich: it is difficult to recall a movie in which Nazism was not orchestrated with a Wagnerian motif. In *Brute Force* (1947), Munsey (Hume Cronyn), a prison captain, tortures an inmate to the Venusberg music from Wagner's *Tannhäuser*. Munsey performs a kind of ritual before the torture, strutting around with his chest sucked in beneath a skintight undershirt. That the captain is a homoerotic sadist is evident in the film, but Wagner's music, with its historical and erotic associations, characterizes him even further. Music unites his lust for power and his need for sex, neither of which he can achieve except through the degradation of others.

Although *Apocalypse, Now* (1979) deals with America's tragic involvement in Vietnam, the film uses Wagner in much the same way it is used in *Brute Force:* as a symbol of sexual energy channeled into militarism. The "Ride of the Valkyries," from *Die Walküre*, orchestrates the parade-of-the-helicopters sequence. Had the same music been used in a World War II movie in which bombs rained down on German cities, American audiences would have applauded; in the light of the Vietnam debacle, however, "The Ride of the Valkyries" is accusatory rather than nationalistic. It is as if Coppola were accusing America of emulating Nazi Germany by invoking the spirit of Wagner to justify war.

The use of Wagner's music in *Apocalypse, Now* is ironic. However, irony is not the easiest of devices to manipulate. It can backfire, becoming blatant, as happens in *The Night Porter* (1974) when two inmates in a Nazi concentration camp perform an act of sodomy to the music of Mozart's *The Magic Flute*. What should have been a devastating moment becomes merely appalling. Far more intelligent is Ingmar Bergman's use of Bach in *Through a Glass Darkly* (1961) when a schizophrenic daughter discovers that her father is using her sickness as material for a novel. The nobility of the music underscores the father's ignoble intentions.

Karin (Harriet Andersson) in *Through a Glass Darkly* (Ingmar Bergman, 1961) when she discovers that her father is using her schizophrenia for his novel. At that moment, the haunting opening of Bach's Suite no. 2 in D Minor for violincello is heard. *(Courtesy MOMA/FSA and Janus Films)*

In some films, classical music constitutes the entire subtext. It is not just a question of repeating motifs but of using music—either one work or several works—from beginning to end. What happens to music in Stanley Kubrick's *A Clockwork Orange* (1971) is what has happened to society. The social order gives way as thugs and disenchanted youths, leather boys and loafers become the citizens of the future. There is a corresponding degeneration of music; it becomes estranged from art, perverted, capable of producing effects its composers never intended.

One of the most innocent songs ever written is "Singin' in the Rain," which brings to mind Gene Kelly sloshing around without missing a tap in the classic 1952 musical of the same name. It is hardly the kind of song we would associate with violence, yet in *A Clockwork Orange* Alex does a soft-shoe to it while brutalizing a writer and his wife.

Rimsky-Korsakov's *Scheherazade* is an exotic piece of music, lush and sensuous, the kind associated with a veiled courtesan on a chaise longue upholstered in leopard skin. Yet this is the music heard when Alex imagines himself as a Roman centurion lashing Christ on his way to Calvary. *Scheherazade* is one of the most pleasurable compositions ever written, as Alex would be the first to admit. But the pleasure we receive from it is clearly not his.

Alex is also a lover of Beethoven's Ninth Symphony, with its ringing affirmation of humanity in the last movement. He knows that such sublime music can only be the result of intense suffering. While Alex listens to it, on one occasion masturbating to it, Kubrick cuts to various shots of Christ, because Alex associates Christ with suffering and suffering with music. Therefore, the sublimity of the music inspires the hearer to make others suffer. "Preposterous!" we say; or, if this is so, how can the love of music be the mark of a cultivated person? It would be better to raze the concert halls and ban recordings. But in Alex's world, where good and evil have lost their meaning as moral terms, music has no value except the one placed on it. In such a society, it makes no difference whether one meditates to Beethoven's music or masturbates to it. Yet Alex is not alone in misusing the classics; his elders have discovered an equally perverted use for the Beethoven Ninth. During his rehabilitation, Alex is forced to watch Nazi films while the last movement of the Ninth is played electronically.

While *A Clockwork Orange* draws on the works of several composers for its musical associations, *Moonstruck* draws on one: Puccini's opera, *La Bohème*. In *La Bohème*, Mimi meets Rodolpho and within minutes they are pouring out their love in a soaring duet. In *Moonstruck*, Loretta (Cher) no sooner meets her fiancé's brother than he whisks her off to bed to the music of *La Bohème*, his favorite opera. Later, he takes her to the Metropolitan Opera House to see it. *Moonstruck* celebrates the passion that brings men and women together, using opera as a point of departure, where the characters experience such powerful emotions that they cannot express them except through song.

Pretty Woman (1990) uses another popular opera, Verdi's *La Traviata*, as a frame of reference. A wealthy entrepreneur (Richard Gere) takes a prostitute (Julia Roberts), with whom he has become involved, to a performance of *La Traviata*. Although she has never seen an opera before, she immediately identifies with the character of Violetta, who belongs to the same profession and also suffers at the hands of men. The film's emotional climax is believable within an operatic context; *Pretty Woman* rewrites the tragic ending of *La Traviata* and allows two people from totally different worlds to (supposedly) live happily ever after.

Close Encounters of the Third Kind illustrates a highly sophisticated use of music. Roy (Richard Dreyfuss), with whom aliens are communicating telepathically, is a mystery to his wife and children. A boy at heart, Roy wants to take his family to see a revival of Disney's *Pinocchio* (1940), in which they profess to have no interest. In a Spielberg film, a movie reference should never be ignored. During the end credits, John Williams's brilliant score segues into "When You Wish Upon a Star" from *Pinocchio*, placing *Close Encounters* within a special context. Roy has gotten his wish: he has become a space cadet and will enjoy the experience of interplanetary travel. But more important, like Pinocchio, who wanted to be a real boy rather than a puppet, Roy will remain, spiritually, a child—indifferent to time, which, like a puppeteer, controls human lives. It is significant that the humans, who had been declared missing and return at the end of the film, look the same as they did when the aliens abducted them. Roy will be leaving a world, dominated by time, for one in which time, as we know it, has no meaning.

A film has an outer and an inner world, a text and a subtext or, if you prefer, a narrative and an infranarrative. Beneath the text woven by the filmmaker's creativity and technology is the subtext, with its network of associations and implications that, when understood, broaden our knowledge of the film. Because what lies beneath the surface is usually more intriguing than what lies above it, one may be tempted to proceed to the subtext before the text is understood. However, just as in literature a work's symbolic level cannot be appreciated before its literal level is clear, so, too, in film the narrative must be grasped before it can be transcended. Only then are we free to seek out the associations—mythic, historical, iconic or visual, musical—that provide access to the film's inner world.

NOTES

[1]W. Y. Tindall, *James Joyce* (New York: Grove Press, 1960), 102.

[2]As quoted in W. Y. Tindall, *A Reader's Guide to James Joyce* (New York: Noonday Press, 1959), 129.

[3]Parker Tyler, *Magic and Myth of the Movies* (New York: Simon & Schuster, 1970), xviii.

[4]Lillian Feder, *Ancient Myth in Modern Poetry* (Princeton: Princeton University Press, 1971), 10–11.

[5]Donald Richie, *George Stevens: An American Romantic* (New York: Museum of Modern Art, 1970), 62.

[6]Michael T. Marsden, "Savior in the Saddle: The Sagebrush Testament," in *Focus on the Western*, ed. Jack Nachbar (Englewood Cliffs, N.J.: Prentice-Hall, 1974), 97.

[7]André Bazin, "The Evolution of the Western," in *What Is Cinema?*, vol. 2, trans. Hugh Gray (Berkeley: University of California Press, 1971), 152.

[8]Pauline Kael, "Introduction," *Bernardo Bertolucci's* Last Tango in Paris: *The Screenplay* (New York: Dell, 1973), 17.

CHAPTER

The Film Director

6

I f film is a collaborative art, no single person should get credit for a particular movie. Yet it is standard practice to speak of "John Ford's *Stagecoach*," or "Alfred Hitchcock's *Psycho*," or to suggest that directors enjoy a preeminence that writers do not by placing their names beside their films: *Ghosts of Mississippi* (1996) is "A Rob Reiner Film"; *The Mirror Has Two Faces* is "A Film by Barbra Streisand." The elevation of the director to the rank of author is an outgrowth of *auteurism*, a theory of filmmaking in which the director is considered the primary creative force behind a film.

When the *New York Times* lists film revivals, the director's name precedes the film's title, just as an author's name precedes the title of his or her book. Certain film critics (e.g., Andrew Sarris, David Denby) still designate films that way; many film historians prefer to place the director's name and release date in parentheses after the film. In the traditional main title, the director's name is the last credit; but it is also the one audiences see before the film begins—a rather subtle way of suggesting what has always been known in the industry: movies are a director's medium. Certainly, movie directors receive a unique form of recognition.

Directors are also accorded retrospectives even though others may have written the scripts of the films for which they are being honored. Then why John Ford's *Stagecoach* and not screenwriter Dudley Nichols's *Stagecoach*? The answer is auteurism.

AUTEURISM

The Beginnings of Auteurism

During the German occupation of France in World War II, the French were denied American movies, but after the war was over they began to rediscover the greatness of the American cinema. The movies Americans often took for granted, the French took seriously. André Bazin wrote appreciatively of William Wyler and Orson Welles; Jean-Luc Godard saw more in the B movies of Monogram studios than did the American kids who saw them as the second half of double bills at their neighborhood theaters.* The rediscovery of American films by the French led to a reconsideration of the director as artist. What impressed the French was the fact that Hollywood directors could be—and frequently were—handed a screenplay, a cast, and a crew (none of which they had personally selected) and still managed to leave the stamp of their personality on the films.

In 1951 André Bazin and Jacques Doniol-Valcroze began publication of *Cahiers du Cinéma*, a journal that evolved into a critical forum for young film enthusiasts (Jean-Luc Godard, François Truffaut, Eric Rohmer, Claude Chabrol, and others), who expressed themselves in its pages and later went on to become directors. *Cahiers du Cinéma* had the reputation of a maverick; it was often pretentious and erratic in its preference for one director over another. Still, whatever one may think of the journal and the eccentric taste of its writers (e.g., Luc Moullet, who found in such films as Edgar G. Ulmer's *Bluebeard* the theme of the loneliness of humanity without God), it moved directors from the background to the foreground, establishing them as creators instead of studio orderlies.

For the first three years of its existence, *Cahiers du Cinéma* had no

---

*Monogram made low-budget movies and "series pictures" (The Bowery Boys, Charlie Chan, Bomba the Jungle Boy, the Cisco Kid). The Monogram product was undistinguished except for an occasional melodrama like *Suspense* (1946) or *The Gangster* (1947).

real editorial policy; in 1954 Truffaut provided it with one in his famous essay "Une certaine tendance du cinéma français," which attacked classic French cinema for preferring literary scripts to shooting scripts, adaptations to original screenplays, studio sets to actual locations, and a team of specialists to a single auteur. Truffaut argued for "a cinema of auteurs"; and so it was that *auteur*, the French word for "author," entered the critical vocabulary of film.

Cahiers du Cinéma now had a policy: *la politique des auteurs*, "the policy of authors," which has had various interpretations, the most common one being that the journal was partial to certain directors (e.g., Orson Welles, Alfred Hitchcock, Jean Renoir) but indifferent to others (e.g., John Huston, René Clair, René Clément). Another interpretation was that *Cahiers du Cinéma*'s favored directors were infallible and incapable of making bad films. Bazin corrected this misconception in 1957, when he pointed out what should have been obvious: a great director can make a dud, and a mediocre director can occasionally make a classic. Essentially, Bazin endorsed the policy of ranking directors, although he was often disturbed by the indiscriminate taste of some of his writers. Bazin summed up his position in the equation: author + subject = work.

That equation was adopted as the critical principle of Andrew Sarris, through whom auteurism entered America. In his essay "Notes on the *Auteur* Theory in 1962,"[1] Sarris defended the ranking of directors as an extension of a policy that has always prevailed in the arts. We rank Shakespeare over Ben Jonson, Beethoven over Brahms, Mozart's *Don Giovanni* over Beethoven's *Fidelio*. It was inevitable that Sarris would establish a ranking order of his own. In *The American Cinema*, he divided American directors into eleven categories, including the "Pantheon" (Charles Chaplin, John Ford, D. W. Griffith, Howard Hawks, Alfred Hitchcock, Orson Welles); "The Far Side of Paradise" (Robert Aldrich, Frank Capra, Samuel Fuller, Vincente Minnelli); "Expressive Esoterica" (Tay Garnett, Arthur Penn, Edgar G. Ulmer); and "Less Than Meets the Eye" (John Huston, Elia Kazan, William Wyler). Despite the historical importance of *The American Cinema*, it is the kind of book that requires periodic revision. The current critical estimate of Huston and Wyler, for example, suggests that there is more to each of them than met Sarris's eye.

Sarris reduced the auteur theory, which is how *la politique des auteurs* came to be known in America, to three principles: (1) an auteur is technically competent; (2) an auteur has a personality that manifests itself in recurring stylistic traits that become his or her signature; and (3) an auteur's films exhibit a tension between the auteur's personality and his or her material—that is, there are aspects of an auteur's personality that will seep into the films, aspects that may not be readily discernible but may come out when a number of the auteur's films are studied and analyzed. Thus, Hitchcock's ambivalence toward women, especially blondes, is not immediately evident; yet after analyzing such films as *The Thirty-nine Steps*, *Saboteur, Psycho,* and *The Birds*, we see that while blondes held a certain fascination for him, he often subjected them to various forms of degradation—being handcuffed to a man, being slashed to death in a shower, having their faces pecked by attacking birds.

On the basis of Sarris's criteria, it is possible to consider certain directors—admittedly, few—as auteurs or surrogate authors of their films. However, film is not the only medium in which auteurism is practiced; forms of auteurism exist in all the performing arts. A ballet lover may refer to Nureyev's *Romeo and Juliet* as opposed to another dancer's, emphasizing not Prokofiev's score but its interpreter. A theatergoer who remembers Al Pacino's Richard III is not remembering Shakespeare's play but the interpretation of the play by a certain actor. Plays are also sometimes designated in terms of the acting companies that produced them. Thus, one theatergoer might ask another, "Did you see the Abbey's *Juno and the Paycock?*," meaning not Sean O'Casey's play but its production by Dublin's Abbey Theatre. A symphony orchestra provides a good analogy for film. If the brass section is mediocre, if the woodwinds fail to come in on time, if the horns sound flat, the conductor shoulders the blame. Critics constantly berate the conductor who "led a sluggish performance of Franck's Symphony in D Minor" or "who failed to elevate the orchestra to the heights the music demanded." When Leonard Bernstein conducted a Mahler symphony, it was no longer Mahler's symphony but Bernstein's. Bernstein took Mahler's work and attempted to realize the composer's intentions and communicated them to the orchestra. If Bernstein succeeded, he was praised; if not, he was criticized. Similarly, if a director is successful at blending the elements that make up a film into an organic whole that realizes the script's intent, he or she is commended; if not, the director is criticized for being unable to achieve the necessary integration.

However, just as not every conductor is a Leonard Bernstein, so not every director is an Alfred Hitchcock. Hitchcock then clearly fulfills the criteria of the auteur: when we designate *Psycho* as Hitchcock's *Psycho*, we mean that Hitchcock has been successful at integrating the efforts of the writer, the cast, and the crew into a reflection of his vision of the material.

The Debate over Auteurism

Even though some film scholars agree that there is such a thing as an Alfred Hitchcock film and therefore there are Hitchcockian elements in the films of others, many would argue against establishing auteurism as a general theory of film on the following grounds:

1. The genesis of a film is often too complex to be attributed to a single person. Some films, in fact, are the result of a producer's conception rather than a director's. Victor Fleming is credited as the director of *Gone with the Wind* (although George Cukor and Sam Wood also had a hand in the direction), yet the film was the brainchild of the producer David O. Selznick; if anything, then, it might be called a David O. Selznick film. The disaster films, *The Poseidon Adventure* (1972) and *The Towering Inferno* (1975), are associated with the producer, Irwin Allen, not with the directors, Ronald Neame and John Guillermin, respectively. Although Val Lewton never directed a single film, he left his mark on everything he produced at RKO (*Cat People, I Walked with a Zombie, The Curse of the Cat People*, and others). Thus, we think of *Cat People* primarily as a Val Lewton film and only secondarily as Jacques Tourneur's.

    If there is a similarity between *Poltergeist* (1982) and *E.T.*, it is because Steven Spielberg, who directed *E.T.*, coauthored and produced *Poltergeist* (although he did not direct it). Directed by Tobe Hooper, *Poltergeist* bears the Spielberg signature and is imbued with the same childlike innocence that characterizes *E.T.* If *Batteries Not Included* (1987), in which aliens come to the aid of tenants whom a greedy developer is pressuring into moving, sounds like Spielberg again, it is because it is a Spielberg production, even though it was directed by Matthew Robbins.

2. Certain films, especially those made when the studios were at their peak (1930–1950), bear the stamp of their studios more than that of any individual and are therefore thought of as "MGM movies" or "Warner Bros. movies." *Singin' in the Rain* is clearly an MGM musical, specifically a musical that came from Arthur Freed's production unit at MGM. If one compares *Singin' in the Rain* with other Arthur Freed productions (e.g, *Easter Parade*, 1948; *On the Town; An American in Paris*), one recognizes a common feature: the integration of the musical numbers with the action. While *Singin' in the Rain* was directed by Stanley Donen and Gene Kelly, film historians consider it an MGM musical or an Arthur Freed production, not a Donen-Kelly film.

3. Films that involve special effects illustrate the limitations of auteurism. When David Denby and Terrence Rafferty reviewed *Who Framed Roger Rabbit* in *New York Magazine* and *The New Yorker*, respectively, each referred to "Robert Zemeckis's *Who Framed Roger Rabbit.*" Yet Zemeckis was not responsible for the animation; the animation director Richard Williams and his staff were. Furthermore, the film was a cooperative venture between

Disney's Touchstone Pictures and Steven Spielberg's Amblin Entertainment. Spielberg is not the kind of producer who remains aloof from a production; in fact, he had certain ideas on how the cartoon figures should look. (For example, he wanted Roger's mouth to resemble Thumper's in *Bambi*.) The answer to the question "Who framed Roger Rabbit?" is easy. The answer to the question "Who made *Who Framed Roger Rabbit?*" is not.

For this reason, not every director can be considered an auteur; comparatively few, in fact, can be. These are the directors whose films are studied in film courses and who are the subjects of books, articles, and retrospectives. Such directors need not write their own script: Woody Allen does; John Ford never did. There have also been directors who worked within the studio system and still made films that were their own. William Wyler made some of his best movies for Samuel Goldwyn—for example, *Dead End* (1937), *Wuthering Heights* (1939). Shortly before Pearl Harbor, he was hired by MGM to direct *Mrs. Miniver*, which dramatizes the impact of World War II on a typical British family. In one sense, *Mrs. Miniver* is an MGM film; it was made by a specific studio because its head, Louis B. Mayer, believed in the "family film." However, Wyler was able to make it a William Wyler film. Wyler always tried to encompass as much as he could in a single shot, thus minimizing cutting. *Mrs. Miniver* is filled with such shots—Kay Miniver sitting on the bed while her husband is off in the dressing room; the Minivers seated at the dinner table while their son is seen talking on the telephone in the alcove; Kay standing on the bridge with the station master below her and water behind him.

Directors who are taught, written about, and honored with retrospectives and tributes have the following in common: their work illustrates the collaborative nature of the medium because they frequently work with the same personnel (writer, stars, cinematographer, editor) in a succession of films; they repeat favorite themes in the same or different genres; they allude to their earlier films; and they borrow from the films of others.

COLLABORATION

From a director's standpoint, collaboration can take several forms, the most common of which are as follows:

1. Collaboration between a director and a screenwriter. Sometimes a director will have the same screenwriter for several movies; undoubtedly, those movies will have certain features in common. Joan Harrison worked on the scripts for Hitchcock's *Rebecca*,

Foreign Correspondent, Suspicion, and *Saboteur,* in all of which the wrong person was under suspicion. Billy Wilder and Charles Brackett coauthored the scripts for three Mitchell Leisen films: *Midnight; Arise, My Love* (1940); and *Hold Back the Dawn* (1941). All three entail some form of deception.

2. Collaboration between a director and a cinematographer. Historically, the most famous was that between D. W. Griffith and Billy Bitzer. Other creative director-cinematographer collaborations have been between Eric von Stroheim and William Daniels (*Blind Husbands,* 1918; *Foolish Wives,* 1921; *Greed,* 1924; *The Merry Widow,* 1925); Josef von Sternberg and Lee Garmes (*Morocco,* 1930; *Dishonored,* 1931; *Shanghai Express,* 1932); Ingmar Bergman and Gunnar Fischer (*Smiles of a Summer Night,* 1955; *The Seventh Seal,* 1957; *Wild Strawberries*).

3. Collaboration between a director and a composer. Examples of this type include John Ford and Alfred Newman (*Arrowsmith,* 1931; *The Hurricane,* 1937; *The Grapes of Wrath; How Green Was My Valley*); Federico Fellini and Nino Rota (*La Strada,* 1954; *La Dolce Vita,* 1960; *8½,* 1963; *Juliet of the Spirits*); and Hitchcock and Bernard Herrmann (*The Wrong Man; Vertigo,* 1958; *Psycho; Marnie*).

4. Collaboration between a director and actor(s). Notable here are John Huston and Humphrey Bogart (*The Maltese Falcon,* 1941; *Across the Pacific,* 1942; *Treasure of the Sierra Madre,* 1948; *Key Largo,* 1948; *The African Queen,* 1951); von Sternberg and Marlene Dietrich (*The Blue Angel,* 1930; *Morocco; Dishonored; Shanghai Express; Blonde Venus,* 1932); Truffaut and Jean-Pierre Léaud (*The 400 Blows; Stolen Kisses; Bed and Board; Day for Night*); Bergman and Liv Ullmann (*Persona,* 1966; *Hour of the Wolf,* 1968; *The Shame,* 1968; *A Passion of Anna,* 1969; *Scenes from a Marriage,* 1973; *Face to Face,* 1976); Billy Wilder and Jack Lemmon (*Some Like It Hot,* 1959; *The Apartment,* 1960; *Irma la Douce,* 1963; *The Fortune Cookie,* 1966; *Avanti!,* 1972; *The Front Page,* 1974; *Buddy Buddy,* 1981); John Ford's stock company (Ward Bond, Victor McLaglen, John Wayne, Maureen O'Hara, Ben Johnson); Woody Allen and Mia Farrow (*Broadway Danny Rose,* 1984; *The Purple Rose of Cairo; Hannah and Her Sisters; Radio Days; September,* 1987; *Another Woman,* 1988; *Crimes and Misdemeanors,* 1989; *Shadows and Fog,* 1992; *Husbands and Wives,* 1992); Martin Scorsese and Robert De Niro (*Mean Streets,* 1973; *Taxi Driver,* 1976; *New York, New York,* 1977; *Raging Bull,* 1980; *The King of Comedy,* 1983; *GoodFellas,* 1990; *Cape Fear,* 1991; *Casino,* 1995).

5. Collaboration between a director and an editor. The collaboration

Billy Wilder with Jack Lemmon, who appeared in six Wilder films. *(Courtesy Margaret Herrick Library of the Academy of Motion Picture Arts and Sciences)*

between Woody Allen and Susan E. Morse is noteworthy for its longevity: *Manhattan* (1979), *Stardust Memories* (1980), *A Midsummer Night's Sex Comedy* (1982), *Zelig* (1983), *Broadway Danny Rose* (1984), *The Purple Rose of Cairo* (1985), *Hannah and Her Sisters* (1986), *Radio Days* (1987), *September* (1987), *Another Woman* (1988), *Crimes and Misdemeanors* (1989), *Shadows and Fog* (1992), *Husbands and Wives* (1992), *Manhattan Murder Mystery* (1993), *Bullets over Broadway* (1994), *Everybody Says I Love You* (1996).

6. Collaboration between a director and a producer. The best examples of this are Wyler and Samuel Goldwyn (*Dead End; Wuthering Heights; The Westerner*, 1940; *The Little Foxes*, 1941); Jacques Tourneur, Robert Wise, and Mark Robson, who directed the films Val Lewton produced for RKO; and William Dieterle and Hal B. Wallis at Paramount (*The Searching Wind*, 1946; *The Accused*, 1948; *Rope of Sand*, 1949; *Paid in Full*, 1950; *Dark City*, 1950; *Red Mountain*, 1951).

7. Collaboration between a director and a studio. Frank Capra and Columbia, Ernst Lubitsch and Paramount, Preston Sturges and Paramount, Raoul Walsh and Warner Bros., Vincente Minnelli and MGM all collaborated in film efforts. Paramount was synonymous with sophisticated comedy during the 1930s and 1940s, and it was such directors as Lubitsch, Sturges, and, to a lesser extent, Leisen who gave Paramount that reputation. Lubitsch could do more with the closing of a bedroom door than most directors could if they kept it open.

VARIETY

A great director need not have a wide repertoire of themes; there is a difference between a varied body of work and a varied number of themes.

The same themes can recur within that body of work, repeated or modified to fit the particular type of film. Billy Wilder's films, for example, center around two major themes: deception and its various forms (disguise, fraud, masquerade), and the impact of one social or political order on another (capitalism/communism, rich/poor, youth/age). Even the scripts that he and Charles Brackett wrote before he started directing reflect these themes: the female commissar of Ernst Lubitsch's *Ninotchka* (1939) who comes in contact with capitalism and falls under its spell; the chorus girl of *Midnight* who impersonates a countess; the female reporter of *Arise, My Love* who rescues a man from prison by pretending to be his wife; the gigolo of *Hold Back the Dawn* who feigns love in order to become an American citizen; the college professors of Howard Hawks's *Ball of Fire* (1941) who find themselves learning slang from a stripper.

Then there are the films that Wilder directed himself:

The Major and the Minor (1942): A woman disguises herself as a twelve-year-old to purchase a train ticket at half fare.
Five Graves to Cairo (1943): A British officer impersonates a lame servant in a desert hotel.
Double Indemnity: An insurance agent tricks a man into signing a policy with a double-indemnity clause; the agent and the client's wife con-

A career woman (Ginger Rogers) disguised as a twelve-year-old in order to ride half-fare to her home in Iowa in The Major and the Minor (1942). *(Courtesy Margaret Herrick Library of the Academy of Motion Picture Arts and Sciences)*

spire to kill her husband to collect on the policy; the agent briefly poses as her husband on board a train.

The Lost Weekend (1945): An alcoholic is continually devising ways of concealing his bottle.

The Emperor Waltz (1948): An Austrian countess meets an American phonograph salesman (a "two social orders" film).

A Foreign Affair (1948): An army captain in postwar Berlin tries to conceal his relationship with a nightclub singer from a visiting congresswoman.

Sunset Boulevard: An aging silent star deludes herself into thinking she can make a comeback as Salome; her kept man conceals his status from his girlfriend.

The Big Carnival (Ace in the Hole): A reporter deceives the victim of a cavein into believing he is the victim's friend.

Stalag 17 (1953): An informer infiltrates a POW camp.

Sabrina (1954): A rich young man courts a chauffeur's daughter (a "two orders" film).

The Seven Year Itch: A summer bachelor plays at being Don Juan.

The Spirit of St. Louis (1957): An atypical Wilder film, which depicts Lindbergh's flight across the Atlantic.

Love in the Afternoon (1957): A May–December romance develops between an older man and a young woman whose father is a detective.

Witness for the Prosecution (1957): A woman tricks a noted barrister into thinking she is a cockney.

Some Like It Hot: Two musicians dress up as women; a millionaire (male) falls in love with one of the disguised men.

The Apartment: A woman with a checkered past masquerades as a virgin.

One, Two, Three: An American Coca-Cola executive and a radical East Berliner clash ideologically.

Irma la Douce: To keep a prostitute from sharing her favors with others, her lover resorts to disguise.

Kiss Me, Stupid (1964): A single female bartender impersonates a married woman; a wife allows her songwriter-husband to think his song succeeded on its own merits although it became a hit because she spent the night with a famous pop singer.

The Fortune Cookie: A TV cameraman is persuaded by his brother-in-law to sue for nonexistent injuries.

The Private Life of Sherlock Holmes: Deception is implicit in any treatment of Holmes.

Avanti!: A married man and the daughter of his late father's mistress arrange to have a yearly rendezvous in Italy, repeating the deception their parents (his father, her mother) had practiced until their death.

The Front Page: An editor will do anything to get his star reporter back, even resorting to a lie that also happens to be one of the most famous curtain lines in the American theater: "The son of a bitch stole my watch."

Fedora (1979): A facially disfigured international movie star passes her daughter off as herself.

Buddy Buddy: To prevent himself from being unmasked, a hit man attempts to save a television censor from suicide.

Variety is achieved more through genre than theme. While deception/disguise is a recurring theme in Wilder's films, it is a theme that manifests itself in farce (*The Major and the Minor, Some Like It Hot, Irma la Douce*), romantic comedy (*Sabrina, Love in the Afternoon, Avanti!*), political comedy (*A Foreign Affair; One, Two, Three*), social comedy (*The Apartment, The Fortune Cookie*), social realism (*The Lost Weekend, The Big Carnival*), espionage and wartime melodrama (*Five Graves to Cairo, Stalag 17*), courtroom melodrama (*Witness for the Prosecution*), gothic melodrama (*Sunset Boulevard*), period pieces (*The Emperor Waltz, The Private Life of Sherlock Holmes*), film noir (*Double Indemnity*).

The films themselves are derived from several sources: novels (*The Lost Weekend, Love in the Afternoon*), plays that are either adaptations (*Stalag 17, Sabrina, The Seven Year Itch, Avanti!*) or almost total rewrites with little of the original left intact (*One, Two, Three; Irma la Douce; Kiss Me, Stupid*), original scripts (*The Emperor Waltz, Sunset Boulevard, The Big Carnival, The Apartment, The Fortune Cookie, The Private Life of Sherlock Holmes*); and other films (*Buddy Buddy*).

REPETITION

A great director, may repeat favorite themes not only in different kinds of movies but also as motifs within those movies. Thus, the deception/disguise theme recurs as various motifs in Wilder's movies:

1. adultery (*Double Indemnity, The Seven Year Itch, Love in the Afternoon, The Apartment, Kiss Me, Stupid, Avanti!*)
2. insurance fraud (*Double Indemnity, The Fortune Cookie*)
3. women physically altering their appearance (*The Major and the Minor, Witness for the Prosecution, Fedora*)
4. men physically altering their appearance (*Some Like It Hot, Irma la Douce*)
5. a woman deceiving the man she loves (*The Major and the Minor, The Apartment, Kiss Me, Stupid, The Private Life of Sherlock Holmes*)

6. a man deceiving the woman he loves (*The Seven Year Itch, Some Like It Hot, Irma la Douce*)
7. men deceiving each other (*Five Graves to Cairo, Double Indemnity, The Lost Weekend, The Big Carnival, The Fortune Cookie, Buddy Buddy*)

Similarly, in the "two orders" films the following motifs can be found:

1. distinctions of class (countess/commoner in *The Emperor Waltz*; common girl/privileged boy in *Sabrina*)
2. distinctions of age (young woman/older man in *Sabrina, Love in the Afternoon, The Apartment,* and *Avanti!*; young man/older woman in *A Foreign Affair* and *Sunset Boulevard*)
3. distinctions based on war (allies/enemy in *Five Graves to Cairo* and *Stalag 17*; victor/vanquished in *A Foreign Affair*)
4. distinctions of ideology (capitalism vs. communism in *One, Two, Three*; freedom vs. fascism in *A Foreign Affair*)

QUOTATIONS

Directors repeat themes, character types, characters' names, or visual motifs. Sometimes repetition is unconscious, but generally it is because directors assume the audience will interpret the repetition as a sign of continuity—not a lack of imagination. Thus, in casting John Wayne to play a character called Lt. Col. Kirby Yorke in *Rio Grande*, John Ford might have hoped the audience remembered that two years earlier Wayne played Captain Kirby Yorke in *Fort Apache*.

The opening credits of Ford's *The Man Who Shot Liberty Valance* are on broken crosses intended to evoke the opening credits of *My Darling Clementine*, which appeared on sign posts. In the years between *Clementine* (1946) and *Liberty Valance* (1962), Ford's vision of the West had changed from romantic to realistic. The stars of *Liberty Valance*, John Wayne and James Stewart, play roles that would have been more suitable for them twenty years earlier; hence the broken crosses to suggest that time has left its mark on both the director and the stars. In *Empire of the Sun*, when a boy is reunited with his parents amid a vast throng of people, Steven Spielberg repeats a composition from a movie he made ten years earlier, *Close Encounters of the Third Kind*, in which a man and a woman pushed their way through a crowd to find each other.

Hitchcock often quotes himself, but his quotes are rarely verbatim. Rowley's fall from the cathedral tower in *Foreign Correspondent* prefigures

Marlene Dietrich as Erika, a cabaret singer in post–World War II Berlin; and John Lund as her lover, Captain John Pringle, in *A Foreign Affair* (1948). *(Copyright ® by Paramount Pictures, Courtesy MCA Publishing Rights, a Division of MCA Inc.)*

Marlene Dietrich as Christine, who meets her future husband, Leonard Vole (Tyrone Power), in a Hamburg nightclub at the end of World War II in *Witness for the Prosecution* (1957). Wilder added the nightclub scene, which does not appear in the Agatha Christie play, to show how the Voles met. He is clearly repeating a plot device from *A Foreign Affair*—the smoke-filled basement nightclub where Pringle came to hear Erika sing. *(Courtesy MOMA/FSA)*

similar falls, but in different contexts, in *Saboteur, Vertigo,* and *North by Northwest.* The airplane wing that becomes a life raft when a plane crashes in the Atlantic in *Foreign Correspondent* yields to the real thing in *Lifeboat* (1944), a totally different kind of film that uses a more conventional form of survival at sea.

In Hitchcock's *Family Plot* (1976) when Blanche (Barbara Harris) and her boyfriend are driving along in a car whose brakes give way, she grabs hold of his necktie, almost strangling him with it. Her action recalls the necktie murders in *Frenzy* (1972). Similarly, when the pair are on a deserted stretch of highway, we almost expect the crop duster from *North by Northwest* to materialize and spray them with bullets. And to avoid detection when in a jewel thief's home, the boyfriend takes the same precautions Marnie took in Hitchcock's film of that name: he removes his shoes and tiptoes past the kitchen. In fact, we wait for him to drop a shoe, as Marnie did. These are old tricks, but they appear in a new setting.

In *Witness for the Prosecution*, Billy Wilder added a flashback to show how Leonard Vole (Tyrone Power) met his wife, Christine (Marlene Dietrich), in a Hamburg nightclub at the end of World War II. Dietrich had the same profession in Wilder's *A Foreign Affair*. Wilder must have had the earlier film in mind when he decided to open up the Agatha Christie play a bit by putting in the flashback. Yet *Witness for the Prosecution* is not *A Foreign Affair*, any more than *Family Plot* is *Frenzy* or *North by Northwest*.

BORROWINGS

Wilder regarded Ernst Lubitsch as the unrivaled master of subtlety. Whenever someone in a Lubitsch film closed a door, drew the curtains, or shut the blinds, one always wondered, "Did they or didn't they?" In *Double Indemnity*, the camera dollies back from Phyllis and Neff as they sit snugly on the sofa in his apartment. "We just sat there," Neff's voice is heard saying. We no more believe him than we believe the Lubitsch heroine who closes the door of her lover's bedroom and in the next shot awakens in her own.

As a rule, great directors are not troubled by the question of originality, because they see themselves as part of a tradition. Although they respect the past, they neither worship it blindly nor lean on it for support; instead, they view it as a legacy on which they can draw. The Odessa steps massacre in *Potemkin* left its mark on many filmmakers, including Busby Berkeley, who paid it a curious tribute in the "Lullaby of Broadway" sequence in *Gold Diggers of 1935*. Hitchcock did the same in *Foreign Correspondent*, in which an assassination was staged on the steps of an Amsterdam conference hall. Brian De Palma paid homage to the Odessa steps sequence in *The Untouchables* (1987), which even includes the careening baby carriage. Most directors are flattered when viewers evidence an awareness of a borrowing or a quote; in fact, in some cases viewers are expected to notice the borrowings so they can appreciate the director's integration of past and present.

HOMAGE TO THE ODESSA STEPS SEQUENCE
The Odessa steps massacre in *Potemkin*. *(Courtesy MOMA/FSA and Janus Films)*

AN INTERVIEW WITH BILLY WILDER

Billy Wilder is an ideal director for study. He directed his first film in 1942; his last in 1981. He is also a true auteur, inasmuch as he coauthored the scripts of all the films he directed. Since *The Big Carnival*, with a few minor exceptions, he produced his own films. Wilder has been the subject of retrospectives, doctoral dissertations, books, articles, and television tributes by the American Film Institute and the Film Society of Lincoln Center. He is a six-time Academy Award winner: twice for direction (*The Lost Weekend, The Apartment*); three times for best screenplay (*The Lost Weekend, Sunset Boulevard,* * *The Apartment*); and once for best picture (*The Apartment*).

D. H. Lawrence said, "Trust the tale, not the teller." Yet the teller can have much to tell, especially one who writes, directs, and produces one's own tales. Wilder told much during an interview on June 11, 1976:

> DICK: The critics who like to minimize the director's role will say that all a director did during the Studio Years was carry out the studio's policy. They would not speak of "Billy Wilder's films" but of "Billy Wilder's Paramount

---

*The *Sunset Boulevard* Oscar was technically for story and screenplay.

Hitchcock's homage to the Odessa steps in *Foreign Correspondent* (1940). *(Courtesy MOMA/FSA)*

period [1942–1954]." When you were at Paramount, were you conscious of turning out a Paramount product?

WILDER: Never, not even in the early days when I did not have script approval and the right of final cut. If this were true, then Lubitsch's pictures, Sturges's pictures, Mitchell Leisen's pictures, my pictures—in fact, all the pictures made during those interesting days at Paramount—would have been the same. They were not. Once Paramount and I agreed on the subject of the movie, the cast, and the budget, and once they realized I would not have censorship problems (and in those days we had to smuggle things past the censors)—once all of this was settled—I was on my own. I wrote the film the way I wanted to, I cut it the way I wanted to. Of course, I may have to give a little when a picture is sold to television and make a cut here or a cut there. But even when I was beginning and did not have the ultimate control I have now, never for a moment did I think of myself as a foreman on the Paramount lot.

You see, the auteur theory, in emphasizing the director who takes over someone else's script, has little to say about a director like myself who writes,

Billy Wilder on the set.
(Courtesy Billy Wilder)

directs, and produces his own. Although I do not belong to the producers' guild (I do, of course, belong to the screenwriters' and directors'), I think I can evaluate the auteur theory better than most critics. Being the writer, director, and producer of a picture, naturally I am the auteur.

DICK: Then you do not accept the auteur theory?

WILDER: I accept it only up to a point. The auteur theory does not emphasize the script. I deeply believe in the script and in the director's getting the maximum out of it. A mediocre director with a great script will still come out on top, but a brilliant director with a poor script will inevitably fail.

DICK: Is it easier to become a director now than it was when you began in the industry?

WILDER: It is much easier now because television provides you with a training ground. In the past, there was no training ground except shorts and a series like MGM's "Crime Does Not Pay," where Fred Zinnemann got his chance. Otherwise, unless you worked on Broadway or had important connections, or unless powerful stars requested you, it was extraordinarily difficult to get a break. You might think that by becoming an assistant director you would stand a good chance of becoming a director. Yet the assistant director had the least chance of ever becoming a director. The dialogue coach, the cameraman, the actor, the actor's relatives stood a better chance of becoming directors.

Of course, all that has changed with television. With the enormous demands it makes on one's time, you can learn by being on the set long enough. And with highly trained crews at his disposal, a director can't make a total ass of himself.

Directing is not Chinese glass blowing or the art of making Inca gold statuettes. It can be learned, and it can be learned quickly if you have a flair and a style for it. It is also an exhausting profession and one that has a finality about it. In the theater, you can rewrite a play during its tryout; in my profession you can't say "Let's reshoot the film" if you don't like it. The sets are down, the actors are in Yugoslavia, and plans have already been made for the picture's distribution.

DICK: Do you have an image in your mind of what the film will look like in its final form?

WILDER: Even though you lose yourself in the picture while you're making it, ultimately it is back to what it was when you did the script, which is proof that the script was good and the choice of material was good. If a film doesn't work—and often it doesn't—it was because I was telling the wrong story or an uninteresting story; I was telling a story that didn't have a chance no matter how brilliantly I might do it. Maybe I chose the right story at the time, but it turned out to be the wrong time for the picture. If I write an article for a magazine, it will be published a few weeks later. The mood of the public has not changed, and there is still interest in the subject. But my picture will not see the light of day for two years, when the mood of the public may be entirely different.

DICK: Are your scripts complete when you begin shooting?

WILDER: They are complete in the sense that I know how the film will end, but I want to see how the first two acts will play before I go on to the third. They are not complete in the sense that every line has been written down. I am always open to suggestions. If a scene does not play well in rehearsal, I will change it. If an actor has a good idea, or even an electrician, I can add it. But you must first have something to add it to.

DICK: Is there any truth to the story that Shirley MacLaine and Jack Lemmon were handed their dialogue for the final scene of *The Apartment* on the last day of shooting?

WILDER: Could be. But we knew very well how it would end: the boy would get what he wanted, give it up, and get the girl. Maybe the actual words were typed the night before. But we did not improvise; I never depend upon improvisation.

DICK: Your films evidence an incredible range—romantic comedy, farce, social drama, film noir, melodrama, biography. Did you aim for such diversity?

WILDER: I know a man who always wears a dark blue suit when he goes out in the evening. It's rather boring, you know. Why not a striped suit once in a while? Sometimes I wonder if I did the wrong thing by experimenting so much. Hitchcock, whom I greatly admire, stayed with one kind of picture. When people go to a Hitchcock movie, they know what to expect. Certain directors develop a style, refine it, and never give it up; they never leave their own neighborhood. I ventured out and tested myself. But whatever kind of film I make, there is always one quality I aim for: a complete simplicity of style, a total lack of pretentiousness; there is not one phony setup in a Billy Wilder picture.

Also, making films is a matter of mood. Now I am in the mood for something a bit serious, so I will do *Fedora*,* which may remind some of *Sunset Boulevard* at least in texture, but it will be quite different.

DICK: It's well known that you write your scripts with a collaborator, but do you ever look upon your editor as a collaborator? I ask because Doane Harrison edited several of your early films.

WILDER: Doane Harrison was an old-time cutter, going back to the time when George Stevens was a cameraman for Hal Roach. He was very close to me when I made *The Major and the Minor;* he taught me a great deal because until then I had spent my life behind the typewriter, not behind the camera.**

DICK: How did you get behind the camera?

WILDER: How I became a director is very interesting. When I was writing scripts with Charles Brackett, we were never allowed on the set when the film was being shot. First of all, directors didn't want writers on the set; and second, we were off writing another picture. I decided to assert myself because I wanted some control over my scripts. So I started to raise hell, and Paramount finally let me direct a picture. Actually, it was no big deal because at that time Paramount was turning out fifty pictures a year. They said, "Let Wilder make a picture and then he'll go back to writing." Everyone expected me to make something "fancy-schmancy." Yet I made something commercial. I brought back the most salable hunk of celluloid I could—*The Major and the Minor.*

You see, unless you control your film, you are also at the mercy of actors. It's easy for an actor to argue with a director who is weak or who isn't convinced about the script. I remember Mr. Brackett and I were working on the script for *Hold Back the Dawn*, which Mitchell Leisen was directing. We had written a very fine scene for Charles Boyer, who was playing an immigrant waiting for his visa to come through. Unkempt and unshaven, Boyer waits in a cheap Mexican hotel. Well, to show the kind of hotel it was and to suggest something about the character Boyer was playing, we included a scene where Boyer makes some cynical remarks to a cockroach climbing up the wall. I assumed the scene would be shot as we had written it. A short time later, I ran into Boyer and asked him how he liked the scene with the cockroach. He said, "We cut that scene." I was shocked. "Why was it cut?" I asked. "How can I talk to a cockroach when the cockroach can't answer?"

Fedora, the first novella in Thomas Tryon's *Crowned Heads* (1976), is about a movie star who does not seem to age.

**Wilder began his career as a reporter in his native Vienna. It was in Berlin in the late 1920s that he turned to screenwriting.

was Boyer's reply. I was so angry I told Brackett, "If that son of a bitch ain't talking to a cockroach, he ain't talking to anybody." We hadn't finished the script yet, so we pared Boyer's remaining scenes down to the bare minimum.

DICK: Is it important for a director to be able to write?

WILDER: It is more important for a director to be able to read. Many directors do not understand the script, and they don't have the nerve to say so. But they go ahead and shoot it, regardless.

DICK: There is a great deal of confusion today about the role of the editor. Did an editor ever change the form of any of your films?

WILDER: No, I learned to shoot with utmost economy, so there is not much an editor can do. I cut the film in the camera. I do not protect myself by shooting the scene eighteen different ways: it exhausts the actors, and the words begin to lose their meaning. I will go over the rushes with the editor and we will discuss them. I may say to him, "I need an additional shot here," but that is the extent of it. The worst that can ever happen is that I must alter my film or add to it.

DICK: Yet some directors rely very heavily on their editors. Dede Allen has become a legend in her own lifetime. Some critics have even said that she bails out Arthur Penn time and time again with her editing.

WILDER: I would not say she "bailed" him out; it was more like the way Maxwell E. Perkins helped Thomas Wolfe reorganize his novels for publication. If an editor bails a director out, it is because he shot crap. Dede Allen fully deserves the billing she gets, because she makes the picture better. It is the same with Verna Fields, who cut *Jaws*. She has the knack of knowing which frames to cut and how fast to cut them.

DICK: You edited *The Front Page* in four days, yet Terrence Malick supposedly spent a year editing *Badlands*.

WILDER: That is because he shot a great deal of film; I don't. I also work with very expensive actors, so I do not have the time. In the case of *Badlands*, you have a crew of very talented beginners who do everything themselves, including moving the camera from place to place. They can go out and shoot where they like; and by the time the sheriff comes around to ask if they have permission, they've gone. I must apply for permission and wait until I get it. If I pick up a chair on the set, I have the unions to contend with. Our approaches are totally different; it's like commedia dell'arte as opposed to the legitimate theater.

DICK: Did you go into producing because you wanted more control over your pictures?

WILDER: Yes, and also because there were so few creative producers. Look at this ad in *The Hollywood Reporter*:

SILVER STREAK
A MARTIN RANSOHOFF-FRANK YABLANS PRODUCTION
AN ARTHUR HILLER FILM
A MILLER-MILKIS-COLIN HIGGINS PICTURE

This is insane. What happens is that somebody buys a property or two people buy it, so their names must appear. If the star becomes involved in the production, then his name appears. The director says it must read "A Bill Friedkin Film" or "Bill Friedkin's Film." Then the schleppers and the hangers-on get into the act. The vanity game is enormous. Even in the theater, it's "a such-and-such production in conjunction with so-and-so." Ultimately, when it's all over, it's Josh Logan's *South Pacific*.

The true producers, like Thalberg, Selznick, and Goldwyn, would add to a picture and enrich it; they were there when you needed them for important decisions. When the picture was finished, they got the maximum exposure for it and arranged for it to be shown in the best theaters.

DICK: Since *Ace in the Hole*, you produced all of your films except for *The Spirit of St. Louis*, which Leland Hayward produced, and *Witness for the Prosecution*, which Arthur Hornblow, Jr., produced. Was there any reason for your not producing these yourself?

WILDER: Leland Hayward was my agent when I first came to Hollywood, so there was no real problem with his producing my film. Arthur Hornblow produced my very first film, *The Major and the Minor*. He was also a friend of Marlene Dietrich, who wanted the part in *Witness for the Prosecution* and asked me to direct so she would be sure to get it.

DICK: How do you feel about directors like Peter Bogdanovich, who pay homage to the work of other directors?

WILDER: You know what we call Bogdanovich? "The Frank Gorshin of directors." He is so steeped in film history that it is difficult for him to find a style of his own.

DICK: Have you ever paid homage to other directors?

WILDER: If I did, it was unconscious.

DICK: What about Lubitsch? There is a Lubitsch quality about *The Emperor Waltz* and *The Private Life of Sherlock Holmes*.

WILDER: I advise everyone to stay away from Lubitsch; he cannot be imitated. I did not set out to make a Lubitsch film in either case. And incidentally, you picked two of my failures. *Holmes* didn't make a ripple. I even had to cut two episodes out of it.

DICK: It is a film that is gaining in popularity. It was recently revived as part of a Sherlock Holmes Film Festival in New York, and those who have never seen it before were quite taken with it.

WILDER: It was, I think, the lushest of the Holmesiana and truest to the period.

DICK: Most of your films employ some form of disguise or deception. Would you agree?

WILDER: Some, but not all. Not in *Double Indemnity*.

DICK: It does appear in the way Neff gets Dietrichson to sign the insurance policy.

WILDER: Yes, I see what you mean. Well, there is a lot of that in *Fedora*, I assure you.

DICK: You said before that you were not conscious of any Lubitsch influence. Were you aware of the fact that in both *Five Graves to Cairo* and *The Private Life of Sherlock Holmes* you used a parasol as part of the plot and as a symbol of femininity? In *Five Graves*, Bramble places it on Mouche's grave; in *Holmes*, Ilse uses her parasol to send messages as well as to say good-bye to Holmes.

WILDER: No, I was not conscious of *Five Graves to Cairo* when I was making *Holmes*. In *Five Graves to Cairo* the parasol was a sentimental touch; there are no flowers in Tobruk, so he brings her a parasol. In *Holmes* Ilse used it for Morse code. And a parasol is so photographable, you know. There is something exquisite about it, especially when it is opened out against the sun. I am very fond of the proper use of props, and I like to make them part of the script. In *The Apartment* I used a broken compact mirror as the means of identifying Shirley MacLaine as the girl Fred MacMurray had been bringing to Jack Lemmon's apartment.

DICK: Were you influenced by the Book of Genesis when you were writing *Ace in the Hole*? I am thinking of the continual emphasis on serpents, the desert as a kind of Eden that turns into a carnival, the rescue operations that take six days.

WILDER: That is a very interesting theory. You see, personally my mind doesn't go that way. And if it did, I couldn't admit it.

DICK: Several years ago you made this statement: "We're just like the guys in Detroit, putting out cars, no matter what anyone thinks we are." This is rather strange coming from a man who is the subject of retrospectives, books, articles, and Ph.D. dissertations. Do you still believe it?

WILDER: I did not mean what people think. How do you interpret it?

DICK: That directors are assembly-line workers.

WILDER: What I meant was that it takes tremendous artistry to put something into an assembly-line product so it will not have that mass-produced look. If someone is writing a poem or composing a symphony, he is doing it himself and on his own time. In our business we are playing for enormous chips supplied by other people. They give me the chips to gamble with, and I in turn am responsible to them. In this kind of situation it takes more artistry to produce something of value—sometimes to sneak in something of value—than it does when you are given as much money as you want, with no strings attached, and told to go to Salzburg and bring back a two-hour film. If I get behind schedule or exceed my budget, or if I indulge myself, after a couple of such pictures I would be flat on my ass. I would not get a chance to work again. I must do something that is hopefully superior, hopefully innovative, and at the same time it must be profitable. I personally believe that anything worthwhile ultimately finds some kind of audience. If somebody says, "This is the goddamnedest greatest picture ever made but no one went to see it," then it is not the goddamnedest greatest picture ever made.

I assure you, I have as many sleepless nights and as many ulcers as the truest of artists. But I have an added burden. If a painter buys a canvas for a couple of dollars and does not like what he has painted on it, he can throw it away. My canvas costs $4 million; if I don't like it, it can't be thrown in the fire. It's going to be shown, reviewed, maybe even play to empty houses. In the theater the producers can decide to close a show on the road and not bring it to Broadway. I can't. I've always said that the trouble with making pictures is that we can't try out in New Haven. If a picture is bad, it will come back to haunt you on the late-late show. Its stench will endure forever.

AN INTERVIEW WITH ALAN ALDA

In the movie industry, when a writer becomes a director, he or she is said to have "gone hyphenate." To use movie jargon, Alan Alda has gone double hyphenate: while Billy Wilder is a writer-director, Alan Alda is an actor-writer-director. Alda's career began on Broadway with major roles in *Purlie Victorious* (1961), *The Owl and the Pussycat* (1964), and *The Apple Tree* (1966), which won him a Tony nomination. When Hollywood beckoned, he began the second phase of his career, appearing in such films as *The Paper Lion* (1968), *The Extraordinary Seaman* (1969), and *The Mephisto Waltz* (1971). When the success of the movie *M*A*S*H* led to the television spin-off in 1972, Alda's already varied career took another direction. As Hawkeye Pierce, Alda became one of television's most popular stars, a favorite among college students, and one of America's most sought-after commencement speakers.

What contributed to *M*A*S*H*'s longevity on television was an emphasis on human relationships that was quite different from the absurdist and often cruel humor of the film. The series underwent a transition from sitcom to human comedy, and Alda played a significant role in the change, first by writing some scripts and then by directing them. By the mid-1970s, Alan Alda was a former Broadway star turned Hollywood actor who was then acting in, writing for, and directing some of the episodes of one of the most popular programs in the history of American television.

By the end of the 1970s, Alda had experience writing for television but had not yet written for the movies. The next stage in an already thriving career was to write his first screenplay, the highly successful *Seduction of Joe Tynan* (1979). However, Alda did not direct *Joe Tynan*. Thus, there was one more height to scale: directing an original screenplay in which he would also appear. He achieved that goal with *The Four Seasons* (1981), which proved to be both a critical and a commercial success. Three other films followed, which he directed and in which he appeared: *Sweet Liberty*, *A New Life*, and *Betsy's Wedding* (1990).

Alda's views on filmmaking are as valuable as Wilder's because, as an

Alan Alda on the set of *Sweet Liberty* (1986). *(Copyright ® Universal Pictures, a Division of Universal City Studios, Inc. Courtesy MCA Publishing Rights, a Division of MCA Inc.)*

actor-writer-director, he understands the needs of three of the key members of the industry.

The following interview took place in Alan Alda's office at Martin Bregman Productions in New York on June 13, 1988:

> DICK: Some writers become writer-directors, or "go hyphenate" as *The Hollywood Reporter* would say, because they want greater control over their scripts. Was that true of yourself?
>
> ALDA: No. I think I became a director because I thought I would love directing; it turned out I did. When I started to direct, I was on *M*A*S*H*. I was eager to direct anything, whether I had written it or not. It would be a chance for me to work under the best conditions, where there were people who could catch me if I fell. Yet I can understand what writers go through when someone else directs their work. Unless a writer and a director are in close touch and are lucky enough to see things the same way, the result may be quite different from what the writer intended. My first *M*A*S*H* script had a very good director, yet the scenes didn't have the point I thought they should; in some cases, the actors didn't get the jokes, and I just had to sit by

helplessly. It's a good idea, in general, for writers to direct their own material, and for directors to write their own material—but only if the directors can write. Unfortunately, there are a lot of directors who can't write but who keep doing it. I have great respect for the written word; that comes from having been an actor first. Since I come from the stage, I would never think of changing a word in a script. And I wouldn't do it as a director, either, unless I consulted with the writer.

DICK: You don't believe, then, that the director is the author of the film, as the auteurists do?

ALDA: I have a problem with the auteur theory; the author of the film is the author of the script. I could understand if, by the auteur theory, you mean that the director contributes something to the film. If the director tells the story successfully through the lens, he or she has contributed something the writer couldn't because the writer told the story on paper. John Wayne contributed something unique to his movies, but you don't call a John Wayne film "A Film by John Wayne." After Marshall Brickman finished directing *Simon*, he was asked if he would like it called "A Film by Marshall Brickman." He replied, "No. It's a film by Kodak."

DICK: An editor also contributes something to the film. How much latitude did you allow William Reynolds, who edited *A New Life?*

ALDA: Since we had to get the film out in a hurry, I gave Bill a lot of latitude. As I watched the rushes, I made detailed notes about preferred takes and angles, and how I saw the scenes fitting together. I didn't sit over his shoulder. Actually, I liked the idea of loosening my grip a little. I think I was able to do it on *A New Life* because I was more secure. I told Bill what my ideas were; if he had a better idea or if he felt one of mine wouldn't work, he would tell me and we would proceed from there. I find that editing is like script writing. You refine what you've written and get other ideas. All the cuts have some of my ideas and some of Bill's.

DICK: Did you allow Michael Economou the same latitude on *Sweet Liberty?*

ALDA: No, and I'm sorry I didn't. The fact that I allowed Bill Reynolds more on *A New Life* represents growth on my part. Whether you have tight reins or loose reins, it all boils down to communication. No matter to whom you are talking—the editor, the cinematographer, the actors—you have to be able to describe what you see. You just can't say to someone, "This is the script; you do it." That's not the job of the director or even the producer; that's what the studio does. The studio says, "I like that script; I like that cast. Here's the money. Go make the movie." From that point on, everybody must start communicating with each other. The producer has to say to the writer or the writer-director, "Do you really need that scene? Do you think these lines are clear?" The producer does not do this to achieve the producer's vision, but the writer-director's. And the writer-director tries to get everyone else to realize the vision he or she has.

DICK: Do you have an image in your mind of how the completed film will look?

ALDA: For *Sweet Liberty* I storyboarded. There was a picture of every scene in the movie. An artist I was working with came back with a storyboard that represented the way he thought everything should look. I said, "Thank you, but that's not the point. They hired me to tell the story as I see it." A storyboard conveys a great deal of information; it's supposed to be a visualization of the script as well as an aid to all the departments involved in shooting the script. What I did was draw stick figures and discuss them with the artist so that he could draw the figures properly. Eighty percent of the film looked like the storyboard.

DICK: What about your relationship with the cinematographer?

ALDA: We would discuss what kind of lens, dolly, or crane we would use. I also had a specific shot list. That part of the job was over before I even got to the set, so we didn't have to waste half the morning wondering whether we would shoot this way or that.

DICK: Did you storyboard *A New Life* also?

ALDA: Not as much, since I didn't have an artist. I just drew stick figures.

DICK: Is storyboarding difficult if you're verbally oriented?

ALDA: No. I think in images. I usually start writing when I have a visual image. Novelists do the same, you know. John Fowles had an image of a woman at the end of a jetty, so he wrote *The French Lieutenant's Woman* to find out who she was.

DICK: Did *The Four Seasons* begin with an image?

ALDA: That film came from several sources. First there was Vivaldi's *Four Seasons*. Wouldn't it be interesting, I thought, to make a movie showing the same people on vacation in each of the four seasons? The musical form would dictate the form of the film. Then I had another image: I envisioned three couples getting out of a car. I kept seeing them getting out of the car and walking somewhere, and doing it over and over. It was like seeing a film in a loop. It haunted me. I had to find out more about those people.

DICK: In the film, the car is a very unobtrusive way of starting the film.

ALDA: Yes, in the credits sequence, one couple picks up the other couples, so that by the time the actual film begins, you know who everyone is.

DICK: Did you plan to have *The Four Seasons* begin in spring and end in winter?

ALDA: It wasn't until after I had written the film that I realized the whole spring-winter progression corresponds to the four stages of friendship. There's a springtime to a friendship when nobody can do any wrong. In the glare of the summer sun, you see your friends as they are. In autumn, illusions fall away like leaves. In winter, you're "frozen" with your friends; you have to accept them as they are or find new ones who won't be a burden to you because you don't know who they are yet. I think this is what happens in the movie, but didn't understand it until I had written it.

DICK: Do you have a complete script at the time of shooting?

ALDA: Absolutely. I have to because I haven't got time to rewrite on the set. That's why I go through about a dozen drafts and am overly particular about what I want to shoot.

DICK: When you were in the theater, you did improvisations as a member of the Second City [a Chicago-based improvisational group]. As a film director, do you improvise?

ALDA: If you mean during filming, very little. I may do a bit in scenes where several people are talking at once. In *A New Life*, I improvised a scene in which the character I play is arguing with a lawyer at a party. We did one episode on *M*A*S*H* that was an improvisation. It was called "The Interview" and consisted of someone interviewing the M*A*S*H unit as if for a documentary. Yet it was a highly controlled situation. We rehearsed for weeks by improvising into a tape recorder; the tape was edited by the writer, Larry Gelbart, who added some of his own jokes, and that became the script. But there were also last-minute questions that we had never heard before; that part of the episode was spot improvisation. There's a great difference between a spot improvisation and a script that has been derived from improvisation. When you're improvising, and it works, it is very hard to repeat the improvisation and get the same effect. It may take fifteen or twenty attempts for it to come to life again. If you're working from a script that came out of an improvisation, it's the same as working from any other script. Filmmakers should know that. There is a difference between improvising during rehearsal and improvising whole scenes in front of the camera. But a lot of young directors who have had little experience working with actors think that improvising is a technique that gets the actors to be more truthful. There's a danger that the values of the script will get lost in the improvisation and that nothing will replace them. Also, if the actors improvise in rehearsal, and something exciting happens, the director assumes that if the actors repeat these lines, the excitement will recur. The director doesn't realize that it wasn't the lines that were exciting but the creative impulse that inspired them. The first time the impulse passes through the actor is thrilling, yet nobody knows the source of that impulse, and to rediscover it takes several more improvisations. You may or may not get it again.

Directors who feel it's the actors' fault if they improvise brilliantly during rehearsal but can't repeat what they did in front of the camera don't realize it has nothing to do with the actors; it's the way the brain works. Something mysterious might happen during an improvisation that brings the scene to life. What happens is that connections are made and impulses arise that should be explored. The actual words that are said are not nearly so important. Improvisation is useful to find out who the characters are and what their pasts have been, and I've used improvisation during rehearsals for that purpose. Once the actors understand their characters—and improvisation is one way of accomplishing this—they may be able to play the scene with more life. Improvisation also gets the actors to feel comfortable with one another and with the director.

DICK: To make them comfortable, would you change dialogue with which they are uncomfortable?

ALDA: That's a traditional way of making actors comfortable. I do it with caution, but I do it. What is important is what the script is communicating and the truth of the relationships expressed in the script. If changing a word here or there doesn't vitiate that truth, then I'm happy to. But if it wrecks the story, makes it illogical, or denies something truthful about the character, I explain to the actor that I can't. It's the director's job to keep the whole picture in mind. Every department may have a wonderful idea, but it might not fit into the whole scheme of the film. However, an actor may be uncomfortable with a line of dialogue, and after a few days of rehearsal, when the context is clear, the actor is not only comfortable with it but would kill to keep it. Improvisation and changing dialogue are only two ways to make actors feel comfortable. The most important thing is for the actors and director to eat dinner together.

DICK: Is that why food is so important in your films?

ALDA: That happens to be the way I am, the way I run my life. A lot of it is devoted to eating.

DICK: Do you believe in eating with the cast because the meal has always been a symbol of unity?

ALDA: That reason never occurred to me. I think that food is an image that comes to me a lot because I like food.

DICK: Since you've written both teleplays and screenplays, is the basic difference between them that the half-hour teleplay is in two acts, while screenplays are not divided into acts?

ALDA: Actually, a screenplay is divided into acts even though the acts may not be indicated as such in the script. Most screenwriters talk in terms of act one, act two, act three. You introduce the situation, complicate it, and resolve it. George S. Kaufman used to say that in act one you get the hero up a tree; in act two you throw stones at him; and in act three you get him down. All stories are like that. You introduce the characters in the beginning, along with their goals; then there are complications in their achieving those goals because everyone wants something different. Thus, it won't be so easy for the main character to get what he or she wants because of the obstacles thrown in the way by the other characters. It's what Aristotle in the *Poetics* called "dramatic action"—action in the sense of the characters' trying to achieve something. The resolution is the final working out of their either getting what they want or not, or getting not what they want but what they need. In that case, they experience growth, sometimes tragic growth. They may no longer be able to do what they did in the past, but they have achieved insight. This may not always be apparent in what I write because I stress relationships and internal struggles, but I'm always thinking in terms of action—dramatic action, not car chases. Someone's always trying to accomplish something, even if it's just to understand something.

It's almost impossible for the actor to act unless the character wants something. That doesn't mean the character has to want something external; it can be internal. It may be peace, tranquillity, or self-knowledge. And a director must know what that goal is. Otherwise, if it's a play, you'll just hear a lot of talking, or if it's a film, you'll see a lot of fancy shots.

The writer must give the character a goal, even if it's a limited goal, as it is in *Rocky*. Rocky only wants to go the distance; the fact that he doesn't win is unimportant. He achieved his goal: he went the distance. An actor shouldn't be allowed to go onstage or before the camera if he or she is playing a character without an objective or a goal. If the character doesn't want something, turn the lights out and save electricity. The scene will go dark anyway if the actors are only feeding each other lines so the author can get the exposition out. Shakespeare knew how to handle exposition: in the opening scene of *Othello*, we learn who Iago, Roderigo, Desdemona, and Othello are without one expository line being uttered. Everything comes out of the action. The actors have not been forced to say to themselves, "Well, we just have to say these lines so the audience will get what's going on."

DICK: You have been speaking of writing, acting, and directing as if they were part of the same process.

ALDA: They are. The actors need an objective that the writer provides and that the director achieves. It's painful for me to see writers and actors at odds with each other. The writers complain, "Those damn actors aren't saying my words right." The actors complain, "Who wrote this crap?" They both work the same way, yet they'll never know it unless they sit down and talk with each other. If actors don't speak the dialogue properly, it's probably because they don't understand it. Writers blame actors because they fail to realize an actor must go through a certain process to absorb in a few days what it may have taken the writer two years to create. Being an actor, a writer, and a director, I understand all three.

DICK: If you had to describe the role of a director to someone outside the industry, how would you do it?

ALDA: A director gives direction; it's inherent in the job title. However, it's not a good idea to direct actors down to the last little movement of their pinkie. It's not only a bad idea; it can also wreck the picture. You must find out how you can communicate your vision to each department so that everyone will give you what you want from their heart. What's the point of hiring an art director if you say, "This is what I want—nothing else." All the art director will do is draw the set you designed. You want to be able to get design ideas from the art director, but those ideas must serve *your* vision. All of this is done through communication. You must be able to describe what you see to everyone, and you should be able to compare what you see happening with what you see can happen. But you must understand the specific capabilities of each department, what each can and cannot do. Actors cannot work from results. The first mistake a director makes is to say to an actor, "Be mysterious." That's a result; mystery is what you experience when the actor is doing the scene right. The director has to find out, with the actor, what the actor is trying to accomplish in terms of the action that will make the actor appear mysterious. You have to find the cause that produces the result. Actors can play a state; they can depict a state of drunkenness, for example. But once an actor establishes that the character is drunk, the actor has to achieve something, even if it's trying not to appear drunk.

DICK: It is possible to learn directing?

ALDA: The only way to learn anything is with a mentor who will go through the steps with you, then let you do it and go over your mistakes. It's like the way my wife and I taught our children to wash their hands. We would put all of our hands under the faucet and rub them back and forth with the soap. Then the kids got the feeling. It's the way an artist guides the hand of a pupil or the way the tennis instructor puts his or her hand over yours on the racket. But you still have to make the shots; still, it's better if you've had hands-on experience with someone who is experienced.

NOTES

[1] The article appeared in *Film Culture* (Winter 1962–1963); it has been reprinted in Gerald Mast, Marshall Cohen, and Leo Braudy, *Film Theory and Criticism*, 4th ed. (New York: Oxford University Press, 1992), 585–88.

CHAPTER

Film and Literature

7

"Film has nothing to do with literature," claimed Ingmar Bergman.[1] Like so many dogmatic statements, this one is only partially true. Certainly a student can analyze a film as he or she analyzes a work of literature—in terms of form, rhythm, imagery, and symbolism. A student does not, however, analyze it in the same way a novel or a poem would be analyzed. A film's rhythm is often determined by the length of the strips of celluloid, not by variations of stressed and unstressed syllables, as in poetry; or by the alternation of description and dialogue, as in fiction. A film's imagery is visual. Imagery in literature is verbal.

A film's form is an inheritance partly from literary narrative and partly from the visual arts. Literature by its very nature implies something written. A screenplay may be literature in the root meaning of the word, but it is rarely literature in the traditional sense (e.g., a literary classic). While many films are works of cinematic art, most screenplays do not qualify as works of literary art. Some film classics, in fact, were even shot without a script (e.g, *The Birth of a Nation, Intolerance*).

While there are some published screenplays that read like literature (Ingmar Bergman's and Woody Allen's, for example), they are not always an accurate representation of the films. In his screenplay of *Through a Glass Darkly*, Bergman has Martin cut his finger; then Martin's wife, Karin, sucks the blood. From the way the incident is described in the screenplay, the reader would assume that Karin is behaving bizarrely. What happens on the screen is far less extreme: Martin cuts his finger, and Karin kisses it. When Bergman wrote the screenplay, he may have envisioned the scene differently. When he directed the scene, he apparently decided to make it less dramatic. Since a screenplay is prefilmic, it may contain material that never reached the screen. Likewise, the film on which it is based may include scenes that were not in the screenplay.

A screenplay can be compared with an opera libretto. While there are many great operas, there are few libretti that deserve to be studied as literature. Just as a libretto needs music, a screenplay needs visualization.

The screenplay is a *play*, but a play intended for the screen; it will therefore have some characteristics of drama. The screenplay is also a form of narrative; thus, it shares certain techniques with fiction. Like a play, a film can have a prologue and an epilogue. In film, however, the prologue can be either in the form of print (an opening title) or it can be dramatized in the form of a credits or precredits sequence. *Opening title* and *credits/precredits sequence* are, of course, terms peculiar to film; even so, they are prologues—in one case, a prologue involving the written word; in the other, a prologue involving visualized action.

Film also uses many techniques that are found in literature, the most famous of which is the flashback.

THE FLASHBACK

In ancient epic, the flashback was a way of incorporating material into the narrative that could not be added in any other way. For example, since the *Odyssey* begins ten years after the end of the Trojan War, the only way Homer could describe Odysseus' postwar adventures was by providing him with an occasion—a banquet—where he could recount them. In the *Aeneid*, Virgil, imitating Homer, likewise has Aeneas summarize at a banquet his seven years abroad.

The flashback has always been a favorite device of authors who start in the middle of an action (Milton's *Paradise Lost*) or whose narratives work from the present back to the past, where the explanation for the present resides (Thomas Pynchon's *V*). In a film, a flashback can be introduced by a slow fade-out/fade-in, a dissolve, a wipe, or a quick cut, and it serves three basic functions: (1) to furnish information that is otherwise unavailable; (2) to dramatize a past event even at the moment it is being narrated because the event cries out for visualization; and (3) to connect past and present when none of the characters are knowledgeable enough to do so.

The first function is self-explanatory, but the others require some examples. In Tennessee Williams's one-act play *Suddenly, Last Summer*, Catherine Holly, in one of the great monologues of the American stage, describes the death of her cousin Sebastian, whose flesh was devoured by the boys he had tried to debauch. The 1959 film version, directed by Joseph L. Mankiewicz, includes the monologue, which is also partly dramatized as it is being delivered. The monologue demands some visualization, and Mankiewicz provides it.

Although most flashbacks are memory flashbacks, not all are. Sometimes we are not within the consciousness of a character, but of the camera, so to speak. *Godfather II* is a flashback film, but not a memory film; no one in the movie is remembering the past, because no one knows enough about it. The purpose of the sequel to *The Godfather* is to integrate the lives of Vito Corleone and his son Michael. Since Vito is dead when the film opens, director Francis Ford Coppola could not crosscut the lives of father and son. Instead, he told Vito's story in flashback. *Godfather II* illustrates the impersonal flashback, which is not the result of a reminiscence, an inquest, or an investigation but, rather, the integration of the past with the present under the supervision of a central omniscience that can be termed the *omniscient camera* or the *omniscient filmmaker*. *Two for the Road* (1967) also illustrates the impersonal flashback. The film crosscuts a European trip a couple is making with incidents from previous trips. Because of the subtle way in which past and present intertwine, we never ask if it is the wife or the husband who is remembering. It is established at the outset that it is the camera—the same camera that had apparently accompanied them on their former jaunts.

While filmmakers have always been partial to the memory flashback, it is often poorly motivated. A character will say something banal like "It seems only yesterday that . . ." and the present will fade out and the past in. In the best memory flashbacks, an object provokes the reminiscence. In *Kitty Foyle* (1940), a glass paperweight with a girl on a sled inside it sets Kitty remembering; in *Penny Serenade*, phonograph records trigger a woman's memories of her marriage; in *Brute Force*, the picture of a woman on a calendar causes four convicts to remember the women in their lives.

There is an unusual flashback in *The Searchers* involving a letter that Martin has written to Laurie. At first, it seems as if the letter is being used to summarize what the audience will not be seeing. But that is not the case.

Some of what is in the letter has already been seen (e.g., the incident of the Indian woman who attached herself to Martin), but most of its contents are dramatized as it is being read. Because the sequence is so long, John Ford obtains some variety by alternating between Martin's voice as he writes the letter and Laurie's as she reads it.

THE FLASHFORWARD

A device that enjoyed popularity with filmmakers beginning in the 1960s was the flashforward, in which some aspect of an event is shown before it occurs. The flashforward is a distant relative of the literary device called *dramatic foreshadowing*, wherein one incident presages another, or some indication is given that an event is going to happen before it actually does. But the true ancestor of the flashforward is a rhetorical device termed *prolepsis*, in which a speaker anticipates and answers an objection before an opponent has even voiced it.

Sometimes what seems to be a flashforward isn't one. During the course of *They Shoot Horses, Don't They?* (1969), the narrator (Michael Sarrazin) speaks directly to the camera—or is he speaking to someone we cannot see? We discover at the end that he is speaking to a judge, explaining why he shot Gloria (Jane Fonda) at her request. The reason flashforwards succeed in *They Shoot Horses* is that from the audience's point of view they exist in the future, but from the narrator's they exist in the past. In retrospect, it becomes apparent that the entire film was a flashback told to a judge.

Because of their anticipatory force, proleptic devices can be dramatically effective. In George Stevens's *The Greatest Story Ever Told* (1965), after Pilate delivers Jesus to be crucified, an off-camera voice is heard saying, "And he suffered under Pontius Pilate." It is a compelling moment in the film, for it elevates a historical event to an article of faith without waiting for the Apostles' Creed to be written.

The way in which the credits appear on the screen often has a foreshadowing character. In *Saboteur*, during the credits the shadow of the saboteur moves from the right of the frame into the center. Billy Wilder used the same technique in *Double Indemnity*; in that film the shadowy figure is on crutches, a prefiguration of the result of Dietrichson's accident, which will make murdering him a bit more complicated.

Sometimes a shot has the impact of a flashforward although it is really a comment on an earlier incident. Well after the midpoint of *The Story of Adele H.*, François Truffaut inserts a shot of Adele on the Isle of Guernsey, gloriously confident as she prepares to sail for Halifax to reclaim the affections of Lieutenant Pinson. Her voice is equally self-assured: "This incredible thing—that a young girl shall walk over the sea, from the Old into the New World, to join her lover—this, I shall accomplish." Obviously this is an Adele we have not seen before, since the film begins with her arrival in Halifax. Truffaut inserts the shot where he does to mark the end of Adele's fruitless quest and the beginning of her descent into madness. If the shot had appeared at the opening, it would simply have been a prologue. Because it appears where it does, it has the force of dramatic irony: Adele did make a journey from the Old World to the New, but it was also a journey from one form of neurotic behavior (obsession) to another (self-inflicted degradation). At the very end of the film, Truffaut repeats the shot, this time drained of its color and looking like a faded photograph. Adele's voyage is now just an item of memorabilia.

POINT OF VIEW

Like a work of literature, a film can be narrated in the first or the third person. A first-person film, one recounted by an "I" in the same way as Dickens's *Great Expectations* is recounted by Pip and Sartre's *Nausea* by Roquentin—that is, an "I" who begins speaking at the outset and continues right up to the end—is rare. (*Double Indemnity* comes close, with all but the very beginning and the very end narrated by Neff.) What generally happens in film is that a voice-over of the "I" is heard at the beginning and perhaps intermittently thereafter. The semidocumentary may seem to be an exception, since it is first-person narration throughout; however, the narrator is not a character but a disembodied voice. When the voice intrudes periodically, it acts like a fade-out, demarcating the film into narrative blocks.

Something similar happens in *Radio Days*, which is narrated by an adult who is seen only as a child in the film. If *Radio Days* has a distinctly literary quality and seems like a filmed short story, it is because continuous first-person narrative calls attention to itself as narrative. There is also a credibility problem if the "I" relates something to which it would not have had access. Despite the excellence of *Radio Days*, even Woody Allen has difficulty explaining how a grade-school boy can know what he does.

A film need not use "I" narration to achieve other first-person effects that suggest the first person without the presence of the narrating "I": subjective camera and subjective sound. (We have already discussed these techniques in chapter 3.) In subjective camera, the camera doubles as a character so that we are aware of both an "I" and an "eye," as in the slasher movies, when the camera looks in through the window from the outside. There the camera is both an "I" (the predator) and an "eye" (the predator's eye and, by extension, ours).

Thus, point of view in subjective camera is not that of an "it" but of an "I," a definite presence relating something to the viewer as an "I" would relate something to a "you." Subjective sound is similar: when a character hears something, the character is no longer a "he" or a "she" but an "I" telling "us" what he or she is thinking or hearing.

It is important to remember that voice-over narration does not necessarily mean a first-person film. Since the voice tends to come and go, one soon forgets there is a narrator. Far more important is to see how film emulates first-person narrative through subjective camera and subjective sound.

Omniscient Author

In fiction, the omniscient author tells the story in the third person, moving from place to place, time to time, and character to character, disclosing or concealing details at will.[2] The film equivalent, omniscient camera, is best seen in multiplot films or films that move back and forth in time. When the camera is omniscient, it behaves very much like an omniscient author. The camera in *Nashville* is omniscient. It can leave a freeway crack-up and move on to a hospital to look in on country singer Barbara Jean recovering from one of her breakdowns. It can abandon the Reese home for the local tavern, a nightclub for a smoker, a church for an automobile graveyard.

Omniscient authors can be intrusive if they pass judgment on what is seen, unintrusive if they suspend judgment. The camera can do likewise because omniscience does not mean impartiality. In *The Day of the Locust*, Homer Simpson (Donald Sutherland) is sitting in a wicker chair in the backyard of his Hollywood home. An orange drops from a bough with the sound of ripe fruit. In the yard above his, a woman looks down on this scene of otherworldly tranquillity. There is ripeness in her face, but it is the overripeness of rotting fruit. The camera has said nothing, but by moving from Homer to the woman, it makes its own comment on Hollywood as the earthly paradise for those who bask in the glow of an endless summer and those who decompose in it.

Instead of traveling back and forth among the characters, authors can select one of them as a "center of consciousness," to use Henry James's phrase, or as a "reflector" through whose eyes readers will view the action. In film, the reflector method works well when the script involves a character trapped by his or her fantasies or victimized by some neurosis. In *The Lost Weekend*, Billy Wilder draws us into the consciousness of Don (Ray Milland), an alcoholic. Don becomes a genuine reflector; we share his experiences even when they are portrayed objectively, as they often are. Early in the film, there is a scene in which Don is watching *La Traviata* and develops an uncontrollable urge to drink during the first-act "Drinking Song." Wilder cuts from Don to the stage, where Violetta and Alfredo are toasting each other, and back again to Don. So far the camera has been objective: what Don has been seeing on the stage is what everyone else in the audience has been seeing. But not everyone in the audience is an alcoholic; thus, Wilder allows the camera to turn subjective at this point as Don sees, superimposed against the stage, the checkroom where his raincoat is hanging, a bottle in one of the pockets. We clearly understand his craving and the effect the "Drinking Song" has had on him.

The Implied Author (Author's Second Self)

Some fiction is written so impersonally that it appears to be authorless. Hemingway's "The Killers" is often cited as the kind of story that seems to have been written by a scientist rather than a novelist. In "The Killers," Hemingway obliterated his actual self and created a second self who mediates between Ernest Hemingway and the story that bears his name. Filmmakers can do likewise; they can suppress or mask their personal feelings so that they do not interfere with the film. This *implied author* method usually results in an impersonal movie because it does not encourage emotional involvement; as a result, this kind of movie does not reach a high level of emotional intensity.

Barry Lyndon is such a film. First, it is Stanley Kubrick's *Barry Lyndon*, not William Makepeace Thackeray's; and it is Kubrick's film completely: he not only produced and directed it but he also wrote the screenplay. To say that Kubrick remains aloof from his characters is not the same as saying that he shuns them. The implied author approach is not emotional evasion; it is emotional noninvolvement. Kubrick was more interested in the characters as embodiments of their age than in the characters as human beings.

In adapting *Barry Lyndon* for the screen, Kubrick was dealing with a novel written in the nineteenth century but set in the eighteenth. Thus, the tone had to be Victorian and the atmosphere neoclassical. Kubrick achieved an eighteenth-century air by framing scenes in the style of painters of that era—Watteau, Dayes, and Gainsborough—and by orchestrating them with selections from Bach, Handel, Vivaldi, and Mozart. He re-created a Victorian tone by using an off-camera narrator whose voice was fittingly snobbish.

Seeing *Barry Lyndon* is like viewing a painting. A great painting draws a viewer toward it; but once the viewer is face-to-face with it, instinctively walks backward to see it from a distance. Kubrick uses the same technique. He begins with a close-up; he then gracefully withdraws until he is satisfied with the distance between the audience and the image. *Barry*

The famous *Barry Lyndon* candlelight. All the candlelight scenes were photographed with a special Zeiss lens and entirely with natural light. *(Courtesy Warner Bros., Inc.)*

Lyndon is like a tour of the world's great museums. The glow of candlelight is not the smoky haze it usually is in most films; specially created lenses give the candlelight in *Barry Lyndon* the look of melting gold. Light floods a window, not in neat spotlighting cones but in a burst of silver. To achieve such beauty, Kubrick had to sacrifice a certain amount of emotion.

FILM ADAPTATION

One common type of film is the adaptation of a novel, a story, or a play. The adaptation, however, occasions the greatest amount of criticism because the material has already appeared in another form that becomes the standard against which the film version is compared; hence, the often repeated charge, "Well, it wasn't the book (or the play)." There is only one answer to that charge: it wasn't intended to be. The adaptation is *a* version, not *the* version, since there can be several film versions of a particular novel or play. Which *Phantom of the Opera* is Gaston Leroux's novel *The Phantom of the Opera?* The 1925 version, the 1943 version, or the 1962 version?

Adaptation is not as simple as one might think. It is a given that the film version will differ from the original. Why else would a filmmaker adapt a work for the screen, and why should audiences be expected to see the adaptation if they have read the book or seen the play? The adaptation must be different—but how different? The adaptation may preserve the essence of the original, even though it alters plot details (perhaps even drastically), adds or eliminates characters, and changes the conclusion so that it is the opposite of what it was in the original.

 ## Adaptations of Novels

The Color Purple (Steven Spielberg, 1986)

Alice Walker's Pulitzer Prize–winning novel, *The Color Purple*, was not easy to adapt for the screen. On one level, it is a novel about written expression and the need to articulate feelings which, if they cannot be expressed orally, must be committed to paper, and, if they cannot be addressed to the right person, must be addressed to God. Clearly, it would be difficult to present this philosophy on the screen, yet the film repeats the exact words with which the novel opens: *"You better not never tell nobody but God. It'll kill your mammy."* These words are addressed to Celie, a fourteen-year-old black girl, by her "Pa." Actually, he is her stepfather, but at this point Celie does not know this. She only knows that Pa, whose real name is Alphonso (in the novel, several characters are not known by their real names), has raped her and that the two children she bore were taken from her shortly after birth.

Forbidden to speak of her suffering and shame to another person,

Whoopi Goldberg as Celie in *The Color Purple* (Steven Spielberg, 1986). *(Courtesy MOMA/FSA and Warner Bros., Inc.)*

Celie begins a series of letters to God. Thus, *The Color Purple* is an epistolary novel, consisting of Celie's letters to God, her sister Nettie's letters to
her, and Celie's letters to Nettie. As we saw in chapter 2, the letter is a
commonly used narrative device. However, a work that is both epistolary
and a justification of the epistolary method must be modified considerably
for the screen. While we can accept hearing some of the correspondence
through voice-over narration or seeing some of it in title form on the
screen, the bulk of the correspondence must be visualized.

Celie's correspondence, in particular, is filled with such drama that
its contents can be visualized linearly, as moviegoers prefer. The story
spans some thirty-four years, and although the novel specifies no particular time frame, the film does: 1909 to (approximately) 1943, with superimposed titles (Spring 1909, Fall 1930) to mark the passing of the years.

Menno Meyjes's screenplay repeats the novel's main episodes, although, like any adaptation, with alterations. Pa gives Celie in marriage to
a man she calls Mr. in her letters, although his name is Albert. When
Nettie spurns Mr.'s advances, he angrily ejects her from the house, sepa-
rating the sisters for more than thirty years. Nettie, who eventually becomes an African missionary, writes to Celie, but Mr. confiscates the
letters. It is only through the blues singer Shug Avery that Celie learns
about the letters and manages to obtain them. Shug also becomes Celie's
lover, offering her the warmth and affection that she has been denied.
Ultimately, Shug's effect on Celie is salutary; soon Celie is a successful
pants manufacturer. Eventually she learns the truth about Pa and is reunited with both Nettie and her children.

Just as a film has a subtext, so does a novel. But while the novel's narrative may transfer well to the screen, its subtext may not do so fully.
Subtextually, the novel *The Color Purple* is about language as a vehicle of
communication. Denied an education, Celie can write only in southern-
black dialect; Nettie, who has been educated, writes in standard English.
Celie's letters provide the narrative; Nettie's provide a perspective and a
commentary on the narrative.

As King-Kok Cheung has shown, the novel is an exploration of the
nature of the written word.[3] When Celie learns that Pa is not her natural
father, her perception of God changes from a "He" to an "it" that transcends gender. Once Celie stops regarding God as a substitute for a correspondent, her letters become more complex as she begins describing
instead of merely recounting and, at times, writing metaphorically instead
of literally. Epistolary change, however, is outside the domain of the film.
Menno Meyjes had to make certain choices, one of which was to give
Nettie's letters a purely narrative function so they could fill in details that
Celie would not have known. Since Nettie's letters are for the most part
nondramatic, Spielberg generates some drama by having them visualized

while Celie is reading them. While Celie is on her porch reading Nettie's description of life in Africa, an elephant appears in the background. When Celie is in church reading about the destruction of an African church, a bulldozer comes through the altar of the church where she is sitting. Concurrent visualization at least suggests the effect of language on the imagination, which is one of the novel's main points.

Not everything, however, can be transferred from novel to film. In the novel, Celie leaves Albert after she discovers that he has withheld Nettie's letters from her. She does the same in the film (although more dramatically as she unleashes all the anger and bitterness that has built up inside her). In the novel, after Celie becomes a successful businessperson, Albert reenters her life. Celie bears him no animosity; indeed, she teaches him to sew, and soon he is making shirts to go with the pants that she sells. Albert even asks her to return to him, but Celie declines. Still, they become friends and remain such. The screenwriter, however, eliminated this reconciliation from the movie.

Although in the novel Celie's behavior is exemplary, most women, especially those who have undergone similar mistreatment, would find her reconciliation with Albert hard to take. While reading the novel, however, one can rethink, reread, and ponder; even though the reader may initially find it troubling that Celie would resume any kind of a relationship with Albert, this feeling may change to understanding once the reader realizes that Celie has grown in such a way that her inner peace and resolve allow her to forgive him.

The reader, however, did not *see* Celie's brutalization or witness Albert's attempt to rape Nettie; the reader was not present when Celie gave birth or when Albert unloosened each of Nettie's fingers as she clung to the doorpost, begging him not to send her away. The moviegoer, on the other hand, has seen all of this, and having seen it, could not accept a Celie who takes her husband back as a companion.

There is another reason for the omission of the Albert-Celie reconciliation in the film: it would eclipse the climactic reconciliation of Celie, Nettie, and Celie's children. The film builds up to this with two other reconciliations, each involving one of the other main female characters: Sofia with her family, and Shug with her father, the Preacher. The free-spirited Sofia leaves her husband and children but is reconciled with them after a lengthy prison sentence—the result of her public refusal to be the maid of the mayor's neurotic wife. In the novel, there is no mention of Shug's father; however, to soften the character of Shug, Meyjes introduces the Preacher, from whom Shug is estranged because of her lifestyle. Meyjes was influenced by an episode in the novel in which Shug states that she never found God in church. The reason might well have had to do with the way God was presented to her, perhaps by a minister; perhaps, even, by a minister who was her father. This is an example of the way an adapter's mind works: the novel affords clues about the character's background that are not developed in the written narrative. These clues can be embroidered to serve the adapter's purpose when the narrative is visualized. In one of the film's many moving scenes, Shug is entertaining servicemen at Harpo's waterfront bar while, across the water, she hears gospel singing from her father's church. Inspired by the music, she and the band make their way to the church, where father and daughter are reconciled. "See, Daddy; sinners have soul," Shug says as they embrace. The two preliminary reconciliations are arranged as emotional peaks, the second surpassing the first and both pointing to the grand reconciliation of the sisters at the end.

Interestingly, in the film Albert plays a role in the sisters' ultimate reunion. While he will not be reunited with Celie, he can change, as he did in the novel; his change must be made more acceptable to a movie audience than his learning to sew, which is symbolic rather than dramatic. Since *The Color Purple* is not a film in which the characters are virtuous or villainous, Albert is given a chance to perform one decent act. When a letter arrives from the immigration department apparently about Nettie's return to America, Albert does not hide it but seeks out the immigration officials and arranges for Nettie's trip. The film, then, comes full circle thematically: Albert, who separated the sisters, is, in a sense, partly responsible for their reunion—which he witnesses from a distance. The film also comes full circle visually. It begins in 1909 with the sisters clapping their hands together in a sunlit field, singing, "Us never part / Us have one heart / Ain't no land / Ain't no sea / Can keep you away from me"; it ends in 1943 with the sisters, now middle-aged women, clapping their hands together in the dusk.

Visually, *The Color Purple* is a film of artful simplicity. While Spielberg has an arsenal of techniques that he has built up from his vast knowledge of film, he does not allow technology to overwhelm the human values of the story. Irises and wipes, two of his favorite devices, are absent, since they are more appropriate to an Indiana Jones movie than to one about a black woman's struggle to achieve a sense of worth. However, Spielberg cannot resist a natural fade-out. When Celie asks Albert whether there is any mail, the camera replies by tracking into the dark interior of the mailbox, causing the screen to go dark.

Anyone directing *The Color Purple* would be confronted with a dilemma about how to film Celie. Although the story is essentially Celie's, she cannot be the visual focus of attention. Since she has been denied a significant role in life, Spielberg puts her in the extremity of the frame or in the background. She is often photographed over someone's shoulder or seen at the window as an onlooker rather than as a participant. When she first sees Albert, for example, it is through a window. (Ironically, after she becomes a success, she glances through her store window and sees Albert in the street, the roles of outsider/insider now reversed.) Celie comes into her space for the first time, in close-up and medium close-up, in the love scene with Shug. As Shug expresses her feelings for Celie, each puts her hands on the other's shoulders, while the camera pans right to a tinkling glass mobile. This scene demonstrates another interesting aspect of the film: the human hand is used as a central image.

In earlier scenes, Celie and Nettie clap their hands together and embrace; in a particularly moving sequence, Nettie's fingers have to be dislodged individually from the doorpost. A hand can offer a gesture of affection or be a means of inflicting pain. If it holds a razor or a knife, it can shave, carve, or kill. Spielberg conjoins two separate incidents from the novel that involve hands and sharp instruments. After Celie discovers that Albert has concealed Nettie's letters from her, she is on the verge of cutting his throat while shaving him, until Shug intervenes. In one of her letters from Africa, Nettie describes a ritual initiation that leaves the face scarred. Spielberg crosscuts Celie's sharpening the razor with the preparations for the ritual, form-cutting from razor to knives, from Celie's holding a razor under Albert's neck to hands holding knives against the faces of the children in Africa. By combining two separate incidents into one crosscut sequence, Spielberg creates a contrast between a crime of murder and a rite of passage. The former is interrupted, the latter completed.

Since every great film should have a subtext, what is *The Color Purple*'s? As has already been suggested, the novel's subtext is the written word and its connection with those who use it. Film cannot deal with a subtext so specifically verbal, but it can suggest written texts. As a victim of oppression, Celie recalls other literary characters who also suffered indignities and abuse, the most famous being Oliver Twist. In the film, Charles Dickens's *Oliver Twist* plays an important role, although it is not even mentioned in the novel.

In the film, Nettie, on her way to school, is intercepted by Albert. Dropping her books, she runs away. One of the books—and a close-up makes certain we see the title—is *Oliver Twist*. This is the same book from which Celie learns to read, and the text that she repeats has special relevance to her own situation: "For the next eight or ten months Oliver was the victim of a systematic course of treachery and deception."

Despite its realistic plot, *Oliver Twist* relies heavily, as most of Dickens's novels do, on coincidence; to some extent, so does *The Color Purple*, although Walker's coincidences are not quite as contrived as Dickens's. For example, the two children whom Celie bears and who are taken from her are raised by a local missionary couple and christened Adam and Olivia. After Albert expels Nettie from the farm, she is befriended by this couple. Nettie accompanies them to Africa, along with Olivia and Adam. Thus, Celie's sister and her children are together; and when Nettie, Olivia, and Adam return to America, Celie is reunited both with the sister she has not seen since she was fourteen and the children she has not seen since their birth.

Menno Meyjes expects the viewer to recognize Oliver Twist and Celie as kin. Both are victims of "treachery and deception," yet through a combination of chance events and spiritual strength, both triumph over adversity, receive their rightful inheritance, and are reconciled with their families. Even if one has not read *Oliver Twist*, Celie evokes every victimized figure (from Joseph of the Old Testament to Cinderella) who ultimately came into his or her own.

On another level, Alice Walker's *The Color Purple* is about God, whose existence is so evident throughout the universe that it cannot be ignored. As Shug explains to Celie, "I think it pisses God off if you walk by the color purple in a field somewhere and don't notice it." God's love of humankind, as manifested in the bounty of creation, is as obvious as the color purple, which is too eye-catching to dismiss.

In the film, the color purple is also the color of nature, the color of natural innocence. The film opens with the sisters racing through a field of purple flowers. When Albert makes his advances toward Nettie, she drops her books on a dusty road strewn with purple petals that presage the end of innocence and the separation of the sisters. At the end of the film, the sisters stand in the same field of purple flowers, now muted in color by the setting sun.

While Shug speaks the same line to Celie in the film as she did in the novel, it is now associated with the opening/closing motif. Celie's worth should be as obvious as the color purple; that it is not is another indication of humankind's inability to see what is most clearly delineated.

As an adaptation, *The Color Purple* retains the integrity of Alice Walker's novel; yet, by devising analogous subtexts, Spielberg and Meyjes have made a genuine film, not a filmed novel.

Emma/Clueless/Emma: Jane Austen from Highbury to Beverly Hills—and Back

Anyone contemplating a screen version of Jane Austen's *Emma* (1815) must deal with the following:

1. A decent but self-absorbed and manipulative heroine, Emma Woodhouse, who lives with her widower father in class-conscious Highbury, not far from London. Emma's social status guarantees her a privileged existence spent, for the most part, in meddling in

Alicia Silverstone (left) as Cher, the Emma figure in *Clueless* (1995); and Stacy Dash as Dionne, Amy Heckerling's substitution for Jane Austen's Jane Fairfax. *(Courtesy Paramount Pictures and MOMA/FSA)*

other people's lives. Emma decides to play matchmaker for the illegitimate Harriet Smith, who idolizes her and never questions her judgment. When a farmer, Robert Martin, shows an interest in Harriet, Emma discourages the relationship. Instead, she steers Harriet toward the vicar, Mr. Elton, who is interested in Emma, not in Harriet. When Elton expresses his true feelings, Emma is shocked. The Emmas of the world do not live in parsonages. Elton eventually finds a wife, who becomes increasingly more overbearing as Emma becomes more understanding after she realizes the consequences of interfering in other people's lives.

2. Emma's foil—her brother-in-law, Mr. Knightley, some sixteen years older than she and capable of seeing her faults as well as reminding her of them. Knightly seems to be the least likely partner for Emma. Austen, however, knows better and artfully brings them together so that the novel can end with their wedding.

3. A world in which men and women eventually make the right match although it may not have been the one the reader had been

expecting. But this is part of Austen's technique: to keep us wondering who will pair off with whom. Harriet—for whom Emma had singled out Elton, and then Frank Churchill—ends up with the man who wanted her from the beginning: Robert Martin. And Frank Churchill, who did not seem especially interested in Jane Fairfax, ends up marrying her. That leaves only Knightley and Emma, whose marriage brings the novel to its conclusion.

For this kind of plot to succeed, each potential relationship must also be probable. One could, for example, imagine the union of Jane and Knightley, or even of Harriet and Knightley; when Elton snubs Harriet at a ball, Knightley saves her from embarrassment by dancing with her. One could also imagine the union of Harriet and Churchill, who rescues her from a band of Gypsies. Austen creates situations that are so realistic that any of these pairings is possible; she also convinces us that the marriage partner each character chooses is the right one.

Clueless (1995)

Anyone updating Emma will naturally alter, discard, or find equivalents for some of the narrative details or even the characters; still, the adapter must be faithful to the spirit, if not the letter, of the novel by including the following:

1. An affluent and motherless household in which Emma is indulged by her father
2. Emma's obsession with meddling and matchmaking
3. Emma's eventual realization that her judgment of others is faulty
4. A sense of uncertainty on the viewer's part about the resolution of the various relationships
5. The union of Emma and a family member who is not a blood relative.

Amy Heckerling, who both wrote and directed Clueless—an unusually intelligent and occasionally touching version of Emma—moves the time ahead to the 1990s and the setting to Beverly Hills. Emma becomes Cher (Alicia Silverstone), who is about five years younger than Austen's heroine and is still a high-school student. Mel, her father, is an affluent lawyer, who indulges Emma's passion for designer clothes and Rodeo Drive shopping sprees. Cher's mother, like Emma's, died soon after she was born; but unlike Emma, Cher has no sister. She does, however, have a slightly older stepbrother (not thirty-seven but around twenty)—Josh, the son of Mel's second wife from a previous marriage. Although Mel and Josh's mother are divorced, Josh is attending UCLA and frequently visits with Mel and Cher. Thus, Cher and Josh see each other frequently—like Emma and Knightley. Moreover, as the script emphasizes (but not overly so), they are not blood relatives.

Because he is a college student with a social conscience, Josh is the equivalent of Knightley, calling Cher's attention to her shortcomings, which include a total indifference to world affairs. After watching a television news report on the war in Bosnia, Cher remarks that she thought there was peace in the Middle East.

Having chosen to make Austen's three couples—with the exception of Josh—high-school students, Heckerling had to find an equivalent for class-conscious Highbury. For Beverly Hills teenagers, the equivalent would be a high school not unlike the one featured in the television series *Beverly Hills 90210*. No one is poor in this school, but there is the right racial, social, and ethnic mix to suggest a microcosmic society where distinctions are made according to dress, grades, sexual orientation, and behavior. In this world, which is not all that different from the so-called real one, Cher and her friend Dionne, with their fashionable clothes and cell phones, legislate for those who are too insecure to be themselves.

Just as Harriet was unable to assert her individuality in *Emma*, so, too, is Tai, her equivalent in *Clueless*. Tai, the new student—a gawky but sexually experienced young woman who thinks of coke not as a soft drink but as a drug—is the perfect candidate for a Cher and Dionne makeover. Tai becomes their creation, with hairstyle, makeup, and clothes selected by them. Just as Harriet was attracted to the farmer Robert Martin in the novel, Tai is drawn to someone like herself—the class clown and skateboarder, Travis. And just as Emma discouraged a relationship with Martin and directed Harriet to Elton, Cher steers Tai toward another Elton. Since Heckerling had deliberately chosen the name of Austen's character, she obviously wanted to replicate two scenes from the novel that involve Elton: one in which he faked concern for Harriet in order to ingratiate himself with Emma; the other in which he shocked Emma by declaring his intentions toward her.

Similarly, Heckerling's Elton is solicitous of Tai because he wants to impress Emma; Heckerling's Elton expresses his feelings for Cher in a car, as his namesake did in a carriage. Cher is so outraged that she bolts from the car and is left in a deserted area, where she is mugged. (A similar incident occurred in the novel when Harriet's purse is taken by Gypsies. Heckerling has Cher's mugger take her purse and cell phone.)

Since Austen hinted at a possible union of Harriet and Knightley in the episode in which he dances with her, Heckerling cleverly has Josh dance with Tai when she is consistently ignored. Finally, when Tai has succeeded in ridding herself of any feelings for Elton—realizing that her true soul mate is Travis—she burns mementos of her infatuation with Elton, as Harriet did in the novel.

Heckerling realized that Austen's Jane Fairfax and Frank Churchill, a talented but financially dependent woman and an affluent but self-indulgent man, could never meet in the setting she had created. Instead, she substitutes an African-American couple, Murray and Dionne; Murray is a chauvinist who insists on calling Dionne "woman," and Dionne is a feminist who resents sexist language. Murray and Dionne become mirror images of Josh and Cher. Each couple must change, abandoning misconceptions in favor of a deeper awareness of the partner's uniqueness—failings included.

Once Heckerling had substituted Dionne and Murray (who clearly have eyes only for each other) for Jane and Churchill, she could suggest nothing between Tai and Murray. Instead, she created the character of Christian, who dresses like James Dean but whose favorite films are *Some Like It Hot*, which revolves around cross-dressing, and *Spartacus* (1960), in which Laurence Olivier plays a homosexual who does not hide his attraction for Antoninus (Tony Curtis). When Christian shows Cher his *Spartacus* video, his interest is not in her but in the film—particularly the Olivier-Curtis scene. Although Christian could easily have become a stereotype, Heckerling understands that Austen's satire is gentle, not vicious. Austen can poke fun at her characters and reveal their shortcomings, but she does not make them objects of ridicule. In a scene that further reveals Cher's lack of insight, Murray explains to her that Christian is gay, using language that is both street-smart and literary (he explicitly refers to Oscar Wilde). To Heckerling's credit, there is no trace of homophobic contempt in his remarks. Murray—and Dionne as well—can accept what Cher cannot even comprehend.

Any version of *Emma* should include three weddings, which poses a problem if the three heroines are still in high school. Thus, the film cannot end with the marriage of Cher and Josh. But it must end with a wedding. What Heckerling has done is to take two characters—Emma's tutor and Mr. Weston, who have just married as the novel begins—and turn them into two unmarried teachers at the high school: Miss Geist and Mr. Hall, who teach political science and debate, respectively. Motivated partly by her desire to get a better grade in debate and partly by her mania for matchmaking, Cher, with Dionne's help, keeps bringing the two teachers closer together until the inevitable occurs. Present at their wedding are the three couples who will be having their own weddings in a few years.

Clueless offers many rewards for those who are able to view it as less a youth-oriented film than a modern version of a classic that takes liberties with the original but always remains faithful to its spirit.

Gwyneth Paltrow (Emma) and Jeremy Northam (Mr. Knightley), in *Emma* (1996). (*Courtesy Miramax Films and the Margaret Herrick Library of the Academy of Motion Picture Arts and Sciences*)

Emma (1996).

A year after *Clueless* was released, a literal adaptation of *Emma* arrived on the screen. In adapting *Emma*, Doug McGrath, who also directed the film, remained faithful to the novel in both spirit and letter, going so far as to use much of Austen's own language. He has also succeeded—in so far as it is possible for film to do this with a third-person narrative and an omniscient point of view—in re-creating the novel on the screen. Through omniscience, Austen could enter the minds of the characters, noting their moods and actions and commenting on them. Despite the freedom that omniscience gives a novelist, however, Austen used it judiciously in *Emma*, preferring to present as much of the action as she could from Emma's point of view. Heckerling realized this and thus used voice-over narration in *Clueless*—but only from Cher, who becomes the real narrator, commenting on her own behavior and gradually reaching some level of self-knowledge. McGrath also uses voice-over, but he has succeeded in making it more than a film convention; for the most part, voice-over occurs when Emma (Gwyneth Paltrow) writes in her diary—the closest any adapter can come to evoking Austen's reflections on her characters. Toward the end of the film, in a scene that does not exist in the novel, we even hear Emma's silent prayer in a chapel.

True to Austen, McGrath portrays Highbury as a world unto itself, insulated from anything as mundane as international affairs. Highbury's parochialism is apparent in the credits, during which a planet spins in the galaxy, growing larger as it moves closer into the frame. We soon recognize it as Earth—but not the planet to which we are accustomed. This planet consists of one country, Britain, which is made up of only London and Highbury; soon London disappears, leaving only Highbury.

McGrath also succeeded in having the actors play the potential couples in such a way that any union might be possible. When Frank Churchill joins Jane Fairfax for a duet, he sings with far greater enthusiasm than he did with Emma, who had accompanied him at the piano earlier. On the other hand, when Harriet lies on the ground after being robbed by Gypsies, Churchill extends his hand to her; McGrath cuts to a close-up of their clasped hands. Are they clasped because he is literally bringing her to her feet? Or is this a sign of a budding romance? And why does Knightley, who tells Emma he cannot dance, dance so well with Harriet?

Like Austen, McGrath makes the picnic at Box Hill the turning point. Churchill insists upon a game in which everyone makes one or two witty remarks or three dull ones. When the garrulous Miss Bates jokes that whatever she says will be dull, Emma replies that, at least on this occasion, her dull comments will be limited in number. Knightley realizes the pain that Emma's words have caused Miss Bates and reproaches her for lack of consideration. It is at this point in both the novel and the film that Emma's remorse makes her determined to rise in Knightley's estimation—something one does only if the other party is worth the effort.

But as well written and directed as *Clueless* and *Emma* are, audience reaction depends, to a great extent, on the performances of the leads. Neither Cher nor Emma can be just the typical spoiled brat or "Daddy's little girl," although each is a bit of both. Nor can they be vicious: glib, insensitive, self-centered, haughty—yes; but deliberately cruel—no. That each moves from the extremes of self-love to love of other is a tribute to the directors and the writers (and in both films the director *is* the writer) but also to the talents of Alicia Silverstone and Gwyneth Paltrow.

Adaptation of Plays

A play must be "opened up" for the screen; this is particularly important in the case of single-set plays, many of which are among the theater's finest: *The Little Foxes, A Streetcar Named Desire, Come Back, Little Sheba, Who's Afraid of Virginia Woolf?, Long Day's Journey into Night*, and others. Musicals like *The King and I* and *Evita* pose fewer problems because of their multiple settings. Here are some of the traditional ways to open up a play in which the action is limited to one or two places:

Dramatize or visualize material that had to be narrated because it could not be shown on the stage. William Inge's play *Picnic* (1953) takes place in a yard between two houses in a small Kansas town. Thus, the Labor Day picnic, which inspired the title (and which is a vital element of the plot), is never seen. Since the play dramatized the way a stranger's arrival on a Labor Day morning altered the lives of all the characters, for the 1956 film version screenwriter Daniel Taradash transferred the most dramatic scenes in the play to the picnic, where the characters revealed their true nature and innermost thoughts. And director Josh Logan used the picnic to provide audiences with a vivid depiction of an end-of-summer ritual in rural America.

Gore Vidal, who adapted Tennessee Williams's *Suddenly, Last Summer* (1958), added more scenes since the play had only one set: a garden. In the play, Catherine Holly had been committed to Lion's View State Asylum because she was considered insane. By showing Catherine (Elizabeth Taylor) at Lion's View, Vidal and director Joseph L. Mankiewicz were also able to portray the horrible conditions that existed there. Since the plot hinges on whether Catherine will be lobotomized, the film opens with a lobotomy being performed in an operating theater. Most important, as Catherine delivers her climactic monologue, in which she recounts the hideous death of her cousin Sebastian, details of the incident and events leading up to it are shown on the screen.

Visualize symbols so that they cease to be abstract. The "streetcar" in *A Streetcar Named Desire* is both symbolic and real. It is the mode of transportation that takes Blanche duBois to her sister's home, where she hoped to escape from a sordid and painful past. Film allows us to see the streetcar, which, from the outset, is associated with Blanche, since it was instrumental in bringing her into an environment where she would eventually be destroyed. In another Tennessee Williams play that became a successful film, *The Night of the Iguana* (1962), the iguana, which is tied to a rope and kept under the porch, could not be seen on the stage; yet it is a symbol of the nonconformist (perhaps the artist), whose movements society tries to restrict because those who deviate from the norm often threaten those who have sworn to uphold it. While it is not really necessary to see the iguana, John Huston, who directed the 1964 movie version, obviously knew that audiences expected it; and seeing the iguana, which does not conform to the traditional notion of beauty, highlights the point that Williams was making.

Move some incidents to other locations to achieve variety. Lillian Hellman had no other choice but to have the villain of her play, *Watch on the Rhine* (1941), killed in the living room, since the entire action was set there. The 1943 movie version transfers the murder to the garage. In the play *Streetcar,* Blanche tells Mitch about the suicide of her husband after they return from the Moon Lake Casino. The film allows Blanche to tell Mitch at the Casino itself.

Create a character from a name merely mentioned in the play or create a new character to pair off with one who does appear in the play. In the film version of *Tea and Sympathy*, Ellie—who in the play is known only as the prostitute with whom Tom Lee failed so abominably that he attempted suicide—not only appears as a character but the encounter between herself and Tom is depicted as well. At the end of the play *The Little Foxes* (1939), Alexandra knows that her mother, Regina, was responsible for her father's death. When the 1941 film version was released, the Production Code required some kind of retribution; thus the original ending, in which Alexandra stays on to remind Regina of what she has done, might make it seem that Regina had not atoned for her actions. In the film, therefore, Alexandra leaves home with a young man, David Hewitt, who did not exist in the play but was created for the film so that Alexandra could be paired off with him—and Regina would be left alone with her guilt.

Not every major play has been adapted for the screen as successfully as *Streetcar*, *Picnic*, and *The Little Foxes*.

In Marsha Norman's Pulitzer Prize–winning one-act play, *'Night Mother* (1983), a daughter tells her mother that she plans to commit suicide that night. The play observes the three unities of Greek tragedy: unity of action (one main plot), unity of place (one setting), and unity of time (the time covered in the play is identical to the time required to perform it). The plot of *'Night, Mother* is structured in such a way that a film version would also have to observe the unities. In the 1986 film version, the action was opened up a bit, but not enough to keep the moving images from becoming static pictures. Paul Newman's 1986 film version of Tennessee Williams's *The Glass Menagerie* had similar problems. Because of his great respect for the text, Newman scarcely opened up the action at all, and the result was like watching a photographed play.

Thus, strict fidelity to a work of literature does not necessarily result in a good film. Purists may be delighted that the text is intact, but moviegoers expect "moving pictures."

THE NATURE OF SCREENWRITING

If adaptation, which is merely one kind of screenwriting, is difficult, screenwriting in general can hardly be easy. Distinguished authors like William Faulkner and F. Scott Fitzgerald tried to write for the screen, but what they produced pales in comparison with their fiction. Fitzgerald genuinely wanted to write film scripts, but those that he wrote either contained dialogue the actors found impossible to speak, or were so cluttered with description that they had to be pruned drastically. Fitzgerald's talent lay in fiction, where he could narrate or describe without dramatizing, rather than in screenwriting, where he would have to suppress the urge to tell everything through words and delegate some authority to the camera.

The ideal screenplay advances the plot in two ways: verbally, through dialogue, and visually, through action. If a screenplay were total dialogue, there would be no difference between a screenplay and a stage play. Screenwriters must visualize the action as they write it. When the visual might be more effective than the verbal, the writer must suppress the desire to rely on dialogue and instead must indicate how the action can be visualized.

Julia has a literate—that is, well written and intelligently executed—script by Alvin Sargent, yet there are parts of the film that contain no dialogue at all. Sargent knew when language was necessary to advance the plot, and when images were. For example, the scene in which Lillian is watching a performance of *Hamlet* in Moscow is crosscut with Julia's murder in Frankfurt. Sargent realized it would be more effective to have the murder take place without any dialogue at all so there would be a contrast with the performance of *Hamlet*, where dialogue is essential. Thus, a further contrast results: verbalized stage violence and nonverbal real violence.

Although it is obvious that a screenplay is intended to be visualized, the consequences of visualization may not be so obvious. One such consequence is the kind of language with which the screenplay is written. Because audiences expect the photographed image to be realistic (as opposed to, say, a painting, which need not be), they also expect the characters to sound realistic. In real life, we point to an object and call it a "this" or a "that." In film, a demonstrative can have a visual antecedent, so that a "this" or a "that" is something the audience sees. When Ellen (Claudette Colbert) sees the blanket partition that Peter (Clark Gable) has arranged between their beds in *It Happened One Night*, she says, "*That* makes it all right," glancing in the direction of the blanket. It is the glance that makes the grammar and the line all right, too. A screenwriter who is not thinking visually might have written: "The fact that you've put up a blanket between the beds makes it all right, I presume." Stage dialogue, which this resembles, tends to be more precise and grammatical than film dialogue; it can also turn off moviegoers.

Screen dialogue is often truncated—that is, sentences are frequently left unfinished, and speech is fragmentary. For this reason, screen language is closer to actual conversation than any other kind of dialogue, even that of the most naturalistic kind of theater. An example of stage dialogue is Nick's lines in Lillian Hellman's *The Autumn Garden:* "These are my oldest friends. I think as one grows older it is more and more necessary to reach out your hand for the sturdy old vines you knew when you were young and let them lead you back to the roots of things that matter." Even though these lines are supposed to sound pompous, they would sound doubly so in a film if they were delivered in close-up or even medium shot. The audience might even laugh. *The Autumn Garden* has never been filmed, even though it is considered Hellman's finest play. Yet if it were, and the screenwriter decided to retain the above lines, they would have to be changed to something like this: "These are my oldest friends. You might call them the vines that bring me back to my roots."

Movie dialogue is more like the exchange between Butch and Sundance in *Butch Cassidy and the Sundance Kid* (1969):

BUTCH: How long you figure we been watching?
SUNDANCE: Awhile.
BUTCH: How much longer before you think they're not after us?
SUNDANCE: A while longer.
BUTCH: How come you're always so talkative?
SUNDANCE: Born blabby.

To appreciate the way a screenwriter economizes on language, you might compare the dialogue in a novel with the dialogue in a movie based on the novel. Often a screenwriter will incorporate dialogue from the novel into the screenplay if the dialogue is appropriate. However, spoken dialogue is not necessarily the same as written dialogue; screen dialogue has to be made compatible with the rhythms of human speech. In both Raymond Chandler's novel *The Big Sleep* and the 1946 film version directed by Howard Hawks, General Sternwood asks detective Philip Marlowe about himself. Here is what Marlowe says in the novel: "I'm thirty-three years old, went to college once and can still speak English if there's any demand for it. There isn't much in my trade. I worked for Mr. Wilde, the District Attorney, as an investigator once. His chief investigator, a man named Bernie Ohls, called me and told me you wanted to see me. I'm unmarried because I don't like policemen's wives."

Compare Marlowe's reply in the film: "I'm thirty-eight years old, went to college once. I can still speak English when there's any demand for it in my business. I worked for the District Attorney's office once. It was Bernie Ohls, his chief investigator, who sent me word you wanted to see me. I'm not married." Since Humphrey Bogart was playing Marlowe, the character's age had to be changed from thirty-three to thirty-eight. But the real difference is the succinctness of the screen version, which imparts the same information as the novel, but more concisely.

Economy of language, which is at the heart of screenwriting, is not the same as ellipsis, in which words are omitted for the sake of balance or parallelism. Ellipsis is rhetorical rather than dramatic, artificial rather than real. In a scene from Elia Kazan's 1976 movie version of F. Scott Fitzgerald's unfinished novel *The Last Tycoon*, the producer Monroe Stahr (Robert De Niro) watches the rushes of a highly sophisticated 1930s movie in which the hero says to the heroine, "I love you," and she replies, "And

I, you." Stahr is furious: "'And I—you!' Who talks like that?" Claudius in *Hamlet* does, for one: "And he to England shall along with you." But that is stage dialogue; in particular, Elizabethan stage dialogue. And nobody talked like that in Elizabethan England, either.

People talk in strands, in words and phrases strung together in a kind of beaded syntax, much the way Neff talks in *Double Indemnity*—in units of thought, where the ideas generate their own rhythm and their own grammar. Sometimes movie characters speak in epigrams, but these are movie, not stage, epigrams. They are memorable because they compress a complex idea into an easily remembered line that is natural for the character to speak and not merely an occasion for the writer to wax clever. At the end of *Now, Voyager* (1942), Charlotte (Bette Davis) says to Jerry (Paul Henreid), "Oh, Jerry, don't let's ask for the moon. We have the stars." By using images (moon, stars) that everyone readily understands, she sums up with marvelous precision humankind's perennial desire to overreach. Yet what Charlotte says is appropriate to the circumstances: Charlotte is happy just to take care of Jerry's daughter even though Jerry can no longer be her lover.

Movie epigrams are not stage epigrams, which tell us more about the playwright's gift for language than about the character's motivation or psychology. In Oscar Wilde's *The Importance of Being Earnest*, Lady Bracknell's line "Hesitation of any kind is a sign of mental decay in the young, of physical weakness in the old" is a stage epigram because it functions not so much as dialogue but as an expression of Wilde's wit. While we may enjoy that wit, we sense that we are hearing the author, not the character.

In *All About Eve*, when Margo Channing says, "Fasten your seat belts; it's going to be a bumpy night," she is parodying the airline cliché "Fasten your seat belts; it's going to be a bumpy flight." Margo's line is not a turn of the phrase but a variation on a phrase already turned. Unlike Oscar Wilde's epigrams, which can be quoted out of context and still sound witty, Margo's "Fasten your seat belts" is the closing line of a specific sequence. Realizing that Eve is now her rival, Margo drinks too much at a party and becomes progressively ill-tempered. Downing one last martini, she sweeps across the room, turns, delivers the line, and exits in the grand manner. The camera, which has been tracking her the whole time, exits in a huff with her. As a curtain line, "Fasten your seat belts" might have fallen flat; as an exit line in a movie, it is ideal, particularly given Bette Davis's memorably corrosive delivery. (Nobody ever says, "Do you remember when Lady Bracknell said, 'Hesitation of any kind is a sign of mental decay in the young, or physical weakness in the old?' " They do say, "Do you remember when Bette Davis said, 'Fasten your seat belts; it's going to be a bumpy night' in *All About Eve?*")

Just as the movie epigram differs from the stage epigram, the movie monologue—an extended speech in which a character reveals important information—differs from the stage monologue. In *All About Eve*, Eve delivers a monologue about her dreary childhood and tragic marriage, playing on the sympathies of her five listeners. Even if Joseph L. Mankiewicz had not directed his own screenplay, a director would have no other choice but to cut to the listeners on certain lines, as Eve either calls her listeners by name or alludes to something about them that causes them to respond. There are some seven cuts in Eve's monologue, yet they are so unobtrusive that by the time Eve finishes speaking, the audience feels it has heard a monologue while it has really witnessed a scene. In the theater, the speech could never be a true monologue, since Eve poses rhetorical questions to her listeners or makes references that necessitate a reaction from them, and these reactions demand close-ups. In the movie there is no question that one listener is moved, another close to tears, a third attentive, a fourth concerned, and a fifth mildly skeptical but ultimately convinced. It is important that we see, and see clearly, each listener's reaction, since Eve is winning each of them over by her tale of woe—a tale, incidentally, that is fabricated.

By its nature, a screenplay is best appreciated after one has seen it brought to the screen. *Patton* (1970) is best remembered for Patton's (George C. Scott's) opening monologue; yet, taken simply as a monologue, it is not on a par with the great stage monologues like Hickey's in Eugene O'Neill's *The Iceman Cometh* or Blanche's in *A Streetcar Named Desire*. However, if, while reading it, one tries to imagine Patton growing progressively larger as he becomes more outrageous, which is what happens on-screen, one can then appreciate how the words were translated into images. Patton progresses from a tiny figure against a gigantic American flag to a face that fills the screen to a tiny figure again. It is like watching the ego puff itself up into bloatedness and then lose air.

One can write a novel by telling a story over several hundred pages without adhering to a strict code; the only division necessary is division by chapter or chapter equivalents. Writing a play requires division into acts and, if necessary, scenes within those acts. If the setting changes in a novel, it can be indicated by a phrase ("Meanwhile, in London . . ."); in a play, a change of location is marked by an act or scene change, as in Lillian Hellman's *The Searching Wind:* Act 1, scene 1, the drawing room of the Hazen house, Washington, D.C.; scene 2, a room in the Grand Hotel, Rome. In a screenplay, structuring the narrative and designating scene changes are even more complicated.

A screenplay follows a specific format. Every screenplay begins with the same two words in capital letters: FADE IN. Fade in on what? Suppose you wanted to fade in on a cabin. That would be your first shot and must be numbered as all shots (or scenes, if they entail more than just a shot) must be. So far, we have FADE IN on shot one, a cabin in the woods. But that instruction is incomplete; shots must be described in terms of place (INTERIOR or EXTERIOR), and time (DAY or NIGHT). Thus, an incomplete opening might be:

FADE IN:
1. INT—CABIN—NIGHT.

What is going on in the cabin? Suppose the first shot is to be of ELISE, the heroine, standing anxiously at the window, waiting for her husband to return. How is she to be shown? What will be the size of her image: CU, LS, MS? To convey anxiety, a CU is necessary. How will the audience know she is waiting for her husband? Voice-over narration (V.O.) will be used to reveal her thoughts. In screenwriting, characters' names or designations (ELISE, CROWD), camera movements (PAN TO), transitions (DISSOLVE TO), the words *sound* (SOUND of laughter), and *sound effects* (SF or SFX) are capitalized. Thus, the first shot as it would be filmed would be described:

FADE IN:
1. INT—CABIN—NIGHT

> **CU** of **ELISE** standing anxiously at window. A storm rages outside.

> ### ELISE (V.O.)
> John said he'd be back by nightfall, but it's close to midnight. Dear God, not now . . . please, not now.

To show John, the screenwriter would have to start a new shot.

2. EXT—MAINE WOODS—NIGHT

> **ELS** of **JOHN** trudging through snow. **SLOW ZOOM IN** to reveal face, weather-beaten but confident.

Note, for example, how Alan Alda observes the rules in this brief excerpt from the credits sequence in his *Four Seasons* screenplay:

7. EXT: VILLAGE STREET—DAY
HIGH SHOT—station wagon makes its way down the street. Over this we HEAR:

> ### DANNY'S VOICE
> Who ate the bread? What the hell is this? You started without me?

8. EXT: 13TH STREET—DAY

The station wagon pulls up to the curb. **CLAUDIA ZELLER** is waiting for them holding a large unfinished painting and a box of supplies. She waves and smiles. Claudia is an Italian from the Bronx. Earthy, intelligent and strong. She gets in the car with the painting, passing it with difficulty over everybody's head as she gets into the back of the car.

> **DANNY**
> You brought your work?

> **CLAUDIA**
> It's almost finished. I'm hot. I'm cooking.
> I can't stop for a whole weekend.

> **DANNY**
> I stopped *my* work for the weekend.

> **CLAUDIA**
> Danny, please, you're a dentist.

> **DANNY**
> (to Anne)
> You hear this? I can sculpt a bicuspid that would fool God
> himself, but I'm just a dentist.

> **CLAUDIA**
> I'll go out in the fields with the cows.
> I'll stay out of everybody's way.

She accidentally sticks the painting in Nick's face. Nick grabs at his eye and winces.

> **CLAUDIA** (cont'd.)
> Oh, Nick, I'm sorry. Are you alright?

> **NICK**
> Fine.
> (to Danny)
> I'm glad you didn't bring your dentist's chair.

> **JACK**
> You hear about Janice and Hal?

CLAUDIA

I just got off the phone with her. It's a nightmare. Drive. Let's get as far away from the whole damn thing as we can.

The station wagon takes off.
CUT TO:

9. EXT: MERRIT PARKWAY—DAY

The station wagon moves down the highway past the greens and reds and yellows of spring.

SPRING MONTAGE:

Crabapple trees spraying blossoms like fountains.

Lilac branches sagging with purple buds.

Dark rain clouds passing over the sun.

Forsythia shimmering in a spring rain, its buds dropping under the weight of the fresh water.

Small wet birds in a nest shaking water drops from nearly featherless wings.

And finally, sunset in the woods. New leaves are everywhere. A rabbit crawls slowly out of its hole and surveys the place.

10. EXT: THE BARN—NIGHT

In the distance the station wagon pulls up to a barn that has been made into a house.

END OPENING TITLES.

Screenwriting is an art that film history, which emphasizes the development of film as a medium, the studio system and the stars that came out of it, and the role of the director in the filmmaking process, has tended to ignore, perhaps because the script is prefilmic. Even though most narrative films start with a script, the script recedes into the background as it changes from a verbal to a visual text, so that by the time the film has been completed, the words have been translated into images. Thus, moviegoers associate dialogue not with the writer but with the actors speaking the lines or with the scenes in which they are spoken. Still, a serious student of film will always look for the screenwriter's name in the credits.

NOTES

[1]Ingmar Bergman, "Film Has Nothing to Do with Literature," in *Film: A Montage of Theories,* ed. Richard Dyer MacCann (New York: E. P. Dutton & Co., 1966), 144.

[2]The terms used throughout the rest of this chapter (*omniscient author, author's implied self, reliable narrator,* and others) come from Wayne C. Booth, *The Rhetoric of Fiction* (Chicago: University of Chicago Press, 1961).

[3]King-Kok Cheung, " 'Don't Tell': Imposed Silences in *The Color Purple* and *The Woman Warrior*," *PMLA* 103 (1988): 162–74.

Film
as Film

F ilm provides an experience that cannot be found elsewhere. It can crystallize an emotion or an idea into a visual image. When film uses language, the words can be integrated with the images so that they become inseparable. Once we see *Casablanca*, a line like "Here's looking at *you*, kid" is irrevocably linked both with its speaker (Humphrey Bogart) and the one to whom it is spoken (Ingrid Bergman). We may not be able to dredge up the exact frame from our memory, but we know that Bogart said it to Bergman, and we can remember the look in their eyes.

When we recall certain films that have left an impression, we visualize them as pictures—sometimes just pictures, at other times talking pictures or even musical pictures. Thus, if we were asked what film is all about, we would probably cite our favorite movie, scene, or shot.

The Third Man ends with what is arguably the most unforgettable snub in film. Anna (Alida Valli) walks down a Vienna road through a drift

The ultimate snub: the ending of *The Third Man* (1949) in which Anna (Alida Valli) walks past Martins (Joseph Cotten) without even a nod in his direction. *(Courtesy MOMA/FSA)*

of leaves, her face immobile, her eyes fixed on a never-ending present. Holly Martins (Joseph Cotten) leans against a cart and lights a cigarette, waiting to be recognized. As the autumn leaves fall in a silent shower, Anna moves out of the frame—and out of Martins's life—without even a glance in his direction. Martins grows progressively smaller until he is nothing but a tiny figure by the side of a road, ready to disappear like the smoke from his cigarette. The ending achieves what only film can: eloquence without words. Not one line of dialogue is spoken: the zither alone speaks as it plays with restrained sadness the famous *"Third Man* Theme."

Someone else might maintain that while the ending of *The Third Man* is impressive, it cannot compete with Isak Borg's final vision in *Wild Strawberries*, in which Sara, his boyhood love, leads him through a meadow to a bay. Across the bay, Isak sees his mother knitting while his father fishes, apparently with some success, for the rod is beginning to curve over the water. They wave at their son, and he smiles back at them. Isak's vision of his parents has the texture of an impressionist painting. Not only is the shot perfectly composed but it also captures the essence of its subject; the shot objectifies eternity as a state into which we do not freeze like figures in a mural but rather melt imperceptibly, the way spring softens into summer or summer ripens into autumn.

It is natural to have a favorite scene; yet scenes are parts of a whole, a fact we tend to forget when we single them out for special consideration. Is there such a thing, we might ask, as a work that, in its totality and not merely in its parts, epitomizes everything peculiar to the art of film? In other words, a work that could never have been possible in any other medium?

Let us examine four films, three of which were created especially for the screen, and one originally for the stage that never reached Broadway.

CASABLANCA
(MICHAEL CURTIZ, 1942)

Before there was *Casablanca*, there was a play called *Everybody Comes to Rick's;* the play, however, was never produced. Even if it had been, it would never have meant to the stage what *Casablanca* means to the screen, despite the fact that the plots are not that dissimilar. In the play, Rick Blaine is the jaded owner of a café in Casablanca. One evening, a woman from his past, Lois Meredith, enters the café with the Czech freedom fighter Victor Laszlo. Although Rick and Lois resume their relationship, Rick begins to develop a political conscience; realizing that Laszlo must continue to fight fascism and that Lois must go with him, Rick makes it possible for the two

Humphrey Bogart and Ingrid Bergman as the legendary lovers in *Casablanca* (1942). *(Courtesy MOMA/FSA and Warner Bros., Inc.)*

of them to fly to Lisbon while he stays behind in Casablanca to meet an uncertain fate at the hands of the Nazis.

In the film, Lois Meredith becomes Ilsa Lund. Also, the Production Code precluded Ilsa's sleeping with Rick as Lois did in the play. The background of World War II determined the way the film ends: Laszlo and Ilsa board the plane, while Rick goes off to join the Free French with his friend, Captain Renault, who was even more indifferent to human concerns than Rick but is now willing to do his bit to stop the Nazis.

If the plot sounds farfetched, it is. Yet generations have responded—and continue to respond—to *Casablanca*'s romanticism because there is a solid mythic foundation beneath a rickety plot, a foundation that constitutes the subtext. While there is no particular myth that describes the subtext, there is a universal one: the myth of regeneration. *Casablanca* argues that as long as there are the uncommitted like Rick, who are capable of change, there is hope for the world. And once the uncommitted have changed, they make it possible for the Victor Laszlos to do what most of us cannot: make the world a better place.

We identify with Rick because we, too, may be more concerned about ourselves than about the world; we also identify with Laszlo because we aspire to his idealism. We even empathize with the patrons of Rick's café, a true cross section of humanity, who show the kind of courage we envy. As the Germans bellow their anthem, the patrons respond defiantly with "La Marseillaise" and drown them out. When Rick tells Ilsa that "the problems of three little people don't amount to a hill of beans in this crazy world," he is admitting that there are times when individual needs must be subordinated to the common good. Yet this is not any man speaking to any woman but Humphrey Bogart speaking to Ingrid Bergman, one icon to another. Each is the perfect embodiment of the character: Bogart, the cynic in need of regeneration; Bergman, the woman with the power to regenerate him.

With two other actors, the effect might not have been the same. Bogart and Bergman have such powerful screen personas that when they play characters like Rick and Ilsa, a coinciding of persona and character results, so that when one thinks of *Casablanca*, one thinks of Humphrey Bogart and Ingrid Bergman and not merely of Rick Blaine and Ilsa Lund.

THE GODFATHER, PART II (FRANCIS FORD COPPOLA, 1974)

In the sequel to Francis Ford Coppola's *The Godfather* (1972), the lives of Vito Corleone and his son Michael are interwoven in a way that is truly cinematic. Since Vito is dead when the film opens, Coppola could not crosscut the lives of father and son, so he tells Vito's story in flashback.

The first time the film moves from the present to the past, from Michael (Al Pacino) to Vito (Robert De Niro), Michael is putting his son to bed. Michael's face is to the *left* of the frame. Slowly the scene dissolves to Vito, his face to the *right* of the frame, as he puts his son Fredo to bed. The transition from son to father, from present to past, is balanced by a movement from left to right. The transition also brings about a corresponding change of rhythm: As the action shifts from 1957 to the turn of the century, the frenetic pace of the present yields to Old World ease. The color also changes as Lake Tahoe dissolves into Little Italy. Michael's world is dark and forbidding; Vito's is bright and sympathetic.

The first flashback ends as it began—with a shot of Vito and his son—and suddenly we are in the late 1950s again with Michael en route to Miami. By ending with a cut instead of another dissolve, Coppola points up the difference between the feverish pace of Michael's life and the tranquillity Vito knew, at least in his early manhood.

The second flashback begins when Michael hears that his wife, Kay, has had a miscarriage, which is later revealed to be an abortion. The scene again dissolves to Little Italy, where Vito is hovering over his son, who is ill with pneumonia. Again, it is a child that effects the transition. Coppola ends the flashback by showing Vito with the young Michael on his lap; then he cuts to a car making its way along a wintry road and proceeding through the forbidding entrance to Michael's Lake Tahoe home. The cut propels us into a present that is so loveless that Kay does not even look up from her sewing to greet her husband.

Coppola could not use a child as a bridge three times in succession. Consequently, the third flashback in *Godfather II* does not spring from a particular image. Coppola merely dissolves a shot of Michael speaking with his mother into one of Vito buying fruit and ends the flashback with the formation of the Genco Importing Company. In the first two flashbacks, it was a cut that restored the action to the present; in the third, it is a dissolve. Just as Vito is about to enter the import business, Coppola dissolves to a congressional investigation at which Michael is being interrogated. By dissolving from the Genco Importing Company to the hearings, Coppola establishes a connection between them. The legitimacy of the Genco Importing Company, the foundation on which Vito built his empire, is now the subject of an investigation. Michael, who has inherited his father's empire along with its foundation, plays the honest businessman who refuses to take the Fifth Amendment, claiming that he has nothing to hide.

The final flashback begins after Kay tells Michael that her miscarriage was really an abortion. Coppola cuts to Vito's return to the Sicilian town of Corleone in order to avenge the murder of his parents, who were victims of Don Ciccio's vendetta. Here the link between present and past is something quite different from a child's being put to bed or the establishment of an import company: the link is death. An admission of abortion becomes the occasion for a flashback of a mafioso's assassination. It is also death that returns the action to the present. As Vito leaves Sicily after killing Don Ciccio, Coppola dissolves to a casket containing the body of Michael's mother, Mama Corleone.

Godfather II interweaves past and present, contrasting them in a way that's peculiar to film: through variations of rhythm, balance, and color.

RAGING BULL (MARTIN SCORSESE, 1980)

The credits begin with the intermezzo from Mascagni's opera *Cavalleria Rusticana*; it is soothing, tranquil music, coming midway in an opera about betrayal, adultery, and murder. The credits are in color, with the title in flamboyant red. During the credits, a boxer in a hooded robe is seen limbering up in the ring in slow motion. The combination of Mascagni's serene music and the eerie sight of a boxer in an otherwise empty ring, moving with the speed of a puppet, prompts us to wonder if this is the raging bull of the title. And if we know that the film is based on the life of Jake La Motta (Robert De Niro), who lost the title of middleweight champion of the world to Sugar Ray Robinson in 1951 (and who was also known to be ill-tempered and violent), we might also ask why Scorsese has created such dreamlike credits and scored them with music that is similarly restful.

Anyone who has learned to read visuals and correlate them with the accompanying soundtrack would sense that perhaps Scorsese is asking the viewer to feel some compassion for the title character, as one might for a once-raging bull that now rages alone because he has become too slow-moving to be a threat.

But poignancy fades as the film begins. Not only does the bull rage but he rages in black and white—and at a pace that is at odds with that of the credits, which look lethargic in comparison. Those expecting a sentimental biopic in color would be taken aback by the changeover to black and white and the opening shots of pounding fists and battered faces. Scorsese has made three artistic choices: to tell La Motta's story in black and white—the same visual style of the great boxing pictures of the past (e.g., *Body and Soul* [1947], *The Set-Up* [1949], and one in which boxing is an important theme and from which Scorsese will quote at the end, *On the*

Robert De Niro as middleweight champion Jake La Motta in *Raging Bull* (1980). *(Courtesy MOMA/FSA)*

Waterfront [1954]); to provide a chronological and historical framework for the narrative through titles introducing each sequence (e.g., "New York, 1964"; "The Bronx, 1941"; "La Motta vs. Robinson, 1943"); and finally to use a framing device, beginning and ending with La Motta, now a night-club performer capitalizing on his former fame, rehearsing a monologue in his dressing room. Everything else—La Motta's career from 1941 on— is enclosed between the prologue and the epilogue, like a series of texts be-tween two bookends.

Segmenting the action requires variations of rhythm, which poses problems, since Scorsese has to shuttle back and forth between La Motta's professional, domestic, and social life. Yet all of these scenes have one common note: violence. La Motta can be almost as violent at home or in a club as he is in the ring. The turbulence of the first sequence, which in-cludes a bloody fight as well as a riot among the spectators, seems to have abated at the beginning of the second, set in the Bronx, where La Motta and his first wife live. However, we soon discover that only the rhythm is different. An argument over the way a steak should be cooked throws La Motta into such a rage that he almost trashes the kitchen. Violence is vio-lence; the occasion determines the manner in which it is expressed.

Scorsese, with the assistance of his extraordinary editor, Thelma Schoonmaker, varies the rhythm so successfully that no single scene—

regardless of where it is set—is the same. When La Motta sees Vicky (Cathy Moriarty), soon to be his second wife, she is at the local pool, looking like a 1940s pinup. The pace slows down, as La Motta fixes his gaze on her. Other men are also aware of her, and Scorsese conveys a men's-club atmosphere by having us hear only the men as they speak. Vicky just moves her lips; to the men, she is only an object. They do not hear her because they do not think of women as human beings enjoying the same freedom of speech as men. Women are meant to be silent; if they speak their mind, a slap across the face ends the conversation.

While *Raging Bull* may seem to be sexually explicit, the love scenes between La Motta and Vicky are antiseptic. She behaves robotically, planting kisses on his face or chest and removing articles of clothing as requested. But there is no real passion; the only lust is on La Motta's part, which is short-lived. Because he has a fight coming up, he cools himself by emptying a pitcher of ice water down his shorts. This is clearly a male universe; there is far more affection between the men, who embrace and kiss freely, than there is between the men and the women. When Jake brings Vicky to his apartment for the first time, Scorsese uses a three-shot to illustrate La Motta's hierarchy of love. La Motta, left of frame, and Vicky, right, stand in profile at the dresser, on which there is a picture of La Motta and his brother Joey (Joe Pesci). The picture stands between them, as does the bond between the brothers after they marry.

Scorsese frequently uses slow motion, but not to give a blow-by-blow breakdown of a fight, as one might expect in a boxing film. Slow motion is used in the fight sequences primarily to reflect the point of view of the boxer, who is so disoriented after a round that nothing looks or moves as it normally would. But Scorsese also uses slow motion outside the ring. When La Motta sees Vicky in a club, it is as if his vision were temporarily altered as she turns into the golden girl of his imagination, moving in a rhythm that is different from that of the real world. It happens again at the Copacabana when she spots some old friends and makes her way to their table.

Segmenting the narrative poses another set of problems: no matter how the rhythm is varied, certain events must be either omitted or telescoped. Scorsese does both. Most of 1944–1947 is reduced to a montage of stills from La Motta's fights and home movies of his marriage and his brother's. But the fact that the films are in color indicates that Scorsese was trying to suggest some of the changes in the media that occurred in the 1941–1964 period—such as color home movies.

The brief switch to color was not accidental, nor were later sequences, set in the 1950s, that showed a television set in La Motta's home. Significantly, the set is not working. Jake's days in the ring are over; likewise, sporting events, once available only on radio, can now be seen by anyone who can afford a television set. Jake can afford one, but television will never be his medium, which was evident in 1951 when viewers saw him lose his title to Sugar Ray Robinson.

Like Steven Spielberg and Woody Allen, Scorsese has an astounding knowledge of movie history. Sometimes he refers to past films by evoking an image of the past (e.g., Vicky wearing a white turban and a white two-piece swimsuit, looking like Lana Turner in *The Postman Always Rings Twice*, 1946) or making a direct reference—Terry's (Marlon Brando) famous speech in *On the Waterfront*, in which he chastizes his brother Charley for making him throw a fight and thus lose his chance to become a contender ("I could have been somebody. I could have been a contender").

At the end of the film, La Motta, a would-be entertainer, sits at his dressing table, staring into the mirror as he rehearses the speech. He is thinking not of Terry or Charley but of his own brother, Joey, from whom he became estranged when, in a moment of irrational jealousy, he accused Joey of committing adultery with Vicky. In both *On the Waterfront* and *Raging Bull*, the brothers were mirror images—similar and opposite, as reflections are. *On the Waterfront*, then, becomes a subtext for *Raging Bull*—another film about brothers who never saw in each other what they should have seen and therefore could never do more than bond in the most primitive way.

Scorsese does not ask us to sympathize with Jake La Motta; he asks us to view La Motta as we might any protagonist who has experienced a tragic fall. Certainly, none of the classical tragic figures (Oedipus, Hamlet, Lear, Othello) were blameless; frankly, one would not want to be around them very long, given their penchant for rage. But La Motta's fall is as real within the context of *Raging Bull* as Othello's is within that of Shakespeare's play.

The end title is an excerpt from St. John's Gospel. After Jesus cures a man who was born blind, the Pharisees summon the man a second time, insisting that his sight was restored by a sinner. The man replies that he does not know whether Jesus was a sinner; he knows only that once he was blind and now he can see.

The next title is a dedication: "Remembering Haig R. Monoogian, Teacher, May 23, 1916–May 28, 1980, with love and affection, Marty." This is a personal reference that a biographer should investigate; perhaps the teacher encouraged Scorsese to look for qualities in La Motta—or someone like him—that would elude others. The dedication aside, the end title suggests that *Raging Bull* might open the eyes of those who expect to find tragic figures only in the classics but not in everyday life. Perhaps they will say, like the man who was formerly blind, "Now I can see."

With its variations of mood, tone, and rhythm; popular songs as background music, reflecting the changing taste of the American public over a twenty-year period; intertitles that identify characters and specify time and place; and an end title exhorting the viewer to see human beings whole before judging them, *Raging Bull* is inconceivable in any form other than film.

NATURAL BORN KILLERS (OLIVER STONE, 1994)

The subject matter of *Natural Born Killers* is clearly repellent: mass murderers who kill wantonly, get away with it, and eventually marry and have a family. However, it is one thing to abhor mass murder, as any responsible human being does, and another to dismiss the range of film techniques that Stone draws on to tell his story. *Natural Born Killers* begins with a pre-credits sequence; the setting is a truck stop somewhere in the Southwest. Two of the patrons, Mickey and Mallory (Woody Harrelson and Juliette Lewis), look like locals, yet an offensive remark by one of the truckers leads to a bloodbath, with only one survivor. It is the couple's policy to spare one eyewitness to add to the ongoing saga of Mickey and Mallory.

Thus, the sequence acts as a prologue, delineating the couple's nature, which remains consistent. Visually, however, the sequence has a more important function: it keeps alternating between black-and-white and color, creating a pattern that predominates throughout the film. Stone deliberately disorients audiences that are accustomed to color by forcing them to see two different worlds: in one, blood is red; in the other, it is black.

Looking at the film in terms of narrative and infranarrative, one might say that, superficially, *Natural Born Killers* is about a murderous couple; on a deeper level, it is about the way the tabloid media capitalizes on the public's fascination with violence by giving Mickey and Mallory the kind of coverage deserved by those who improve society, not those who subvert it.

Proceeding from this position to an even stronger one, a viewer might argue that Stone illustrates visually how the media—specifically television—presents violence. To a generation accustomed to color television and color film, violence in monochrome seems unnatural. But it is not a question of violence being unnatural but of violence drained of color—specifically, the color of blood. The sight of blood-splattered walls in black and white has a distancing effect: dark splotches on a white surface are not blood; in fact, they resemble something a young artist might create who has become infatuated with abstract expressionism.

Understandably, audiences perceive Mickey and Mallory as villains; Stone, however, would argue differently. Who are the real villains: those

Woody Harrelson and Juliette Lewis, as Mickey and Mallory, in *Natural Born Killers* (1994). *(Courtesy Warner Bros., Inc. and MOMA/FSA)*

who kill or those who publicize the killers, going so far as to televise a live interview with them that precipitates a prison riot and leaves corridors strewn with corpses? Even a television reporter (Robert Downey, Jr.) becomes so caught up in the violence that he joins the couple, who manage to escape and finally kill him. When he pleads that the couple has been known to leave one survivor, Mickey agrees, pointing to the video camera before shooting him. The camera, then, can be either hero or villain; in the hands of a master, it can produce a masterpiece; in the hands of an opportunist, it can cause death. But, as the reporter said earlier, "The media is like the weather, except that it is man-made." What Stone is really saying, then, is that humans may have a capacity for violence, but so does their creation—the media. Since the media has resources and technology that are unavailable to most humans, its capacity—and culpability—may be even greater.

Mickey and Mallory are products of a media culture, as Stone illustrates by using comic-book animation, subliminal cutting of the sort seen on MTV, where lyrics-evoking images flash in and out, and often grainy photography giving the impression of a film that has been projected so often that it looks scratchy and washed-out. Anyone who's interested in probing the deeper meaning of *Natural Born Killers* (and wondering why someone of Stone's stature would have made such a movie, as, two decades earlier, others wondered the same about Stanley Kubrick when he made *A Clockwork Orange*) might ponder the following: why do shots of Mickey and Mallory as children appear periodically? Why, when the film has barely begun, does Stone put the main action on hold to present a parodistic sitcom, "I Love Mallory," in which we are introduced to her foul-mouthed father, passive mother, and creepy kid brother, and discover that the father has abused his wife physically and his daughter sexually?

One answer is that Stone is exploiting the full potential of film, stopping the narrative proper to interpolate a subnarrative. But that is just a complex way of saying that Americans who delight in dysfunctional families (and are willing to watch them bare their souls on trash television) would tune in to "I Love Mallory" if it ever became a sitcom. And what is one to make of the scene in which the couple marry themselves on a bridge, as a breeze carries Mallory's bridal veil into the sky? That innocence ended when the media invaded our lives? And if a film is the sum of its parts, are Mickey and Mallory not the sum of theirs? Why are there so many canted shots in the film—shots that look lopsided, off-kilter, and alien to the way we perceive reality? If technology can skewer reality, perhaps human beings can be as off-center as a canted shot.

Stone does not provide the answers; he leaves them to you. To suggest one way of looking at the film, he offers a concluding montage of shots from the film, as well as those of Rodney King, Lorena Bobbitt, and O. J. Simpson—none of whom appeared in *Natural Born Killers*. The acquittal of the Los Angeles police officers responsible for the beating of Rodney King after the first trial led to one of the worst riots in American history in 1992; Lorena Bobbitt severed her husband's penis in 1993; at the time *Natural Born Killers* was released, Simpson was the prime suspect in the murders of his wife, Nicole, and Ron Goldman. King was a victim of police brutality; Bobbitt, an abused wife; and Simpson, the most famous of all, a suspect in the so-called crime of the century. All became media figures. Is Stone perhaps suggesting that a country born of a revolution and lacking a mythology of its own is so fascinated by violence and the mythic types it produces that it makes little difference whether they are victims, perpetrators, or suspects?

If you have a particular candidate for film as film, first ask the following questions: Could it have been anything other than a film—a novel, a short story, or a play, for example—and have been as effective? Perhaps it might have made a better novel than a film. If it is an adaptation of a work of literature, is it so different from its source that, for all practical purposes, it is an original work? Or, if it is a faithful adaptation, does the film version deepen or enhance the source, bringing out details that the author only suggested? How much of the film is told through images or camera movement without recourse to dialogue? If everything is conveyed through dialogue, the same effect might have been achieved if the film had been a novel or a play. Do the camera and script collaborate, with each doing what it does best so that word and image are allies rather than enemies? What is the infranarrative, or subtext? Without one, the film would have exhausted itself in a single viewing. It is not a question of whether the movie is a masterpiece but of whether the moviemaker has drawn on the treasury of techniques available to anyone who wants to tell a story visually. No one would call *Natural Born Killer* a masterpiece, yet it is difficult to ignore Stone's visual arsenal, even though he draws on it to bombard audiences with images they would probably rather not see.

The infranarrative enriches the film, causing the viewer to return to it. If, on the other hand, a film remains entirely on a superficial level—with visuals to match—and everything it has to offer can be absorbed in one viewing, it is just a diversion.

CHAPTER

Film Criticism

Theory and Practice

M ost criticism from Aristotle to John Dryden is really theory of literature. Students reading Aristotle's *Poetics* for the first time may be disappointed if they expect a detailed analysis of a Greek tragedy. In the *Poetics*, Aristotle was practicing legislative criticism. He was setting forth certain principles (art as imitation, plot as soul, the tragic hero as midway between perfect goodness and utter depravity) and establishing various categories and distinctions (the simple versus the complex plot, the kinds of recognition). But he was not explicating a text or exploring its levels of meaning.

In *On the Sublime*, Longinus analyzed one of Sappho's poems, but most of the work is also legislative: how to achieve the sublime, how not to achieve it, what elements of the sublime can be learned, what elements are innate. Horace's *Ars Poetica* also ignores practical criticism, as does Sir Philip Sidney's *An Apology for Poetry*, which by its very title is a defense of an art rather than an interpretation of it.

Descriptive criticism, which is based on the analysis of a literary work, is relatively new; it began in 1688 with Dryden's *An Essay of Dramatic Poesy*, and not very successfully at that. Dryden was superb when he championed the cause of English drama, but deficient when he tried to analyze a particular English play, Ben Jonson's *The Silent Woman*. The kind of criticism to which most of us are accustomed—where a text is examined line by line, image by image—started with the New Critics (John Crowe Ransom, Cleanth Brooks, Robert Penn Warren, and others), who focused almost exclusively on the work, ignoring the historical milieu out of which it came as well as the author's biography.

Early film criticism was also theoretical and reflected the basic premises of literary criticism—namely, that criticizing a medium requires a knowledge of what the medium can and cannot do, and that this knowledge is obtained through theory.

THE HISTORY OF FILM CRITICISM

The Russians

Film criticism really began in Russia with the Revolution of 1917. It is true that before that time newspapers had reviewers, that in 1915 Vachel Lindsay published *The Art of the Moving Picture*, and that in 1916 Hugo Munsterberg's *The Photoplay: A Psychological Study* appeared. But no filmmaker attempted to explain the nature of his craft until Lev Kuleshov started writing in 1917. In the famous Kuleshov Workshop at the State Film School in Moscow, which included such famous pupils as V. I. Pudovkin and briefly Sergei Eisenstein, Kuleshov performed various experiments in montage, which he defined alternately as "the joining of shots into a predetermined order," "the alternation of shots," and "the organization of cinematic material." To show how editing can alter the face of objective reality, Kuleshov intercut a close-up of an actor's neutral face with three different shots: (1) a bowl of soup, (2) a woman in a coffin, and (3) a little girl with a toy bear. Audiences marveled at the actor's "versatility" in expressing (1) hunger, (2) sorrow at his mother's death, and (3) joy at the sight of his daughter.

Pudovkin continued in his teacher's footsteps. He idolized Kuleshov, and made the extravagant claim that while others made films, Kuleshov made cinematography. Kuleshov was not infallible; although much of his theory still has value, some of it is misleading. His belief that the shot is the equivalent of the word has led to a misunderstanding of what the shot can and cannot say; his comparison between a sentence and a sequence limits the sequence to imparting only the information of which a sentence is capable; his view that the way a film is put together is more important than what it means is equivalent to the fallacy that form is more significant than content.

To his credit, Kuleshov was critical of the way Russian directors shot scenes. A great admirer of American films, he contrasted American "fast montage" with Russian "slow montage." He envisioned a suicide scene in which a despondent man would sit down at his desk, remove a pistol from the drawer, press it to his forehead, and pull the trigger. The American director would fragment the scene by breaking it up into its components: a close-up of the man's agonized face, a shot of his hand reaching into the drawer, an extreme close-up of the man's eyes, and, finally, the firing of the pistol. The Russian director would simply film the scene as if it were taking place on the stage.

What Kuleshov meant by montage in this example was nothing other than the editing technique that D. W. Griffith had perfected. Thus, when Kuleshov said montage developed in America, he was speaking the truth. Pudovkin continued to explore the implications of montage, which at this stage still meant editing. He argued that the foundation of film art is editing and that a film is not "shot" but "built" from individual strips of celluloid. Pudovkin was intrigued by what happens when two different shots are combined within the same narrative context. For example, in *Tol'able David* (1921), a tramp enters a house, sees a kitten, and immediately wants to drop a stone on it. Pudovkin read the scene in this way: Tramp + Kitten = Sadist.

To Eisenstein, Pudovkin was incorrect: The equation was not $A + B = C$, but $A \times B = Y$. Shots are meant to collide, not join together. With Eisenstein, montage was no longer a matter of combining shots or of alternating them but of making them collide with each other: $A \times B = Y$; fox $\times$ businessman = cunning. In *Tol'able David*, when director Henry King cuts from the tramp to the kitten, both the tramp and the kitten are part of the same scene; in *Strike* (1924), when Eisenstein juxtaposes the face of a man and the picture of a fox, the fox is not an integral part of the scene as the kitten is in *Tol'able David*. To King, the kitten is a character; to Eisenstein, the fox is a metaphor.

The Grammarians

As new terms (*montage, dissolve, wipe,* and so on) entered the vocabulary of film, definitions became necessary to explain their functions. In 1935 Raymond Spottiswoode published *A Grammar of the Film*, whose purpose was "to make as precise as possible the language and grammar of film."[1] Spottiswoode was critical of some of the ways in which film expressed itself. He had little use for the wipe because, unlike the cut, which is imperceptible, the wipe calls attention to itself. He believed that while dissolves could be justified, they generally interfered with the film's rhythm because they slurred over the bridge between shots and altered the tone of a scene. Although *A Grammar of the Film* was a serious attempt to analyze film techniques, much of it is passé by today's standards. One no longer speaks of "credit titles," and what were once known as "strip titles" are now "subtitles."

The Apologists

Spottiswoode combined a study of film terminology with a defense of the medium, arguing that movies can only become an art if they first become part of a nation's cultural life and that critics must help film develop a national character. He was forced to defend film, as Sidney was forced to defend poetry 350 years earlier, against its detractors, who called moviegoers "celluloid nitwits." However, few defenses of the filmmaker are as eloquent as Rudolf Arnheim's in *Film as Art*:

> [The filmmaker] shows the world not only as it appears objectively but also subjectively. He creates new realities, in which things can be multiplied, turns their movements and actions backward, distorts them, retards or accelerates them. . . . He breathes life into stone and bids it move. Of chaotic and illimitable space he creates pictures . . . as subjective and complex as painting.[2]

To Arnheim, the fact that photography is limited is precisely what makes film an art. Because photography is incapable of perfect reproduction, film ceases to be a mere replica of reality and becomes reality's ally or enemy but never its equivalent. Film is the art of partial illusion, the same illusion that exists on the stage, where we accept a room with only three walls. In a silent film, we accept characters who speak but cannot be heard; in a black-and-white film, we ignore the absence of color.

Because film is capable of distortion, it is not a purely realistic medium. To the doubters who think the camera reproduces the object as it is, Arnheim explains how the camera's ability to approach an object from different and unusual angles creates effects that are ordinarily found in great painting. "Art begins where mechanical reproduction leaves off,"[3] and Arnheim had no doubt that film was art.

The Realists

Since the first film critics based their theories on the silents, they were more sympathetic to montage than the critics who came of age with the talkies. Sound brought spoken dialogue, and once the pictures learned to talk they were not so docile as they were when they were silent. Russian montage was not well suited to the narrative sound film, in which the combination of happy face and flowing brook could break dramatic continuity or destroy verisimilitude.

"There are cases in which montage far from being the essence of cinema is indeed its negation," wrote André Bazin,[4] whose early death in 1958 was an irreparable loss to film criticism. What bothered Bazin about montage was its inability to offer more than a limited and frequently distorted view of reality. Bazin discerned two main traditions in film: montage and mise-en-scène, or the cut as opposed to the long take. It was mise-en-scène that he championed, and it was the mise-en-scène directors (Jean Renoir, William Wyler, Orson Welles, and others) whom he favored.

Mise-en-scène, a term derived from the theater, is difficult to translate because it signifies a variety of things. It means staging a film with the same feeling for style and detail that a theater director (*metteur-en-scène*) brings to a play; it means that the director stages the action, positions the actors within the frame, dresses them in costumes suitable to the era and mood of the film, provides them with decor that is similarly evocative—in short, blends all the elements of filmmaking, from acting and makeup to the composition of the shots, into a whole to give as close an approximation of reality as he or she can.

Directors who work within the mise-en-scène tradition achieve a high degree of realism by shooting certain scenes in long take. In fact, some of the finest camera work in film is a result of the long take. The opening of *Touch of Evil* derives its power from being an uninterrupted tracking shot. The long take was particularly evident in *The Best Years of Our Lives* (William Wyler, 1946), a 172–minute movie with 190 shots per hour; the average film has between 300 and 400 per hour. Wyler filmed several scenes without making a single cut, creating action and reaction within the same shot. Bazin justly admired the famous ending: the wedding of Wilma (Cathy O'Donnell) and Homer (Harold Russell). All of the principals are present: Al and Milly Stephenson (Fredric March and Myrna Loy); their daughter Peggy (Teresa Wright); and Fred Derry (Dana Andrews), Homer's best man. Fred and Peggy are in love, but his inability to find a job has prevented their marriage. As Homer and Wilma exchange vows, Fred turns in the direction of Peggy, who is standing with her parents. At that moment, Wyler brings everyone into the frame. The vows seem equally applicable to Fred and Peggy; the result is the illusion of a double wedding. A cut at any point during the scene would have shattered that illusion.

Another scene Bazin praised was the one in which Fred phones Peggy to terminate their relationship. Fred, Al Stephenson, and Homer

In the celebrated long take from *The Best Years of Our Lives* (1946), William Wyler brings all the principals into the frame for the wedding of Homer (Harold Russell) and Wilma (Cathy O'Donnell). *(Courtesy Samuel Goldwyn Productions)*

are in a bar, where Homer is playing the piano. In one unbroken movement, the camera goes from the piano to the phone booth, pausing only for a quick look at Al. Another director might have used several cuts or allowed us to overhear the conversation between Fred and Peggy. The fact that Wyler did neither reinforces Bazin's thesis that Wyler did not have imitators, only disciples.

Bazin wanted film to encompass as much reality as possible, but mise-en-scène cannot produce realism by itself; it needs *deep focus*, a technique in which background and foreground are in focus at the same time. Thus, mise-en-scène and deep focus are allies. Deep focus has three other advantages for Bazin: (1) it brings spectators into closer contact with the image; (2) it is intellectually more challenging than montage, which manipulates spectators and annihilates their freedom of choice by making them see only what the filmmaker wants them to see (deep focus, by contrast, presents spectators with the whole image, from which they may choose to see only a part, such as the foreground); and (3) it allows for ambiguity, which is absolutely essential to works of art, whereas montage re-

Anatomy of Film

duces a scene to one meaning (smiling face + babbling brook admits of only one interpretation).

Bazin never expressed his theory of film in a full-scale critical work, but only in the form of essays and articles, not all of which have been translated into English. Yet it is clear that he was moving toward an aesthetics of realism. Bazin was especially impressed by the neorealistic Italian films that appeared after World War II—for example, Roberto Rossellini's *Open City* (1945) and *Paisan* (1946), and Vittorio De Sica's *The Bicycle Thief* (1947). He saw these films as showing the same respect for reality that deep focus does. Neorealism and deep focus have the same purpose: to keep reality intact. In a neorealistic film, Eisensteinian montage is impossible; nothing can be added to the existing reality. The cutting must follow the script, which cannot tolerate juxtapositions.

Initially, it was film's realism that caused its adversaries to regard it as a copy of nature. To Siegfried Kracauer, film's ability to capture reality, far from being a handicap, is its greatest asset. Just as in the *Poetics* Aristotle determined the nature of art before he discussed the nature of tragedy, Kracauer began his epochal *Theory of Film* not with film itself but with its parent—photography.

Kracauer is unwilling to call photography an art for the same reason he is unwilling to call film an art: the photographer lacks the artist's freedom to create his or her own inner vision. Both the photographer and the filmmaker are more dependent on the material world than either the painter or the poet. In art, the raw material of nature disappears; in film, it remains.

Kracauer's reluctance to elevate film to an art form follows inevitably from his belief that film is better equipped to record physical reality than any other medium. Consequently, film should stay on the surface of reality, for when it tries to penetrate the surface, it becomes uncinematic. Parker Tyler challenged Kracauer's thesis by showing that film has successfully explored such themes as split personality (*Persona*) and the impossibility of certitude (*Blow-Up*) by moving from the surface into the realms of human consciousness, where the camera once feared to tread. Kracauer would probably agree with Tyler but then add: "*Persona* and *Blow-Up* are uncinematic," meaning not that they are inferior films (quite the contrary), but that they deal with a form of reality that is better suited to the novel. Kracauer's position is thoroughly classical. Each form reaches its highest stage of development when it accomplishes what no other form can.

To Kracauer, films are either cinematic or uncinematic. The more they reflect the material world, the more cinematic they are; as soon as they forsake physical reality for spiritual reality, they become less cinematic. Thus, he would call the following genres uncinematic by nature: (1)

the historical film because it is an artificial reproduction of a bygone age; (2) the fantasy film because of its otherworldliness; and (3) the literary adaptation because in a novel or a drama the physical world is not the only one that matters—there is the inner world of the characters, which the camera has difficulty entering.

Because film evolved from photography, it shares with it four characteristics: (1) an affinity for unstaged reality, (2) a penchant for the fortuitous and the random, (3) a sense of endlessness, and (4) a preference for the indeterminate. A fifth characteristic is peculiar to film alone: an ability to capture the open-ended flow of life as it appears in the stream of situations and occurrences that constitute human existence. Kracauer is not saying that film must never attempt to stage reality or that it must always deal with such themes as chance encounters and unpredictable events. He means only that film favors nature in the raw and resists the artificial; thus, film balks at being made to resemble a play. As we have seen, shooting a film from the point of view of a spectator in an orchestra seat is entirely different from shooting it from the point of view of the camera eye, which can look up, down, around, over, under, and beyond what it sees. Naturally, photography favors the fortuitous; some of the most memorable pictures ever taken were the result of the photographer's being in the right place at the right time.

When Kracauer says that film has a liking for the fortuitous, he does not mean that the camera will record whatever passes in front of its lens; he does mean that a good many movies involve chance occurrences on streets, in the badlands of the West, on ships, in airports, railroad stations, hotel lobbies, and so forth. Film tends toward the endless because physical reality is seemingly without end; thus, in a movie a change of scene may be a change of continent. The filmmaker had to learn how to bridge vast distances by creating such transitions as the fade and the dissolve.

Film is indeterminate because physical reality is indeterminate. The juxtaposition of laughing face and flowing brook evokes the same response the world over. But what of the meal of wild strawberries and milk that Mia offers the Knight in *The Seventh Seal?* Bergman has not falsified reality by making the strawberries and milk other than what they are. The context of the scene changes the strawberries and milk from picnic food to food for a eucharistic meal; it also changes those eating the food into communicants. Reality's indeterminacy is one of the glories of film, where an object can be both itself and a symbol at the same time. The strawberries and milk never cease to be what they are: a means of sustenance. The scene determines the *kind* of sustenance: spiritual as well as physical.

Toward the end of *Theory of Film*, Kracauer distills the essence of his thesis into a myth. It is not an original myth but the old one of Perseus and Medusa's head. Because the sight of Medusa's head turned men to stone,

Athena warned Perseus not to look directly at it but only at the reflection on his shield:

> Now of all the existing media the cinema alone holds up a mirror to nature. Hence our dependence on it for the reflection of happenings which would petrify us were we to encounter them in real life. The film screen is Athena's polished shield.[5]

Hence, the complete title of Kracauer's book: *Theory of Film: The Redemption of Physical Reality.* Kracauer does not believe that film deals only with nature in the raw as opposed to nature transfigured. Nature in the raw, of course, is film's starting point, as it must be; for nature in the raw—physical reality—is to film what language in the raw—words—is to literature: the means by which the work comes into being. Yet how does film redeem physical reality? The very fact that Kracauer speaks of holding a mirror up to nature, a polished mirror at that, provides the answer. A polished mirror will not catch a reflection of the physical universe as it is but as something better than it is; it catches a higher form of reality, one that is no less real than what we see around us but is superior to it. How can art imitate nature and improve it? Aristotle never tells us. How can film mirror reality and redeem it? Kracauer never tells us. For the answer, we must examine the works of artists who knew the secret of working within the material universe without becoming mired in it.

The Auteurists

It was in the late 1950s that the cult of the director arose, resulting in a spate of books on the great and the not so great auteurs. Presently, there is a book, a section of a book, an encyclopedia entry, or a monograph on every director who made some contribution to the art of film, even if it was only directing a Republic western with verve and style, as Joe Kane did. That contribution could be revolutionary, as in the case of D. W. Griffith, or minor, as in the case of Edgar G. Ulmer. Yet if there can be critical studies of minor authors, there can be critical studies of minor directors. Minor does not mean mediocre; one's influence on a particular art form may not be pervasive, but it can nonetheless be noteworthy.

As we saw in chapter 6, auteurism is merely *one* way of looking at film. It enables those who need a "handle," so to speak, on film to have one. Certainly it is much simpler to deal with a work of known rather than unknown authorship; among other things, it affords a sense of control and security. Even though it is common knowledge that Shakespeare wrote *Hamlet* and Dickens *Great Expectations,* we still speak of "Shakespeare's *Hamlet*" and "Dickens's *Great Expectations.*" To be able to say "Hitchcock's

Psycho" means we can approach *Psycho* in the same way we might approach *Hamlet;* just as a literary scholar can discuss *Hamlet* within the broader context of Shakespeare's plays, we can approach *Psycho* within the context of Hitchcock's work instead of viewing it merely as a horror film or as the prototype of the modern slasher film.

There are, of course, drawbacks to auteurism. The auteurist approach cannot be applied unilaterally. It would be something of a joke to write, "Edward Bernds's *Bowery Boys Meet the Monster* (1954)," although confirmed auteurists would think nothing of it. Whatever one may think of Edward Bernds (a competent director) or the film, such a designation is bound to strike non-auteurists as laughable.

Auteurists can teach us something about the way directors repeat compositions, framings, and certain types of shots. Frank Capra's love of bells, which ranges from the tolling bells in *Lost Horizon* (1937) to the bell on the Christmas tree in *It's a Wonderful Life* (1946), led to his using the bell as the logo of his short-lived production company, Liberty Films. No doubt Capra associated bells with the spirit of freedom and a feeling of joy. Hitchcock's high shots, or "God's eye shots," may be a vestige of his Roman Catholicism or merely an attempt to suggest an unseen, omnipotent presence peering down at the world. At any rate, the high shot is a favorite Hitchcockian device, as is irising in D. W. Griffith, double framing in John Ford, long takes in Orson Welles and William Wyler, and a claustrophobic atmosphere in Edgar G. Ulmer. If writers in the auteurist tradition can deepen our understanding of a director's style, they have served film well. However, auteurism can only be considered a way of approaching film, specifically of approaching the films of selected directors.

The Mythographers

Parker Tyler was the first film critic to understand how mythic the movies are. In *The Hollywood Hallucination*, Tyler explained the extraordinary appeal of stars like Greta Garbo and Marlene Dietrich: they were mystery women, phantom ladies, moon goddesses like Diana. Their inaccessibility made them more desirable than they really were. If they ever loved a man, they could love him only in myth, where they would never have to yield. Even if a man broke down their resistance, we could never believe these goddesses could offer him anything more than fairy-tale love.

To Tyler, even Mickey Mouse cartoons had mythic underpinnings. Intelligent moviegoers watch an animated mouse without feeling their intelligence has been insulted because they instinctively recognize some myth, some universal pattern of experience, behind the cartoon. Tyler identified it as the Frankenstein myth, which is based on an even older myth of the artist who creates a human being out of inert matter (e.g.,

Prometheus, who molded man from earth; Pygmalion, who carved Galatea out of marble). We understand intuitively that Mickey Mouse is someone's creation. Tyler cited other similarities between Mickey Mouse and the Frankenstein monster: both are mechanized beings; both are factory products (Mickey, the product of the Disney factory; the monster, of Frankenstein's laboratory); both obey their masters. There is also a difference between them: in *Frankenstein,* the monster turns on his maker, but Mickey always remains an amiable mouse.

We identify with the underdogs in animated cartoons because they have the same problems we do. We forget that they are ducks, mice, or pigs and think of them as humans running the same obstacle course as ourselves and encountering the same frustrations. Yet, Tyler asks, is it not the same situation in gangster films? Don't we empathize with the Little Caesars, the Dillingers, the Bonnies and the Clydes? Many moviegoers find gangsters sympathetic for various reasons: they are nonconformists who flaunt morality; their lives are colorful; they are upwardly mobile, often beginning at the bottom with petty crime and moving up the ladder of notoriety to bank heists and bloodbaths. Hollywood tends to humanize its gangsters, and to Tyler humanization equals glorification. Interestingly, Tyler made no distinction between Superman and the gangster. Who gave Superman the right to take the law into his hands? He is only a newspaper reporter, not a police officer. Yet we look the other way when Clark Kent ducks into a phone booth and emerges as Superman; or, rather, our unconscious looks the other way as a reporter becomes a disrupter of the normal order.

In *Magic and Myth of the Movies,* Tyler continued to explore the ways in which the unconscious sees films and to show how we accept certain actions in a movie that we would not tolerate in real life. Physical pain is never humorous, yet we laugh when comics slip on banana peels or get pies thrown in their faces. We do not laugh because we are sadistic; the comics give us the right to laugh by becoming scapegoats for our sake and suffering indignities on our behalf. It is the same with comics who distort their faces and mock themselves: they laugh at themselves first so that we can laugh with them. Yet if we read their actions correctly, the rubber-faced clowns are really asking for our approval, our love. They humiliate themselves to win our applause.

Tyler saw the stars of the 1930s and 1940s as gods and goddesses. Because the screen made them immortal, they could not die; they only underwent a ritual death, like the vegetation deities who die in winter and are resurrected in spring. A star can never really die because divinity makes death impossible. The almost universal interest in films of the past supports Tyler's thesis. Humphrey Bogart will live as long as his films are shown, and there is little likelihood that the world will call a moratorium on movies. To see Bogart in *Casablanca* is to see a man in his prime, not a man who died of cancer in 1957. In *The Happy Ending* (1969), the heroine's husband accuses her of mooning over *Casablanca* whenever it is on television. When he reminds her that practically the entire cast is dead, she replies that Humphrey Bogart, Peter Lorre, Sidney Greenstreet, and Claude Rains are more alive than either of them.

The Semioticians

Semiotics emphasizes the way a film transmits its meaning through signs and codes.[6] Its approach is similar to that of the myth critics, who search out universal patterns and archetypal themes. Semiotics is also the theoretical side of structuralism, which is not so much a new discipline as a new approach to older disciplines such as linguistics, anthropology, psychoanalysis, and rhetoric, disciplines that are more concerned with signs than with objects. Thus, structuralists are invariably attracted to myth because myths are the first structures, the first messages of a culture.

But myths are coded; they are invisible patterns, "offstage voices," as Roland Barthes might call them. The structuralist tries to bring the voice from the wings to center stage. Myths remain coded until they become transparent; then society discards them as clichés. The reason myths were such unifying forces in ancient societies is that they resisted decoding. Frequently they appeared in binary form, reflecting the dualism inherent in nature (spirit/matter, male/female, life/death) and in culture (urban/rural, endogamy/exogamy, freedom/imprisonment). The great myths are inexhaustibly bipolar; they resist any attempt to reduce them to a single meaning. Oppositeness is at the heart of Greek mythology—which is one reason it is constantly being reinterpreted. The Oedipus myth, for example, embodies the polarities knowledge/ignorance, wife/mother, old order/new order, rationalism/mysticism, sight/blindness. Myths such as this are deathless because they are founded on natural, not artificial, opposites.

It is understandable that semiotics would be in such vogue today. Semiotics is studied in the university and in adult-education centers, where "Semiotics for the Layperson" teaches students to translate the signs they encounter in daily life: the TV commercials that promise a world where young and old, white and black will stand together if they drink Pepsi or chew Juicy Fruit gum; the clothing ads that build sexual potency into their product; the body language that is spoken at parties but not always understood.

In *Mythologies*, Roland Barthes sees signs everywhere. A person's hairstyle can designate the class and era to which he or she belongs. In Joseph L. Mankiewicz's *Julius Caesar* (1953), the fringed hair of the characters was a sign of their "Roman-ness." Wrestling abounds in signs. The wrestler with the fleshy, sagging body telegraphs certain messages to the spectator: repulsiveness, cruelty, cowardice. The wrestler's body determines the way he acts in the ring. The conventions of wrestling (the armlock, the twisting of the leg) are all parodies of tragedy. Just as the mask of tragedy is an exaggeration of the human face, so too is wrestling an exaggeration of human suffering. The opponent who lies flat on his back with his arms outstretched has been crucified. In wrestling defeat reaches the nadir of humiliation—crucifixion.

Even our detergents speak to us, according to Barthes. Chlorinated detergents proclaim they are absolute; as liquid fire, they blaze a path through the dirt and annihilate it. Powdered detergents are more selective; they liberate the dirt. Foam detergents, on the other hand, are useless. They are luxury items, airy and immaterial, as impractical as bubble bath.

If detergents talk, so does food. Fish-and-chips speak of nostalgia, of the British bearing up under the Blitz; steak speaks of virility, and if it is served rare and swimming in blood, of ambrosia that produces godlike strength. (In Jacques Tourneur's *Experiment Perilous* [1944], a woman on a train orders steak for a male passenger because she assumes that steak is a man's dish.)

On the surface, semiotics seems rather easy to understand. There is a signifier (say, a gold band) and the signified (marriage); there is denotation, by which a word keeps its literal meaning ("He lit the *fire*"), and connotation, by which it takes on other meanings ("She was consumed by the *fire* of passion"); there is *langue*, language system that can be verbal (English, German, and so on) or nonverbal (the "language" of poker, falconry, and so on), and there is *parole* (speech), the actual practice of a language system.

The problems begin when one attempts to apply this terminology to film. In film, what are the signifiers? Can a movie denote and connote, or in film does denotation become connotation? There is also the haunting question: Is film a language system? To Christian Metz, the best known of the film semioticians, film is not *langue*.[7] In language, a word can acquire a different meaning merely by the addition of a single letter—for example, *d* or *r* added to *love*. But film has no words. Metz rightly rejects the shot-as-word theory and compares the shot to the sentence. Like a gifted child, film skipped the parts of speech and moved to a higher grade. But if film has no parts of speech, then it has no grammar. We know "He see the man" is ungrammatical in standard, edited English; but what is ungrammatical in a movie? Using a dissolve instead of a cut?

Another difference is that in words there is a distance between the signifier and the signified. *Sadness* can be broken up into its signifier (the sound săd'něs) and its signified (the concept of unhappiness). But in film the signified cannot be disengaged from the signifier. In a movie, the sound of sadness is not săd'něs but a child weeping, a man wailing, an American secretary sitting alone in an outdoor café in Venice while couples stroll past her. In a movie, sadness is not a concept but an actual situation (a sad family) or an attribute of a specific person (a sad man). For the same reason, denotation and connotation are not distinct in film. A movie denotes and connotes at the same time. When Isak Borg raises a glass of wine in Bergman's *Wild Strawberries*, he is Isak Borg who at that moment is having lunch with his daughter-in-law and some young hitchhikers; he is also Isak Borg the priest-figure officiating at a communion service and elevating not a wineglass but a chalice.

Metz claims that film is "like" language because it communicates. But how does it communicate? In two ways: syntagmatically and paradigmatically. A *syntagm* is a unit of actual relationship; thus, *syntagmatic relationships* result when the units of a statement or the units in a filmic chain follow each other in order. If we analyze the way the subplots of *Nashville* interconnect or trace the rise of a character such as Mildred Pierce from housewife to restaurant owner, we are approaching the film syntagmatically.

A *paradigm* is a unit of potential relationship; thus *paradigmatic relationships* are associative, not sequential. They are not concerned with the order of the links in the chain but with the meanings we associate with them. If we associate Frank Serpico with Jesus Christ or the madness that erupted at the Hollywood premiere in *The Day of the Locust* with the outbreak of World War II, we are approaching the film paradigmatically. Because paradigmatic relationships are independent of the order in which the events occur, they can also exist between scenes taking place at different times within the film. Shane's ride of vengeance at the end of George Stevens's film of the same name should, by its horizontal movement, recall the first appearance of Wilson the gunfighter, who also rode horizontally across the frame; yet it also contrasts with the way Shane rode down into the valley at the beginning of the film. If we associate descent with something positive (the desire to reform) and horizontal movement with something negative (the desire to murder), then we have made a paradigmatic connection.

It is not enough for the semiotician simply to isolate syntagmas and paradigms; the movie relays its messages through codes that the filmmaker used and that the semiotician must now reconstruct. There are all kinds of codes: codes of dress, color, lighting, and so forth. In certain simplistic westerns, we may discover that white and black attire mean hero and villain, respectively; in other westerns, the dress code will yield to a landscape code, in which the signifier (Monument Valley) becomes the signified (America in microcosm).

Transportation codes are particularly meaningful in discovering a filmmaker's intentions. Karel Reisz saw the car as a vehicle charged with associations of death in *Isadora* (1969); in *Two for the Road*, the particular car in which the couple is traveling is related to a particular stage in their marriage. In *The Wild One* (1954), the motorcycle is the embodiment of raw virility, fascism, and arrested sexuality; but in *Easy Rider* (1969), the motorcycle epitomizes young, disenchanted America in the late 1960s. The Yuppies of the 1980s, however, do not travel by motorcycle; they go cross-country in a motor home in *Lost in America* (1985), in which *Easy Rider* is mentioned so reverentially that the idealistic sixties becomes the yardstick by which to measure the materialistic eighties.

Cigarettes in the movies of the 1930s and 1940s were the epitome of cool and sophistication: Humphrey Bogart in a trench coat and fedora, speaking with a cigarette between his lips; Bette Davis, brandishing her cigarette as if it were a scepter. The sight of so many stars smoking, which made cigarettes an essential part of one's wardrobe, influenced countless moviegoers to take up the habit.

His Girl Friday represents one of the few films in which the cigarette is not just an accessory but a sign of belonging to a special group. The film is a reworking of the famous stage play *The Front Page*, which depicts the various machinations to which a newspaper editor, Walter Burns, resorts to keep his star reporter, Hildy Johnson. For *His Girl Friday*, Howard Hawks turned Hildy, a male in the play, into a woman (played by Rosalind Russell). Although Hildy insists that she wishes to give up the newspaper business and marry an insurance salesman, Walter knows otherwise. There are many ways in which Hawks makes it clear that Hildy belongs in Walter's world; her striped suits, for example, which make her look more like a "newspaper man" (which is what she calls herself) than a female journalist. But cigarettes are another sign of belonging. When Walter, Hildy, and Hildy's fiancé, Bruce, are at a restaurant, Hildy and Walter keep blowing their cigarette smoke in his face, making him distinctly uncomfortable. When Hildy interviews a prisoner, she offers him a cigarette, which the prisoner declines. The prisoner does not belong to the newspaper world, in which the cigarette is almost like a badge or a press card.

Sometimes codes are not quite so easy to decipher. Whenever Marlene Dietrich wore a tuxedo in a movie, as she did in *Morocco* and *Blonde Venus*, both directed by Josef von Sternberg, 1930s audiences were taken aback at the sight of such a sensuous woman in men's clothes. A dress code was operating, but what did it mean? In *Morocco*, it meant that a strange form of defeminization had taken place by which Dietrich had become the essence of Hollywood Woman (seductive, smoldering) decked out with the trappings of Hollywood Man (debonair, aggressive). Thus, the Dietrich figure in a tuxedo became androgynous.

Critics who are influenced by semiotics use a specialized vocabulary. For example, they do not think of film narrative solely in terms of plot.

Marlene Dietrich looking androgynous in *Blonde Venus* (1932). *(Copyright ® Paramount Pictures, Courtesy MCA Publishing Rights, a Division of MCA Inc.)*

They distinguish between *plot*, *diegesis*, and *discourse*. The plot, or what Aristotle in the *Poetics* called the *mythos*, is the ordered arrangement of the incidents in terms of a beginning, a middle, and an end. The diegesis is the story that is recounted, embodying everything pertaining to the story regardless of how much of it actually appears on the screen. The party in *Notorious* is an all-evening affair, but on the screen it lasts only ten minutes. Thus, there is a difference between diegetic time (all evening) and film time (ten minutes). The discourse is the manner in which the story reaches the audience. That story includes what is dramatized as well as what is implied; it is based on a script that is brought to the screen by a team who have broken down the action into various codes (color codes, dress codes, lighting codes, codes of manners); it is the result of the interaction between an "I" and a "You," between the one telling the story (the filmmaker) and the one perceiving it (the filmgoer); it is the result of decisions made before, during, and after production. Thus, the main title and the end credits would be very much a part of the film's discourse; a credits sequence, which is visualized action, is part of the plot (the film's structure) and diegesis (the film's world).

While semioticians have shown how complex film narrative is, one should remember that it is perfectly possible to write good film criticism without resorting to critical jargon. If it is understood properly, Aristotle's concept of plot is as applicable to film narrative as it is to literary narrative. "Plot is the structure of events," Aristotle wrote. Note that he does not call the plot the story line, as many would, but the *shape* of the story line and the *form* it takes. To Aristotle, the plot is the soul of the work—the source of its life. Remove the plot from a work of fiction and it ceases to be a work of fiction; remove it from a narrative film and it ceases to be a narrative film. Soul is structure; it is the harmony that exists when all the parts work together. Once plot is understood as the nucleus around which the incidents, the characters, the theme, and the setting gather, and the source from which they draw their life, it can then be perceived as the soul of the work and something quite distinct from the story line, which is a bodily part.

Semiotics is to film what linguistics is to literature. A knowledge of linguistics can be helpful in reading dialect literature or in interpreting poetry, since poets coin new words and use old ones in startlingly new ways. However, literature can be analyzed quite successfully without the terminology of linguistics. Similarly, semiotics can enhance our perception of a film by disclosing the way signs and codes operate in it, yet film can be discussed intelligently without resorting to the vocabulary of semiotics.

Feminist Criticism

Feminist film criticism, whose practitioners include Laura Mulvey, Julia LeSage, Annette Kuhn, and E. Ann Kaplan, is indebted to the work of French psychologist Jacques Lacan, especially for his theory of the mirror stage of development. Briefly stated, the image a child sees reflected in a mirror produces ambivalent feelings. The child is attracted to the image because it is an ideal image, but repelled by it because the real can never be the ideal; the ideal is *other than* real. The Hollywood studio system, a male-created and male-dominated industry, never seems to have gone beyond the mirror stage. In the classic Hollywood film, the separation of real and ideal made woman the other, an object rather than a subject. Specifically, the woman was an object of the male gaze; she was an exhibit or a spectacle rendered in terms of anatomy (bosom, legs, mouth, posterior) and fractured representation (close-ups, extreme close-ups). The idealization of woman (soft focus, front lighting, lenses smeared with Vaseline or covered with gauze to give the face a glow) originates in the fear of castration. It was as if the male had unconsciously struck a bargain with the female: if she would not deprive him of his potency, he would glorify her image. In this way, the universe would remain phallocentric, dominated by the symbol of male potency, the phallus, which, according to Lacan, is a signifier. The phallus represents male power as well as male presence, as opposed to female helplessness and female absence. Since the female lacks the organ on which the signifier depends, she denotes absence—the absence of power, authority, and speech. Speech is phallocentric, the prerogative of the male; speechlessness is the state of the female. Thus, even when women speak, they are passive; it might be more accurate to use the passive voice.

Although the woman's film of the 1930s and 1940s placed the woman at the center of the action, feminists would still argue that, despite woman's pivotal role, it is the male who sets the plot in motion. *Dark Victory*, a key woman's film, is ostensibly the story of Judith Traherne's acceptace of death from brain cancer. After Dr. Steele, a neurosurgeon, has diagnosed Judith's condition, she reluctantly submits to surgery. Later she falls in love with Steele, who cannot bear to tell her that the operation was unsuccessful and her condition is terminal. Judith learns the truth by accidentally coming upon her medical record. Embittered, she turns on Steele, indulges in self-pity and drink, but finally returns to him, begging his forgiveness. Forgiveness for what, one might ask? She is the one who is going to die, not he. Judith even goes to his apartment and admits that she has been a "fool." That visit, however, results in her marriage to Steele, without which the plot cannot be resolved. Judith knows that blindness will precede death. When her eyesight suddenly fails, she does not tell Steele, who must depart for an important medical meeting, but manages to help him pack while continuing to behave normally. The ending of *Dark Victory* would have been impossible without the character of Steele, for it is Judith's marriage to him that gives her the courage to face not just death but death alone.

Like all theories, phallocentrism and the mirror stage cannot be proved scientifically. Thus, they may strike one as either probable or improbable. One can also argue that women were depicted as goddesses endowed with an aura denied to men because Hollywood believed that attractive women were "good box office." Women liked seeing themselves on the screen, and men liked seeing women on the screen. When both sexes were happy, the studio system thrived.

One cannot ignore Hollywood's ambivalence toward women. As Laura Mulvey states in an influential article, "woman . . . stands in patriarchal culture as signifier of the male other."[8] When woman is the object of the male gaze, she is given the full treatment; she is exquisitely gowned and impeccably coiffured. Her face is bathed in light that cleanses it of imperfections. A close-up transforms her image into a portrait. Woman as movie star is Other as Ideal, and the ideal should be idealized. However, other is also not-I, and in a phallocentric world, what is not-I is not Male.

As not-male, woman is often relegated to a subordinate position in the frame. In westerns, she is frequently behind the hero, serving him or standing in the background looking terrified as he takes on the villain. When the hero rides off at the end, she becomes part of the landscape in the extreme long shot that concludes the film.

Although the industry is still male-dominated, and women are still objects of the male gaze in slasher, macho, and exploitation films, several talented women directors (e.g., Gillian Armstrong, Penny Marshall, and Amy Heckerling) have succeeded in ignoring "the gaze," with its dominance-submission pattern, along with the polarities (active/passive, speech/speechlessness, voyeur/fetish) that the gaze creates. In Armstrong's remake of *Little Women* (1994), Marmee and her daughters look and act as if they can survive a father's absence. In *A League of Their Own* (1992), Marshall not only treats each of the women on the team as an individual; she also uses the opportunity to portray the main male character, an alcoholic ex–ball player (Tom Hanks), not as a caricature but as a failure worthy of our compassion. Heckerling is unusually perceptive in depicting adolescents, especially in *Fast Times at Ridgemont High* (1982) and *Clueless* (discussed in chapter 8). Students of film should attempt to test the validity of "the gaze" by comparing the portrayal of women in films directed by women with those directed by men; they might also compare the way male directors portray men on the screen with the way women do.

The Reviewers

A film reviewer is not necessarily a film critic; few reviewers can be considered critics if, by critic, we mean a representative of the most insightful approach possible. If Alexander Pope's standards are applied to contemporary reviewers, only a handful would qualify as critics. Pope expected the critic to know everything about the work under evaluation:

> You then whose judgment the right course would steer,
> Know well each ancient's proper character;
> His fable, subject, scope in every page;
> Religion, country, genius of his age:
> Without all these at once before your eyes,
> Cavil you may, but never criticise.
>
> —*An Essay on Criticism* (I, 118–23)

Film reviewers write for newspapers and magazines or deliver their reviews on television and radio. Film reviewing, then, is a branch of print and broadcast journalism. Movies are a form of news; thus, they should be covered. The question is, by whom? Ideally, by someone who's knowledgeable about film. However, it often happens that the film reviewer of a local newspaper is a reporter who was assigned to the movie beat because there happened to be an opening in that department. A major newspaper, on the other hand, is likely to have several reviewers who know film and have a wholeness of vision that is reflected in their reviews. They can relate the film being reviewed to other films of its kind, to the director's or the stars' previous work, to the writer's former scripts. Their reviews are not valentines studded with superlatives; rather, they offer a reasoned and balanced judgment of a film so that if they use words like "greatest" or "best," we know they are not being hyperbolic.

Television critics are a special breed: limited sometimes to a mere minute of air time, they are almost forced to be glib to keep the viewer from switching channels. Thus, to base one's knowledge of film criticism on television reviewing is to limit criticism to one-liners.

Americans need and want film reviews. This was true even at the turn of the century, when the public was so hungry for some kind of film review that it even accepted plot summaries and naive accounts of the wonders of celluloid. By 1904, the *Philadelphia Inquirer* was reviewing movies: its review of *The Great Train Robbery* (1903) was superficial ("There is a great amount of shooting"), but at least it was a beginning. By 1906, the first film journals had been started. In 1909, the *New York Times* ran its first movie review, an archly written piece on D. W. Griffith's *Pippa Passes*; from that time on, film reviewing became a regular department in the *Times*. Since there were no special qualifications for reviewing films, anyone could write about them, and often did. Frank Woods, an advertising salesperson for the *New York Dramatic Mirror*, wrote a movie column in the *Mirror* under the pseudonym "The Spectator" from 1908 to 1912; later he went on to become a leading screenwriter.

Before he became a major playwright, Robert E. Sherwood served as film critic for *Life* magazine from 1920 to 1928. Men of letters such as Edmund Wilson, Joseph Wood Krutch, and Mark Van Doren also wrote occasional film criticism. However, Wilson, Krutch, and Van Doren made their reputations in literary criticism, not movie reviewing. The first writer to achieve a national reputation for movie reviewing was James Agee, who between 1941 and 1948 reviewed for both *Time* magazine and the *Nation*. In addition to being a critic, Agee was also a novelist, a poet, and a screenwriter; thus, his reviews had a literacy not generally found in movie columns. Agee could be vicious, but generally he was honest and regarded himself as an amateur conversing with his readers.

Agee's early death at forty-five prevented his leaving behind a fully developed theory of film; yet he demonstrated in outline, if not in detail, what a critic should be. It is clear from his review of Michael Curtiz's *Mission to Moscow* (1943), made when Russia was an American ally, that he sensed the film's importance, not as art but as pro-Soviet propaganda. Although *Mission to Moscow* justified Stalin's purge trials, Agee was unmoved by the film's rationalizations. Instead, he wrote:

> About the trials I am not qualified to speak. On surface falsifications of fact and atmosphere I might, but on the one crucial question, whether Trotsky and Trotskyists were or were not involved with Germany and Japan in a plot to overthrow the government and to partition the country, I am capable of no sensible opinion. I neither believe it nor disbelieve it.[9]

One imagines Agee would have been the kind of critic who could take a film on its own terms, however political those terms may be. His charge that *Mission to Moscow* indulges its audience is more damning than five paragraphs of invective. Agee was not the kind of critic who catered to prejudices and yearned to make his audience a reflection of himself, but the kind who believed that readers have the right instincts within them and only need the proper guidance to bring them forth.

Whether Agee would have become an auteurist is problematic. He was certainly conscious of the role of the director, as is evident from his review of Preston Sturges's *Hail the Conquering Hero* (1944). Sturges's mother was a bohemian who gave her son a charmed life: private schools and early exposure to opera, theater, and ballet. His foster father was a down-to-earth Chicago millionaire. Agee saw Sturges as a man torn between his mother's love of the arts and his foster father's success in business. Thus in his films, Sturges was always floundering between art and popular entertainment, tending more to the latter than to the former. Agee realized that he was doing something quite unusual when he invoked a director's life as background for his films. Here is one of those tantalizing glimpses into the kind of critic Agee might have become. He seemed to be on the right track with Sturges. In *Sullivan's Travels*, John L. Sullivan (Joel McCrea), a liberal director who may well be Sturges's persona, abandons social-consciousness films for comedies because "there's a lot to be said for making people laugh." In *The Palm Beach Story*, Sturges was completely ambivalent toward money, satirizing the gold diggers and the frivolous rich alike but resolving their problems before the fade-out.

Agee was not afraid to express admiration for B films. He must have known that Val Lewton's movies would someday be classics, for he hailed *The Curse of the Cat People* and *Youth Runs Wild*, also a Lewton production, as the best "fiction films" of 1944. He also wrote favorably of Robert Siodmak's *Phantom Lady* (1944), now regarded as a model of film noir.

Another important reviewer was Bosley Crowther.[10] Of all the newspaper reviewers of his era, he carried the greatest weight because from 1940 through 1967 he wrote for the *New York Times*. Since Crowther reviewed for the most prestigious paper in America, he did not waste his time on what he deemed to be "junk." Whereas Agee saw more in Val Lewton films than calculated fright, Crowther saw nothing in them. *Cat People*, he felt, was "labored and obvious"; and although he found *The Curse of the Cat People* sensitive, it did not make his Ten Best list.

Crowther wrote for that anomaly known as the *New York Times* reader: someone who was educated but not pedantic, conservative but not a book burner, liberal without endorsing every cause as right, a believer in human values without being a teary sentimentalist. Crowther had these qualities himself. When the National Legion of Decency condemned Roberto Rossellini's *The Miracle* (1948) as an affront to the Virgin Birth, Crowther praised it as a work of art. But in the 1960s, his influence began to wane. The movies were changing, and so were audiences. One of the last reviews Crowther wrote before his retirement was of *Bonnie and Clyde*. The review gave no indication of the sane judgments of which he was capable. Unable to see the film as a commentary on the Great Depression, he branded it as cheap, pointless, and marred by violence.

Dwight Macdonald, who devoted more than forty years of his life to movie reviewing, defined the concept of *film critic*: A critic will judge the film's quality, prove its quality, and compare the film with other films, giving it its proper place within the history of motion pictures.[11] Note how Richard Corliss of *Time* meets these criteria in his review of *Evita*. He compares the film with the stage musical, locates a subtext (class distinction), contrasts Madonna's performances in *Evita* and *Dick Tracy*, and places the film within the context of the modern—as opposed to the classic—musical.

She stands on the balcony of the Casa Rosada in Buenos Aires, the night humid with portent, the masses chanting her name, as she sings her calculated confession. "And as for fortune, and as for fame,/ I never invited them in,/ Though they seemed to the world they were all I desired."

Well, maybe they were what two famous women desired. María Eva Ibarguren Duarte de Perón kept her eye on the spotlight, her hand tightening around the cojones of power. And Madonna fought like hell for the right to incarnate, in one of the era's most vivid musical dramas, a woman whose career and notoriety mirror her own: model for steamy photos, singer on the radio, movie actress of disputed pedigree, sexual adventurer. In both these stars one can see the great goad of ambition, the ability to enthrall and outrage. So, there's tabloid poetry in the fact that—50 years after Juan Perón's election as President of Argentina, 20 years after the release of the original album of the musical, and after numerous false starts of film projects that had nearly every female but Queen Latifah rumored for the lead—Madonna should step out on the balcony in *Evita*.

It's a relief to say that Alan Parker's film, which opens on Christmas Day, is a pretty damn fine one, well cast and handsomely visualized—easily the best adaptation of a Broadway-style musical in decades. It is faithful to the sting and breadth of Tim Rice's libretto, to the ravishing Andrew Lloyd Webber score that synthesizes Broadway, opera and pop with the lilt of Latino lounge music. But this *Evita* is not just a long, complex music video; it works and breathes like a real movie, with characters worthy of our affection and deepest suspicions. For at the heart of the drama is Rice's fascinated ambivalence toward the prototype couple of criminal celebrity and toward the culture that needs them to play out fantasies of success, overreaching greed, the instructive death at an early age.

Evita is not so much about Argentine politics as about the English obsession with class. Eva, the illegitimate daughter of an estate manager whose funeral her servant mother was forbidden to attend, gets back at the middle class with her upwardly nubile conquest of the military aristocracy. Our guide in this revenge melodrama is a sardonic, Rice-like narrator (Antonio Banderas), offering keys to the allure of Santa Evita, first lady, holy whore.

As a teenager in 1936 Eva makes her first conquest, the troubadour Agustín Magaldi (Jimmy Nail), whom she accompanies to Buenos Aires, a glittering Hollywood of hope for Eva. Her gift for attracting men of position leads her to Juan Perón (Jonathan Pryce), a junta colonel who becomes Argentina's President in 1946. Eva's glamour—less a natural attribute than a triumph of her will—and her urge to help the poor humanize Perón's stolid majesty; they also come close to bankrupting the country, even as they drain her. She fulfills the rock-age hagiography: live big, die young, and leave a memory that time can transform into gaudy myth.

Parker has filmed the story in the suave, dark tones of a film-noir musical. Buenos Aires becomes a character in the movie less by re-creating period exteriors than by focusing on the extras' faces—gorgeous, pensive reflections of Eva's sultry magnetism. But this is, essentially, a three-character play, demanding that the stars must sing, swagger and act with style. Pryce, consummate pro, lives fully in all three realms. Banderas parades his sex appeal as the one man who is not a father figure to Evita; he is the skeptical stud who can match her arrogance with his own.

Madonna once again confounds our expectations—and, at times, exasperations. At first a star more famous for attitude than for voice, she proved, in the 1990 *Dick Tracy*, equal to the sere demands of Stephen Sondheim's songs. Here again she does a tough score proud. Lacking the vocal vigor of Elaine Paige's West End Evita, Madonna plays Evita with a poignant weariness, as if death has shrouded her from infancy. And dressed in sumptuous gowns or feeling life seep away, she has more than just a little bit of star quality. Just before Eva's death, she sings the film's one new tune, which sounds eerily like an act of faith: *You Must Love Me*. But love or hate Madonna-Eva, she is a magnet for all eyes. You must watch her. And to find the soul of the modern musical for once on the big screen, you must see *Evita*.

Richard Corliss, *Time* (December 16, 1996)

Naturally, not all reviewers can fulfill Macdonald's criteria as well as Corliss does. Several, however, can: Andrew Sarris, David Denby, Stanley Kauffman, and perhaps the most famous of all, Pauline Kael.

The best of Pauline Kael's criticism has been collected in *For Keeps: 30 Years of Movies* (1994). Because she identifies with the moviegoer, she is sometimes forced to assume an egalitarian, even an anti-intellectual pose. She constantly laments the teaching of film in the university, claiming that an overly scholarly approach will kill "movies" (her favorite term for the medium, because in America we never say "I'm going to the films" but "I'm going to the movies"). She scorns pretentiousness, believing that films like *Last Year at Marienbad* (1961) will drive moviegoers out of the theaters. She champions American movies, yet she is not chauvinistic; she merely feels that they come closer to what movies ought to be than do most European films. Although she scorns auteurism, she has favorite directors, among them Robert Altman and Sam Peckinpah. She may have written for *The New Yorker*, but there is no wordiness in her style; there is wit, however, which may explain her long association with that magazine.

If Pauline Kael sounds like a mass of contradictions, it is because on the one hand, she writes about an art form that, in its inception, was not taken seriously; movies were "flickers," and nothing more. On the other hand, she is writing about an art form that is now not only taken seriously but is the subject of undergraduate and graduate study. Thus, she maintains a "one of the people" stand by addressing the reader as a "you," a form of address that David Denby has also adopted. "What you keep reacting to is the film's exuberant doodles," she wrote of *Bull Durham* (1988). Yet, as a critic whose knowledge of the other arts is on a par with her knowledge of film, she is more than just one of the people; she is the people at their most perceptive; she is the ideal moviegoer.

This does not mean that she cannot make mistakes. No critic is infallible; one should remember that Tolstoy refused to consider Shakespeare a classic, and T. S. Eliot made the extravagant claim that Virgil's *Aeneid* is the only true classic of Western literature. Kael can also be hyperbolic when she feels strongly about a movie: she once compared the evening *Last Tango in Paris* closed the 1972 New York Film Festival with the evening Igor Stravinsky's *The Rite of Spring* premiered, calling each date a cultural landmark. Because she disapproves of auteurism (although she has favorite auteurs), she set out to discredit Orson Welles as the auteur of *Citizen Kane* in her essay, "Raising Kane" (1971), which first appeared in *The New Yorker* and then as the introduction to *The Citizen Kane Book*. Subsequent criticism, notably by Robert Carringer, has shown that Kael was not entirely correct in attributing the script wholly to Herman J. Mankiewicz. Kael certainly has her blind spots; she either failed, or refused, to see how Welles impressed his personality on *Citizen Kane* by drawing on his stage and radio experience (especially overlapping dialogue and musical bridges) to combine the best of both media in the film.

To her credit, Kael at least has a philosophy of film: it is a people's art form. Moviegoers loathe sham; they prefer "movies" to "cinema"; they want theorizing kept to a minimum; they cannot bear to see their values mocked. Thus, Kael reacted negatively to *A Clockwork Orange* because it argued that humankind's capacity for evil is never exhausted. Kael, who believes in people (or at least moviegoers), could not accept that. Consequently, she accused Stanley Kubrick of "sucking up to the thugs in the audience."[12]

Pauline Kael wrote what are really essay-reviews. Her method is to reconstruct the film, incorporating her own impressions, comparisons with other films, and frequently comparisons with other art forms. Those who dislike Kael claim that in reconstructing the film she creates an antifilm that bears little resemblance to the original. If Kael does this, and it is not often, readers are at least afforded an X ray of her thoughts so that they can experience what was going on in her mind when she saw the film and later when she was writing about it. We may not always be able to see every movie we read about. What reviewers as critics can do is suggest how we might have reacted during the film and when reflecting on it. Pauline Kael can provide this vicarious experience better than most of her colleagues.

PRACTICAL CRITICISM

If fiction is a house with many windows, as Henry James alleged, then criticism is a house with many doors, each with its own key. No school of literary criticism has a monopoly on interpretation; each offers its own peculiar access to the work. The New Criticism stresses the text; historical criticism places the text within its time; biographical criticism, within the context of the author's life; Marxist criticism, within the framework of the class struggle; psychoanalytic criticism, within the workings of the unconscious; myth criticism, within the universal dreams of humankind.

That criticism is an applied art is evident from the various ways in which a film historian, an auteurist, a myth critic, and a social historian might interpret *Citizen Kane*.

The history of *Citizen Kane* is filled with so many untruths and half-truths that uncovering the real truth about the film is as complex as Thompson's attempt to solve the enigma of "Rosebud." The popular assumption that RKO was in such a state of financial instability that its president, George J. Schaefer, wooed Orson Welles, the boy wonder of stage and radio, to Hollywood in the hope of working wonders for the studio, is one such untruth. In "A History of RKO Radio Pictures, Incorporated, 1928–1942" Richard B. Jewell has shown that in 1940, the year RKO signed Welles, its finances were in good shape.[13] Furthermore, the studio had a tradition of hiring stage personalities such as Katharine Hepburn, George Gershwin, and the director Garson Kanin; thus, RKO's hiring Welles was not inconsistent with studio policy, although his being given the right of final cut was inconsistent with Hollywood policy in general.

Although one may never know whose idea it was—Welles's or Herman J. Mankiewicz's—to make a movie based on the life of newspaper tycoon William Randolph Hearst, films about the rise of an entrepreneur from obscurity to renown were not unknown. Since Mankiewicz, who wrote the first two drafts of *Citizen Kane* (which he entitled *American*), had been writing for the movies since 1926, he may well have been influenced by the script Preston Sturges wrote for *The Power and the Glory* (1933), which dealt with a Kane-like railroad magnate. Thomas Garner (Spencer Tracy) in *The Power and the Glory* is as enigmatic as the master of Xanadu. Moreover, there are points of contact between both films: the Horatio Alger theme, the flashbacks following the tycoon's death, violations of chronology, and the extremes of admiration and contempt that both men inspired.

Mankiewicz, however, was not wholly responsible for the script of the film that ultimately became *Citizen Kane*. Pauline Kael's "Raising Kane" is in error on this point.[14] In an attempt to refocus attention on Mankiewicz, whom Welles has eclipsed, Kael downplayed Welles's contribution even to the point of undermining its orginality. What other critics consider Wellesian, she would attribute to Gregg Toland's cinematography. Kael invites us to compare *Kane* with *Mad Love* (1935), a Peter Lorre "mad doctor" movie, which Toland photographed and which has certain features in common with *Kane*: gothic sets, a physical resemblance between the bald Lorre and the bald Welles in *Kane*'s final scenes, cavernous rooms, and even a white cockatoo.

"Raising Kane," which has occasioned controversy since its publication, has been superceded by what appears to be the definitive work on the subject, Robert L. Carringer's *The Making of Citizen Kane*. Consequently, we now know that "Mankiewicz . . . wrote the first two drafts. His principal contributions were the story frame, a cast of characters, various individual scenes, and a good share of the dialogue. . . . Welles added the narrative brilliance—the visual and verbal wit, the stylistic fluidity, and such stunningly original strokes as the newspaper montages and the breakfast table sequence."[15] Unlike Kael, who exalted Mankiewicz at the expense of Welles, Carringer is perfectly willing to credit Mankiewicz for a contribution of "fundamental importance" but, knowing what he does about the film's genesis, cannot attribute the script solely to him.

Nor can Carringer allow the myth to persist that Gregg Toland determined how *Citizen Kane* would be photographed. Carringer proves that Welles and Toland were in total agreement as to how the film would be shot; it was not to resemble a typical Hollywood movie but rather it would display all the techniques at which Toland excelled (low angles, deep focus, high-contrast photography, and the like). Deep focus, long takes, and a paucity of close-ups would also serve Welles's purpose. One must never forget that Welles came from the theater; hence, deep focus and long takes would be as close as he could come to duplicating stage drama. Since stage actors project more forcefully than film actors, a preponderance of close-ups would reveal their lack of film experience. One must also never forget that the leading roles were played by members of Welles's Mercury Theatre. Finally, it should be remembered that the Mercury Theatre had a weekly radio series, *The Mercury Theatre on the Air*, which Welles hosted and in which he frequently appeared. *Citizen Kane* contains examples of a common radio-drama device, the cross fade, in which a character begins a sentence in one place and someone else finishes it in another.

Although *Citizen Kane* is not always thought of in terms of RKO, it was an RKO product. As Carringer demonstrates, the glass paperweight that is so crucial to the plot is not that different from a similar paperweight that appeared in an earlier RKO film, *Kitty Foyle*. In both films, the paperweight has a snow motif that conjures up memories of childhood. Since both paperweights were made by the RKO property department, it is unlikely that Mankiewicz or Mankiewicz/Welles hit upon the paperweight idea without some prior knowledge of *Kitty Foyle*.

Knowledge of a film's production history makes it possible to speak authoritatively about the film. Without such knowledge, one runs the risk of crediting the wrong individuals with contributions that others have made.

The Auteurist

Like many a first film, *Citizen Kane* contains within it the director's major themes and preoccupations. Here it is Welles's ambivalence toward wealth

The glass paperweight in *Kitty Foyle* (1940) that probably inspired the one in Citizen Kane. *(Courtesy WCFTR)*

and his fascination with corruption. Welles's world is full of potentates, of men who are larger than life: Kane, Bannister of *The Lady from Shanghai*, Gregori Arkadin of *Mr. Arkadin* (1955), and their alter egos in the director's Shakespearean films (*Macbeth*, 1948; *Othello*, 1952; and *Chimes at Midnight*, 1967).

Wealth assumes various forms in Welles's films: Kane's Xanadu, the Amberson mansion in *The Magnificent Ambersons*, the yacht in *The Lady from Shanghai*, the castle of Dunsinane in *Macbeth*, the castle at San Tirso in *Mr. Arkadin*, and Henry IV's court in *Chimes at Midnight*. Conversely, symbols of squalor also recur: Mary Kane's boardinghouse, the boardinghouse to which George and Aunt Fanny retreat in *The Magnificent Ambersons*, the Mexican fleabag in *Touch of Evil*, K's flat in *The Trial* (1963).

There are certain Wellesian artifacts that characterize the rich, the corrupt, and the guilty: mirrors (*Kane*, *The Lady from Shanghai*, *Othello*); corridors (*Kane*, *Macbeth*, *The Trial*); staircases (*Kane*, *The Magnificent Ambersons*); chauffeured cars (*Kane*) and private planes (*Mr. Arkadin*).

Another Wellesian theme is the war of the worlds. The extraordinary world encroaches on the ordinary, and the fortuitous and the irrational confront the stable and the orderly. In *Kane*, Susan Alexander gives up a secure but mediocre existence to enter Kane's erratic world, in which she clearly does not belong. In Welles's other films, the two worlds are reflected in various ways: the automobile confronts the horse and buggy in *The Magnificent Ambersons*; Nazism brings disorder to a quiet Connecticut town in *The Stranger* (1946); an Irish sailor is exposed to the idle but murderous rich in *The Lady from Shanghai*; an ordinary couple is thrown into a nightmarish world of drugs and violence in *Touch of Evil*; the little man is introduced to fascist bureaucracy in *The Trial*. Even in the Shakespearean cycle, worlds collide: Macbeth's and Lady Macbeth's, Macbeth's and Macduff's (*Macbeth*); Othello's and Iago's, Othello's and Desdemona's (*Othello*); Falstaff's and Henry's, Falstaff's and Hal's (*Chimes at Midnight*).

The Wellesian king-figure dies as he lived—in style: Kane's arms solemnly folded on his breast, Othello's bier carried aloft, Henry IV expiring on his throne. Even the Wellesian villain goes out in the grand manner: from the top of a tower (*The Stranger*), in a maze of mirrors (*The Lady from Shanghai*), plunging through space (*Mr. Arkadin*).

As Welles's first film, *Kane* represents the beginning of the Wellesian style that would continue to manifest itself visually (long takes, dichotomy of light and darkness, recurring mirror and snow imagery) and aurally (overlapping dialogue, cross fades) in his later work. The three-minute-long take that begins *Touch of Evil* had its origin in the camera's moving up the gate of Xanadu at the opening of *Citizen Kane* and in the camera's craning up the billboard advertising Susan Alexander Kane's appearance at El Rancho, moving over to the skylight, then shooting down at Susan seated at a table. Kane's multiple image reflected in the panels of the mirrored corridor anticipates the multiple images of Elsa and Bannister in the climax of *The Lady from Shanghai*. Welles's ambiguous attitude toward light (source of knowledge and sign of its absence; symbol of innocence and illusion as well as the glare of reality) runs throughout his films. Susan, a study in white with her blond hair and gleaming white skin, is a symbol of innocence exploited. The light that floods her face makes her even more pathetic; so does the light that masks the face of the doomed Isabel in *The Magnificent Ambersons*. Conversely, the light that hardens the face of the already hardened (and blond) Elsa Bannister in *The Lady from Shanghai* mocks the symbol of innocence by its profusion.

Like *Kane*, other Welles films open in darkness or semidarkness (*The Lady from Shanghai, The Stranger, Macbeth, Touch of Evil*). Darkness can suggest womblike withdrawal (the dimly lit Xanadu) as well as a universe unilluminated by grace or providence (*The Lady from Shanghai, Touch of Evil*).

For a true appreciation of *Kane*, one must know how, as the first expression of Welles's visual and aural style, it foreshadowed themes and techniques that reappear in his subsequent films.

The Myth Critic

Every leading character in *Citizen Kane* is the incarnation of a mythological figure. Kane himself is a Zeus type. Zeus, who never had a childhood, was whisked off to Crete by his mother so that his wicked father, Cronus, would not devour him as he had done his other children. Charles Foster

Kane was also deprived of a normal boyhood. When he was a child, his mother entrusted him to a guardian so that he could have the life she could never give him.

Neither Zeus nor Kane was happily married. Zeus's marriage to Hera may have been made on Olympus, but it was not blessed with tranquillity. Kane's marriage to the cool, patrician beauty Emily Norton was no different. A president's niece, Emily was socially superior to her husband and showed it by her demeanor. Thus, Kane looked for love elsewhere, finding it briefly in an aspiring but untalented singer, Susan Alexander. Zeus also sought other women, rarely appearing to them as himself but taking other forms (a bull, a swan, a husband away from the war). Kane also conceals himself by diluting his importance when he describes his job to Susan, preferring that she love him for himself: "I run a couple of newspapers. How about you?"

When Kane tries to make Susan into an opera star, he steps out of the role of Zeus and into that of Pygmalion. But he becomes a Pygmalion in reverse. The sculptor Pygmalion fell in love with his own creation, which miraculously came to life. Welles inverts the myth, making Kane into an anti-Pygmalion who fashions a puppet for himself out of a living woman.

Zeus replaced his father's tyranny with the enlightened rule of the Olympians. Kane must fight his surrogate father (Thatcher, his guardian), who embodies the worst qualities of the privileged class. When Thatcher asks Kane what he would like to have been, Kane replies, "Everything you hate." In fact, Kane is always fighting Cronus in some form: Thatcher, the elderly owner of *The Inquirer* that he takes over, the political boss Jim Gettys. When he is not clashing with Cronus, he is battling Prometheus in the person of Leland, who sees him for what he is: "You don't care about anything except you."

Ultimately, Zeus became another Cronus: authoritarian, misanthropic, vindictive, fearful of having his power usurped, and, finally, aloof. Kane gradually grows more and more like Thatcher-Cronus; although he wants to benefit humanity, he has become too corrupted by wealth to do so. In the *Iliad*, Zeus, weary of all the infighting among the Olympians, frequently retired to the topmost peak of Mount Ida; Kane, disillusioned by political defeat, broken friendships, and Susan's failure as an opera star, retires to the seclusion of Xanadu.

If it is viewed as myth, *Kane*'s universality is more evident than it would be if the film were studied as a historical artifact or as the work of an auteur.

The Social Historian

As Machiavelli noted in *The Prince*, half of our affairs are governed by fortune (*fortuna*); the other half, by personal endeavor (*virtù*). It was by pure chance that Mary Kane, the owner of a boardinghouse, acquired the Colorado Lode. A boarder, unable to pay his rent, gave her a deed to an abandoned mine shaft that turned out to be the world's third-richest gold mine. Once fortuna places something in our path, virtù must take over. Unfortunately, Mary Kane's virtù was diseased; married to a failure, she did not want her son, Charles, to become a replica of his father. Therefore, she entrusted the boy to the care of Walter P. Thatcher, a noted financier; in so doing, she deprived Charles of a normal childhood so that he could enjoy a life befitting a millionaire.

The American dream can become a nightmare. Charles Foster Kane first tries to redeem himself. When he assumes control of the *New York Inquirer*, he begins exposing trusts and slumlords. He tells his guardian: "It is my duty—I'll let you in on a secret—it is also my pleasure—to see to it that decent hard-working people of this community aren't robbed blind by a pack of money-mad pirates!"

Kane is a principled muckraker. He also refuses to run the newspaper as if it were his private enterprise; instead, he delegates authority. He even writes a Declaration of Principles, promising his readers an honest newspaper. However, while he is writing it, his face is shrouded in darkness. Kane is clearly irredeemable.

There is no salvation for Kane because he is heir to his mother's belief that the purchasing power of money is infinite. Just as his mother bought him a privileged life, Kane buys his second wife an operatic career as well as an opera house, forcing her into a role for which she has no talent. Finally, to achieve the seclusion he requires, he buys a pleasure dome on the Florida Gulf Coast.

Who is Charles Foster Kane? After his death, the press called him a plutocrat; his guardian branded him a communist; the Union Square demagogues labeled him a fascist. Then there is Kane's view of himself: "I am, always will be, and always have been one thing: an American."

The popular conception of Kane, confused and contradictory, is no different from the popular conception of America: the republic to which we pledge allegiance, the democracy we claim we are, the empire others perceive us to be. The three faces of America become Kane's three faces. First, he is the republican editor who delegates authority to his representatives; then, he is the democratic leader, promising in his Declaration of Principles to be a champion of human rights; finally, he is the imperialist, bald and gowned, an Oriental potentate living in splendor at Xanadu. *Citizen Kane* forces us to watch the transformation of the country through the transformation of one man.

While each interpretation is valid as far as it goes, one could easily write an essay combining all of them by recounting details about the film's production history, showing how *Kane*'s visual style is repeated in Welles's

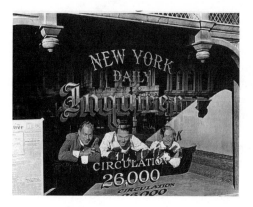

THE THREE FACES OF KANE
The republican Kane flanked by
Leland, his drama critic (Joseph
Cotten), and Bernstein, his
managing editor (Everett Sloane).
(Courtesy MOMA/FSA)

other films, relating its archetypal plot to well-known myths, and noting its ambivalence about a society that encourages "rags-to-riches" optimism and places material values before spiritual ones.

GUIDELINES FOR FILM CRITICISM

There is no one way to criticize film. After a lifetime of reviewing, Dwight Macdonald wondered whether the norms that had once served him were still valid. Since Macdonald's guidelines are among the best that a contemporary critic can offer a student of film, it is worthwhile to repeat them here. They represent ways of approaching film, however, not ironclad laws. Thus, there will be exceptions; some of the guidelines may not be applicable to a particular film, as Macdonald is the first to admit. Still, it is easier to deal with exceptions when one has standards by which to measure them than would be the case if one had no standards at all. The following excerpt from Macdonald's work, *Dwight Macdonald on Movies*, summarizes his guidelines succinctly:

> I know something about cinema after forty years, and being a congenital critic, I know what I like and why. But I can't explain the *why* except in terms of the specific work under consideration, on which I'm copious enough. The general theory, the larger view, the gestalt—these have always eluded me. Whether this gap in my critical armor be called an idiosyncrasy or, less charitably, a personal failing, it has always been most definitely there.
>
> But people, especially undergraduates hot for certainty, keep asking me what rules, principles or standards I judge movies by—a fair question to which I can never think of an answer. Years ago, some forgotten but evi-

dently sharp stimulus spurred me to put some guidelines down on paper. The result, hitherto unprinted for reasons which will become clear, was:

(1) Are the characters consistent, and in fact are there characters at all?

(2) Is it true to life?

(3) Is the photography cliché, or is it adapted to the particular film and therefore original?

(4) Do the parts go together; do they add up to something; is there a rhythm established so that there is form, shape, climax, building up tension and exploding it?

(5) Is there a mind behind it; is there a feeling that a single intelligence has imposed his own view on the material?

The last two questions rough out some vague sort of meaning, and the third is sound, if truistic. But I can't account for the first two being there at all, let alone in the lead-off place. Many films I admire are not "true to life" unless that stretchable term is strained beyond normal usage: *Broken Blossoms, Children of Paradise, Zéro de Conduite, Caligari, On Approval,* Eisenstein's *Ivan*

The democratic Kane as Man of the People. *(Courtesy MOMA/FSA)*

The Imperial Kane as Master of Xanadu. *(Courtesy MOMA/FSA)*

the Terrible. And some have no "characters" at all, consistent or no: *Potemkin, Arsenal, October, Intolerance, Marienbad, Orpheus, Olympia.* The comedies of Keaton, Chaplin, Lubitsch, the Marx Brothers and W. C. Fields occupy a middle ground. They have "consistent characters" all right, and they are also "true to life." But the consistency is always extreme and sometimes compulsive and obsessed (W. C., Groucho, Buster), and the truth is abstract. In short, they are so highly stylized . . . that they are constantly floating up from terra firma into the empyrean of art, right before my astonished and delighted eyes.[16]

If philosophy begins with wonder, as Plato claimed, so too does film criticism—with a sense of amazement that pictures can move, and the desire to explain how the moving picture can be a work of art. Even though you know the pictures do not move miraculously, never lose that childlike sense of wonder that you felt when you saw your first movie. Realize that when you are asked to write about a movie you are sharing in an ancient art, the art of criticism, that goes back to the fourth century B.C. Although film criticism is in its infancy compared to literary criticism, it works from the same principle: the desire to explain structurally, descriptively, psychologically, or ideologically how a work of art functions. The papers you write will be on limited topics; they always are: "Deep Focus in *Citizen*

Kane, "The Chronology of *Citizen Kane,*" "Expressionism vs. Realism in *Citizen Kane.*" Yet if you peruse scholarly journals such as *Film Criticism, Film Quarterly,* and *Literature/Film Quarterly,* you will discover articles by film scholars that are equally specific. One would have to write a book in order to articulate a philosophy of film. Still, when you write your papers, at least try to relate your particular topic to the whole film, showing how deep focus figures in the film's overall meaning, how the alternation between expressionism and realism is part of the film's tension, or how the jumbled chronology reflects the film's attitude toward Kane's life and biography in general.

Think of the parts in relation to the whole. This is what *Anatomy of Film* has attempted to do: to proceed from the components of narrative film to the total film and, finally, to ways of interpreting film. Whether you pursue film criticism professionally or simply as a moviegoer, remember that a work of art possesses integrity or wholeness. A film is a totality; even if it is approached piecemeal, it does not lose its integrity, although that integrity may be hard to discern unless the parts are reassembled.

Alexander Pope has been quoted earlier in this chapter because Pope, who was not even twenty when he wrote *An Essay on Criticism,* formulated principles that are still relevant. As you might expect, he also had something to say about focusing on the whole rather than the parts:

> 'T is not a lip or eye we beauty call,
> But the joint force and full result of all.
>
> —*An Essay on Criticism,* (II, 45–46)

No matter what kind of critic you become or what kinds of critics you read, relate your approach and theirs to the film as a whole.

NOTES

[1] Raymond Spottiswoode, *A Grammar of the Film: An Analysis of Film Technique* (Berkeley: University of California Press, 1969), 29.

[2] Rudolf Arnheim, *Film as Art* (Berkeley: University of California Press, 1974), 133.

[3] Ibid., 57.

[4] André Bazin, *What Is Cinema?* Vol. 1, trans. Hugh Gray (Berkeley: University of California Press, 1967), 50.

[5] Siegfried Kracauer, *Theory of Film: The Redemption of Physical Reality* (New York: Oxford University Press/Galaxy Books, 1965), 305.

[6] One of the best general studies of semiotics is Kaja Silverman, *The Subject of Semiotics* (New York: Oxford University Press, 1983); on film semiotics, see J. Dudley Andrew, *The Major Film Theories: An Introduction* (New York: Oxford University Press, 1976), 212–41. Also recommended is the structuralism issue of *College English* (October 1975).

[7]Christian Metz, *Film Language: A Semiotics of the Cinema*, trans. Michael Taylor (New York: Oxford University Press, 1974), 105.

[8]Laura Mulvey, "Visual Pleasure and Narrative Cinema," in *Film Theory and Criticism*, 4th ed., ed. Gerald Mast, Marshall Cohen, and Leo Braudy (New York: Oxford University Press, 1992), 747.

[9]James Agee, *Agee on Film: Reviews and Comments by James Agee* (New York: Grosset & Dunlap, 1969), 39.

[10]On Crowther's career, see Frank E. Beaver, *Bosley Crowther: Social Critic of the Film* (New York: Arno Press, 1974).

[11]Dwight Macdonald, *Dwight Macdonald on Movies* (Englewood Cliffs, N.J.: Prentice-Hall, 1969), 471.

[12]Pauline Kael, *Deeper into Movies* (Boston: Atlantic-Little, Brown, 1974), 378.

[13]Richard B. Jewell, "A History of RKO Radio Pictures, Incorporated, 1928–1942" (Ph.D. diss., University of Southern California Press, 1978).

[14]Pauline Kael, "Raising Kane," *The Citizen Kane Book* (Boston: Little Brown, 1971), 1–84.

[15]Robert L. Carringer, *The Making of Citizen Kane* (Berkeley: University of California Press, 1985), 35.

[16]Macdonald, *Dwight Macdonald on Movies*, ix–x.

APPENDIX

Films Discussed and Directors

Film	Director
Abraham Lincoln (1930)	D. W. Griffith
The Accused (1948)	William Dieterle
An Act of Murder (1948)	Michael Gordon
Address Unknown (1944)	William Cameron Menzies
Against All Odds (1984)	Taylor Hackford
The Age of Innocence (1993)	Martin Scorsese
Alice Doesn't Live Here Anymore (1975)	Martin Scorsese
*All About Eve (1950)	Joseph L. Mankiewicz
All the President's Men (1976)	Alan J. Pakula
Amadeus (1984)	Milŏs Forman
*An American in Paris (1951)	Vincente Minnelli
And Now Tomorrow (1944)	Irving Pichel
Angels with Dirty Faces (1938)	Michael Curtiz
À Nous la Liberté (1931)	René Clair

---

*Films chosen for the Library of Congress's National Film Registry (1989–), created to single out films of historical and cultural significance.

The Apartment (1960)	Billy Wilder
Apocalypse Now (1979)	Francis Ford Coppola
Arise, My Love (1940)	Mitchell Leisen
Avanti! (1972)	Billy Wilder
**The Awful Truth* (1937)	Leo McCarey
The Bad and the Beautiful (1952)	Vincente Minnelli
**Badlands* (1973)	Terrence Malick
Ball of Fire (1941)	Howard Hawks
The Barkleys of Broadway (1949)	Charles Walters
Barry Lyndon (1975)	Stanley Kubrick
Beauty and the Beast (1992)	Gary Trousdale and Kirk Wise
Beginning of the End (1957)	Bert I. Gordon
**The Best Years of Our Lives* (1946)	William Wyler
The Big Carnival (1951)	Billy Wilder
The Big Sleep (1946)	Howard Hawks
The Birds (1963)	Alfred Hitchcock
**The Birth of a Nation* (1915)	D. W. Griffith
The Bishop's Wife (1947)	Henry Koster
The Blob (1958)	Irving S. Yeaworth, Jr.
Blonde Venus (1932)	Josef von Sternberg
The Blue Angel (1930)	Josef von Sternberg
Bluebeard (1944)	Edgar G. Ulmer
Body and Soul (1947)	Robert Rossen
Body Heat (1981)	Lawrence Kasdan
**Bonnie and Clyde* (1967)	Arthur Penn
The Bravados (1957)	Henry King
Breathless (1959)	Jean-Luc Godard
Bride of Frankenstein (1935)	James Whale
Brief Encounter (1946)	David Lean
Brigadoon (1954)	Vincente Minnelli
**Bringing Up Baby* (1938)	Howard Hawks
Broken Arrow (1950)	Delmer Daves
**Broken Blossoms* (1919)	D. W. Griffith
Broken Lance (1954)	Edward Dmytryk
Brute Force (1947)	Jules Dassin
Buddy Buddy (1981)	Billy Wilder
Burnt Offerings (1976)	Dan Curtis
Butch Cassidy and the Sundance Kid (1969)	George Roy Hill
The Cabinet of Dr. Caligari (1919)	Robert Weine
Cape Fear (1991)	Martin Scorsese

Carrie (1976)	Brian De Palma
Casablanca (1942)	Michael Curtiz
Cat People (1942)	Jacques Tourneur
Caught (1949)	Max Ophuls
Chimes at Midnight (1967)	Orson Welles
Chinatown (1974)	Roman Polanski
Citizen Kane (1941)	Orson Welles
A Clockwork Orange (1971)	Stanley Kubrick
Close Encounters of the Third Kind (1977)	Steven Spielberg
Clueless (1995)	Amy Heckerling
Colorado Territory (1949)	Raoul Walsh
The Color Purple (1986)	Steven Spielberg
Coney Island (1943)	Walter Lang
The Corn Is Green (1944)	Irving Rapper
Cover Girl (1944)	Charles Vidor
Creature from the Black Lagoon (1954)	Jack Arnold
Criss Cross (1949)	Robert Siodmak
The Crying Game (1992)	Neil Jordan
The Curse of the Cat People (1944)	Gunther von Fritsch and Robert Wise
Dances with Wolves (1990)	Kevin Costner
Dark Passage (1947)	Delmer Daves
Dark Victory (1939)	Edmund Goulding
The Day of the Locust (1975)	John Schlesinger
The Day the Earth Stood Still (1951)	Robert Wise
The Dead (1987)	John Huston
Dead Reckoning (1947)	John Cromwell
Detour (1946)	Edgar G. Ulmer
Dog Day Afternoon (1975)	Sidney Lumet
A Doll's House (1973)	Patrick Garland
Double Indemnity (1944)	Billy Wilder
Dracula's Daughter (1936)	Lambert Hillyer
Dr. Cyclops (1940)	Ernest Schoedsack
Dream Street (1921)	D. W. Griffith
Dressed to Kill (1980)	Brian De Palma
Dr. Jekyll and Mr. Hyde (1932)	Rouben Mamoulian
Duel in the Sun (1947)	King Vidor
Easter Parade (1948)	Charles Walters
Easy Living (1937)	Mitchell Leisen
Easy Rider (1969)	Dennis Hopper
Emma (1996)	Doug McGrath

The Emperor Waltz (1948)	Billy Wilder
Empire of the Sun (1987)	Steven Spielberg
*E.T.: The Extra-Terrestrial (1982)	Steven Spielberg
Evita (1996)	Alan Parker
Experiment Perilous (1944)	Jacques Tourneur
Family Plot (1976)	Alfred Hitchcock
*Fantasia (1940)	Ben Sharpsteen
Fatal Attraction (1989)	Adrian Lyne
Fedora (1979)	Billy Wilder
The First Time (1952)	Frank Tashlin
Five Graves to Cairo (1943)	Billy Wilder
Flying Down to Rio (1933)	Thornton Freeland
A Foreign Affair (1948)	Billy Wilder
Foreign Correspondent (1940)	Alfred Hitchcock
Forever Amber (1947)	Otto Preminger
Forrest Gump (1994)	Robert Zemeckis
Fort Apache (1948)	John Ford
The Fortune Cookie (1966)	Billy Wilder
42nd Street (1933)	Lloyd Bacon
The 400 Blows (1959)	François Truffaut
The Four Seasons (1981)	Alan Alda
Four Weddings and a Funeral (1994)	Mike Newell
*Frankenstein (1931)	James Whale
French Kiss (1995)	Lawrence Kasdan
Frenzy (1972)	Alfred Hitchcock
Friday the 13th (1980)	Sean S. Cunningham
The Front (1975)	Martin Ritt
The Front Page (1974)	Billy Wilder
The Giant Claw (1957)	Fred S. Sears
Gilda (1946)	Charles Vidor
The Glass Menagerie (1986)	Paul Newman
*The Godfather, Part II (1974)	Francis Ford Coppola
Gold Diggers of 1933 (1933)	Mervyn LeRoy
Gold Diggers of 1935 (1935)	Busby Berkeley
*Gone with the Wind (1939)	Victor Fleming
GoodFellas (1989)	Martin Scorsese
*The Grapes of Wrath (1940)	John Ford
The Greatest Story Ever Told (1965)	George Stevens
Great Expectations (1946)	David Lean
The Great Lie (1941)	Edmund Goulding

*The Great Train Robbery (1903)   E. S. Porter
The Green Berets (1968)   John Wayne / Ray Kellogg
The Grifters (1990)   Stephen Frears
Gun Crazy (1949)   Joseph H. Lewis

Hail the Conquering Hero (1944)   Preston Sturges
Halloween (1978)   John Carpenter
Hannah and Her Sisters (1986)   Woody Allen
The Happy Ending (1968)   Richard Brooks
Hello Frisco, Hello (1943)   H. Bruce Humberstone
Hennessy (1975)   Don Sharp
He Ran All the Way (1951)   John Berry
*High Noon (1952)   Fred Zinnemann
High Sierra (1941)   Raoul Walsh
High Society (1956)   Charles Walters
Hiroshima Mon Amour (1959)   Alain Resnais
*His Girl Friday (1940)   Howard Hawks
Hold Back the Dawn (1941)   Mitchell Leisen
The House on Carroll Street (1988)   Peter Yates
*How Green Was My Valley (1941)   John Ford
How to Marry a Millionaire (1953)   Jean Negulesco
Hustle (1975)   Robert Aldrich

I Confess (1952)   Alfred Hitchcock
I Married a Monster from Outer Space (1958)   Gene Fowler, Jr.
Indiana Jones and the Temple of Doom (1985)   Steven Spielberg
*Intolerance (1916)   D. W. Griffith
*Invasion of the Body Snatchers (1956)   Don Siegel
Isadora (1969)   Karl Reisz
It Came from Outer Space (1953)   Jack Arnold
*It Happened One Night (1934)   Frank Capra
*It's a Wonderful Life (1946)   Frank Capra
I Walked with a Zombie (1943)   Jacques Tourneur

Jane Eyre (1944)   Robert Stevenson
Jezebel (1938)   William Wyler
Johnny Guitar (1954)   Nicholas Ray
The Jolson Story (1946)   Alfred E. Green
Jules et Jim (1961)   François Truffaut
Julia (1977)   Fred Zinnemann
Juliet of the Spirits (1965)   Federico Fellini
Julius Caesar (1953)   Joseph L. Mankiewicz

King and Country (1964)	Joseph Losey
*King Kong (1933)	Merian C. Cooper and
	Ernest B. Schoedsack
Kiss Me, Stupid (1964)	Billy Wilder
Kitty Foyle (1940)	Sam Wood
Knock on any Door (1949)	Nicholas Ray
Lacombe, Lucien (1974)	Louis Malle
Lady and the Monster (1944)	George Sherman
Lady Be Good (1941)	Norman Z. McLeod
*The Lady Eve (1941)	Preston Sturges
The Lady from Shanghai (1948)	Orson Welles
Lady in the Dark (1944)	Mitchell Leisen
Lady in the Lake (1946)	Robert Montgomery
Lady in White (1988)	Frank Laloggia
The Last Emperor (1987)	Bernardo Bertolucci
The Last Picture Show (1971)	Peter Bogdanovich
Last Tango in Paris (1972)	Bernardo Bertolucci
The Last Temptation of Christ (1988)	Martin Scorsese
Last Train from Gun Hill (1956)	John Sturges
The Last Tycoon (1976)	Elia Kazan
L'Atalante (1934)	Jean Vigo
A League of Their Own (1992)	Penny Marshall
*Letter from an Unknown Woman (1948)	Max Ophuls
A Letter to Three Wives (1949)	Joseph L. Mankiewicz
Lifeboat (1944)	Alfred Hitchcock
Little Big Man (1970)	Arthur Penn
The Little Foxes (1941)	William Wyler
Little Women (1994)	Gillian Armstrong
The Locket (1946)	John Brahm
Long Day's Journey into Night (1962)	Sidney Lumet
Look Who's Talking (1989)	Amy Heckerling
Lost Horizon (1937)	Frank Capra
Lost in America (1985)	Albert Brooks
The Lost Weekend (1945)	Billy Wilder
Love in the Afternoon (1957)	Billy Wilder
M (1931)	Fritz Lang
Macbeth (1948)	Orson Welles
Mad Love (1935)	Karl Freund
*The Magnificent Ambersons (1942)	Orson Welles
The Major and the Minor (1942)	Billy Wilder

Malcolm X (1992)	Spike Lee
The Man from Laramie (1955)	Anthony Mann
Manhattan (1979)	Woody Allen
The Man Who Shot Liberty Valance (1962)	John Ford
Marnie (1964)	Alfred Hitchcock
Married to the Mob (1988)	Jonathan Demme
*M*A*S*H (1970)	Robert Altman
McCabe and Mrs. Miller (1971)	Robert Altman
Medium Cool (1969)	Haskell Wexler
Meet John Doe (1941)	Frank Capra
*Meet Me in St. Louis (1944)	Vincente Minnelli
Meet Nero Wolfe (1936)	Herbert Biberman
The Merry Widow (1934)	Ernst Lubitsch
Midnight (1939)	Mitchell Leisen
*Mildred Pierce (1945)	Michael Curtiz
The Miracle (1948)	Roberto Rossellini
The Mirror Has Two Faces (1996)	Barbra Streisand
Mission to Moscow (1943)	Michael Curtiz
*Modern Times (1936)	Charlie Chaplin
Moon over Miami (1941)	Walter Lang
Moonstruck (1987)	Norman Jewison
*Morocco (1930)	Josef von Sternberg
Mr. Arkadin (1955)	Orson Welles
Mr. Deeds Goes to Town (1936)	Frank Capra
Mr. Skeffington (1944)	Vincent Sherman
Mrs. Miniver (1942)	William Wyler
*Mr. Smith Goes to Washington (1939)	Frank Capra
Mulholland Falls (1996)	Leo Tamahori
The Mummy (1932)	Karl Freund
Murder on the Orient Express (1974)	Sidney Lumet
*My Darling Clementine (1946)	John Ford
My Reputation (1946)	Curtis Bernhardt
The Naked City (1948)	Jules Dassin
The Naked Dawn (1955)	Edgar G. Ulmer
Natural Born Killers (1994)	Oliver Stone
A New Life (1988)	Alan Alda
'Night, Mother (1986)	Tom Moore
*The Night of the Hunter (1955)	Charles Laughton
The Night of the Iguana (1964)	John Huston
The Night Porter (1974)	Liliana Cavani
*Ninotchka (1939)	Ernst Lubitsch

North by Northwest (1959)	Alfred Hitchcock
No Sad Songs for Me (1950)	Rudolph Maté
Now, Voyager (1942)	Irving Rapper
Of Mice and Men (1939)	Lewis Milestone
Old Acquaintance (1943)	Vincent Sherman
The Old Maid (1938)	Edmund Goulding
One, Two, Three (1962)	Billy Wilder
Only You (1994)	Norman Jewison
On the Town (1949)	Gene Kelly and Stanley Donen
On the Waterfront (1954)	Elia Kazan
Othello (1952)	Orson Welles
Out of the Past (1947)	Jacques Tourneur
The Palm Beach Story (1942)	Preston Sturges
The Passenger (1974)	Michelangelo Antonioni
Patton (1970)	Franklin Schaffner
Peggy Sue Got Married (1986)	Francis Ford Coppola
Penny Serenade (1941)	George Stevens
The Petty Girl (1950)	Henry Levin
The Philadelphia Story (1940)	George Cukor
Phone Call from a Stranger (1951)	Jean Negulesco
Picnic (1956)	Joshua Logan
The Picture of Dorian Gray (1945)	Albert Lewin
Pinocchio (1940)	Ben Sharpsteen and Hamilton Luske
Platoon (1986)	Oliver Stone
The Player (1992)	Robert Altman
Postcards from the Edge (1994)	Mike Nichols
The Postman Always Rings Twice (1946)	Tay Garnett
Potemkin (1925)	Sergei Eisenstein
The Power and the Glory (1933)	William K. Howard
The Preacher's Wife (1996)	Penny Marshall
Pretty Woman (1990)	Gary Marshall
Priscilla, Queen of the Desert (1994)	Stephen Elliott
The Private Life of Sherlock Holmes (1970)	Billy Wilder
Psycho (1960)	Alfred Hitchcock
The Purple Heart (1944)	Lewis Milestone
The Purple Rose of Cairo (1985)	Woody Allen
Pursued (1947)	Raoul Walsh
The Quiet Man (1952)	John Ford
Radio Days (1987)	Woody Allen

Raging Bull (1981)　　　　　　　　　Martin Scorsese
Raiders of the Lost Ark (1981)　　　Steven Spielberg
Rebecca (1940)　　　　　　　　　　　Alfred Hitchcock
Rebel Without a Cause (1956)　　　Nicholas Ray
Red River (1948)　　　　　　　　　　Howard Hawks
The Red Shoes (1948)　　　　　　　Michael Powell
Rhapsody in Blue (1945)　　　　　　Irving Rapper
The Roaring Twenties (1939)　　　Raoul Walsh
Romeo and Juliet (1996)　　　　　　Baz Luhrmann
Rope (1948)　　　　　　　　　　　　Alfred Hitchcock

Saboteur (1942)　　　　　　　　　　Alfred Hitchcock
Sabrina (1954)　　　　　　　　　　　Billy Wilder
Sabrina (1995)　　　　　　　　　　　Sydney Pollack
Sahara (1943)　　　　　　　　　　　Zoltan Korda
Scarface (1932)　　　　　　　　　　Howard Hawks
Schindler's List (1993)　　　　　　Steven Spielberg
The Searchers (1956)　　　　　　　John Ford
The Secret Garden (1949)　　　　　Fred M. Wilcox
September Affair (1950)　　　　　　William Dieterle
The Set-Up (1947)　　　　　　　　　Robert Wise
The Seventh Seal (1957)　　　　　　Ingmar Bergman
The Seven Year Itch (1955)　　　　Billy Wilder
Shane (1953)　　　　　　　　　　　George Stevens
She Wore a Yellow Ribbon (1949)　John Ford
Shock Corridor (1963)　　　　　　　Samuel Fuller
Show Boat (1936)　　　　　　　　　James Whale
Singin' in the Rain (1952)　　　　Gene Kelly and Stanley Donen
Snow White and the Seven Dwarfs　Ben Sharpsteen
　(1937)
Soldier Blue (1970)　　　　　　　　Ralph Nelson
Some Like It Hot (1959)　　　　　　Billy Wilder
The Song of Bernadette (1943)　　Henry King
Sorry, Wrong Number (1948)　　　Anatole Litvak
Spartacus (1960)　　　　　　　　　Stanley Kubrick
Spellbound (1945)　　　　　　　　　Alfred Hitchcock
The Spirit of St. Louis (1957)　　Billy Wilder
Stagecoach (1939)　　　　　　　　　John Ford
Stage Fright (1950)　　　　　　　　Alfred Hitchcock
Stalag 17 (1951)　　　　　　　　　Billy Wilder
A Star Is Born (1954)　　　　　　　George Cukor
A Star Is Born (1976)　　　　　　　Frank Pierson
Star Spangled Rhythm (1942)　　　George Marshall
Star Wars (1977)　　　　　　　　　George Lucas

Stella Dallas (1937)	King Vidor
The Story of Adele H. (1975)	François Truffaut
The Stranger (1946)	Orson Welles
A Streetcar Named Desire (1951)	Elia Kazan
Suddenly, Last Summer (1959)	Joseph L. Mankiewicz
*Sullivan's Travels (1941)	Preston Sturges
*Sunset Boulevard (1950)	Billy Wilder
Sweet Liberty (1986)	Alan Alda
*Swing Time (1936)	George Stevens
Take a Letter, Darling (1942)	Mitchell Leisen
A Tale of Two Cities (1935)	Jack Conway
Tarantula (1955)	Jack Arnold
Tea and Sympathy (1956)	Vincente Minnelli
Tell It to the Judge (1949)	Norman Foster
That's Life! (1985)	Blake Edwards
Thelma and Louise (1991)	Ridley Scott
There's No Business Like Show Business (1954)	Walter Lang
They All Kissed the Bride (1942)	Alexander Hall
They Died with Their Boots On (1941)	Raoul Walsh
They Shoot Horses, Don't They? (1969)	Sydney Pollack
The Thing (1951)	Christian Nyby
The Thin Man (1934)	W. S. Van Dyke
The Third Man (1949)	Sir Carol Reed
This Island Earth (1955)	Joseph Newman
Through a Glass Darkly (1961)	Ingmar Bergman
Till the Clouds Roll By (1946)	Richard Whorf
Time after Time (1976)	Nicholas Meyer
The Tin Star (1956)	Anthony Mann
Tol'able David (1921)	Henry King
Tora! Tora! Tora! (1970)	Richard Fleischer
*Touch of Evil (1958)	Orson Welles
Twelve O'Clock High (1949)	Henry King
Two for the Road (1967)	Stanley Donen
The Two Mrs. Carrolls (1947)	Peter Godfrey
*2001: A Space Odyssey (1968)	Stanley Kubrick
Two Weeks in Another Town (1962)	Vincente Minnelli
Ulzana's Raid (1972)	Robert Aldrich
The Umbrellas of Cherbourg (1964)	Jacques Demy
The Unbearable Lightness of Being (1988)	Philip Kaufman
Une Femme Douce (1969)	Robert Bresson
The Uninvited (1944)	Lewis Allen

An Unmarried Woman (1978)	Paul Mazursky
The Untouchables (1987)	Brian De Palma
The Vagabond King (1956)	Michael Curtiz
Viridiana (1961)	Luis Buñuel
Wabash Avenue (1950)	Henry Koster
Wagonmaster (1950)	John Ford
A Walk in the Sun (1945)	Lewis Milestone
War of the Worlds (1953)	Byron Haskins
Watch on the Rhine (1943)	Herman Shumlin
Waterworld (1995)	Kevin Reynolds
When Willie Comes Marching Home (1950)	John Ford
While You Were Sleeping (1994)	Jon Turteltaub
White Heat (1949)	Raoul Walsh
Who Framed Roger Rabbit (1988)	Robert Zemeckis
The Wild Bunch (1968)	Sam Peckinpah
The Wild One (1954)	Laslo Benedek
Wild Strawberries (1957)	Ingmar Bergman
Witness for the Prosecution (1957)	Billy Wilder
*The Wizard of Oz (1939)	Victor Fleming
The Wolf Man (1941)	George Waggner
A Woman of Affairs (1928)	Clarence Brown
Woman of the Year (1942)	George Stevens
Women in Love (1970)	Ken Russell
The Wrong Man (1957)	Alfred Hitchcock
Ziegfeld Follies (1946)	Vincente Minnelli

Sample Student Paper

Art vs. Violence in
A Clockwork Orange

DAVID GOULDSTONE

Stanley Kubrick's adaptation of Anthony Burgess's novel received the New York Film Critics award for the best film of 1971. It was acclaimed as much for its aesthetic qualities as for the moral questions that it raised. Kubrick incorporated music from various classical compositions at critical moments in the film to highlight the tensions and ambiguities that he wanted to illustrate. He used the music of Rossini and Beethoven (which inspire Alex's dreams of mayhem and destruction) as a background to the senseless violence that Alex and his friends commit.

When Alex and his clique fight a rival gang, the violence of both groups is given a perverse beauty through stylish choreography and music from Rossini's "Thieving Magpie." Consequently, the audience is torn between the viciousness of the fight and the beauty of its visualization, experiencing a sense of uncertainty and ambiguity. This is intentional on Kubrick's part; it is his attempt to estrange the audience from the victims of the encounters. Perhaps he is using this tension to illustrate the variety and contradictions of human nature. While society may condemn acts of violence, there is, nevertheless, an innately aggressive aspect of human nature. Kubrick's use of music, therefore, retrieves this tendency from the audience's unconscious, thereby causing moral uncertainty.

Thus, we don't know whether to sing along with Alex to the music of "Singin' in the Rain," kicking our feet in time with his, or to be repelled by his brutality. Kubrick even has the kindness to remind us of our uncertainty at the end, leaving "Singin' in the Rain" resonating in our ears and forcing us to choose between memories of the fleet-footed Gene Kelly dancing across the puddles or of Alex's cruel feet stomping his victim.

Interestingly, Kubrick plays with our attitude toward Alex in a similar way. First he incites our contempt as we witness Alex's relentless cruelty; then our sympathy as he is betrayed and spiritually crucified; and finally our uncertainty as he "rises" again. We can detest his adoration of "ultraviolence," yet the undeniable charm of his Elizabethan dialect and his love of "Ludwig van" prevent us from rejecting him completely. Alex is, paradoxically, a cultured barbarian, which is, perhaps, what Kubrick is accusing us all of being.

The film exudes aesthetic appeal. As one critic wrote, "Mr. Kubrick constantly uses . . . a wide-angle lens to distort space relationships within scenes," contending that the director intends to separate people and images from the environment and emphasize their distinctions (Canby, 193). Kubrick creates a surreal, dreamlike atmosphere from the start. First, we are greeted by the face of Alex (one eye ringed with fake lashes); then we take in his environment. Kubrick may have used this surreal technique to represent the drug-induced vision of Alex and his gang when they are at the milk bar. Kubrick reverts to a realistic style when they are not high; for example, during the day or when Alex is sent to prison.

On the surface, the film is futuristic, but, in truth, it is a critique of contemporary society. The clothes and the setting have a futuristic look, but Kubrick refuses to comfort the audience by implying that the events are in the distant future.

Alex's final line, "I was cured, all right!" mocks the therapy that society prescribed for him. Alex has returned to his old self with the help of the very people who tried to destroy his soul and his freedom of choice. It is an ironic redemption for Alex, who has risen, fallen, and risen again in a world that is no less sick than he is. Consequently, it is impossible for such a society to offer Alex any salvation. Therefore, when he once again dreams of rape and violence to the music of Beethoven's Ninth Symphony, we accept the fact that he is back to "normal." Quite simply, it was futile to expect that the cause of his condition—society—could also be his cure.

Works Cited

Canby, Vincent. "'A Clockwork Orange' Dazzles the Senses and Mind." Rev. of A Clockwork Orange. New York Times 20 December 1971. Rpt. New York Times Film Reviews (1971–1972). New York: New York Times and Arno Press, 1973. 193.

A Clockwork Orange. Dir. Stanley Kubrick. With Malcolm McDowell, Patrick Magee, and Adrienne Cori. Warner Bros. 1971.

A Basic Film Library

III

Since film studies entered the college curriculum in the 1960s, the number of film books has multiplied to such an extent that even film journals cannot review all of them. Anyone interested in going beyond the boundaries of an introductory film course will naturally be in a quandary. Unable to read, much less own, all the books listed in the standard bibliographies, you may want to know which are essential or, to use a distinction made in syllabuses, which are required—rather than suggested—reading. Because personal preference plays a role in any recommendation, I have chosen to identify certain areas in which one should be knowledgeable and suggested the best books for acquiring that knowledge easily.

Film History

A basic film library should include a comprehensive history of film such as David Cook, *A History of the Narrative Film*, 3rd ed. (New York: Norton,

1996). You should also be aware of Scribner's extraordinary History of the American Cinema series, which, when complete, promises to be authoritative. The University of California Press has already published some of the volumes in paperback: Charles Musser, *The Emergence of Cinema: The American Screen to 1907* (1994); Eileen Bowser, *The Transformation of Cinema: 1907–1915* (1994); Richard Koszarski, *An Evening's Entertainment: The Age of the Silent Feature Picture, 1915–1928* (1994); and Tino Balio, *Grand Design: Hollywood as a Modern Business Enterprise 1930–1939* (1995). There are also illustrations in these books that have not been reproduced elsewhere.

Film history is being made daily; thus, no text can supply the latest information about the industry or clarify the current status of the studios. Anyone seeking up-to-the-minute news of the world of film should read the *Hollywood Reporter* and *Variety* (which is published weekly and, on the West Coast, daily) along with such magazines as *Vanity Fair* and *The New Yorker*, which frequently run informative pieces on the industry. Since movies are now considered a business, changes in the industry are not reported in the entertainment section of the *New York Times* but in the business pages.

Film Criticism

Admittedly, some film criticism is impenetrable. Fortunately, J. Dudley Andrew, *The Major Film Theories: An Introduction* (New York: Oxford University Press, 1976), describes the various schools of criticism with great clarity. In Gerald Mast, Marshall Cohen, and Leo Braudy, eds., *Film Theory and Criticism: Introductory Readings*, 4th ed. (New York: Oxford University Press, 1992)—an anthology cited in the text—the major theories, with examples, are arranged in sections, each prefaced by a short introduction.

Auteur Studies

Because of its historical significance, Andrew Sarris, *The New American Cinema: Directors and Directions 1929–1968* (New York: Dutton, 1968. Rpt. New York: DaCapo, 1996), is a book one should own. Unfortunately, it has not been revised; thus, Sarris's ranking of a director may not reflect current critical opinion. For those who are interested in a particular director, Twayne Publishers has a book in its filmmakers series on every major director, American and international, and many of the minor ones, too.

Biographies

A good film biography should include some analysis of the subject's work. One of the best film biographies is Donald Spoto, *The Dark Side of Genius:*

The Life of Alfred Hitchcock (Boston: Little, Brown, 1983), which illustrates the similarity between Hitchcock's life and his art. The result is a portrait of a tortured genius who translated the tension between his religious scruples and his sexual repression into film art. Spoto has written other well-researched biographies of such figures as Tennessee Williams, Sir Laurence Olivier, James Dean, and Elizabeth Taylor. His most scholarly is *Marilyn: The Biography* (New York: HarperCollins, 1993), which concludes through medical evidence that the star did not commit suicide, despite what is commonly thought.

Autobiographies

Film autobiographies are often suspect because, too often, they are just catalogs of love affairs and anecdotes, offering little or no information about the medium in which the autobiographer became famous. One exception is Lillian Gish, *The Movies, Mr. Griffith and Me* (Englewood Cliffs: Prentice-Hall, 1969), a charmingly written memoir about the early days of moviemaking. Equally readable is Frank Capra, *The Name Above the Title* (New York: Macmillan, 1971. Rpt. New York: DaCapo, 1997), a moving account of a Sicilian immigrant's rise from obscurity to fame. Like any autobiographer (Benjamin Franklin is the prime example), Capra engaged in embellishment and omission, as Joseph McBride has shown in *Frank Capra: The Catastrophe of Success* (New York: Simon & Schuster, 1992).

Studio History

To understand what is meant by Hollywood's golden age—roughly the years from 1930 to the end of the 1950s—one should know something about the studios and their heads. The best introduction to that era is Thomas Schatz, *The Genius of the System: Hollywood Filmmaking in the Studio Era* (New York: Pantheon, 1988). Each of the major studios has been the subject of a coffee-table book with a year-by-year history of the studio and capsule summaries and stills of the films. *The MGM Story, The United Artists Story, The Paramount Story, The Warner Bros. Story,* and others have been published by Crown Publishers. They are often found on remainder counters in bookstores or included among publishers' clearances. Since these books are lavishly illustrated and moderately informative, they are worth owning. The best studio book is *The RKO Story* (Random House Value Publishing Inc., 1984) by film scholar Richard B. Jewell, who drew on the vast knowledge of Vernon S. Harbin, RKO archivist and Hollywood historian.

Unfortunately, the industry now refers to the golden age as "old" Hollywood. For an introduction to "new" or corporate Hollywood, where the studios are subsidiaries of conglomerates (Warner Bros. of Time

Warner, Paramount of Viacom, Columbia of Sony, and so on), read Peter Bart, *Fade Out: The Calamitous Final Days of MGM* (New York: Morrow, 1990) and Nancy Griffith and Kim Masters, *Hit and Run: How Jon Peters and Peter Guber Took Sony for a Ride in Hollywood* (New York: Simon & Schuster, 1996). Taken together, these books provide a study in contrast with Schatz's.

Reference Works

It is possible to purchase inexpensive reference works. Truly indispensable is *Halliwell's Filmgoer's and Video Viewer's Companion*, 9th ed. (New York: Perennial Library, 1990). Alphabetically arranged entries from Bud Abbott to Adolph Zukor provide not only biographical information on stars, writers, directors, and so forth, but also definitions of film terms and descriptions of familiar themes and genres. No lover of film can afford to be without Leonard Maltin's *Movie and Video Guide*, published by Penguin and updated annually. Maltin not only includes capsule summaries of more than 19,000 films but also the most current mail-order sources for video-cassettes and laser discs.

There is also no substitute for browsing in such bookstores as Barnes & Noble, Borders, and B. Dalton, which offer a wide selection of film books.

Finally, every film library is eclectic. Yours will probably combine the traditional and the personal; the latter will make your library unique because it will reflect what you truly believe film is.

Index

Abraham Lincoln, 39
Accused, The, 33
Ace in the Hole. See The Big Carnival
Act of Murder, An, 22
adaptations, 200–13
Address Unknown, 48–49
Agee, James, 254–55
Age of Innocence, The
  iris shots in, 73
  linear sequence in, 60–61
  main title of, 12
  moving shots in, 54
  overlapping sound in, 25
Alda, Alan, 14, 73, 184–91
Alice Doesn't Live Here Anymore, 117
All About Eve, 3, 216–17
Allen, Irwin, 166
Allen, Woody
  credits sequence, 15, 60
  and improvisation, 8
  intertitles in *Hannah and Her Sisters*, 19
  and reflexive film, 113

and R-rating for language, 127
and voice-over, 27
  See also Radio Days
All the President's Men, 22, 39–40, 41
Altman, Robert, 6, 8, 115
Amadeus, 44
American Cinema, The, 164
American montage, 63, 75, 237
Amityville Horror, The, 120
amour fou, 108
And Now Tomorrow, 23
Andrew, J. Dudley, 286
Angels with Dirty Faces, 104–5
angle-shots. *See* shots
animated musicals, 96
Antonioni, Michelangelo, 54
Apocalypse Now, 158
Apollo 13, 3
Armstrong, Gillian, 253
Arnheim, Rudolph, 80, 238
Arthur, Jean, 111, 135
Ashman, Howard, 96–97
associative sequences. *See* sequences

Astaire, Fred, 84, 91–96
atomic bomb films, 125–126
auteurism, 162–67, 243–44, 258, 261–63
authors, directors as. *See* auteurism
Awful Truth, The, 111

back lighting. *See* lighting
backstage musicals. *See* show-business musicals
Back Street, 118–119
Bad and the Beautiful, The, 115
Badlands, 30, 181
Balio, Tino, 286
Barkleys of Broadway, The, 93
Barry Lyndon, 31, 57, 198–99
Bart, Peter, 288
Barthes, Roland, 245–46
Bass, Saul and Elaine, 12
Bates, Alan, 58–59
Baxter, John, 124
Bazin, André, 136–37, 163–64, 239–41
Beauty and the Beast, 96–97
Bergman, Ingmar, 44–45, 192, 193, 242
Bergman, Ingrid, 5–6, 66, 224–25
Berkeley, Busby, 175
Bernstein, Walter, 14, 114
Bertolucci, Bernardo, 12, 148–50
Best Years of Our Lives, The, 239–240
Beyond Formula, 99
Bicycle Thief, The, 241
Big Carnival, The, 137–38, 183
Birds, The, 21, 124
Birth of a Nation, The, 6, 18–19, 71–72, 193
Biskind, Peter, 124
Bittersweet, 92
black-and-white. *See* color
Blow-Up, 241
Blue Angel, The, 132
Bluebeard, 47, 163
Blue Dahlia, The, 40
Bobker, Lee, 79

Body and Soul, 227
Body Heat, 109
Bogart, Humphrey
  in *Casablanca*, 20–21, 139, 222–25, 245–46
  in *Dark Passage*, 41–43
  in *High Sierra*, 104, 139–41
  as icon, 139–41
  in *Sabrina*, 152–54
  in *Sahara*, 49, 139
  in *The Two Mrs. Carrolls*, 68
Bogdanovich, Peter, 15, 72, 182
Bonnie and Clyde, 105, 256
Boomerang, 30
Bowser, Eileen, 286
boxing films, 227–31
Brando, Marlon, 49, 148–50
Braudy, Leo, 286
Breathless, 64–65, 72
Bresson, Robert, 29
Bride of Frankenstein, 122–23, 125
Brief Encounter, 157–58
Brigadoon, 94
Bringing Up Baby, 110–12
Broken Blossoms, 18, 37, 72
budgets, 183
Bull Durham, 258
Buñuel, Luis, 49
Burnt Offerings, 120
Butch Cassidy and the Sundance Kid, 119–20, 215

Cabinet of Dr. Caligari, The, 121–22
Cagney, James, 104–5
Cahiers du Cinéma, 163–64
Canby, Vincent, 283
Cape Fear, 114
Capra, Frank, 63–64
  and bells, 244
  biographies of, 287
  end title in *Prelude to War*, 17
  iconography in *Meet John Doe*, 49
  time in *Meet John Doe*, 6
  use of montage sequence, 63–64
  use of music, 157
  wipes in films of, 69–70

Carrie, 47, 82, 122–23
Carringer, Robert, 259, 260–61
Carroll, Leo G., 43
cars, 248–249
Carson, Jack, 106–7
Casablanca, 8, 20–21, 155, 222–25
case studies, 222–234
Cat People
  as collaborative effort, 166
  noise in, 22–23
  nursery tune in, 156
  recalling cults, 125
  repetitive voice in, 33–34
  synchronization in, 24
  as transformation myth, 132–34
Cats, 94
Caught, 67
censorship
  and double entendres, 112
  end of Production Code, 119
  Production Code and crime,
    103
  and voice-over confession, 32
  and the woman's film, 117–18
Chan, Jackie, 14–15
Chaplin, 15
Chaplin, Charles, 114
characters
  in crime films, 103
  goals needed in, 189–90
  in horror films, 120
  in science fiction, 124
  in screwball comedies, 111–12
  in westerns, 100–101
  in the woman's film, 117–20
Cheung, King-Kok, 201
Children's Hour, The, 119
Chinatown, 150–51
Chorus Line, A, 94
Christ imagery, 49
  in *Clockwork Orange, A*, 159
  in Eisenstein's montage, 74
  in *Raging Bull*, 230
  in *Serpico*, 141–42
  in *Shane*, 134–36
cigarettes, 249

Citizen Kane
  auteurist critique of, 261–63
  color symbolism in, 81–82
  curtain calls in, 15–16
  deep focus in, 50–51
  example of tone, 78
  high-angle shot in, 50
  history of, 260–62
  lighting in, 87–88
  low-angle shot in, 39
  multiple narrators in, 28
  myth critique of, 263–64
  paperweight scene, 261–62
  printed word in, 20–21
  rhythm in, 75–77
  script of, 3
  social history critique of, 264–66
  sound in, 23
  tilt shots in, 54–55
  See also Welles, Orson
class distinctions, 111–12, 116
clocks, 6
Clockwork Orange, A, 159–60, 259,
  282–84
Close Encounters of the Third Kind,
  124, 160, 173
close shot, 36
close-up, 36, 37
clothing
  in gangster films, 103
  in westerns, 100–101
Clueless, 206–10, 253
Coen, Ethan, 3
Coen, Joel, 3
Cohen, Marshall, 286
Colbert, Claudette, 110, 214
collaborative efforts, 166–69, 181
color
  black-and-white, 80–82, 84,
    227–30, 231
  deepening the narrative with, 82–83
  used in horror films, 121–23
  See also colorization
Colorado Territory, 68–69
colorization, 83–84
Color Purple, The, 200–205

comedies
  of manners, 151–54
  musical, 92
  screwball, 110–13
Coming Home, 119–20
computer graphics, 77–78
computer screen, 22
Coney Island, 93–94
conflict, 4–5
contrast cuts. *See* cuts
Conway, Jack, 27–28
Cook, David, 285–86
Coppola, Francis Ford, 72–73, 225–27
Corliss, Richard, 256–58
Corn Is Green, The, 116
Cover Girl, 56, 94, 96
Cowan, Jerome, 66–67
crane shot. *See* shots
Crawford, Joan, 106, 116
creature films, 124–25
credits sequence, 12–13, 193
  in *Manhattan*, 60
  in *Raging Bull*, 227
  in semi-documentaries, 30
  in *Touch of Evil*, 53
  in *The Wild Bunch*, 59
  See also end credits; precredits
    sequence
crime films, 103–105, 245
Criss Cross, 106
critic, definition of, 256–58
criticism
  apologist, 238
  auteurist, 243–44, 261–63
  biographical, 259
  descriptive, 236
  example of, 256–58
  feminist, 251–53
  grammarian, 237–38
  guidelines for, 166–69, 266–69
  historical, 260–61
  Marxist, 259
  myth-oriented, 244–46, 263–64
  psychoanalytic, 259
  realist, 238–43
  reviewers and, 253–59

  Russian, 236–37
  semiotician, 246–51
  social history approach, 264–66
cross cuts. *See* cuts
Crossfire, 86
Crowther, Bosley, 256
Crying Game, The, 47–48
Cry of the City, 11
Cukor, George, 8, 92–93
Curse of Frankenstein, 122
Curtiz, Michael, 224–25, 255
cuts, 64–65, 214, 217
cutting, 74–78

dance musicals, 91, 94
Dances with Wolves, 20, 103
Dark Passage, 41–43
Dark Victory, 22, 23, 116–17, 252
Darling, 64
Davis, Bette, 66–67
  in *All About Eve*, 3, 138, 216–17
  in *Dark Victory*, 22, 23
  in *Jezebel*, 80
  in *Mr. Skeffington*, 66–67
  in *Now, Voyager*, 216
  roles in woman's films, 115–16
Day of the Locust, The, 146–47, 197, 248
Day the Earth Stood Still, The, 124
Dead, The, 40, 42
Dean, James, 82–83, 138, 141, 287
Death of a Salesman, 90
death scenes, 101–5, 108, 156
deep focus, 240–41
Denby, David, 258
DeNiro, Robert, 227–31
DePalma, Brian, 73, 175
depth, sense of, 85–86
DeSica, Vittorio, 241
Detective, 115
Detour, 45–46, 51, 65, 107–9
dialogue
  in comedies, 112
  screen vs. novel, 215–16
  screen vs. theater, 214–16
Dietrich, Marlene
  effect of side lighting on, 87

as myth, 144, 244
in *Stage Fright*, 55
wearing tuxedos, 249–50
directors
auteurism vs. collaboration,
165–67, 185–86
borrowings, 175, 230
collaboration, 166–69
interviews with, 176–91
list of discussed, 271–81
as primary creative force, 162–65
themes, motifs, and quotes, 169–75
working with actors, 190
Dirty Harry, 75
disaster films, 166
dissolves. *See* transitions
Dmytryk, Edward, 80
Dog Day Afternoon, 17–18
Doll's House, A, 78
dolly shot. *See* shots
double framing. *See* framing
Double Indemnity
Dietrich persona in, 144–45
first person narration in, 28–29
Liebestod in, 108–9
subtle sex scene in, 175
Dr. Cyclops, 125
Dr. Jekyll and Mr. Hyde, 54, 69–70,
74
Dr. Zhivago, 23
Dracula's Daughter, 55
dreams, 132
Dream Street, 87
Dressed to Kill, 73
Duel in the Sun, 156
Dwight Macdonald on Movies, 266–68

Easy Living, 91, 110–12, 147–48
Easy Rider, 248–49
editing, 78–80, 181
continuity, 73
definition, 79–80
montage, 74–75, 237, 239, 241
rhythm, 75–76, 228–29
space, 77–79
theme, 78

time, 76–77, 225–27
tone, 78
Edwards, Blake, 9–10
Eisenstein, Sergei, 5, 46, 74–75,
236–37
elliptical sequences. *See* sequences
Emma, 205–207, 210–11
Emperor Waltz, The, 92, 182
Empire of the Sun, 16, 73, 173
Empire Strikes Back, The, 16
end credits, 14–16
epigrams, 216
epigraphs, use of, 16, 18
epilogue, end title as, 17
Escape from Alcatraz, 75
establishing shots. *See* shots
E.T. the Extra-Terrestrial, 124, 166
Everyone Says I Love You, 127
Evita, 138–39, 211, 256–58

fade-out. *See* fades
fades. *See* transitions
Fast Times at Ridgemont High, 253
Fatal Attraction, 109
Faulkner, William, 213
Feder, Lillian, 131
Fellini, Federico, 82
female bonding, 119–20
fill light. *See* lighting
film
criticism, 235–70
defining, 2
exploiting full potential of, 222–34
historians, 260–61
as narrative text, 2–4, 6
recommended reading about, 285–
288
silent, 3, 19
Filmguide to Psycho, 4
film noir, 86, 105–109, 255
films
about films (*see* reflexive films)
list of discussed, 271–81
First Time, The, 27
Fitzgerald, F. Scott, 213
Five Graves to Cairo, 183

flashbacks, 19, 193–95, 226–27
flashforwards, 195–96
Fleming, Victor. *See Gone with the Wind*
Fletcher, Louise, 142–44
Flying Down to Rio, 91
focus, 50–51, 240–41
Ford, John, 3, 27, 38, 52
  continuity between films, 173
  double-framing, 244
  use of black-and-white in westerns, 84
  use of elliptical sequence, 61
Forrest Gump, 12–13, 26, 77–78
Forever Amber, 24
For Keeps: 30 Years of Movies, 258
Forman, Milŏs, 142–44
form cuts. *See* cuts
form dissolves. *See* transitions
Fort Apache, 84, 100
42nd Street, 93
400 Blows, The, 58, 149
Four Seasons, The, 12, 187
Four Weddings and a Funeral, 20
frame-within-a-frame. *See* framing
framing, 45–54
  double, 52
  frame-within-a-frame, 52
  masked, 52
  in *Raging Bull*, 227
Frankenstein, 122–23, 244–45
Freed, Arthur, 166
freezing. *See* shots
French Kiss, 15, 112
Friday the 13th, 123
frigidity, 133
Front, The, 12, 14
Fuller, Samuel, 18
full shot, 37

gangster films. *See* crime films
Garbo, Greta, 87, 244
Genesis myth. *See* myth
genres, literary vs. film, 89–92
Ghost, 22
Gibbs, Anthony, 79–80

Gish, Lillian, 37, 287
Glass Menagerie, The, 213
Godard, Jean-Luc, 64–65, 72, 115, 149, 163
Godfather, Part II, The, 20, 83, 194, 225–27
Gone with the Wind
  as collaborative effort, 8–9, 166
  commentative sound in, 23
  repetitive voice in, 34
  use of color in, 84
GoodFellas
  long take in, 53
  subjective camera in, 40
  titles and credits in, 15, 16–19
Goodwins, Leslie, 122
Gouldstone, David, 282–84
Grapes of Wrath, The, 15, 21, 40
graphics, 8–22
Greatest Story Ever Told, The, 195
Great Expectations, 33
Great Lie, The, 116
Great Train Robbery, The, 101
Griffith, D. W.
  close-ups and long shots, 37, 39
  intertitles, 18–19
  iris use by, 72, 244
  montage technique of, 237
  and parallel cutting, 76–78
  use of side lighting, 87
Griffith, Nancy, 288
Grifters, The, 109
Gun Crazy, 106, 109
guns, 105

Hail the Conquering Hero, 255
hairstyles, 143–44, 246
Halliwell's Filmgoer's and Video Viewer's Companion, 288
Hannah and Her Sisters, 19
Harbin, Vernon S., 287
Harrelson, Woody, 231–34
Harrison, Doane, 180
Hawks, Howard, 110–11
hearing-impaired character, 20
Heckerling, Amy, 207–209, 210, 253

Hellman, Lillian, 212
Hello Frisco, Hello, 93
Hennessy, 16–17
Hepburn, Katharine, 43, 57, 112, 118, 138
heroin addiction, 119
high-key lighting. *See* lighting
High Noon, 6, 98
High Sierra, 68–69, 105, 139–41
Hill, George Roy, 72
Hiroshima Mon Amour, 33
His Girl Friday, 111, 249
Hitchcock, Alfred
  associative sequences, 61–63
  as auteur, 165
  biography of, 286–87
  borrowings, 175–77
  close-ups, use of, 37
  dissolve used in *North by Northwest*, 67
  end title in *The Wrong Man*, 17
  form dissolve in *The Wrong Man*, 69
  God's eye view shots, 38–39, 244
  long takes in *Rope*, 52–53
  musical leitmotif, 156
  point-of-view shot, 43
  printed word in *The Birds*, 21
  quotations from earlier work, 173–75
  and repetitive voice, 33–34
  tilting and panning, 55
  use of color in *Marnie*, 82
  and use of sound, 23
  and wipes, 70
  See also Notorious; Psycho
Hoffman, Dustin, 22, 39–40, 41
Hold Back the Dawn, 180
Hollywood Hallucination, The, 244
Hollywood Reporter, 286
homosexuality, 119
Horizons West, 98
horror films, 34–35, 37, 86, 120–23
House of Wax, 122
House on Carroll Street, The, 114
House on 92nd Street, The, 30
How Green Was My Valley, 61

Hustle, 13
Huston, John, 212

iconic associations, 138–44
I Married a Monster from Outer Space, 124
improvisation, 8, 188
Indiana Jones and the Last Crusade, 65
Indiana Jones and the Temple of Doom, 9, 16
Indians, 103
intellectual associations, 144–55
intertitles. *See* titles
Intolerance, 18, 72, 77, 193
Invasion of the Body Snatchers, 75, 125–26
Italian films, 241
It Came from Beneath the Sea, 124
It Came from Outer Space, 124
It Happened One Night, 69, 110–12, 147, 214
It's a Wonderful Life, 244
I Walked with a Zombie, 34–35, 166

Jane Eyre, 54, 69
Jewell, Richard B., 287
Jezebel, 80, 82–83, 84
Johnson, Ben, 113–14, 135
Johnson, William, 124
Johnston, Eric, 32
Jolson Story, The, 93
Jordan, Neil, 47–48
Jules and Jim, 49, 50
Julia
  depicting women's friendship, 117, 119
  dialogue in, 214
  high angle-shot in, 38, 40
Juliet of the Spirits, 82
jump cuts. *See* cuts

Kael, Pauline, 2, 148, 258–59, 260
Kaplan, E. Ann, 251
Kauffman, Stanley, 258
Kaufmann, Philip, 19
Kelly, Gene, 92, 94, 96, 166

King and Country, 64, 68
King Kong, 16, 132
Kitses, James, 98
Kitty Foyle, 194, 261–62
Koszarski, Richard, 286
Kracauer, Siegfried, 241–43
Kubrick, Stanley
  use of music, 159–60, 282–84
  See also 2001: A Space Odyssey;
    Barry Lyndon
Kuhn, Annette, 251
Kuleshov, Lev, 236–37

Lacan, Jacques, 251
Lacombe, Lucien, 16
Ladd, Alan, 40, 68, 100–101, 134–37
Lady and the Monster, The, 34
Lady Be Good, 91, 93
Lady Eve, The, 12, 64, 111–12
Lady from Shanghai, The, 262–64
Lady in the Lake, 41, 44
Lady in White, 120
Lang, Fritz, 25
Lang, Walter, 93–94
language. See semiotics
Last Emperor, The, 12
Last of the Mohicans, The, 20
Last Picture Show, The, 15–16, 68,
  113–14
Last Tango in Paris, 148–50
Last Temptation of Christ, The, 17
L'Atalante, 150
Lawson, John Howard, 2
League of Their Own, A, 253
Léaud, Jean-Pierre, 58, 148–50
Lee, Spike, 26
Legion of Decency, The, 34–35
Leisen, Mitchell, 91, 111, 180
leitmotif, musical, 155–61
LeSage, Julia, 251
Letter, The, 31
Letter from an Unknown Woman,
  32–33, 56–57
Letter to Three Wives, A, 23, 31
Lewis, Joseph H., 106
Lewis, Juliette, 231–34

Lewton, Val, 166, 255
library, basic film, 285–88
Liebestod (love-death), 108, 156
lighting, 84–88, 106–7, 121
Lincoln, a History, 18
Lindsay, Vachel, 236
linear sequences. See sequences
literature
  adaptations, 199–213
  flashbacks and flashforwards, 193–
    196
  point of view, 196–99
  screenplay and, 192–93
Little Foxes, The, 52, 156, 211–12
Little Women, 253
Locket, The, 109
Logan, Josh, 211–12
logos, studio, 9–11
Lonely Villa, The, 76–77
Long Day's Journey into Night, 57, 211
long shot, 37, 38
long takes. See shots
Look Who's Talking, 27
Lost Horizon, 244
Lost Weekend, The, 197–98
Loves of Carmen, The, 49
low-key lighting. See lighting
Lubitsch, Ernst, 81, 175, 182
Lucas, George, 126
Lumet, Sidney, 57, 141

M, 25
Macdonald, Dwight, 166–69, 256
Madonna, 138–39, 256–58
Magic and Myth of the Movies, 245–46
Magnificent Ambersons, The, 72, 262
main titles, 11–16
Major and the Minor, The, 170, 180, 182
Making of Citizen Kane, The, 260–61
Malcolm X, 26
Malick, Terrence, 181
Maltin, Leonard, 288
Mamoulian, Rouben, 54, 69–70, 74
Manhattan, 60
Mankiewicz, Herman J., 3, 259,
  260–61

Mankiewicz, Joseph L., 3, 23, 193, 212
Man Who Shot Liberty Valance, The,
    84, 98, 173
Man with the Golden Arm, The, 119
Marnie, 23, 40, 82
Married to the Mob, 14
Marshall, Penny, 253
M*A*S*H, 49, 51, 184, 185
masked framing. *See* framing
Mast, Gerald, 286
Masters, Kim, 288
matriarchs, 154
McBride, Joseph, 287
McGrath, Doug, 210–11
Medium Cool, 26
Meet John Doe, 6, 49
Meet Me in St. Louis, 85
melodramas, 86
Menken, Alan, 96–97
mentors, 191
Menzies, William Cameron, 8–9
Merry Widow, The, 81
metamorphoses, in horror films, 120
Metz, Christian, 247–48
Meyjes, Menno, 201–205
Mickey Mouse, 244–45
Midnight, 111
Mildred Pierce, 106–7
Milestone, Lewis, 13
Minnelli, Vincente, 32, 92, 94, 115
Miracle, The, 256
mirrors, 108
mise-en-scène, 239
Mission to Moscow, 255
Modern Times, 114
Monogram studios, 163
monologues, 217
montage sequences. *See* American
    montage; sequences
Moonstruck, 64, 160
morphing, 77–78
motorcycles, 248–49
Mr. Deeds Goes to Town, 69, 75
Mr. Skeffington, 66–67, 157
Mr. Smith Goes to Washington, 63–64,
    69, 75

Mrs. Miniver, 65–66, 167
Mulholland Falls, 109
Mulvey, Laura, 251–53
Mummy's Curse, The, 122
Munsterberg, Hugo, 236
Murder, My Sweet, 28, 105–6
Murder on the Orient Express, 34
music
    background, 23
    classical, 157–61
    dramas with, 92–93
    as element of subtext, 155–61
    as postlude, 15
    Wagner's, 158
musicals, 84, 91–97
Musser, Charles, 286
My Darling Clementine, 38, 84, 91,
    97–98
My Man Godfrey, 111–12
My Reputation, 117
myths, 244–46
    Apollo-Hercules, 136
    in *Citizen Kane,* 263–64
    definition of, 130–32
    Frankenstein, 244–45
    genesis, 137–38, 183
    knight-errant, 136–37
    savior, 134–37
    and science fiction, 126
    transformation, 132–34

Naked City, The, 30–31
Naked Dawn, The, 38
Naremore, James, 4
narration
    as confession, 32
    disembodied voice, 30–31
    epistolary, 31–33
    ex machina, 34–35
    first person, 28–30, 32–33
    omniscient, 31
    repetitive, 33–34
    subjective voice, 33
    voice-over, 26–28, 35, 210
narrative film. *See* film
Nashville, 6

Natural Born Killers, 231–34
Naughty Marietta, 92
Neal, Tom, 45–46, 51
Net, The, 22
New Criticism, 259
New Faces of 1952, 92
New Life, A, 63, 186–88
New York, New York, 91, 93
New Yorker, The, 166, 258–59, 286
New York Times, 254, 256, 286
Nicholson, Jack, 54
Nickelodeon, 6, 22, 72, 114
'Night Mother, 213
Night of the Iguana, The, 212
North by Northwest, 55, 63, 67, 70, 174
No Sad Songs for Me, 116
Nothing Sacred, 111
Notorious
   associative sequence in, 61–62
   close-up in, 37
   fades in, 66
   scenes and sequences, 59–60
   time and suspense in, 5–6
Now, Voyager, 216

Of Mice and Men, 13
Old Acquaintance, 117, 119
Old Maid, The, 117
One Flew over the Cuckoo's Nest,
   142–44
Only You, 112
On the Town, 92
On the Waterfront, 49, 119, 227–30
Open City, 241
operettas, 92
Ophuls, Max, 32–33, 56–57, 67

Pacino, Al, 17–18, 141–42, 165
Paisan, 241
Palm Beach Story, The, 111–12, 255
paper. *See* student paper, sample
paradigm, 248
parallel cuts. *See* cuts
parody, 49, 51
Passenger, The, 54, 55

Patton, 217
Peckinpah, Sam, 59, 101
Peggy Sue Got Married, 73
Penny Serenade, 72, 194
Persona, 241
Petty Girl, The, 69
Phantom Lady, 255
Phantom of the Opera, 199
Phantom of the Rue Morgue, 122
Philadelphia Inquirer, 254
Phone Call from a Stranger, 13
photography, 242
Picnic, 211–12
Picture of Dorian Gray, The, 16
Pinocchio, 96
Platoon, 32
Player, The, 115
plots
   diegesis, discourse and, 250–51
   of film noir, 109
   of horror films, 120–23
   of musicals, 92–97
   of science-fiction films, 124–26
   of westerns, 100
   of woman's films, 116–20
point of view
   first person, 196–97
   implied author, 198–99
   omniscient author, 197–98
   slow motion to depict, 229
Polanski, Roman, 122–23, 150
Porter, E. S., 101
Postcards from the Edge, 13–14, 15
postludes, 15
Potemkin, 5, 46, 74–75, 175–76
precredits sequence, 13
Prelude to War, 17
Pretty Woman, 160
printed word, 20–22
Priscilla, Queen of the Desert, 15
Private Life of Sherlock Holmes, The,
   156, 182
producer, role of the, 182
Production Code. *See* censorship
profanity, 119

Psycho, 244
  extreme close-ups in, 37
  main title, 12, 16
  as parent of slasher films, 123
  shower scene, 3–4
  subjective voice in, 33
  wipe in, 37
Public Enemy, The, 104
Pudovkin, V. I., 236–37
Purple Rose of Cairo, The, 113
Pursued, 91

Quiet Man, The, 52

rack focus. *See* focus
Radio Days, 15, 27, 45, 196
Raging Bull, 19, 227–31
Raiders of the Lost Ark, 114
ratings, 34–35, 79
rating system, 119
Ray, Nicholas, 82–83, 100
realism, 238–42
Rebecca, 33–34, 62–63, 70
Rebel Without a Cause, 82–83
Red Dawn, 20
Redford, Robert, 22, 39–40, 41
Red River, 113–14
reflexive films, 113–15
Reisz, Karel, 78–79, 248–49
remakes, 151–55
Return of the Jedi, The, 16
reviewers. *See* criticism
revues, 92
Robbins, Matthew, 166
Rocky, 189–90
Rogers, Ginger, 84, 91, 95
Romeo and Juliet, 5
Rope, 52–53
Rosemary's Baby, 122–23, 125
Rossellini, Roberto, 241, 256
Rumble in the Bronx, 14–15

Saboteur
  close-up in, 37
  credits in, 195

crosscut in, 64
  fall in, 114, 174
Sabrina, 151–54
Sabrina Fair, 151–54
Sahara, 49
Sargent, Alvin, 214
Sarris, Andrew, 164–65, 258, 286
scenes. *See* sequences
Schatz, Thomas, 287
Schindler's List, 83
Schlesinger, John, 146
science-fiction films, 124–27
Science Fiction in the Cinema, 124
Scorsese, Martin
  portrayal of widow in *Alice Doesn't
    Live Here Anymore*, 117
  remaking *Cape Fear*, 114
  and techniques of the past, 72
  and titles, 17–19
  use of subjective camera, 40
  *See also The Age of Innocence;
    GoodFellas; Raging Bull*
screenwriting, 213–21
script, importance of, 3, 178–79
Searchers, The, 3, 52, 98–102, 194–95
Secret Garden, The, 83
Seeing Is Believing, 124
semidocumentaries, 30–31
semiotics, 246–51
sequences
  associative, 61–63
  elliptical, 61
  linear, 60–61
  montage, 63–64, 233 (*see also*
    American montage; editing)
  See also credits sequences; precred-
    its sequences
Serpico, 141–42, 248
Set-Up, The, 6, 227
Seventh Seal, The, 242
Seven Year Itch, The, 12, 157–58
Shane, 38, 68, 100–101, 134–37, 248
She Wore a Yellow Ribbon, 102
Shock Corridor, 18
shoot-outs, 101–2

shots
  canted, 46–48
  close-ups and extreme close-ups,
    37–38
  crane, 56, 57
  dolly, 56
  establishing, 37
  framing, 45–54
  high and low angle, 38–40
  iris, 70–73
  long and extreme long, 37
  long takes, 52–53, 239
  moving, 54–57
  point-of-view, 37
  subjective, 40–43
  three-shot in *Raging Bull*, 229
  tilting and panning, 54–55
  tracking, 56–57
  types of, 36–37
  zoom and freeze, 57–59
Show Boat, 6
show-business musicals, 93–94
side lighting. *See* lighting
Siegel, Don, 75, 125–26
silent film. *See* film
Silverstone, Alicia, 207–209, 211
Singin' in the Rain, 92, 166
Siodmak, Robert, 11, 255
Slaves, 78
Snow White and the Seven Dwarfs, 96
Solomon, Stanley, 99
Song of Bernadette, The, 67, 87
songs, 93–94
Sorry, Wrong Number, 28
sound, 8–9, 22–35
  actual and commentative, 23
  asynchronization, 24–25
  off screen vs. on screen, 23
  overlapping, 25–26
  synchronization, 24
sound effects, 22–23
Sous les toits de Paris, 150
space. *See* editing
Spellbound, 43
Spielberg, Steven
  humanization of science fiction, 126

  logo in film, 9
  match cut, 65
  Raiders of the Lost Ark, 83
  repetition from earlier film, 173
  signature characteristics, 166–67
  use of color in *Schindler's List*, 83
  wipes, irises and fades, 72–73
  See also The Color Purple
Spoto, Donald, 286–87
Spottiswoode, Raymond, 237–38
Stagecoach, 84, 91, 98–100, 163
Stage Fright, 55
Stanwyck, Barbara, 29, 68, 116, 144
Star Is Born, A, 87, 91, 92–93, 115
Star Spangled Rhythm, 92
Star Wars trilogy, 16, 73, 126
Steadicam, 57
Stella Dallas, 116
Stevens, George, 38, 68, 72, 195
Stevens, K. T., 48–49
Sting, The, 72
Stone, Oliver, 231–34
Story of Adele H., The, 31–32, 195–96
straight cuts. *See* cuts
stream of consciousness, 33
Streetcar Named Desire, A, 24, 90,
  211–12
Strike, 237
structuralism, 246
student paper, sample, 282–84
Student Prince, The, 92
studios, 166, 287
Sturges, Preston, 12, 64, 88, 255
subtext
  defined, 128–30
  film history as, 148–51
  historical, 146–48
  iconic associations, 138–44
  intellectual associations, 144–45
  musical associations, 155–61
  mythic associations, 130–37, 225
  relating remake to original film,
    151–55
subtitles. *See* titles
Suddenly, Last Summer, 43, 119, 194,
  212

Sullivan's Travels, 88, 111, 112, 255
Sunset Boulevard, 3, 28, 87, 115
Suspicion, 37
Sweet Liberty, 14, 73, 114, 185–87
Swing Time, 95, 127
syntagm, 248

Tale of Two Cities, A, 27–28
Taradash, Daniel, 211–12
Tea and Sympathy, 32, 212–13
Technique of Film Editing, The, 79–80
television, 178–79, 189
terms, defining unfamiliar, 18
text, movie as, 6–7
That's Life!, 9–10
Thelma and Louise, 120
themes, 78, 169–75
Theory of Film: The Redemption of Physical Reality, 241–43
There's No Business Like Show Business, 93
These Three, 119
They Shoot Horses, Don't They?, 195
Thing, The, 124
Thin Man, The, 54, 69
Third Man, The, 47, 222–23
This Island Earth, 124
thoughts, revealing, 18–19
Three Days of the Condor, 26
Three Little Words, 93
Till the Clouds Roll By, 94
tilt shots. *See* shots
time, 4–6
  See also editing
Time After Time, 51
Time magazine, 254, 256–58
Tindall, William York, 131
titles
  dedication, 230
  end, 17–18
  intertitles, 18–20, 227–28
  main, 11–16
  opening, 16–17, 193
  roll-up, 16
  subtitles, 20
  vs. voice-over, 27–28

Tol'able David, 237
Toland, Gregg, 260–61
tone, 78
  See also editing
Tora! Tora! Tora!, 20
Touch of Evil, 53, 54, 239, 262–63
Tourneur, Jacques. *See Cat People*
tracking shot. *See* shots
tragedy, 89–90
transitions
  dissolves, 67–68
  fades, 65–67
  form dissolves, 69
  irising in and out, 70–73
  metaphorical dissolves, 67–68
  wipes, 69–70
Truffaut, François
  and *auteurism*, 163–64
  comment as flashforward, 195–96
  composition in *Jules and Jim*, 49
  epistolary voice use, 31–32
  and Jean-Pierre Léaud, 149
  use of iris shot, 72
Twelve O'Clock High, 80–81
Two for the Road, 194, 248–49
Two Mrs. Carrolls, The, 68
2001: A Space Odyssey, 65, 126
Two Weeks in Another Town, 114
Tyler, Parker, 132, 241–42, 244–46

Ulmer, Edgar G., 38, 45–47, 163, 244
Umbrellas of Cherbourg, The, 92
Unbearable Lightness of Being, The, 19–20
Une Femme Douce, 29
Uninvited, The, 120
Unmarried Woman, An, 119–20

Vanity Fair, 286
Variety, 286
Vidal, Gore, 212
Vidor, King, 116
Vietnam War films, 102–3
vignettes, 19
violence, 228, 231–33, 282–84
Viridiana, 49, 51

voice-over. *See* narration
Vorkapich, Slavko, 75

Wagonmaster, 84, 100
Walk in the Sun, A, 32
Wallis, Hal, 8
Walsh, Raoul
  and crime films, 103–5
  western whodunit by, 91
  See also High Sierra
War of the Worlds, 124
Washington montage, 63–64
Watch on the Rhine, 212
Waterworld, 10–11
Wayne, John, 98–99, 102, 113–14,
  138, 173
Welles, Orson
  iris used in *The Magnificent
    Ambersons*, 72
  and *The Lady from Shanghai*, 108
  light in, 263
  long takes, 53, 244, 263
  and moving camera, 54
  Pauline Kael's view of, 258–59
  style, summarized, 263
  symbolic objects, 262
  themes, 261–62
  See also Citizen Kane
westerns, 38, 84, 97–103
Wexler, Haskell, 26
Whale, James, 6, 122
When Willie Comes Marching Home,
  27, 39
While You Were Sleeping, 112–13
White Heat, 105
Who Framed Roger Rabbit, 150–51,
  166
Wild Bunch, The, 59

Wild Child, The, 72
Wilder, Billy, 3, 12, 92, 152
  an interview with, 176–184
  and Lubitsch, 182–83
  omniscient author in *The Lost
    Weekend*, 197–98
  opinion of *auteur* theory, 178
  themes, motifs, and quotations,
    170–73, 175, 179–80, 182
  use of musical leitmotif, 156
  *See also The Big Carnival; Double
    Indemnity*
Wild Strawberries, 44–45, 223, 248
Williams, Richard, 166–67
wipes. *See* transitions
Wise, Robert, 6
Witness for the Prosecution, 174–75, 182
Wizard of Oz, The, 83
Woman of Affairs, A, 19
Woman of the Year, 118
woman's film, the, 115–120
women, depiction of, 251–53
Women in Love, 58–59
Wood, Sam, 8
World War II montages, 63
Wrong Man, The, 17, 69
Wyler, William
  characteristic shots, 52, 167
  color used in *Jezebel*, 80
  long takes, 244
  *See also The Best Years of Our Lives;
    Mrs. Miniver*

Zanuck, Darryl F., 15
Zemeckis, Robert, 26, 150–51, 166
Ziegfeld Follies, 92
Zinnemann, Fred, 6, 98
zooming. *See* shots